# BETTY GRABLE

Publicity pose for the movie *A Yank in the R.A.F.*, 1941. Collection of the author.

# BETTY GRABLE

## A Bio-Bibliography

### Larry Billman

Bio-Bibliographies in the Performing Arts, Number 40
*James Robert Parish, Series Adviser*

**GREENWOOD PRESS**
Westport, Connecticut • London

**Library of Congress Cataloging-in-Publication Data**

Billman, Larry.
  Betty Grable : a bio-bibliography / Larry Billman.
    p.  cm.—(Bio-bibliographies in the performing arts, ISSN
  0892-5550 ; no. 40)
  Includes bibliographical references and index.
  ISBN 0-313-28156-4 (alk. paper)
    1. Grable, Betty, 1916-1973.  2. Grable, Betty, 1916-1973—
  Bibliography.   3. Motion picture actors and actresses—United
  States—Biography.     I. Title.  II. Series.
  PN2287.G66B55  1993
  791.43'028'092—dc20
  [B]        93-17579

British Library Cataloguing in Publication Data is available.

Library of Congress Catalog Card Number: 93-17579
ISBN: 0-313-28156-4
ISSN: 0892-5550

First published in 1993

Greenwood Press, 88 Post Road West, Westport, CT 06881
An imprint of Greenwood Publishing Group, Inc.

Printed in the United States of America

The paper used in this book complies with the
Permanent Paper Standard issued by the National
Information Standards Organization (Z39.48-1984).

10 9 8 7 6 5 4 3 2 1

Dedicated to my parents, Harry and La Vone Billman,
who lovingly introduced me to all of life's pleasures,
among them Betty Grable.

# Contents

# Illustrations

# Preface

Betty Grable will forever remain a fond part of the collective American memory - smiling at us from over her shoulder - representing the War years as the "Pin Up Girl Supreme" that many young American men were willing to fight for. Her upswept blonde cotton candy curls, million dollar legs and white, one-piece bathing suit have been the subject of "Pop" artists for fifty years to represent Hollywood, the Movies, World War II and the American culture. The New Yorker Magazine once defined entertainment as: "Mickey Mouse's adventures and Betty Grable's legs." The old cliche about American ideals was almost revised to say: "Mom, the Flag, Apple Pie and Betty Grable."

In a career which spanned 35 years and 83 shorts and feature films, her good natured performances were the perfect Saturday night film fare of the families of the 1940's, escaping the reality of World War II and its horrors. Admittedly, her forties films were merely escapist vehicles, but "A" films all - usually glowing in eye-popping Technicolor to take advantage of the sunflower yellow blonde hair, the sky blue eyes, the ruby red lips and the peaches and cream complexion. During the 1940's and early 1950's, Americans religiously went to see "a Betty Grable movie" because they knew she promised a good time at the local cinema.

Betty Grable's great success was with American audiences. Europe and the Orient did not hold her in the same esteem since Musicals were never wildly successful abroad and her appeal was basically American. She seemed to know better than anyone else at her studio, 20th Century Fox, what her loyal fans wanted to see. Her only flops were films which tried to achieve to something else.

Her performances were always of a spunky, self-reliant, no-nonsense American working girl who was out to "better" herself: get a better job, achieve show business success, find a worthy man. While other glamour stars of the period, such as Lana Turner and Rita Hayworth, were reluctant to portray mothers on the screen, Betty happily did it. One of her biggest successes was a nostalgic vaudeville musical called <u>Mother Wore Tights</u> (1947). Her loyal fans knew she would fill the bill, playing a Mother realistically - and also filling the tights to perfection. After all, America had seen her happily cradling her very own daughters in dozens of fan magazines. Not only would Betty be a great girlfriend and/or wife, her many fans felt she'd also be a perfect Mother.

The film studios and publicity machines of the period worked overtime to create the myth of the exotic, unapproachable "Love Goddess": Greta Garbo, Marlene Dietrich, Hedy Lamarr, Rita Hayworth, Ava Gardner and Lana Turner. But Grable's personna was in the "One of the Guys/Girl Next Door/Kid Sister" categories with Barbara Stanwyck, Ann Sheridan and Carole Lombard. Like Jean Harlow before her, she was a blonde with "Attitude." Yet, her musical talents set her apart. She was a softer Betty Hutton, a prettier June Allyson and, as author Ethan Mordden states in <u>The Hollywood Musical</u>, "Betty Grable was a big Judy, the happy Judy that Garland herself seldom projected."(B127)

Her facial features were small and delicate, with her nose being a bit too large for the rest of her face when studied clinically. The outlandish hair styles and various shades of blonde which studio hairstylists created for her over the years were artificial and often bizarre. But, her coloration, beautifully proportioned body and the sincere joy of life which radiated from her smile made her tremendously appealing to audiences of the time.

Grable's "White Hot Blonde" sex appeal bridged the transition of Sex Goddesses from Jean Harlow to Marilyn Monroe. It has been said that Monroe admired and tried to copy Grable - her walk, her way of speaking and singing. Although Grable's breasts were ample, she neither flaunted them - nor ignored them. Betty's sex appeal was the wholesome lure of sister, girlfriend and wife, not hussy or hooker. She exuded physical fitness in her energetic dance routines. She was honest, appealing, natural. Her simple and straightforward acting allowed audiences to accept some of the weakest and most implausible storylines in films.

Because of the binding control of the studio system in filmdom's halcyon days, Betty was never costarred with the great male musical film stars of the "Golden Days of the Movie Musical." A co-Fox contractee, Dan Dailey, finally became her partner in a series of films which began in the late 1940's. But the author personally feels that she should have costarred with Gene Kelly and Fred Astaire. Ironically, she did appear in two Astaire films (<u>The Gay Divorcee</u> and <u>Follow the Fleet</u>). In <u>The Gay Divorcee</u> (1934), she performs a madly nonsensical song and dance called, "LET'S K-KNOCK K-KNEES" with Edward Everett Horton. Fred Astaire enters the scene at the conclusion of the number and speaks to Horton. Watching the film now, we wish he would notice Grable, talk to her...and sweep her into his arms, spinning into a glorious adagio routine. Several film vehicles would have been fitting for an Astaire/Grable pairing (<u>Easter Parade</u>, <u>Let's Dance</u>, <u>The Barkleys of Broadway</u>), but it never was to be. Or had she been under contract to MGM, what would a teaming with Gene Kelly in <u>For Me and My Gal</u> or <u>The Pirate</u> have been? Several modern film historians agree that she could have effectively done many of Judy Garland's film roles. Only in our dreams.

Her friendships with Tyrone Power, Cesar Romero, George Montgomery; her romances with Artie Shaw, George Raft, and Victor Mature and her marriages to Jackie Coogan and Harry James linked her with some of the most popular male celebrities of the time and gave the movie magazines ample gossip to talk about as they chronicled the nightlife of the era. The eventual Grable/James marriage was a press agent's dream - one which unfortunately turned out to be a nightmare for Grable as James gambled, womanized and drank his way out of their marriage. If she was the "Pin Up Girl," he became the cliche of the "Irresponsible Musician." But she survived, loving Harry till the end of her life.

She was a professional "Workhorse" who performed for fifty one of the fifty six years she lived. She appeared with dance bands, in Vaudeville and made thirty three feature and eighteen short films before finally getting the leading role in a "Good Neighbor Policy" color jamboree called Down Argentine Way (1940) which would finally make her a star. The reigning Fox "Blonde-and-Song" star of the time, Alice Faye, was unavailable, so Betty was given a chance. Ironically, Grable would be replaced by Marilyn Monroe, the next "Blonde" waiting in Fox's wings. Gentlemen Prefer Blondes should have been a Grable vehicle. It wasn't...and the rest is history. The iron hand of studio control and the American fettish against age and maturity ushered in the next bombshell. Betty did get to appear with Marilyn in How To Marry a Millionaire (1953), giving Marilyn support and friendship, from all reports. Somehow, Betty knew that the wheel of fortune was spinning and gracefully moved on, leaving Fox and films.

For nearly thirty years, she rarely complained about the roles she was given. She merely reported for work every day, doing the job expected of her by the Moguls and the fans. While other major female stars of the era such as Bette Davis and Olivia De Havilland bravely rebelled at scripts, co-stars and directors, Betty plugged away in her routine musical formula films. It wasn't until the 1950's that she began seriously questioning Fox's decisions, causing her unhappiness and putting her on suspension for refusing to do roles that Fox chief Darryl Zanuck wanted to cast her in. Rebellion finally arrived, but not until she had earned millions of dollars for the studio and found personal happiness as a wife and mother.

She rejected several films which might have moved her career into other areas, the most famous one being the Oscar Award winning role of "Sophie" in The Razor's Edge (1946) which went to Anne Baxter. Perhaps she was correct. But it is interesting to theorize what might have happened had she taken a chance at more dramatic roles. Directors such as Henry King thought she had great dramatic potential. She just wouldn't take herself seriously, nor did her critics and fans.

Betty approached her film work with a sense of joy and a professional attitude. Co-workers, such as choreographer (and Astaire alter ego) Hermes Pan remembered: "You couldn't do much with Betty outside of letting her be Betty Grable ...she could move and she had beautiful legs, and she had a certain magnetism when she was on screen. Her color was beautiful and she was pleasant to watch." (B93).

Before she died tragically of cancer in 1973, she toured the country in Hello Dolly, bringing her beauty and joy to millions of fans around America. Admittedly, her performance as "Dolly Levi" was not one which stretched her talents, but rather, one which allowed audiences to see the real Betty Grable on stage...singing, dancing and giving them a glimpse of her famous "Gams." It also allowed them a glimpse of her heart. It was a perfect vehicle for her. One which earned her many standing ovations. Her many years of live stage, vaudeville and nightclub experiences insured consistently strong stage performances.

Betty Grable's right leg is immortalized in cement with her handprints and autograph at Mann's Chinese Theater; her name blazes from a golden star on the Hollywood Walk of Fame and her "Peek-a-Boo-Pin-Up" photo peers at us from countless books, posters, photographs and art works. Critics of the time never praised her singing, dancing or acting abilities. Instead, their reviews always mentioned her legs ("Gams" or "Stems") and the stages of undress which she appeared in. Her career in retrospect has not been treated kindly by modern film historians, claiming that her films were "Fluff that does not hold up when viewed today." They have not given her due credit for the position she held: Number one box office Female for ten years, highest salaried woman in the United States in 1946-'47 and epitome of American womanhood for millions of men and women.

Betty Grable and her career personify professionalism and the erotic physicality of a very gentle time. She led the way to Marilyn Monroe, Doris Day, Madonna...and the next blonde "Flavor of the Month." Although announcements are often made about a television feature being planned about her life, (with current blonde personalities Loni Anderson, Ann Jillian and Pia Zadora being mentioned to portray America's "Pin Up Girl") none of the projects have become reality. Who could truly impersonate Betty Grable? Several current actresses might be able to sing the songs, dance the dances and manage a physical impression of her, but who possesses her unique personality and infectious likableness?

Her "Pin Up" pose continues to find its way into Pop Art. For the 1992 release of Cool World, a combined animation and live action comedy, the logo art work is clearly based on Betty's famous pose. Although the blonde depicted wears a mini skirt and has a contemporary hairstyle, the "Peek-A-Boo" look over her shoulder and the stance is definitely Grable.

In the history of the American musical film, Betty Grable firmly holds her niche as the quintessential Pin Up Blonde who could dance a little, sing a little and yet, make millions of fans care a lot. Biographers have turned her into an Icon - although all recollections of her by co-workers and friends prove she was a very vulnerable and caring human being. The showing of her films on cable television and the release of the "Betty Grable" series of videos and laser discs are introducing her and her unique joy to new generations. But it is the men and women who grew up during the 1940's that truly remember the essence of Grable. Just mention her name and they smile, their heads suddenly filling with wonderful memories of music, dancing, beauty and happiness. This is her legacy.

It is the author's intent in this book to go beyond the popular pin up image and to document all phases of Miss Grable's life and career in film and the often ignored details of her extensive stage, nightclub, television and radio work for fans and film historians. Through research and interviews with personal friends and co-workers, a serious attempt has also been made to collect and notate little-known facts and anecdotes about her life and personality. Because of the author's respect and admiration for the actress and her work, the more sensational or disparaging aspects and rumors of her life are only mentioned, with a conscious attempt to not alter the truth. The "Truth" is that Betty Grable was a human being like the rest of us, with strengths and weaknesses. This book attempts to concentrate on and document those strengths.

The book is divided into 13 major sections:

1.  A short biography.

2.  A chronology of the highlights in her life.

3.  A complete listing of her work in films, the medium for which she is best known. The films are listed in chronological order, with short films interspersed among feature films. A complete listing of cast and credits, plot summary, selected excerpts from reviews, anecdotes and comments about the making of the film or its cast and staff, Academy Award nominations and awards and existing audio and video recordings.

4.  Appearances on television listed chronologically, with cast and credits, synopses or contents, excerpts from reviews, comments and audio and video recordings.

5.  Appearances on radio listed chronologically, with available cast and credits, synopses or summarized contents, comments and audio recordings.

6.  A chronological listing of her appearances on stage, including vaudeville, big band paticipation and legitimate theatrical comedies and musicals with cast and credits, synopsis, reviews, and comments.

7.  A separate listing of her nightclub appearances, listed chronologically with cast and sporadic credits, contents, reviews and comments.

8.  A videography of existing commercial video tapes and laser discs available of her films and television appearances, cross referenced in the appropriate sections.

9.  A discography of existing audio recordings of her film, television and radio appearances on both vinyl

and compact disc, cross referenced in the appropriate sections.

10.    A selected listing of commercially available collectible items.

11.    A list of miscellaneous data: location of her Hollywood Walk of Fame Star, leg and hand prints, her funeral, her burial, residential addresses over the years, her vital statistics, the products she advertised, films she was offered or announced to appear in, awards and honors, songs associated with her and songs which mention her name.

12.    An annotated bibliography of books and magazine articles containing intensive or unusual information about her life and work, cross referenced throughout the various sections.

13.    A complete index of names, places and important titles listed throughout the book.

# Acknowledgments

A book like this is a collaborative effort. The facts are all out there somewhere, but without the many people and institutions who supplied them to me, they never would have found their way onto these pages.

Thanks to fellow film biographers and historians Margie Schultz, Ann V. Mc Kee and Brenda Scott Royce for their friendship, advice, support and valuable information. Chris Lembesis offered me information from his extensive radio logs and I am grateful for his help and patience. Miles Krueger of the Institute of the American Musical allowed me access to his hallowed halls - and his legendary expertise. And to James Robert Parish, a master of chronicling the details of film history and personalities, my deepest gratitude for acting as my mentor and guiding me.

To Betty Grable's friends and co-workers Ray Aghayan, Donn Arden, Buddy Bryan, Harvey Church, Roy Clark, Roberta Tennes Deutsch, Fluff Le Coque, Rebecca Mann, Pete Menefee, Miriam Nelson, Robert Osborne, Cesar Romero and Dee Dee Wood - none of whom had a bad word to say about the lady - I enjoyed every minute of our interviews as you shared your personal memories with me.

Invaluable research sources include the resources and staffs of the Anaheim City Library, Beverly Hills Library, Brea City Library, Los Angeles Central Library, Santa Ana City Library, the Academy of Motion Pictures Arts and Sciences Library and The Billy Rose Theatre Collection at the New York Public Library. Haunting memorabilia shops became a way of life for me and among the most pleasant and helpful were Music and Memories, Aladdin Books, Larry Edmunds Bookshop, Movie World, Book City, Cinema Collections (all located in California) and the Tampa Antiquarian Book Co., a treasure of a little store in Florida. Gratitude to Aggie Carroll, whose clippings and photos allowed me to reconstruct Miss Grable's career from the press of the time.

Thank you to Amy Mihill, Publicity Manager for the Municipal Theatre Association of St. Louis for her help in locating material about Miss Grable's appearance at the Muny Opera. And to John Behrens, CBS historian extraordinaire and

Yuien Chen and Pamela Panio of the NBC News Archives, who, in this day of busy schedules and accelerating indifference to the past, took a moment to listen to my request - and fill it, supplying so many of the details about Miss Grable's radio and television participation. Thank you.

My gratitude to the many friends who helped, supported and encouraged me: John Frayer, Richard De Neut, Sylvia Lewis, Jim Smith, John and Mary Jo Ludin, Yoshi Hashimoto and Richard and Ava McKenzie. And to the beautiful ladies in my life: Tomo, Sekiya, Saadia and Aki, who shared me with a "Pin Up Girl" for eighteen months. To my sister, Nancy Thompson, thank you for letting me steal your autographed Grable picture those oh-so-many years ago. Special thanks to Legh Townsend for her proofreading and invaluable expertise.

Sincere thanks to my original Greenwood editor, Lynn Taylor, for her expertise and guidance and to George F. Butler, who inherited me and my work when he arrived at Greenwood, continuing the excellent attention and advice. Liz Leiba and her production team are to be thanked for their additional eyes and suggestions.

And, finally, to Bob Isoz, a longtime fan and intimate friend of Miss Grable's, who supplied me with information, clippings and reviews, photos, anecdotes, viewings of her rare short film appearances and his trust. Most of all, for his smile whenever he spoke of her which gave me a rare insight into what kind of special lady she must have been. I hope I have honored his love for her.

# Biography

## 1. A STAGE MOTHER IS BORN

On December 18, 1916, Elizabeth Ruth Grable was born in south St. Louis to John Conn Grable and Lillian Hoffman Grable. Some biographers have listed her name at birth as: "Ruth Elizabeth" yet her certificate of baptism into the Episcopal Church reads: "Elizabeth Ruth." An older sister, Marjorie, had been born to the couple on April 17, 1909 and a brother, John Carl, had been born in 1914. Unfortunately, John was to contract pneumonia when he was twenty-two months old. He died while Lillian was pregnant with baby Elizabeth. Betty never got to see her brother.

Lillian Grable was to become one of filmdom's most famous "Stage Mothers," taking her place in Hollywood infamy along with Ginger Rogers' mother, Lela and Judy Garland's domineering mother, Ethel. The classic "Stage Mother" often is a combination of frustration over the lot life had given her, unhappiness in her marriage and vicarious dreams of stardom. Add to that Lillian's physical disabilities and you have the plot for driving ambition equalling Medea. Betty always defended Lillian and never cursed her mother or her memory when she got older, undoubtedly realizing that without Lillian, there might never have been a "Pin Up" girl. Lillian's ambition was to drive her second child to fame, fortune and often, frustration.

Lillian had been born on May 29, 1890 to Charles and Elizabeth Hoffman. Charles was an accomplished cellist and his musical ability had been passed on to Lillian in the form of what first daughter Marjorie remembers as a "lovely singing Voice" (B207). But Lillian was not one to sing and dance. She would be cursed with a "stiff hip," which made her an ambulatory cripple. No official diagnosis had ever been made of her condition, although it was suspected she may have had polio as a child. Nevertheless, for the rest of her life, she would have to rely on crutches, canes and wheelchairs to help her move, a bizarre juxtaposition to Betty's easy physicality. Lillian's bitterness about her affliction was often reflected in the way she drove Betty to success. She would readily use her condition to produce shame, pity and obedience in those around her.

Betty's father, called "Conn," was an easy going man of German extraction who was one of St. Louis' many "South Side Dutch," as the Germans in the area were called. He was a bookkeeper when Betty was born and he patiently endured the separations from wife and daughter as Betty was taken away from St. Louis at an early age to try for the Gold Ring of show business in California. He and Lillian would eventually separate - another show business cliche when young performers are involved. Lillian put all of her hopes into her talented offspring's future. A terrible burden for a youngster, but a classic one.

Lillian had tried to make a performer out of Marjorie, but she did not seem to have natural abilities, so every lesson available was given to Betty. Betty was later to comment: "I've had every kind of lesson there was except eccentric dancing. Tap dancing, toe dancing, ballet dancing, acrobatic dancing, twirling, ice skating, roller skating. I can even play the Saxophone - and not bad either." Lillian realized that this bright, blonde baby at a very early age, would be her ticket out of the unhappiness she felt surrounding her. If the youngster hesitated or rebelled, the promise of a "Horseback ride on Sunday" always got Betty to her dance classes. Horses were to become a major love in Grable's life.

In 1920, when Betty was four years old, Conn became a grain broker on the Board of Trade and his financial gain allowed the family to move to the Forest Park Hotel in one of St. Louis' more fashionable neighborhoods. There, Lillian visited with vaudevillians who were appearing at nearby theatres, asking their advice and displaying her golden-haired prodigy. Lillian even had a special platform constructed in the foyer of the Grable apartment where little Betty could practice her dancing (B160). Lillian would ask Betty to perform everywhere and anywhere - and Betty would obligingly pop up on a table and go into her song and dance. While other relatives and neighbors might look askance at little Betty's "showing off," Lillian successfully removed any twinges of bashfulness from Betty's psyche.

When she reached school age, Betty was enrolled in Mary Institute, a well-regarded grammar school for young ladies. At the same time, Betty began appearing in local stage productions, finally working her way into the Mary Institute's annual Christmas shows at the Odeon Theater, and vaudeville performances at the Missouri Theater, where she shared the bill with major stars like Jack Haley, Frank Fay and Jane Froman.

Leaving Mary Institute in 1928, she enrolled in Eugene Field Grammar School, where Donn Arden (who was to become the acknowledged master of Nightclub spectacles) was a schoolmate. They also attended Mrs. Clark's dance studio together ("not in the same class") and Arden related how all of Betty's classmates were jealous when Lillian would arrive several times a week at the grammar school, whisper to the teacher that Betty had a stage appearance that afternoon and the adorable blonde youngster would be allowed to go to the

cloakroom, get her coat and leave for work. One of young
Betty's jobs was in the chorus of a show at the Missouri
Theater featuring Ed Lowry and Ginger Rogers.

After a scouting trip to California in the summer
of 1928, Lillian found the opportunity to move her talented
youngster to Hollywood in 1929 when Betty was thirteen.
Lillian assured Conn that this was the natural move for a
child as talented as Betty and Conn agreed. By then, his
career had progressed to successful stockbroker and he felt
that he could not leave St. Louis. Marjorie was attending the
University of Missouri, where she would meet her future
husband, David Arnold. So, like "Mama Rose" in the musical
Gypsy, Lillian left - leaving Conn and Marjorie behind. In
California, Betty was immediately enrolled in the Hollywood
Professional School and began dance classes with Ernest
Belcher (Marge Champion's father and film dance pioneer),
Eduardo Cansino (Rita Hayworth's father) and Albertina Rasch
(famed Broadway choreographer who was creating dance numbers
for Fox and MGM.) Sister Marjorie evidently didn't resent
Betty's talent, but instead was pleased that the pressure was
off of her to perform (B151).

With the wild success of the talking picture, 1929 was
the year of the Star-Studded Revue and the birth of the
Technicolor musical in Hollywood. Broadway stars and
composers were all moving West to the "Gold Rush" of the
Movie Musical. Lillian and Betty arrived there just in time.
A talent scout attended Belcher's dance school and noticed
Betty, inviting her to a dance audition at the Fox Studios.
As Betty was only 5'4" tall, Lillian advised her to "Stand
next to the smallest girl...It was like a poker game in which
you're holding four aces...I knew Betty had what they wanted"
(B120). Lying about Betty's age, Lillian managed to get her a
one year stock contract as part of the Fox chorus at $50 a
week. She danced in Happy Days and Let's Go Places (1929),
and Movietone Follies of 1930. They were chorus roles, but
Lillian wanted Betty to start getting experience...and making
contacts. Although pleased with Betty's dancing abilities,
the studio was not happy when they found out she had lied
about her age to work illegally and her contract was broken.

A new opportunity arrived when she was signed to
appear in Whoopee (1930), an Eddie Cantor film co-produced by
the great Flo Ziegfeld himself and introducing the genius of
dance director Busby Berkeley to films. Fourteen year old
Betty managed to get out of the chorus for this, being given
dialogue to speak and lyrics to sing in a featured solo. She
also danced in the chorus of Kiki (1931), hired by dance
director Berkeley.

When Betty was not busily working at the film studios,
Lillian made certain that she was appearing in "Amateur
Nights" at Los Angeles theaters, as well as such nearby
cities as Long Beach and Compton. To insure constant
exposure, Lillian also insisted that Betty make as many
publicity and personal appearances as possible: throwing the
first ball at baseball games, posing for cheesecake photos
and appearing at benefits. These early days as a film starlet
were filled with as much self-promotion as Lillian could
encourage.

The film work continued into 1931 with work in a

series of shorts, directed by Roscoe "Fatty" Arbuckle, whose popular film career had been shattered by a sex scandal in 1921. He was now directing short films for Educational Pictures under the name of "William Goodrich." Several biographers have written that to avoid the blemishing of Betty's name, Lillian insisted that she appear in the films under the name of "Frances Dean." The films themselves smack of exploitation, with such provocative titles as Ex-Sweeties, Crashing Hollywood and Once A Hero. But, it was work. A Twentieth Century Fox press release in 1947 discussed the name change, stating that it was made while Betty was under contract to Goldwyn. Betty was quoted as telling the studio publicist: "Anyway, they huddled with Mr. Goldwyn, and I believe it was Vicki Baum, the writer, who came up with the monicker they pinned on me...'Frances Dean.' I thought it was silly since there were already a couple of very popular leading ladies in pictures called Frances Dee and Frances Dade. I figured nothing would come of it, because I was just a dancing stock girl. But they gave it the old A-1 treatment complete with bathing suit art, and re-christened me as though I were a battleship!" (B197). She did not, however, make any appearances in Goldwyn films under the name.

For Palmy Days (1931), another Eddie Cantor starrer at United Artists, Betty auditioned with over 1500 female hopefuls and was selected by Busby Berkeley - along with Jane Wyman, Paulette Goddard and Virginia Bruce - to become one of the original "Goldwyn Girls." While filming Palmy Days, Betty met dashing, suave George Raft. Betty was sixteen and Raft was thirty six. They were to begin a long romantic relationship. George realized that Betty was very young when they met and he reportedly respected her inexperience, saying: "I'm giving her up till she grows up." She also was too young to realize that he was married to a woman who, because of her religious beliefs, would not give him a divorce, despite their loveless relationship. Lillian must have known about Raft's marital situation, but perhaps felt that her daughter's association with the up-and-coming film star might be advantageous to Betty's career. And his status as a married man would keep him from taking her darling daughter/mealticket away from her. So, Lillian allowed the flirtation and eventual courtship.

During 1932, Betty continued to appear in shorts for Educational and MGM (Lady, Please!, Hollywood Luck, The Flirty Sleepwalker, Hollywood Lights, Over The Counter). She also worked for RKO and Chesterfield in bit parts in three feature films released that year (The Greeks Had a Word For Them, The Age of Consent and Probation.) She finally was elevated to "Leading Lady" status at RKO in Hold 'Em Jail, costarring with Wheeler and Woolsey, a popular comedy team of the time, also released in 1932. In Pin Up, The Tragedy of Betty Grable (B151), one of the two full length Grable biographies, author Spero Pastos writes that in 1932, while living at the Canterbury Apartments, a major Los Angeles earthquake forced the residents to leave the shaking building and seek safety in a small park nearby. There, Lillian mingled with Dick Powell and famed vaudeville comic Bert Wheeler of the comedy team of Wheeler and Woolsey. Lillian spoke at great length to Wheeler, singing her daughter's praises and asking for his advice. This conversation supposedly led Betty to a role in Hold 'Em Jail and a long association with the team. The only problem with this story is that the famous Los Angeles earthquake happened six months after Betty had made Hold 'Em Jail. But somehow a relationship was created with the comedy pair (perhaps from her childhood association with them in St. Louis?) which led her to work often with the team.

As Jean Harlow had recently caused a sensation on the silver screen, teenaged Betty was appropriately tinted platinum blonde and her eyebrows alluringly plucked and pencilled. Many of the up-and-coming film ladies of the day emulated the style, among them Bette Davis.

Another unique opportunity arrived when Betty was cast in Tattle Tales, a musical stage revue starring comedian Frank Fay and his then-wife, Barbara Stanwyck. During an Out-of-town tryout tour, the show played in San Francisco, Santa Barbara and Los Angeles. Betty was easily accepted into the energetic crowd of working youngsters and even made a nightclub appearance with the Rocky Twins, an androgynous pair of entertainers, at the Christie Hotel in Hollywood while they were appearing in Tattle Tales at the Belasco Theater in Los Angeles. In May, 1933, the show moved to Broadway, where it opened on June 1 at the Broadhurst Theater, but by then, Betty had already taken the next step toward her goal and did not travel with the show to New York.

Ted Fiorito, famed Band Leader, happened to see Tattle Tales in San Francisco, singled out Betty and reputedly goaded by Lillian (B207), asked her to join the band as a vocalist. Although Betty protested that she could not sing, Fiorito felt that her beauty and dancing talents would be a welcome addition to his band. She would learn to sing. For the next nine months, Betty toured with the group to San Francisco, Santa Monica and Los Angeles. Although Lillian strictly chaperoned sixteen year old Betty and all of her beaus, trying to keep the tight reins on her budding beauty, Betty managed to fall in love with one of the band members, drummer Charlie Price. When the Fiorito job ended, Betty sang with Jay Whidden and Hal Grayson's bands.

In 1933, my Mother, La Vone Harden, was a member of "The Pal's Club," a social organization of young people at the Wilshire Blvd Christian Church in Los Angeles. Another Pal's Club member, Ginjie (Virginia) Overbeck, was a friend of young Betty Grable. During the Summer, Ginjie brought Betty and her sister, Marjorie, to the Pal's Club meetings and social events. One Summer afternon, La Vone drove them to the beach, since she was the only one who had a car. La Vone remembers Betty was working with the Ted Fiorito Orchestra at the Santa Monica Beach Club at the time. "Betty was as blonde as her sister was brunette, but they both had the most beautiful skin and complexions," La Vone reminisced. "Betty also had a boyfriend with her - they rode in the rumble seat - a kid with a lot of freckles, but I don't remember his name. Betty wore a bright pink dance leotard...I think it was a leotard because I don't remember having bathing suits which were as revealing as this one was in those days. When she went into the water, the pink suit became nearly transparent. You should have seen the boys gather from all over the beach when she came out of the water!" Mother remembers her as being bright, vivacious and a very luminous young girl.

Betty's ongoing film releases in 1933 included The Kid From Spain for RKO, Cavalcade for Twentieth Century Fox (a film which was to win the Academy Award for "Best Film of 1932-33"); Child of Manhattan, a melodrama for Columbia; Melody Cruise, a feature for RKO; What Price Innocence? (Columbia - her largest purely dramatic role) and singing with Fiorito's band at Monogram in Sweetheart of Sigma Chi and Air Tonic, a short for RKO. Although she was getting valuable experience and making lots of contacts, becoming a very visible working actress, her roles were still going from leads with the minor studios to bit parts with the majors.

1934 was a promising year for the struggling teenager. Early in the year, four shorts she had made for Columbia and Warner Brothers were released (Elmer Steps Out, Love Detectives, Business is a Pleasure and Susie's Affairs) and she was cast in the first of two Fred Astaire and Ginger Rogers films she would make, The Gay Divorcee. In the highly successful film, she was selected to perform a featured song and dance number with Edward Everett Horton, "LET'S K-NOCK K-NEES." Co-star Horton observed: "We all knew there was something special about her - something appealing that made you feel good inside" (B151).

Because of her eye-catching work in The Gay Divorcee, Betty was given a five year contract with RKO in 1934, where she was given a small role in By Your Leave. She also appeared in a small role in the MGM feature film Student Tour (on loan from RKO) and managed a brief vaudeville appearance with Bert Wheeler between pictures.

RKO co-starred her in three of their 1935 short films (A Night at the Biltmore Bowl, Drawing Rumors and A Quiet Fourth), hoping to offer her exposure to audiences and give her confidence in front of the camera. The only feature film appearances she made that year for RKO was in The Nitwits (again with Wheeler and Woolsey) and Old Man Rhythm, being sixth billed and leading one of the film's musical numbers. Her largest role that year was as co-star in an Astor short (The Spirit of 1976), receiving the best reviews of her career.

Conn finally felt that he was able to make the move to California, so the family was briefly reunited in 1935.

On loan to Paramount for an ample role in Collegiate (released in 1936), she was still seeing Charlie Price, as evidenced from this mention in the Hollywood Reporter in 1935: "Young Betty Grable was borrowed for a Paramount Picture Collegiate. She had an extra glow when she reported for work. Friends say that it was because Grable was in love with a guy named Charlie Mace (sic), a member of Ted Fiorito's Band"(B208). Between other romances, she continued to date George Raft, whose career was thriving.

While enjoying a summer cruise to Catalina, Betty was introduced to Jackie Coogan by Bill Carey, a member of the Ted Fiorito Band. She was attracted to Coogan, the former child star who was trying to secure a career as an adult. He was handsome, famous and talented and helped Betty become a woman, although this relationship threatened Lillian's stranglehold on her. They costarred in a touring vaudeville show, Hollywood Secrets (December, 1935 to April, 1936) and made Sunkist Stars at Palm Springs, a 1936 short for MGM, fell in love and announced their engagement.

Betty's film career, however, was floundering. Her on screen personna was not energetic enough for the popular image of the ingenue like Olivia De Havilland and Loretta Young, not intense enough for the heavily dramatic roles of Bette Davis and Miriam Hopkins, nor sophisticated enough for the "Femme Fatale" roles that Marlene Dietrich and Greta Garbo were playing. Her singing was pleasant, but certainly not in the league with Jeanette MacDonald or Grace Moore. Her dancing was versatile but without the unique impact of Eleanor Powell or Ruby Keeler. She was hardly uninhibited or raucous enough to be a comedienne like Joan Blondell or Carole Lombard and she was just pretty enough to prohibit her being classified as a "Character Actress." Too young for romantic pairings with the leading male stars of the day and too old to be heralded as a "Child Star" like Shirley Temple and Judy Garland. Betty Grable in 1936 was a young actress in search of her film personality.

In her second Astaire and Rogers film, Follow The Fleet, released in 1936, she was barely noticeable as part of a vocal trio, vividly illustrating that RKO did not know quite how to take advantage of her and her talents. After a featured dramatic role in Don't Turn 'Em Loose in 1936, Betty was loaned to Twentieth Century Fox, for the college musical Pigskin Parade. Her RKO contract was not renewed.

Hoping that she had possibilities to be a money-making leading lady, Paramount signed her at $600 a week to be featured in a raft of their musicals: This Way Please; Thrill of a Lifetime (1937); College Swing; Give Me A Sailor and Campus Confessions (1938). Ethan Mordden has this to say about the College Musical genre in The Hollywood Musical: "Then there was the college musical, made entirely of quartets, student bands and devout dancers. The film musical pursued youth and candor, and academe promised a great deal of it: students have no grandeur, no bitterness, and, in the Hollywood version, they spend so little time in classes that there's plenty of time for dizzy deans, nutty professors, perhaps a college widow. College Swing (1938) has more staff in it than students" (B127). Higher education was on the nation's mind and Hollywood was never one to ignore a timely topic. College equalled football. This popular film formula gave Betty the opportunity to portray an appealing coed several times. She even admitted: "I used to wake up yelling 'Rah Rah for Oat Meal!'" At nineteen, she was one of the few featured film performers who could actually have been enrolled in college.

July 1937 to February 1938 were filled with twenty six semi-regular appearances on the radio program Song Time with future film costar John Payne. This would be the most active radio exposure she would receive during her entire career.

While making films at Paramount with Coogan, a studio worker was quoted at the time about their romance: "They just sat and looked at each other at parties. Then they'd go outside and hold hands, and there was nothing mamma could do about it" (B120). Without Lillian's approval, they married on December 20, 1937, two days after Betty reached her twenty-

first birthday. The highly publicized newlyweds worked
together in two feature films for Paramount: College Swing
(1938) and Million Dollar Legs - a prophetic title for Miss
Grable (1939), and made radio appearances. Their greatest
impact, however, was made as a popular staple of Hollywood's
"Brat Pack" of the time. "Dining, dancing and romancing" at
Hollywood's nightspots, their images and names were
constantly seen in fan magazines and society columns. They
were young, famous, beautiful and perceived by America as
privileged and carefree. The truth was quite different.

At the same time, Jackie was going through traumatic
court appearances to gain the money he had earned as a child
star. His father had been killed in 1936 and he bitterly
battled his mother for his rightful share of his earnings.
His subsequent trial would cause "The Child Actor's Bill"
(dubbed "The Coogan Law") to be enacted and to protect all
future child film performers. The pressures of the trial and
both of their careers finally scuttled their dreams of
happiness. Betty had to pay for the wedding reception and
although both were receiving $1000 per week on their
Paramount contract, Jackie only worked two weeks. At her
divorce hearing, she stated that she had sold many of their
possessions to pay off some of his personal debts. They were
married less than two years. But Jackie had allowed Betty to
leave Lillian's control and move on her way to independence.

Conn also was released from Lillian's grip when she
divorced him on July 7, 1939.

In 1939, she was to co-star opposite Jack Benny in Man
About Town at Paramount, but illness caused her to be
replaced by friend Dorothy Lamour. She recovered in time to
make a featured appearance in the film. Even though Campus
Dormitory was announced for her, once again, she was cast
into the sea of "Free-lancers" as her Paramount contract was
not renewed. She returned briefly to RKO for a comic role in
The Day the Bookies Wept before she made the career decision
which would change her life.


2. BROADWAY BABY


Betty Grable was to work for nearly every major studio
in Hollywood, before studio mogul Darryl F. Zanuck would
finally recognize her potential and find her a home at
Twentieth Century Fox.

Jack Haley had asked Betty to appear with him at the
Golden Gate Exposition in San Francisco in July of 1939.
Spotting Betty in some newspaper photos taken to publicize
her appearance with Haley (B19), Darryl F. Zanuck signed her
to a contract at Fox, but at the time, was unsure of what to
do with her. Also during that auspicious appearance in San
Francisco, super-agent Louis Shurr, who was looking for a
beautiful dancer for a Broadway package he was putting
together, saw Betty and recommended her to producer Buddy De
Sylva, for Cole Porter's newest show, Dubarry Was a Lady
(B39).

There must have been lots of discussions with Lillian,
her agent and other trusted advisors. What was a starlet to

do? She had languished for ten years in Hollywood, trying her very best to make an impression in fifty one film projects, but failing to find her niche. Even the new contract with Fox did not promise much. She must have been reminded of her unhappy marriage with Coogan in every nightspot in town. So, Betty looked her future squarely in the eye and was "Broadway Bound."

Before she left California, she had to appear in court on October 11, 1939 for her final divorce proceedings against Coogan. She suprised everyone by appearing on the arm of Artie Shaw, famed band-leader (and Casanova), for moral support. Charismatic Shaw was to be linked romantically with some of Hollywood's loveliest stars: Lana Turner, Ava Gardner, Evelyn Keyes and Judy Garland. Since Betty's divorce from Jackie would not be final until November 11, 1940, marriage to Shaw was out of the question - for now. On October 26, 1939, Hollywood Gossip Queen Louella Parsons wrote that Shaw was about to sign with Fox to make films with Grable: "For as we told you before anyone else printed it, Betty will be Mrs. Shaw when she gets her final decree."

In _Dubarry Was A Lady_, Betty played the soubrette lead. Ethel Merman and Bert Lahr were the stars, but Betty was about to cause a sensation on the "Great White Way." The show had tryouts in New Haven, Boston and Philadelphia and then, on December 6, 1939, opened on Broadway just a few days before Betty's twenty-third birthday. Betty received glowing reviews, as well as the prestigious cover of _Life_ magazine. Her career gamble had paid off. All of New York and Hollywood were talking about little Betty Grable and her Broadway "Smash." Cole Porter said of her at the time: "If the show accomplished nothing else, it once and for all made it unnecessary to identify Miss Grable as 'Jackie Coogan's Ex'"(B39). Everyone loved Betty, including the star, Ethel Merman, who was not known to have much sympathy for younger, prettier co-stars. Ethel and Betty surprisingly became good friends and spent many evenings together at the Stork Club, where Artie Shaw squired Betty and Ethel visited her then-fiance, owner Sherman Billingsly, as camera bulbs flashed and columnists scribbled furiously.

Although Betty was often seen with producer Buddy De Sylva, her romance with Artie Shaw continued. But Artie was almost as famous for his playing with women as he was for playing his clarinet. While Betty was performing in New York, Artie began a romance with Judy Garland in California. In one of Hollywood's most famous "Slapstick" scenarios, Betty and Judy, both fully convinced that Artie was in love with them, awoke on the morning of February 12, 1940, to read in the newspapers that Artie had married Lana Turner. According to the luscious, just-turned twenty year old Miss Turner, longtime beau Greg Bautzer had broken a date with her on the evening of February 11th. Artie had phoned for a first date and they had eloped to Las Vegas. Both Judy and Betty were devastated and hysterical phone calls from the two girls to mutual friend Phil Silvers heated up the East and West Coast phone lines that fateful morning (B46).

During her appearances in _Dubarry_, it was publicized that she was engaged to Alexis Thompson, a rich Canadian, who had given her a ruby and diamond ring. It was obviously an attempt to let Shaw know that she had recovered from his ungallant behavior.

While healing her romantic wounds in New York, Betty tried songwriting. She also made some disparaging remarks about Hollywood not knowing exactly what to do with her in a newspaper interview. Darryl Zanuck read the remarks and a propitious chain of events began.

Reigning musical queen Alice Faye was about to star in the latest Fox Technicolor Latin American extravaganza Down Argentine Way. Suddenly, an emergency appendectomy for Miss Faye left the film without a star. Remembering his newest little blonde contractee, and having the intuitive hunch that this role might introduce his latest star to the filmgoing public with tremendous impact, Zanuck called Betty Grable back to Hollywood to star in Down Argentine Way. It has been conjectured that Fox could have waited a week or two for Faye's recovery but Alice was already beginning to get tired of her Film Stardom treadmill. As she later told costume designer/producer Ray Aghayan when they worked together on The Dinah Shore television show in the 1960's: "The limo would pick me up about four o clock in the morning. I'd go into make-up and hair styling, where I would sleep while they fixed me up and then I would walk onto the set. I didn't know which movie I was making. I just said my lines, walked down the staircase and sang my songs. It was all the same movie anyway. One morning, I was still so sleepy, I almost fell down the stairs. That's when I decided to quit. "The "Queen of Fox" was ready to abdicate and Zanuck sensed he had found her successor in Broadway's latest darling, Betty Grable.

As too often happens, Betty Grable had to go to Broadway and make a success for Hollywood to recognize her potential. The snob appeal of the Broadway stage was still very powerful in Hollywood, so Betty's gamble won her the greatest chance of her career. Her new-found confidence also showed on the screen in the film. She added spunk and energy to her beauty and singing and dancing talents as she "held her own" with co-stars Don Ameche, Charlotte Greenwood and Carmen Miranda's auspicious film debut. There is a moment in the film, as she begins to sing and dance the title number "DOWN ARGENTINE WAY," that even today is recognized as the moment Betty Grable was ready for stardom. She nearly burns the screen with her intensity and appeal.

While filming Down Argentine Way, Betty showed her songwriting efforts ("ALLURE" and "I'M NOT WORRIED") to film composers Mack Gordon and Harry Warren. With their advice, she managed to get them published by the Irving Berlin Company in  New York. Betty dove into the film with all of her energy and radiating in glorious Technicolor, she found her niche. Finally, in her fifty-second film, Miss Grable was to become a star! And a published songwriter! (B18).

Down Argentine Way, released in 1940, was to be the beginning of more than a decade of Grable's routine Fox color frivolities. They were not "Book" musicals where the songs and dances came naturally out of the story line as a continuation, but "Backstage" musicals where the only excuse to sing and dance would be rehearsals or performance. While the American musical theatre and the MGM movie musical team under the inspired leadership of Arthur Freed would move ahead to the more creative form of musical construction, Fox remained in the "Good Old Days" with Warner Brothers, Paramount and Columbia. Betty would not be asked to stretch her skills or credibility for the rest of her career - something which would eventually spell the end to her career and make her film efforts seem frivolous to later critics and biographers.

She would simply go on to make over 100 million dollars for Twentieth Century Fox.

## 3. PIN UP GIRL

As the public responded to Betty's new found fame, the emphasis on her physical attributes was continued by the Fox publicity team. During the next few years, she would be named "The Screen's Most Beautiful Blonde," "The Actress With the Best Figure," "Miss Ideal America" and a statuette of her would be named "The Spirit of Hollywood." As Betty was no stranger to publicity stunts, she patiently posed for photos and made publicity appearances - with Lillian close at hand.

The Publicity machinery of the studio system during those years worked overtime creating catchy names for their female stars. Starting with Clara Bow being named the "The It Girl," Jean Harlow was dubbed "The Platinum Blonde," Ann Sheridan became "The Ooomph Girl," Vivian Blaine - "The Cherry Blonde" and the madness reached its height with would-be starlet Chilli Williams being dubbed "The Polka Dot Girl." Grable was about to find her lasting name, but the public would bestow it on her.

Before her next Fox film, she made a prestigious "personal appearance" with Ken Murray at the Chicago Theater, while <u>Down Argentine Way</u> played in a nearby theater.

Her next film in 1940, <u>Tin Pan Alley</u>, paired her with Alice Faye and it is the only time moviegoers got to see "The Queen" and "The Intended" appear together. They remained life-long friends.

As a full-fledged movie personality, she was rushed from film to film in the next two years: <u>Moon Over Miami</u>, <u>A Yank in the R.A.F.</u>, <u>I Wake Up Screaming</u> and a short, <u>Hedda Hopper's Hollywood</u> in 1941; <u>Song of the Islands</u>, <u>Footlight Serenade</u>, and <u>Springtime in the Rockies</u> in 1942. Betty became "The Queen of the Fox Lot," with Lillian never far away. Lillian's visits to the soundstage during the shooting of each film continued, while cruel remarks were constantly made about her "lurking, limping" visits by studio workers. Although acclaimed as a movie queen, Betty Grable was still chaperoned by her doting Mother.

World War II was raging around the globe and escapist films were being manufactured in Hollywood as quickly as possible. Betty's ingratiating freshness and beauty appealed strongly to the American G.I.s stationed overseas and her films were eagerly requested by the lonely servicemen. She was also one of the film exhibitors' favorites, so Fox was constantly announcing new projects for their biggest star. When Alice Faye became pregnant, <u>My Gal Sal</u> was announced for Grable, but the starring role eventually was played by Rita

Hayworth (on loan from Columbia). There was also <u>Weekend in Havana</u>, with a conflict with Betty's busy schedule trading the role back to Faye.

Although she never toured outside the United States for the U.S.O., Betty actively participated in War efforts, appearing at Camps across the country and at Bond Rallys where she auctioned off her nylons for thousands of dollars (B8). Volunteering at the Hollywood Canteen, a club for servicemen staffed entirely by film stars and studio workers, she "Jitterbugged" the night away with hundreds of soldiers, sailors and marines. On Opening Night of the Canteen, it was reported that she changed partners forty six times in ten minutes in a "Tag Dance."

Betty was now a major star, with honors and accolades coming her way. But, along with glory also came the headaches of notoriety. In 1941, she was the intended victim of three Pennsylvania originated extortion plots. One was perpetrated by an 18 year boy, who called himself "The Yellow Hornet," from Washington, Pa. and demanded $2,000. The second, from a lady also from Washington Pa., also demanded $2,000. The third came from a twenty four year old singing waiter from Philadelphia. His demands were for $8,500. Betty learned quickly that fame had its price (B102 and B158).

On the screen, she was paired with all of Fox's biggest male heartthrobs: Tyrone Power, Don Ameche, Cesar Romero, Victor Mature and John Payne. Fan magazines of the period were filled with photos and print about her romantic nightclub hops with Oleg Cassini, Desi Arnaz, Mature and the ever-present George Raft, who once again figured importantly in her life after her unhappiness with Artie Shaw. She told Louella Parsons: "I would have married George Raft a week after I met him, I was so desperately in love with him. But, when you wait two and a half years, there doesn't seem to be any future in a romance with a married man...I don't expect to get over George today, tomorrow, or next week. But I do know there's no turning back"(B32).

Cesar Romero, one of Betty's co-stars in <u>Springtime in the Rockies</u> (and who would subsequently go on to co-star in three more of her films), told the author in a telephone interview that working with Betty was always a pleasure. "She was a complete professional and always fun to be around." He admitted that he would have liked to have been romantically involved with her. They often spent time together at social functions and appeared at studio sponsored events. "I tried and I tried, but she was in love with George Raft at the time, so it just didn't work out."

But a new man was about to come into her life.

Harry Haag James was born in Albany, Georgia on March 15, 1916 to a circus bandmaster father and a trapeze artist mother. At the age of five, young Harry was billed as "The Human Eel" and performed contortions in the circus. He began studying the drums and trumpet and, while still in his teens, became leader of the circus band. He then joined Ben Pollack's Orchestra and his unique trumpet virtuosity led him to a spot with Benny Goodman. After several best-selling records, he started his own band and by 1943 was one of the most popular names in American music.

Betty first met Harry James during her appearance with

Ken Murray in Chicago in October, 1940. Working together in Springtime in the Rockies, and volunteering at the Hollywood Canteen, their relationship blossomed into love.

Because he was married and the father of two young sons, he and Betty had to wait until his divorce became final. On July 5, 1943, in a little church on the property of the Frontier Hotel in Las Vegas, they were wed at 4:15 a.m. after a series of comic mishaps which delayed their arrival at the wedding site (B101). Surprisingly, her status as Mrs. James did not damage her popularity, but rather, enhanced it. "The Girl Next Door" became America's "Perfect Wife." All of the pieces of Betty's life were seemingly coming together. Named the Number One female box office attraction in 1942, 1943, and 1944 - Betty's name would consistently appear on the "Top Ten" box office lists for the next ten years. Her fan mail often totalled 10,000 letters per week. In 1942, she had sent 54,000 autographed photos to soldiers at Camp Robinson, Arkansas, in response to their 54,000 letters (B194). In a valuable publicity stunt, Fox Studios insured her famous legs with Lloyd's of London for $1,000,000 - and - she was pregnant.

On March 4, 1944, daughter Victoria was born, named after the character Betty had played in Springtime in the Rockies, a sentimental film for Mr. and Mrs. James.

Coney Island and Sweet Rosie O' Grady, Grable's first two "turn-of-the-century" musicals were released in 1943. Following the formula which Fox had successfully used of nostalgic period settings for Alice Faye in In Old Chicago (1938), Lillian Russell (1940) and Hello, Frisco, Hello (1943), the backstage "Gay 90's" locales were slightly adapted for Grable's saucy energy and dance ability, with ample opportunity for brief costumes to show off her valuable physical assets. In both films, the storylines allowed Betty to make the transition from brassy saloon queen to elegant Broadway star. She also made a guest appearance in Four Jills In a Jeep (1944), singing what would become one of her "Signature" songs, "CUDDLE UP A LITTLE CLOSER" from Coney Island. These successful films proved that Betty still had time for being a movie star, as well as mommy.

At the same time, a cheesecake photo of her, taken by photographer Frank Powolny, was to become the visual image of World War II. Millions of copies of the photo found their way to American Servicemen stationed overseas, as well as enemy troops. The story of the photo, like all good Hollywood legends, is muddled and contradictory.

Powolny himself erroneously recounted (B151) that he made the shot in the summer of 1941 - although the date on prints of the photo in various printings is "1943." The photographer said that Betty usually insisted on only one shot of each pose to give her pictures spontaneity but Powolny remembers he asked Grable for a "back" shot. She posed once and he asked for a second pose, to get a harder swing in her body. That is his version of the legend. Friends and co-workers have stated that Grable was pregnant at the time (which she would abort) and tried to hide her stomach. Other poses in the sitting, however, prove this to be untrue. Another well-rehashed version has Grable getting anxious during the photo shoot, turning her back to the camera and saying "That's it!," before she walked out of the studio.

Other claims: it was a shot used for <u>Sweet Rosie O'Grady</u> costume designers to create period wardrobe - complete with a garter on one of her legs which was later air-brushed out of the shot and/or it was the basis of a pose to be overpainted with period hat, costume and hairdo for a "Police Gazette" cover for the film (B126). Another story claimed that Fox studio chief Darryl F. Zanuck had entered the photo studio unexpectedly, greeted Betty and she turned around to saucily smile at him. Somewhere, in all of these stories, lies reality. Whatever the truth, the photo made history. The term "Pinup" simply described the action of pinning the photo of an object of admiration (or lust) on the wall by young men and women of celebrities about whom the fan could fantasize. Betty Grable became the quintessential "Pin Up," even giving the word new meaning.

<u>Pin Up Girl</u>, released in 1944, capitalized on that image and millions of Grable fans flocked to the film to see Betty in all of her female glory. Despite her being a wife and a mother, Betty now became a part of the erotic conscience of America, appearing in Tijuana Bibles (pornographic cartoon booklets) and smutty jokes of the period: "What is your favorite Los Angeles Newspaper?" "<u>Examiner</u>." "What newspaper do you read every day?" "<u>Examiner</u>." "What would you do if you found Betty Grable in the bath tub?" "<u>Examiner</u>." G.I.s were singing: "I want a girl just like the girl that married Harry  James!" Her wholesome sex-appeal ripened as her life and career did.

Betty's superstar status at Twentieth Century Fox is well described in <u>Zanuck, Hollywood's Last Tycoon</u> by Leo Guild (B69):"The stockholders complained about Zanuck putting alot of money into his pet projects and hiring the most expensive people in town for them. Zanuck had an answer for them. Walking through the 20th Century Fox lot one day, two important stockholders accompanied Zanuck. Betty Grable walked toward them from a distance. Zanuck pointed at her and said: 'See that girl? See those legs? They're celebrated and are a surefire commodity. They can always be depended upon to pay for the experiments that sometimes do and sometimes don't pan out.'" He was also quoted as saying when one of Fox's film budgets grew out of proportion: "If this one doesn't get off the nut, I'll never make another film without Grable in it"(B120). Betty never publicly revealed her relationship with the studio head, but it is known that she annually gave his children lavish gifts and admitted that Zanuck was the first studio executive to actually talk to her.

Asked about her reason for success by "fan mag" writers, Betty described her appeal thusly: "I'm strictly a song-and-dance girl. I'm no Bette Davis nor am I out to prove anything with histrionics. I just want to make pictures that people will like...My voice is just a voice. When it comes to dancing, I'm just average, maybe a little bit below...People like to hear me sing, see me dance and watch my legs - my legs made me."

Because of her "Gypsy" background and experiences and her hilarious sense of humor and profane comments, she was well-loved by all of the "Little People" on the studio lot: dancers (especially the chorus boys who she could "camp" with), crew, commissary employees and wardrobe women. She never behaved like the unapproachable star, but felt more comfortable as one of the gang. At the Fox commissary, she would not eat in the Executive lounge, instead choosing the main room with all her lesser co-workers. It is well-known Hollywood lore that the waitresses loved her and Carmen Miranda the most of all of the Fox stars. She did, however, cause constant havoc with costume designers such as Charles Le Maire, Orry Kelly and Jean Louis, who have been very vocal in recent books (B23) and interviews about their trials with her. Evidently, she was very opinionated about their creative draping of her famous form and had little regard for the correct period of her costumes. Instead, she was concerned with how her body could be displayed to its best advantage. After she had made life miserable for the designer, she was welcomed with open arms by the fitters and seamstresses in the Wardrobe department.

Hollywood's passion for the horse races was a topic for much of the gossip of the day. All of the major film studios' telephone bills skyrocketed during racing season. The _Hollywood Reporter_ and _Daily Variety_ began printing racing charts and such filmdom giants as Louis B. Mayer, Fred Astaire, Bing Crosby, Harry Warner, Spencer Tracy, Robert Taylor, Errol Flynn and Myron Selznick were proud horseowners. Having been introduced to the horse races by George Raft, Betty took Harry to the racetrack. They found that they had a mutual love of raising horses and betting on the races at Hollywood Park, Santa Anita and Del Mar racetracks. Harry's first purchase was half interest in a horse named "Devil Egg" and in its first race, it paid $114 to "Win." They purchased a sixty-two acre ranch in Calabasas for raising and breeding eighteen horses and then purchased 108 additional acres, naming it "The Baby J Ranch." Their first four horses were dubbed: "James Session," "Big Noise," "Count Cool" and "Mister Bluebird." Although Conn and Lillian were divorced, Betty continued to look after her father and had him co-manage the ranch, along with Harry's father. Lillian was also still on the payroll as "Secretary." Homes for Lillian were constantly purchased in Beverly Hills. The well-knotted ties could not be broken.

In 1945-'46, Betty starred in _Billy Rose's Diamond Horseshoe_, _The Dolly Sisters_, and made a surprise guest appearance in _Do You Love Me?_, Harry's first leading film role. Although Grable continued to be the perfectly obedient contract star, never complaining about the roles given her or being late or absent from work, Zanuck slipped another musical blonde into the wings, June Haver...just in case she might be needed. After all, Alice Faye had abdicated, hadn't she? When Faye turned it down, Betty and June were co-starred in _The Dolly Sisters_, a highly fictional account of the lives of two flamboyant Hungarian sisters who were musical comedy stars of the early 1900's. Miss Haver, a deeply religious girl, would eventually leave films and join a convent for a brief period. Betty wasn't sure that religion and the sexual politics of the "Casting Couch" worked together and secretly joked about Haver's overly religious attitude. Famous on the lot for her ribald sense of humor and "truck driver's" vocabulary, Betty and other female Fox stars reportedly said:

"June Haver is the only girl on the Fox lot with a crucifix in one hand - and a rubber in the other." Years later, Grable would also complain to <u>Hollywood Reporter</u> columnist, TV critic and friend, Robert Osborne, that because she worked from instinct and energy, her first "takes" were always her best. She felt that newcomer Haver had purposely ruined all of the early "takes," weakening Grable's on-screen performances. During the only time in her career, Grable sensed the competition and verbally revealed a dislike for a younger co-worker. But her animosity never showed on the screen and co-workers state that she was always amiable to the younger newcomer.

Fox also intended to star Grable in two more "Betty Grable formula" films in 1945, <u>Doll Face</u> and <u>Nob Hill</u>. Her busy schedule did not allow her to make the films, the roles going to Vivian Blaine. Grable encouraged Blaine, as she had all other newcomers, except Haver. <u>Nob Hill</u> would have co-starred Betty with George Raft, a reunion she perhaps did not relish.

The formula for a "Betty Grable" film was simple: garish Technicolor, a bouncy musical score performed in a backstage setting, a dark leading man, male and female comic sidekicks and Betty breezily portraying a spirited, scantily dressed young woman who must attain success and a husband within 90 minutes or less (B128). When viewed today, the films almost seem to be based on a single scenario, the characters and performers interchangeable. They were spewed out methodically by 20th Century Fox's filmmaking machinery to be the "A" slot of the then-popular double feature.

But the movies - and more importantly, the moviegoers - were changing. The War was reshaping American attitudes and Zanuck felt that they would no longer accept the film trifles of the past. At his first board meeting after returning from military service, Zanuck announced: "...when the boys come home from the battlefields overseas, you will find they have changed...Oh yes, I recognize that there'll always be a market for Betty Grable and Lana Turner and all of that tit stuff...We've got to start making movies that entertain but at the same time match the new climate of the times" (B48). In 1945, Zanuck offered Betty the role of "Sophie," the tragic alcoholic in <u>The Razor's Edge</u>. Betty turned the role down, saying: "Oh, come on. When Sophie drowns herself, my fans would expect me to surface two minutes later with lily pads in my hair, singing a love song." The role went to Anne Baxter, who would win an Academy Award for "Best Supporting Actress." Another film, <u>No Wedding Ring</u>, was announced for Betty, but never filmed. She did appear in two Fox shorts, <u>All Star Bond Rally</u> (1945 - in a number deleted from <u>Footlight Serenade</u>) and <u>Hollywood Park</u> (1946).

On May 20, 1947, a second daughter, Jessica, was born. The James' purchased another sixty-nine acre ranch in Woodland Hills. The family was now complete. Betty enjoyed her domestic life at their palatial home and two ranches. As the girls grew up, she made an attempt (possibly for Lillian's benefit) to enroll Vicki and Jessica in music and dance classes. As neither little girl expressed an interest - or natural ability - she quickly removed them and allowed them to enjoy the simple pleasures of other little girls

(B59, B161). Betty dubbed them "The Tomboy and the Lady."

The Treasury Department reported that for the year 1946-'47, Betty Grable's salary of $300,000 made her the highest salaried woman in the United States. Harry's big band tours unfortunately kept him away from home most of the time, but Betty kept busy. In 1947, she starred in <u>The Shocking Miss Pilgrim</u>, one of Fox's first serious attempts at a "Book" musical as they tried to compete with MGM's success with the genre. Unfortunately, the "Book" was weak, and although the music was by George and Ira Gershwin, it was uncompleted music which had languished in their "unused" files for many years. The characters and setting were drab, the production values weak and the highly-touted Gerswhin score minor. For their misguided efforts, Fox received over 100,000 complaint letters that Betty had not displayed her famous "Gams."

Conversely, 1947 also saw the release of Betty's greatest critical and financial success. In <u>Mother Wore Tights</u>, Betty was finally teamed with a male co-star who met and matched her musical talents, Dan Dailey. She had expected Fred Astaire or James Cagney, but she and Dailey made a splendid team. They went on to make three more successful films and became lifelong friends. Going back to her early "Formula," the musical numbers were all presented in a "performance" context and the period setting allowed her to repeatedly show her world-famous legs as she cavorted with Dailey in turn-of-the-century musical numbers which brought back pleasant memories of <u>Coney Island</u>, <u>Sweet Rosie O' Grady</u> and <u>The Dolly Sisters</u>.

To capitalize on her fame, struggling Astor Pictures released a series of her early 1930's shorts in <u>Hollywood Bound</u> in 1947, similar to the compilation they had released featuring Bing Crosby's early short film appearances.

In 1948, she appeared in <u>That Lady in Ermine</u>, an old fashioned Operetta, which was to be directed by Ernst Lubitsch, who had guided Maurice Chevalier and Jeanette MacDonald to fame in sexy, romantic musicals years before. Unfortunately, not only had he lost his famous "Lubitsch Touch," but he was very ill and suffered a heart attack only eight days into filming, being replaced by Otto Preminger - never famous for a "light fluff" touch in his work. The musical numbers all evolved out of the plot but needed a more classically based score than composers Leo Robin and Frederick Hollander contributed. Betty's light, "Pop" voice and her non-singing costar, Douglas Fairbanks, Jr. were miscast in roles that should have been played by such light-opera performers as Deanna Durbin and Dennis Morgan - neither under contract to Fox.

During the filming, co-star Fairbanks celebrated a birthday and Betty's ribald sense of humor was present at the party: "About five-o-clock in the afternoon, champagne and a cake were brought out, and, in keeping with their picture title, Betty Grable presented her co-star with an ermine-lined jock strap. Later in the filming, Grable had a birthday, and Fairbanks gave her an ermine-lined chastity belt"(Walter Abel, taped interview in New York City, January 5, 1979, B16).

Her next film, <u>When My Baby Smiles at Me</u> (1948), was set in the more familiar Grable territories of Vaudeville and

Burlesque, but attempted heavier drama - which paid off for co-star Dan Dailey with an Oscar nomination for "Best Actor." Rid of the cumbersome hoop skirts and cloying hairstyle of That Lady in Ermine, Betty gave a vibrant, relaxed performance which matched Dailey's intensity. However, Betty Grable was just not the sort of superstar who received "Oscar" recognition.

In 1949, her floundering career suffered from another serious miscalculation. She was miscast in The Beautiful Blonde From Bashful Bend, a satirical comedy/western, directed by the once-brilliant Preston Sturges, who had recently signed a producer/director/screenwriter contract with Fox. During his glory days at Paramount, Sturges was responsible for such film classics as Sullivan's Travels, The Miracle at Morgan's Creek and Hail The Conquering Hero. The movie flopped badly, as once again, Grable was handed a director-in-a-career-decline for her latest film. Her dissatisfaction with her career and Fox's handling of it began to grow along with her apathy. "Betting on the ponies" became a more important outlet for her interest.

Betty angrily begged Zanuck to return to more familiar territory for her fans and so, abandoning experimentation, Fox remade Coney Island as Wabash Avenue in 1950. Once again, Betty was box-office magic. The director, Henry Koster, had nothing but praise for her work (B93) and loyal fans returned in droves to the movie theaters to see Betty in more familiar territory, strutting and bumping her way through the Gay 90's.

Her later radio appearances during the 1940's and '50's on such Hollywood originated programs as the Lux Radio Theatre and Screen Guild Theatre were usually in edited versions of her film roles. It is speculated that because of her busy film schedule and Fox's tight reigns on her other activities, she did not appear on the radio as often as most other popular stars of the time. Not having a susidiary recording company like MGM, Fox also ignored enormous potential revenue by not releasing records of Grable's movie song hits. Instead, they allowed recording companies to reap the benefits by having her most popular songs recorded by other (usually male) singers. The only commercial recording she made of one of her hits was "I CAN'T BEGIN TO TELL YOU" from The Dolly Sisters with Harry James, done under an assumed name ("Ruth Haag") in 1945. It was probably done as an "inside joke," rather than in defiance of Fox's contractual limitations.

Her film career continued with My Blue Heaven (1950) and Call Me Mister (1951) both with Dan Dailey. She sang, she danced and she wore revealing costumes for all of her fans and scored Box Office successes. However, her apathy toward moviemaking was beginning to show. Caring more about marriage, motherhood and her mutual passion with Harry for the racetrack, reports began circulating that Miss Grable was merely "phoning it in." It was common knowledge on the Fox lot that "Betty Grable was far more interested in playing the horses than she was in learning her lines or rehearsing." For a scene in Call Me Mister, she and Benay Venuta were supposed to enter an office. The scene, as usual, was shot out of sequence, and just before they started shooting,

Venuta asked Grable, "Betty, have we met this guy before?" Grable turned on her charm and said, "Who knows, Benay? Let's just hit the marks" (Benay Venuta, taped interview in New York, January 5, 1979 - B16).

Co-star and close friend Dan Dailey had this to say about her and her attitude at the time: "I always called Betty 'Princess' 'cause that's how I felt about her. Betty was class. She was a true star. She could light up before the camera. If she had wanted she could have become a great dancer. I'd be suggesting new routines and she'd holler 'Who are you, the Director?' She was lazy I guess. Loved that racetrack. But great for the business and wonderful to work with" (B83).

A new challenge finally arrived for Betty when she filmed <u>Meet Me After The Show</u>, released in 1951, working for the first time with dynamic jazz choreographer Jack Cole and his assistant, Gwen Verdon. Jack and Betty got along well, with Cole trying to stretch her abilities. However, Betty was commonly perceived as Hollywood's "Good Old Girl" who did not want to reach for results, as described in the following exchange from <u>People Will Talk</u>: John Kobal:"...how adventurous, how creative could you be with her?" Hermes Pan: "You couldn't do much with Betty outside of letting her be Betty Grable. Pin-up girl, cute blonde who sang and danced..." J. K.: "Jack Cole once said that Betty Grable was really underrated and that she could do a lot of things that she wasn't allowed to." H. P.:"I don't really agree, because I worked with Betty on so many films and I can't imagine her doing something lyrical...even flowing...No, as I say, she was so...Betty Grable" (B92).

Fox next ordered her to make <u>The Girl Next Door</u> (working title: <u>Father Does a Strip</u>), a formula piece with Dailey. Wanting some time off, she refused and for the first time was placed on suspension on May 2, 1951. June Haver took the role and upon completion, left films and joined a convent. She was eventually to leave the religious life and marry Fred MacMurray (which caused Grable to caustically remark to Alice Faye: "She found out Nun was spelled "N-O-N-E!").

Struggling to keep Grable on the Box Office Top-Ten list and her profits pouring into 20th Century Fox, Darryl Zanuck then tried to get Betty to accept a role in <u>Blaze of Glory</u> (which became <u>Pickup on South Street</u>) with Richard Widmark, an exploitive property mixing gangsters and Communists. The original actress, Shelley Winters, was pregnant and Zanuck needed a replacement. Betty rejected it, saying: "I have lasted in this business by doing films that were good for me...pictures that my fans wanted to see me in. In <u>Blaze of Glory</u> they wanted me to play a B-Girl who picked up men in bars, I didn't think that was right for me" (B208). Jean Peters took the role and Betty was placed on suspension again - for eight months.

Things at home were not going well either. A series of troublesome lawsuits regarding the ranch (B107-109) plagued Betty and Harry and strained their finances. He continued traveling with his band, and rumors of his flirtations grew.

The "Glory Days" were over.

## 4.  MORE BLONDES WAITING IN THE WINGS

Since June Haver had left the studio to enter a convent, waiting in Fox's wings was the next "Fox Blonde," a bombshell named Marilyn Monroe. When Fox purchased the Broadway success <u>Gentlemen Prefer Blondes</u>, Betty assumed it was for her, although Judy Holliday had been mentioned for the role. When Monroe was announced as the lead, Hollywood gossipers immediately flew to Betty's side. When asked if she was jealous of Marilyn, Betty said: "Nonsense. I love working in pictures. I have no plans to retire. A lot of people think I'm jealous of Marilyn. That's not true. However, I was told that <u>Gentlemen Prefer Blondes</u> was bought for me. Naturally, I wanted to do it. Who wouldn't? But they gave it to Marilyn - and that was her good fortune...When Judy Garland bowed out of <u>Annie Get Your Gun</u>, I was dying to do that part. Twentieth wouldn't let me. In all the years I've been with Fox, I have never worked off the lot" (B208). As graceful as her answers were, it was obvious that Betty was not happy and beginning to read the cruel handwriting on the wall.

In 1953, she costarred with Dale Robertson in <u>The Farmer Takes A Wife</u>, a musicalized version of a Fox property first filmed in 1935. This proved to be an half-hearted attempt to capture the charm and success of such "Americana" stage musicals as <u>Oklahoma</u>, <u>Carousel</u> and <u>Paint Your Wagon</u>. But the film had an undistinguished screenplay and the wrong choreographer (jazz-oriented Jack Cole, who was Fox's dance director at the time.) Grable was to bitterly dub it "The Farmer Takes A Dump" in later years.

By 1953, Television had taken a serious toll on moviegoing and Hollywood was scared. They tried everything: 3-D, Cinerama and Cinemascope to lure moviegoers out of the comforts of their houses and back into the movie theaters. Fox released their second Cinemascope feature as <u>How To Marry A Millionaire</u>, with Betty, Marilyn Monroe and Lauren Bacall. As three gold-digging beauties, the fabulous blondes got great reviews and even better boxoffice receipts.

Betty attacked the film with new vigor and dedication, giving a performance which showed how well she would have handled "Lorelei Lee" in <u>Gentlemen Prefer Blondes</u>, receiving the best reviews of her career. Although Marilyn had been given Grable's former, plush dressing room, Betty went out of her way to make Marilyn comfortable, inviting her over to the house for dinner and late-night pep talks. This time, Betty welcomed the "Usurper." The super-professional attitude on the set among the three blondes is well documented in a letter from screenwriter Nunnally Johnson to a friend: "The three girls are a good story. Everybody went around with their fingers in their ears blabbering about what temperament there would be on the set, and needless to say, the gossip columnists, those lice, have done everything possible to forment trouble for us...But it hasn't worked in the least...Betty Bacall fell in love with Grable and now knows she's the funniest clown she ever had the pleasure of knowing. Which is not far from true. Miss Grable is a real hooligan, and is a fine salty, bawdy girl, without an ounce of pretense about her. In addition, she's giving a better performance than anything she ever did before" (B86).

In the 1990 video documentary <u>Marilyn Monroe - Beyond the Myth</u>, actress Celeste Holm remembered working with Monroe in <u>All About Eve</u> (1950) in her interview:"Marilyn ...wanted so much to be a movie star. So much, that in all her spare time, she watched Betty Grable movies. That's what she did. And the result of that was if you look now at a Betty Grable movie you will see that Marilyn Monroe was giving an imitation." Max Showalter, under contract to Fox as "Casey Adams" and who would eventually co-star with Grable onstage in <u>Hello Dolly</u> had also worked with Monroe in <u>Niagara</u>. He told identical stories about Marilyn consciously copying Grable's style. Marilyn herself told Columnist confidant Sidney Skolsky: "Jane Russell and Betty Grable are the two actresses I've worked with that I like."

It is ironic that Darryl F. Zanuck never truly appreciated his "Fox Blondes" - the ladies who built and bankrolled 20th Century Fox: Shirley Temple, Sonja Henie, Alice Faye, Betty Grable and Marilyn Monroe. His own personal tastes ran toward brooding, European brunettes Bella Darvi, Juliette Greco and Genevieve Gilles - three ladies he unsuccessfully tried to get the public to accept and acclaim as stars. But, the American public loved their Blondes. For all of Zanuck's creative brilliance, he never fully appreciated his greatest assets. As each of the Blondes became older, they were cruelly dumped, making room for the next one.

Through mutual agreement, Betty's contract with Fox was ended. Leaving Twentieth Century Fox for the first time in fifteen years on July 1, 1953, Betty Grable tore up her contract in front of Darryl Zanuck and gathered her personal belongings from her dressing room. Unlike Alice Faye who had left happily, co-workers reported that Betty Grable wept.

Being a sincere professional who realized what fate had in store for her, and wanting to salvage her marriage and family, Betty immediately launched into public appearances with Harry in Las Vegas and around America and sitting on the sidelines while he toured with his band. Their marriage was no longer working. His excessive drinking, gambling and womanizing and her shattered film career had taken their toll. She must have felt that if they were on tour together, she could control his roving eye. In the <u>Modern Screen</u> article "Miss Grable Steps Out" written while she was rehearsing her nightclub debut with James (B166), she said: "I won't sign another studio contract unless I have the right to do outside pictures of my own choosing...TV? Maybe yes, maybe no; it all depends. I'm the kind of girl who never plans her career. I just let nature take its course."

In 1954, Betty was invited by Columbia to make <u>Three For the Show</u>, her only Cinemascope musical. Teamed with up-and-coming Jack Lemmon and Marge and Gower Champion, Betty did her best to appear enthused about the project, although her father, Conn, died of Uremic poisoning on January 25, 1954, the day that filming began. Harry even showed up on that first day of filming, as he had in their happier days, trying to present a show of support for the press and the fans.

For what was to be her final film, in 1955, Betty was

asked back to Fox to co-star with Sheree North (Zanuck's latest "Blonde-in-the-wings" positioned there as a threat to Monroe) in How To Be Very, Very Popular, a film which wasn't popular with anyone - cast, critics or audiences. Marilyn Monroe had originally been announced as Betty's co-star, but refused to do the film. It was a sad "Swan Song" for a lady who had reigned supreme for over twenty years in American films.

### 5.  BACK ON THE "BOARDS"

Betty enjoyed a rare period of complete rest, accompanying Harry on his band tours and spending time with her growing daughters in the relaxed life on the ranch. Realizing it was inevitable, she began appearing on television. Making her debut in the audience of The Walter Winchell Show in 1953, she signed with Harry for a series of prestigious appearances on Shower of Stars for CBS. Miriam Nelson, associate producer and co-choreographer for Betty's first live musical show with James and Mario Lanza, remembers that the creative staff agonized over how they could be sure to show her legs and wonderful figure as they were creating her number "DIGA-DIGA-DOO." "When we told Betty that we wanted to show her legs, she said: 'I don't wanna show my legs. That's just what they expect!'" She relented and showed her legs - and was terrified of the live telecast, Miriam remembers.

From 1956 to 1960, she would alternate between TV and nightclub appearances, primarily in Las Vegas. She and Harry spent so much time in that city that they decided to move there, purchasing a home at 38 Country Club Lane, on the Desert Inn Golf Course. Victoria and Jessica were to spend their high school years in the blossoming Nevada town. This would not be a happy time for the girls, with the younger Jessica beginning to rebel against her parents. Betty is remembered as being a very strict, rather distant mother by Jessica in Pin Up - The Tragedy of Betty Grable (B151). The girls are quoted that their mother insisted on a definite double standard with her daughters when it came to profanity, being very careful never to let her famed ribald jokes and comments be spoken in front of them. Friends maintain that Betty tried her very best to raise the girls, but that her failing career and fragile ego were her priorities. An often-absent father did not ease the situation.

When Samuel Goldwyn announced that he was to make the film version of Guys and Dolls, Betty campaigned vigorously for the role of "Miss Adelaide," something she felt would make a triumphant return to films. Producer Goldwyn agreed. The then-mighty talent agency MCA had even proposed a boxoffice blockbuster package of clients Grable, Clark Gable, Bob Hope and Jane Russell for the film. However, on the morning she was to have a second meeting with Goldwyn, one of her beloved dogs took ill and she went to the Vet instead. Goldwyn was angered at being "stood up" and cast Vivian Blaine, who had created the role on Broadway.

20th Century Fox approached Grable about portraying

Tuesday Weld's mother in <u>Teenage Rebel</u>, a film version of the hit Broadway play <u>Roomful of Roses</u>. There must have been great satisfaction to turn their offer down, the film eventually being made with Ginger Rogers and Betty Lou Keim in 1956.

In 1956, Betty eagerly accepted straight roles in the television comedies <u>Cleopatra Collins</u> and <u>On the Twentieth Century</u>. Betty Grable was still a "hot item," so there was great publicity about her non-singing and dancing television appearances. The harsh critical roastings drove her back to basically musical appearances on the popular Musical Variety shows of the time.

After appearing at the El Rancho Vegas hotel in a duo act, she and Harry began to go their separate ways - he on tour with his big band and she on tour with her solo nightclub act. During the prolific nightclub "Boom" of the Fities and Sixties, most of Hollywood's former musical stars who were suddenly unemployed because of the demise of the Movie Musical began making nightclub appearances (Ann Sothern, Judy Garland, Eleanor Powell, Ginger Rogers, Betty Hutton, Mitzi Gaynor). The large salaries being offered even lured many not-so-musically proficient film celebrities as Tallulah Bankhead, Zsa Zsa Gabor, Mamie Van Doren and Terry Moore to take their chances with live audiences, often with disastrous results.

Grable's highly successful act consisted of musical numbers from her biggest film hits. The loyal fans flocked to see her, whether in Las Vegas, Chicago, Miami or New York's Latin Quarter, where she created a sensation, receiving a major review in <u>Time</u> magazine (B190) and other nationwide attention. Back onstage where her career had begun, Betty always delivered professionally energetic performances, treating the "Gypsies" who backed her up with respect and love. She toured continually from 1958-'61 with variations of the act, finally stopping when the critics began to mention her age.

Although she maintained lifelong female friends (Betty Ritz, Paula Stone and Alice Faye), she was often more comfortable in the company of men. She began surrounding herself with loyal fans Michael Levitt, Bob Isoz and Jeff Parker, energetic young men she had allowed into her personal life. They accompanied her everywhere, enjoying her good humor and being overwhelmed by her never-ending generosity.

Lillian was still an important part of her life. One day, while driving with Bob Isoz, an erroneous report came over the radio that she had been killed in a car accident coming back from the race track. Immediately, she thought of Lillian. "We've got to stop. I have to call my Mother.", she said. Lillian was still a strong influence and Betty had once confessed to Bob, "I did this all for my Mother and I don't regret it."

In 1964, Betty starred in two airings of <u>The Hollywood Palace</u> for A.B.C. <u>The Hollywood Palace</u> was nothing more than videoed Vaudeville and Betty felt right at home in her old element. Pete Menefee, now an Emmy Award winning costume designer, had started his career as a dancer in films and television. He remembered this about his appearance with the blonde star on a 1965 <u>Palace</u>: "In the Opening number, she recreated her famous "Pin Up Girl" pose and then the boys...there was a bunch of us...escorted her down the stairs. Some fortune teller had once told her that she would die from a fall from a staircase, so she was very nervous. Marc and Dee Dee (choreographers Marc Breaux and Dee Dee Wood) had to convince her there was no danger." This is an odd phobia, since Betty appeared on staircases throughout most of her career. Dee Dee Wood remembers her being "terrified at the studio...but take her to lunch and get a couple of drinks in her and she was great fun."

Her daughters were now grown and on August 17, 1964, Vicki married William Bevins, a fellow student at the University of Arizona. In July, 1965, Jessica rebelliously left home and married Ron Yahner. With Harry away on tour and their relationship quickly dissolving and her daughters starting families of their own, Betty tried to keep herself active. In 1962-'64, she returned to her first legitimate stage shows since <u>Dubarry Was A Lady</u>, appearing in stage productions of <u>Guys and Dolls</u> and <u>High Button Shoes</u> with Dan Dailey or Hugh O' Brien in Las Vegas and at Melodyland, a theatre-in-the-round across the street from Disneyland, in Anaheim. There were also an appearance on <u>The Andy Williams Show</u>.

The next two years, unfortunately, were to be filled with great personal tragedy. On December 4, 1964 Lillian died at the age of seventy-five of a heart attack and on October 7, 1965, Betty divorced Harry James after twenty-two years of marriage. The major influences in Betty's life were now gone. The void must have been deep and wide after so many years of living in the shadows of her mother's strong influence and the ups-and-downs of her volatile relationship with a man she would always love.

Professionally, she accepted a welcome offer from producer David Merrick and Director-Choreographer Gower Champion to star in one of the road companies of <u>Hello Dolly</u>. Composer Jerry Herman, a longtime Grable fan, was delighted with Betty's casting as "Dolly Levi" which took her on tour; to Las Vegas; on a second tour and back to Broadway on June 12, 1967...twenty eight years since her New York debut in <u>Dubarry Was a Lady</u>. Although the show had several touring companies and stars (Dorothy Lamour, Martha Raye, Ginger Rogers, Mary Martin, Ethel Merman, Pearl Bailey), Betty's production during 1965-'67 consistently made money for producer Merrick. At the stage door, she would be met by legions of older gentlemen who revealed that her pinup photo had helped them make it through the War. It was a time of triumph for her as the fans let her know she was not forgotten. However, she began having difficulties with "Opening Night" colds and a husky vocal quality, but rarely missed a performance (B14).

Emotionally uninvolved for the first time in twenty-two years, Betty reportedly became romantically linked with Bob Remick, a younger dancer in <u>Hello Dolly</u>. She often joked about their age difference, but Remick looked after her and gave her much-needed love and affection (B1).

Her Las Vegas home was always filled with friends and co-workers - usually the "Gypsies" that populated the desert town. Robert Osborne remembers that the house contained only one photo which represented Betty Grable's life and career. It was a photo of Betty and Louis Armstrong together, taken one night onstage during her Hello Dolly performances when Armstrong joined her onstage for a curtain call. She floated plastic ducks in her pool and laughingly told Osborne: "If I'd been at Metro, they would have been real swans!" She planned many late-night parties at the house, often asking dancer Jeff Parker to show old musical films from his vast personal collection. One evening, a party was planned after Debbie Reynold's last show. When Debbie, Jeff, Osborne and others arrived at 2:30 a.m., apologizing for the late hours, Betty greeted them at the door saying: "Only 2:30? Jesus Christ, June Haver's been at Mass for two hours!"

The highly publicized amounts of money she had made in the 1940's were gone, so she was forced to continue working. Her and Harry's obsessive love of the racetrack and gambling had depleted her reserve over the years, as she paid off debts and tried to keep her Las Vegas home and personal expenses going. The horses and ranches were gone, the Beverly Hills homes had been long ago sold. But, for so many years, she had lived like a "star" - she wasn't about to stop now. Her great generosity to others also needed financing.

The two full-length biographies written about her (B151 and B207) are filled with tales of excessive drinking, hence the cruel legacy often voiced today that "she died drunk and broke." There are no documented stories of her not being able to perform, substance abuse treatment or arrests due to drunkenness, although there are many about long evenings at Vegas lounges, restaurants and nightclubs where the liquor flowed freely. During her heydey, the image of a movie star included a cigarette in one hand and a martini in the other. She had been one of the most photographed examples of that lifestyle. And so, she was often seen, surrounded by cheerful friends and fans, laughing, smoking, drinking - and picking up the tab.

Robert Osborne described her as "A Movie Star. She always looked like one, she thought like one and she lived like one." That extravagant lifestyle needed money.

During 1968, she appeared with long-time admirer Carol Burnett and co-worker Martha Raye on The Carol Burnett Show. She also enjoyed making multiple appearances on the guest panel of The Hollywood Squares. Her television appearances were now nearly ignored by the press.

In 1969, Betty made her first trip to Europe when she travelled to Glasgow and London, to star in a new musical, Belle Starr, written by comedian-composer Steve Allen. While there, she made self-depreciating comments to James Green of the Evening News: "People who take themselves too seriously in this business cause themselves a lot of unhappiness. As a dancer I couldn't outdance Ginger Rogers or Eleanor Powell. As a singer I'm no rival to Doris Day. As an actress I don't take myself too seriously. I had a little bit of looks without being in the big beauty league. Maybe I had sincerity. And warmth. Those qualities are essential. I don't think I've ever had a good review. My films didn't get them either. Yet they did well at the Box Office...All I want to do is please the public. I'm a professional and always set out to do the best I can. They paid me for raising my skirt, not playing Sarah Bernhardt...You know, I used to wake up in the middle of the night wondering how long it would be before they found me out and ran me off the lot!"

As much as she would have wanted a big "Hit" in a new musical, Belle Starr was not to fulfill her wishes. The show was panned severely by the London Theatre critics, despite nightly standing ovations from her loyal British fans (B178). So, in defeat, Betty returned to America, Las Vegas and dinner theatres. From 1970 to 1972 she travelled with Bob Remick throughout the United States, as she acted in successful dinner theater productions of Born Yesterday.

In 1972, she was invited to appear on the 44th annual Academy Awards telecast on April 18th. Producer Howard Koch was determined to bring back some of the old Hollywood magic to the proceedings and invited Betty to be a presenter - as well as receive a tribute on the show. "LIGHTS, CAMERA, ACTION," a special piece of musical material written by Billy Barnes and sung by Joel Grey as the telecast's "Opening Number," featured a Betty Grable "Look-alike," who received a tremendous reaction from the audience. When the real Betty Grable appeared, on the arm of former co-star Dick Haymes to present the award for the "Best Musical Score," the audience showed their excitement. At fifty-five, she was still America's "Pin Up Queen Supreme" and nostalgia filled the air. She did not, however, look healthy that evening and had difficulty breathing. Ironically, this was her last major public appearance, giving her fans their final glimpse of the lady who had brought them so much happiness. She soon checked into St. John's Hospital in Los Angeles for tests.

The tests proved that the price of her heavy smoking habits finally had weakened her system and on May 6, 1972, exploratory surgery was performed on her neck to determine if cancer had spread to her lymph glands. She had received an offer to star in No. No. Nanette in Australia but her illness forced her to turn the offer down. Dire reports about the extent of her illness in the Hollywood columns frightened and infuriated her. Was she really dying? Remick was at her bedside constantly, as well as good friends Betty Ritz and Paula Stone. The operation was completed and Betty was allowed to go home.

She continued to make hopeful plans for live appearances, but the body which had brought her fame and fortune now told her that things were not well. Her operation had only temporarily halted the spread of cancer through her system. The cobalt treatments she received to stop the spread of the "Big C," as she called it, caused her hair to fall out and the cortisone she was given made her bloated. But, she made plans to do Born Yesterday in a Dinner Theatre in Florida in January of 1972. Her optimistic spirits just wouldn't let her give up.

Performing was very difficult for her, with Bob Remick often having to carry her to and from the stage. She never let the audience know how ill she was and the moment the curtain went up, the smile appeared. She gave her best until she couldn't muster up her "best" anymore. Finally, she was taken back to St. John's Hospital.

At the hospital, nurses and workers all fell in love with her as she bravely battled for her life. Worried that her fabled backside might be viewed by strangers through the slit in her hospital gown, she was reassured by one of the nurses: "Don't worry. Nobody's looking." Her fabled "Pin Up" pose must have flashed before her eyes as she answered: "They would've once."

On July 2, 1973, Betty Grable died, at 5:15 in the afternoon. She missed the genuine appreciation of the retrospectives, honors and television documentaries which came into fashion later when "nostalgia" became respectable. In 1973, Betty Grable was merely an ex-actress. Had she survived into the 1980's and 90's, she would have been the subject of respect and awe.

At her funeral, on July 5, 1973 at the All Saints Episcopal Church in Beverly Hills, a visibily grieving Harry James sat with daughters Victoria Bevins and Jessica Yahner, most probably remembering his wedding day to Betty on July 5, 1943. Although he had remarried and was now the father of a new son, Betty and he often met for lunch or talked on the phone since their divorce. Ironically, he was to die exactly ten years later on July 5, 1983. Other mourners included first husband Jackie Coogan, co-stars and friends Alice Faye, Dan Dailey, Dorothy Lamour, Mitzi Gaynor, Patsy Kelly and director George Seaton. June Haver also attended, respectfully ignoring the animosity she must have sensed from the lady who would no longer make cruel remarks about her.

Rev. Talley H. Jarrett Jr. of St. Peter's Episcopal Church in Del Mar delivered the eulogy. He had been Betty's pastor in Las Vegas. His words included the important part she had played in building morale during World War II: "We loved Betty Grable. Betty was one of those who shined even in darkness...She had a zest for life that made her one of the most popular women who ever lived. Well we remember her for her contributions to the morale of this land during some pretty dark days in World War II. She kept up our spirits and made us proud to be Americans - she was America to all of us." His words were honest and heartfelt.

The beautiful body which had inspired thousands of accolades and miles of press over the years was placed in "The Sanctuary of Dawn" in the Inglewood Memorial Park. Despite her self-professed meager talents, the "something special" that was Betty Grable would forever triumph amidst the dreaded excess of her Technicolor frivolities. Swathed in some of the most elaborate costumes ever imagined and topped by an escalating series of improbable hairdos, she was never swallowed up by it all. She transcended the inane scripts, the kitschy settings and the contrived musical sequences to take her rightful place in film folklore. From the darkness of thousands of movie screens, Betty Grable had shone into the hearts and minds of several generations - illuminating any dark spots in the soul and letting the common man share the simple joy of beauty, music and dance.

Betty, Harry, Victoria, and Jessica James, 1950. Collection of Bob Izoz.

# Chronology

1916
March 15 - Harry James born in Albany, Georgia.

December 18 - Betty Grable born at 3955 Lafayette Street, south St. Louis, Mo.

1920
Betty begins dance classes at Clark's Dance School.

1922
Begins school at Mary Institute and makes her first stage appearances at the Ambassador and Odeon Theaters.

1924
Wins the Charleston contest at the Missouri Theater.

1928
The Family goes to Hollywood for summer vacation.

1929
Spring - mother Lillian and Betty move permanently to Hollywood. She appears in her first film, dancing in the Fox chorus: Happy Days and Let's Go Places.

December 18 - she is thirteen years old.

1930
Betty attends Le Conte Jr. High School and Lawlor's Professional School for Children.

March 28 - signs a contract with Samuel Goldwyn.

Films released: New Movietone Follies, Whoopee.

1931
Dances in the chorus of a musical revue at the Hillstreet Theatre.

Film Releases: Kiki, Ex-Sweeties, Crashing Hollywood, Once A Hero and Palmy Days, where she meets George Raft. She adopts the stage name:

"Frances Dean."

1932        Film Releases: <u>The Greeks Had A Word For Them</u>,
            <u>Lady, Please!</u>, <u>Hollywood Luck</u>, <u>The Flirty
            Sleepwalker</u>, <u>Hollywood Lights</u>, <u>The Age of
            Consent</u>, <u>Hold 'Em Jail</u>, <u>Over The Counter</u> and
            <u>Probation</u>.

            December 18, she is sixteen.

            December 29 - <u>Tattle Tales</u> open at the Belasco
            Theater, L.A.

1933        Appears with the Ted Fiorito, Hal Grayson and
            the Jay Whidden Bands (May, 1933 - May, 1934).

            Film releases: <u>The Kid From Spain</u>, <u>Cavalcade</u>,
            <u>Child of Manhattan</u>, <u>Melody Cruise</u>, <u>What Price
            Innocence?</u>, <u>Sweetheart of Sigma Chi</u>, <u>Air Tonic</u>.

1934        She signs a contract with RKO. Film releases:
            <u>Elmer Steps Out</u>, <u>Love Detectives</u>, <u>Business Is A
            Pleasure</u>, <u>Susie's Affairs</u>, <u>The Gay Divorcee</u>,
            <u>Student Tour</u>, <u>By Your Leave</u>,

            On December 18, she is eighteen.

1935        January 25 - Appears in a vaudeville unit with
            Bert Wheeler in Chicago.

            Late summer - Bill Carey from the Ted Fiorito
            Band introduces her to Jackie Coogan on a boat
            to Catalina.

            Conn arrives from St. Louis to join Lillian and
            Betty in Hollywood.

            December 20 - She stars with Jackie Coogan in
            <u>Hollywood Secrets</u> vaudeville unit, tours for
            fourteen weeks.

            Film Releases: <u>The Spirit of 1976</u>, <u>The Nitwits</u>,
            <u>A Night At The Hollywood Bowl</u>, <u>Drawing Rumors</u>,
            <u>Old Man Rhythm</u>, <u>A Quiet Fourth</u>.

1936        Film releases: <u>Collegiate</u>, <u>Follow The Fleet</u>,
            <u>Sunkist Stars at Palm Springs</u>, <u>Don't Turn 'Em
            Loose</u>, <u>Pigskin Parade</u>.

1937        Signs a contract with Paramount Studios. Film
            Releases: <u>This Way Please</u>.

            On December 18, she is twenty one.

            December 20 - She marries Jackie Coogan, St.
            Brendan's Church, L.A.

1938        May 31 - Lillian and Conn separate.

Films: <u>Thrill of a Lifetime</u>, <u>College Swing</u>, <u>Give Me A Sailor</u>, <u>Campus Confessions</u>.

**1939**   January 20 - Betty announces her separation from Jackie Coogan.

June 1 - Lillian divorces Conn (married November 17, 1907).

July 21 - Appears with Jack Haley at the San Francisco Expo. She is spotted by agent Louis Shurr and signed for <u>Dubarry Was A Lady</u>. At the same time, a newspaper picture of her causes Darryl F. Zanuck to give her a contract with Twentieth Century Fox.

July 30 - Betty begins divorce proceedings against Coogan.

August 4 - Appears in a vaudeville unit with Eddie "Rochester" Anderson.

October 11 - interlocutory decree from Coogan given. She begins dating Artie Shaw.

October - rehearsals begin for <u>Dubarry Was A Lady</u>. The show opens out-of-town on November 9th in New Haven. Opens on Broadway December 6th.

Film Releases: <u>Man About Town</u>, <u>Million Dollar Legs</u>, <u>The Day The Bookies Wept</u>.

**1940**   February 8 - Artie Shaw marries Lana Turner.

June 7 - Alice Faye's appendectomy operation.

June 24 - Betty reports to Fox for work on <u>Down Argentine Way</u>.

October 25 - Appears at the Chicago Theater with Ken Murray for two weeks, where she meets Harry James.

November 19 - Her divorce from Coogan becomes final.

Film Releases: <u>Down Argentine Way</u>, <u>Tin Pan Alley</u>.

**1941**   She becomes a victim of three Extortion plots: #1. "Yellow Hornet," James Willard Porter, 18 of Washington, Pa. wants $2000. #2. James Thompson, 24, of Philadelphia wants $8,500. #3. Betty Westlake of Washington, Pa. wants $2,000.

On December 18, she is twenty five.

Film Releases: <u>Hedda Hopper's Hollywood</u>, <u>Moon</u>

<u>Over Miami, A Yank in the R.A.F.</u>, <u>I Wake Up Screaming</u>

1942   October - The Hollywood Canteen opens, where she is reunited with Harry James. She is named Captain of "The Comedians" playing football against "The Leading Men" (Rita Hayworth is their captain) at L.A. Coliseum for War Charities.

December 24 - After the Christmas party at the Hollywood Canteen, Harry James drives her home.

Film releases: <u>Footlight Serenade</u>, <u>Song of The Islands</u>, <u>Springtime in the Rockies</u>.

1943   February 15 - The hand-and-leg imprinting ceremony at Grauman's Chinese Theater in Hollywood.

July 2 - Harry's divorce from his wife is final.

July 5 - She marries Harry James at the Baptist Little Church of the West, Las Vegas at 4:15 a.m.

Frank Powolny takes the famous "Pin Up" shot.

October - She and Harry buy a house at the corner of Coldwater Canyon and Heather (Bert Lahr's former home).

Film Releases: <u>Coney Island</u>, <u>Sweet Rosie O'Grady</u>.

1944   March 3 - Daughter Victoria Elizabeth is born at the Cedars of Lebanon Hospital, Los Angeles at 4:45 a.m. The baby weighs seven pounds and twelve ounces.

Film Releases: <u>Four Jills in a Jeep</u>, <u>Pin Up Girl</u>.

1945   She is announced as the highest paid Fox Star ($208,000) and Darryl Zanuck offers her a role in <u>The Razor's Edge</u>. She declines. She purchases a home for Lillian at 257 Rodeo Drive in Beverly Hills.

Film Releases: <u>Billy Rose's Diamond Horseshoe</u>, <u>The Dolly Sisters</u>, <u>All Star Bond Rally</u>.

1946   On December 18, she turns thirty.

Film Releases: <u>Do You Love Me?</u>, <u>Hollywood Park</u>, <u>The Shocking Miss Pilgrim</u>.

1947   May 20 - Second daughter Jessica is born at the

Cedars of Lebanon Hospital in Los Angeles.
Harry is doing a "One-nighter" in Atlanta.
Jessica weighs six pounds and fourteen ounces.

Betty is announced as the highest paid female in
the U.S.($320,000) - even more than studio boss,
Darryl F. Zanuck! She and Harry open the "Baby
J. Stables." They designate Conn as the manager.

Film Releases: <u>Mother Wore Tights</u>, <u>Hollywood
Bound</u>.

1948    Film Releases: <u>That Lady in Ermine</u>, <u>When My Baby
Smiles At Me</u>.

1949    Film Releases: <u>The Beautiful Blonde From Bashful
Bend</u>.

1950    Film Releases: <u>Wabash Avenue</u>, <u>My Blue Heaven</u>.

1951    May 2 - Suspended by Fox for 6-8 weeks for
refusing to do <u>Father Does a Strip</u> (which
becomes <u>The Girl Next Door</u>).

December 18, she is thirty five.

Film Releases: <u>Call Me Mister</u>, <u>Meet Me After The
Show</u>.

1952    No Grable films are released this year. She is
unhappily assigned to <u>Pick Up On South Street</u>,
which she refuses.

September - she goes on suspension for six
months.

1953    March 6 - her suspension ends.

May 10 - She makes her television debut on <u>The
Walter Winchell Show</u>.

July 1 - she tears up her contract and leaves
Fox.

November 27 - Does a live tour with Harry,
playing Chicago and Detroit.

Film Releases: <u>The Farmer Takes a Wife</u>, <u>How To
Marry a Millionaire</u>.

1954    January 25 - Father Conn dies of uremic
poisoning. Betty begins filming on <u>Three For The
Show</u>.

Television Appearances: <u>Shower Of Stars</u>
(September 30 and November 18).

She and Harry buy a home in Las Vegas.

**1955**   February 17 - Betty injures her ankle and is replaced by Shirley MacLaine on Shower of Stars.

June 9 - Third Shower of Stars appearance.

Samuel Goldwyn sees Three For The Show and offers her Guys and Dolls.

July - First meeting with Goldwyn. She misses the second meeting and the offer is withdrawn. Her role is played by Vivian Blaine.

December 27 - Bob Hope Chevy Show.

Film Releases: Three For The Show, How To Be Very, Very Popular.

**1956**   February 15 - She begins her successful nightclub appearances at the El Rancho Vegas with Harry.

March 9 - Cleopatra Collins, TV comedy.

April 7 - Twentieth Century with Orson Welles.

May 13 - Appears as one "Hollywood Mothers of the Year" on the Ed Sullivan Show.

June 17 - Bob Hope Special.

November 2 - Dinah Shore Show.

On December 18, she is forty.

**1957**   January 22 - Appears with Harry on KTLA'S 10th Anniversary tv show.

January 25 - Bob Hope Special.

September 25 - Ed Sullivan Show.

October 29 - Eddie Fisher Show.

December 31 - opens at the Desert Inn, premiere of her solo nightclub act.

**1958**   February 3 - Appears with Harry on the Lucille Ball Desi Arnaz Comedy Show.

February 18 - Jerry Lewis Show.

March 26 - Academy Awards Show with Harry.

April 17 - Shower of Stars with Harry.

November 21 - Another appearance on the Bob Hope Show.

Nightclub appearances at the Moulin Rouge, Hollywood; Desert Inn, Las Vegas; Puerto Rico; Cal Neva Lodge, Lake Tahoe.

1959        Tours with her nightlub act: Latin Quarter, Miami; Flamingo, Las Vegas; Mapes Hotel, Reno.

March 8 - <u>Dinah Shore Chevy Show</u>.

April 7 - Opens triumphantly at the Latin Quarter in New York.

November 22 - a return visit to the <u>Dinah Shore Chevy Show</u>.

1960        April 3 - <u>Dinah Shore Chevy Show</u>.

June 7 - <u>Ford Star Time</u> with George Burns.

June 8 - She begins an appearance at the El Rancho Vegas but on July 17, the hotel burns down.

Other nightclub appearances: Deauville, Miami; Sahara, Las Vegas; Lubbock, Texas; Puerto Rico.

December 14 - <u>Perry Como's Kraft Music Hall</u>.

1961        She continues nightclub appearances throughout the U.S. (Flamingo, Las Vegas.)

On December 18, she is forty five.

1962        November 8 - <u>The Andy Williams Show</u>.

December 22 - <u>Guys and Dolls</u> opens at the Dunes Hotel, Las Vegas, with Dan Dailey.

1963        July 5 - She and Harry celebrate their 20th wedding anniversary.

September 23 - <u>Guys and Dolls</u> at Melodyland, Anaheim.

1964        May 5 - <u>Guys and Dolls</u> opens at the Coconut Grove Playhouse, Miami.

August 15 - Daughter Victoria marries William Wiley Bevins.

September 29 - <u>High Button Shoes</u> opens at Melodyland.

October 24 - She appears on <u>The Hollywood Palace</u>.

December 4 - Lillian dies of a heart attack.

December 26 - Another appearance on <u>The Hollywood Palace</u>.

1965        June 15 - <u>The Tonight Show</u>.

July - Second daughter Jessica leaves home and marries Ron Yahner.

August 29 - She is the "Secret Guest" on <u>What's My Line?"</u>

October 7 - Betty is granted a divorce from Harry.

October - <u>Hello Dolly</u> rehearsals begin in N.Y.

November 3 - She joins the Mary Martin Company and they open in Chattanooga, Tenneseee.

December 23 - <u>Hello Dolly</u> opens in Vegas at the Riviera Hotel.

1966        September - <u>Hello Dolly</u> closes in Vegas, goes on tour.

December 18 -  She celebrates her 50th birthday in Fort Wayne, Indiana.

1967        June 12 - <u>Hello Dolly</u> opens in New York.

June 18 - Appears on <u>What's My Line?</u>

Her Agent tries to get the film version of <u>Hello Dolly</u> for her and Dan Dailey.

1968        January 8 - Harry marries Joan Boyd.

February 3 - She appears on <u>The Carol Burnett Show</u>.

June - July - She appears in <u>Guys and Dolls</u> throughout the U.S.

1969        April 1 - <u>Belle Starr</u> opens in Glasgow, Scotland and then moves to London for a critical panning.

Multiple appearances on <u>Hollywood Squares</u> (September 8 - 12, October 13 - 17, November 17 - 21). She also is guest panelist on <u>Name Droppers</u> (October 6 - 10).

1970        March 23 - 27, guest panelist on <u>Hollywood Squares</u>.

Summer stock tour with <u>Born Yesterday</u>.

1971        She films a very successful <u>Geritol Commercial</u>.

August 30 - September 5 - Appears at the St. Louis Municipal Opera in This is Show Business with Dorothy Lamour.

Replaces Pearl Bailey in Hello Dolly! in Atlanta and Toledo.

On December 18, she is fifty five.

1972     February 29 - Appears on television in Those Fabulous Fordies.

Spring -   She is hospitalized for tests.

April 10 - Makes her final live television appearance on the 44th Annual Academy Awards.

September - Undergoes stomach surgery.

December 18 - She is fifty six.

1973     January 24 - Born Yesterday at the Alhambra Dinner Theater, Florida.

July 2 - Betty Grable dies at 5:15 p.m.

July 5 - Funeral, All Saints Epsicopal Church, 1:00 p.m.

The legendary "Pinup" girl photo, 1943. Photograph by Frank Powolny.

# Filmography

## F1.  Happy Days

(Fox, Release date: December 23, 1929) 86 minutes, "Grandeur" 70 mm.

CREDITS:
Director, Benjamin Stoloff; script, Sidney Lanfield, Edwin Burke; photography, Lucien Andriot, John Schmitz (Grandeur camera, J.O. Taylor); editor, Clyde Carruth; art director, Jack Schulze; costumes, Sophie Wachner; musical numbers staged by Earl Lindsay.

SONGS:
"MONA;" "SNAKE HIPS;" "CRAZY FEET;" "HAPPY DAYS" by Con Conrad, Sidney Mitchell and Archie Gottler
"MINSTREL MEMORIES;" "I'M ON A DIET OF LOVE" by L. Wolfe Gilbert and Abel Baer
"WE'LL BUILD A LITTLE WORLD OF OUR OWN;" "A TOAST TO THE GIRL I LOVE;" "DREAM ON A PIECE OF WEDDING CAKE" by James Hanley and James Brockman
"VIC AND EDDIE" by Harry Stoddard and Marcy Klauber

CAST:
Marjorie White (Margie); Charles E. Evans (Colonel Billy Batcher); Richard Keene (Dick); Stuart Erwin (Jig); Martha Lee Sparks (Nancy Lee); Clifford Dempsey (Sheriff Benton); Minstrel ensemble: Frank Albertson, Warner Baxter, Rex Bell, El Brendel, Walter Catlett, William Collier, Charles Farrell, Janet Gaynor, George Jessel, Dixie Lee, Edmund Lowe, Sharon Lynn, Victor McLaglen, Tom Pastricola, Ann Pennington, Will Rogers, David Rollins, Nick Stuart; George McFarlane and James J. Corbett (Interlocutors); Betty Grable (member of the Fox chorus).

SYNOPSIS:
Margie, a Mississippi riverboat soubrette (Marjorie White) tries to persuade all of the performers who were apprentices on the Showboat to come together and perform a benefit Minstrel show in Memphis to raise money to save the riverboat

from bankruptcy and closure. She succeeds and the rest of the film becomes a musical revue, featuring most of Fox's stars.

REVIEWS:
PHOTOPLAY, May 1930: "...Fox's latest in the big parade of photoplay revues. It wears a minstrel suit and carries a huge red banner. A bunch of entertainers band together to help an old showman save his troupe. And what an entertainment! Happy Days was shown at the Roxy, New York, on the wide Grandeur screen, and made everybody gasp."

NEW YORK TIMES, 2.14.30 - Mordaunt Hall: "In one of the features a bevy of dancing girls suddenly appears from two giant shoes. In another there is a giant baby carriage with about a dozen crying infants, and in a third a wedding cake that makes the players look like Lilliputians."

COMMENTS:
- Betty appears in blackface in the chorus of "MINSTREL MEMORIES" as part of the the Fox Dancing Chorus.
- The film was originally shown at New York's Roxy Theatre in a 70mm Grandeur system print. The film was advertised as "William Fox's first Grandeur Audible Picture!" 24 years later, Betty would appear in Fox's first Cinemascope film, How To Marry A Millionaire (although released after The Robe, Darryl F. Zanuck's personal production.)

## F2.    Let's Go Places

(Fox, Release date: December 30, 1929) 70 minutes

CREDITS:
Director: Frank Strayer; screenplay, William K. Wells; based on a story by Andrew Bennison;  camera, Conrad Wells, editor, Al De Gaetano; dance director, Danny Dare.

SONGS:
"REACH OUT FOR A RAINBOW;" "UM, UM IN THE MOOONLIGHT;" "OUT IN THE COLD;" "HOLLYWOOD NIGHTS" and "PARADE OF THE BLUES" by Sidney Mitchell, Archie Gottler and Con Conrad
"LET'S GO PLACES" by Cliff Friend and Jimmy Monaco
"FASCINATING DEVIL" and "SNOWBALL MAN" by Joe Mc Carthy and Jimmy Monaco
"BOOP-BOOP-A-DOOPA-DO TROT" by Johnny Burke and George Little

CAST:
Joseph Wagstaff (Paul Adams); Lola Lane (Marjorie Lorraine); Sharon Lynn (Virginia Gordon); Frank Richardson (J. Speed Quinn); Walter Catlett (Rex Wardell); Dixie Lee (Dixie);  Charles Judels (DuBonnet);  Ilka Chase (Mrs DuBonnet); Larry Steers (Ben King); Betty Grable (Chorus Girl); Eddie Kane (Frenchman).

SYNOPSIS:
Paul Adams (Joseph Wagstaff) is a young and ambitious singer on his way to Hollywood. When he arrives, he is mistaken for a famous operatic tenor, Dubonnet (Charles Judels). Staying

at his look-alike's Hollywood mansion, he begins a film
career and falls in love with chorine Marjorie Lorraine (Lola
Lane). When the genuine tenor's wife (Ilka Chase) claims him,
trouble begins. Finally, the real opera star arrives and Paul
discovers that the man he is impersonating is his Uncle, so
all is forgiven.

REVIEWS:
VARIETY, 3.5.30: "Production reaches its climax in 'PARADE
OF THE BLUES' done as a studio sequence with technicians and
cameras in view at the start. It's a double exposure, with
chorus in miniature shown stamping on a huge drum as the same
chorus parades below in larger dimensions."

NEW YORK TIMES, 3.1.30: "...as there are scenes in a
Hollywood studio it has been easy to give a long stretch of
dancing girls presumed to be in a kind of Antarctic cafe,
where the beauties suddenly appear from gigantic snowballs
and are ready to trip the light fantastic for the applauding
multitude."

COMMENTS:
- Once again, Betty does chorus work.
- Rather than the over-worked theatrical "Backstage" story,
Let's Go Places was announced by Fox to be one of the first
films with a "Behind-the-scenes-in-Hollywood" story, showing
how films are made. It never quite lived up to its publicity
promise, however.

## F3.    Fox Movietone Follies of 1930

(Fox, Release date: April 21, 1930) 70 minutes

CREDITS:
Director, Benjamin Stoloff; screenplay, William K. Wells;
camera, L.W. O'Connell; editor, Clyde Carruth; art
director, Steven Goosen; music director, Arthur Kay; dance
directors, Danny Dare, Max Scheck and Maurice Kussell.

SONGS:
"CHEER UP AND SMILE;" "DOIN' THE DERBY" and "HERE COMES
EMILY BROWN" by Jack Meskill and Con Conrad
"I'D LOVE TO BE A TALKING PICTURE QUEEN" by James Brockman,
Joseph Mc Carthy and James Hanley
"YOU'LL GIVE IN" by Joseph Mc Carthy and James Hanley
"I FEEL A CERTAIN FEELIN' COMING ON" and "BASHFUL" by Cliff
Friend and James V. Monaco

CAST:
El Brendel (Alex Svenson); Marjorie White (Vera Fontaine);
Frank Richardson (George Randall); Noel Francis (Gloria De
Witt); William Collier,Jr. (Conrad Sterling); Miriam Seegar
(Mary Mason); Huntley Gordon (Marvin Kingsley); Paul
Nicholson (Lee Hubert); Yola D'Avril (Maid); Betty Grable
(member of the Fox chorus).

SYNOPSIS:
Playboy Conrad Sterling (William Collier, Jr.) causes a fuss

in a nightclub and is written about in the newspapers. Mary Mason (Miriam Seegar), a musical comedy chorus girl, thought that she loved him but is so upset at all of the negative publicity, she refuses to see him. Sterling manages to convince the producer of Mary's latest show to have the cast rehearse at his uncle's lavish mansion so that he can spend some time with Mary and convince her that they were meant for each other. Mary realizes how much trouble Sterling has gone to with his romantic plot to bring them together and all ends happily.

REVIEWS:
PHOTOPLAY, July 1930: "By 1930 the Fox Follies is just another revue. Good enough as such things go, but there have been so many. However, if you like revues, you'll like this. Some fair songs; plenty of high comedy by Marjorie White and El Brendel...and a series of big spectacular scenes."

VARIETY, 6.25.30: "Hybrid rich boy-virtuous chorus girl meller and a hodge podge of the musical revue stuff. It is the strangest combination ever seen on the screen...whatever it is, it is a poor picture that evidences no excuses for its budget."

NEW YORK TIMES, 6.22.30 - Mordaunt Hall: "There are many lavish scenes with dancing girls, but, unfortunately, there is little idea of sound perspective; for when a person is at a distance from the camera or close to it the singing is of the same volume."

COMMENTS:
- Betty appears in the Fox chorus.
- This film is sometimes titled Fox New Movietone Follies and New Movietone Follies of 1930, as the original (William Fox Movietone Follies of 1929) was released the previous year, also in the "Grandeur" 70 mm process.

## F4.   Whoopee

(UA, Release date: September 1, 1930) 94 minutes, Technicolor

CREDITS:
Producers, Florenz Ziegfeld, Samuel Goldwyn; director, Thornton Freeland; screenplay, William Conselman; based on the musical play Whoopee by William Anthony McGuire; adapted from the play The Nervous Wreck by Owen Davis; from a story "The Wreck" by E. J. Rath; camera, Lee Garmes, Ray Rennahan, Gregg Toland; editor, Stuart Heisler; interior decoration, Richard Day; costumes, John Harkrider; musical director, Alfred Newman; production scored and played by George Olsen and His Music; dances and ensembles staged by Busby Berkeley.

SONGS:
"MAKING WHOOPEE;" "STETSON;" "THE SONG OF THE SETTING SUN;" "MISSION NUMBER;" "MAKIN' WAFFLES;" "MY BABY JUST CARES FOR ME;" "INVOCATION TO THE MOUNTAIN GOD;" "MOJAVE WAR

DANCE" and "A GIRLFRIEND OF A BOYFRIEND OF MINE" by Walter Donaldson and Gus Kahn
"I'LL STILL BELONG TO YOU" by Edward Eliscu and Nacio Herb Brown

CAST:
Eddie Cantor (Henry Williams); Eleanor Hunt (Sally Morgan); Paul Gregory (Wanenis); John Rutherford (Sheriff Bob Wells); Ethel Shutta (Mary Custer); Spencer Charters (Jerome Underwood); Chief Caupolican (Black Eagle); Albert Hackett (Chester Underwood); Will H. Philbrick (Andy Mc Nabb); Walter Law (Judd Morgan); Marian Marsh (Harriet Underwood); Dorothy Knapp, Jeanne Morgan, Virginia Bruce, Muriel Finley, Ernestine Mahoney, Christine Maple, Jane Keithly, Mary Ashcraft, Georgia Lerch and Betty Stockton (Showgirls); The George Olsen Band (Themselves); Jacques Cartier, Joyzelle, Betty Grable (Dancers).

SYNOPSIS:
Henry Williams (Eddie Cantor) is a hypochondriac who finds himself on an Arizona dude ranch being cared for by Nurse Custer (Ethel Shutta). She proposes to him, but believing himself to be near death, the frail Henry turns her down. Sheriff Bob Wells (Jack Rutherford) is about to be married to Sally Morgan (Eleanor Hunt), when her childhood sweetheart, Wanenis (Paul Gregory), arrives home from college. Because he is a "Half-Breed," they can never wed, but Sally decides to escape her impending marriage with Henry's aid. They arrive at a nearby ranch, followed by the Sheriff, his posse and the lovesick Nurse Custer. Henry and Sally escape once again, to the Indian Village, where Wanenis finds out he was an abandoned "Paleface" baby, so he and Sally can wed. All ends happily, with the frail Henry in Nurse Custer's strong arms.

REVIEWS:
PHOTOPLAY, October 1930: "It's Sam Goldwyn at his best, Flo Ziegfeld at his best. You can't beat a team like that. Don't say you're fed up on musical comedies. Go to see Whoopee instead. The million and a half spent on it is justified. Ziegfeld brought his most beautiful show girls with him and Hollywood gave its very best...will make you forget Hoover's advice to sit tight because better times are coming. Heck! They are here!"

VARIETY, 10.8.30: "...has everything a laughable high-class musical comedy should have, including Technicolor all the way...aided by superb photography, nifty number staging by Busby Berkeley inclusive of one fine overhead shot on the girls, besides the Lady Godiva stuff of the gals riding down the trail astride horses."

NEW YORK TIMES, 10.1.30 - Mordaunt Hall: "There are fascinating groups of dancers, photographed from directly above, that are remarkably effective."

COMMENTS:
- Fourteen year old Betty leads the Chorus Girls in "THE COWBOY NUMBER" in the opening sequence of this early color

film. She begins the song with a solo, gets playful with some of the Cowboys - even lassoos one of them - and serves as the centerpiece for several Busby Berkeley overhead patterns. On March 28, 1930, she signed a contract with Samuel Goldwyn for $50 per week for the film, co-signed by Lillian, since Betty was a minor.

- In several interviews conducted with Busby Berkeley in the 1970's, he remembers "Discovering" Grable when she was fifteen or sixteen years old (depending on the interview) and casting her in a featured spot in the film. There are several versions of her age printed in many books (B157, B185), but judging from her chronology and when the film was made, she could not be any older than fourteen.

- The film is not much more than a photographed version of one of Cantor's greatest stage successes, with many cast members repeating their roles on film. The lavish "Indian" number is probably one of the best examples of a <u>Ziegfeld Follies</u> number captured on film. The partnership of Sam Goldwyn and Florenz Ziegfeld was a first for both. The friendly relations finally frayed when Ziegfeld insisted on top billing, with Goldwyn barring him from the soundstage during filming.

- Ethel Shutta, playing the determined nurse who is in love with Cantor, performs a very exhuberant "STETSON" song and dance in the film. She later made a sensational comeback on Broadway in 1971 in Stephen Sondheim's <u>Follies</u>, performing the song "BROADWAY BABY."

- <u>Whoopee</u> marked the film debut of Busby Berkeley's cinematic dance innovations.

- The plot began as a story called "The Wreck" by E.J.Rath (the pseudonym for a husband-and-wife writing team), became <u>The Nervous Wreck</u> on Broadway in 1923 and then was filmed in 1926 before being musicalized in 1928. It was remade in 1944 by Goldwyn as <u>Up In Arms</u>, introducing Danny Kaye in his film debut in the Cantor role.

- Filmed at a cost of 1.3 million dollars, the film earned 2.7 million dollars at the box-office. Goldwyn charged $5.00 per ticket during its first run.

ACADEMY AWARDS: Nomination for Interior Decoration - Richard Day.
VIDEO: Embassy Home Entertainment (V36)
RECORDING: "COWBOY NUMBER" on "Betty Grable" (D1)

**F5.   Kiki**

(UA, Release date: March 6, 1931) 96 minutes

CREDITS:
Producer, Joseph M. Schenck; director-screenplay, Sam Taylor; based on the play by David Belasco, from the French play by Andre Picardi; assistant director, Earle Brown; camera; Karl Struss; editor, Allen McNeil; dance director, Busby Berkeley.

CAST:
Mary Pickford (Kiki); Reginald Denny (Victor Randall); Joseph Cawthorn (Alfred Rapp); Margaret Livingston

(Paulette Valle); Phil Tead (Eddie); Fred Walton (Bunson); Edwin Maxwell (Dr. Smiley); Betty Grable (chorus girl).

SYNOPSIS:
Kiki (Mary Pickford) is a fiery French Chorus girl chasing an impressario, Victor Randall (Reginald Denny), whose ex-wife, Paulette (Margaret Livingston), is a Follies star. Kiki loses her job in the chorus for biting another chorine but begs to get her job back, promising to behave. On Opening Night of the new show, she is so enamored with Victor, sitting in the audience, that she ruins the dance routine and Paulette's performance. Victor mistakenly installs her in an apartment out of pity, and then begins trying desperately to get rid of her. She pretends to be in a trance to save herself from being evicted and her perserverance finally pays off and she wins the man she loves.

REVIEWS:
VARIETY, 3.11.31: "The discrepency is that the star is characterizing what was meant to be a pretty rough chorister might as well be doing an innocent if tempestuous child.  The result is that Miss Pickford is again 'cute'...women will undoubtedly fawn over the star...as she looks particularly well in boy's regalia."

NEW YORK TIMES, 3.6.31: "If Mary Pickford is the whole show in Kiki...it is more a tribute to the inexhaustible energy and verve of that comedienne than any dubious quality in the rest of the film."

MOTION PICTURE GUIDE, 1987: "Fifteen year old Betty Grable already was showing her great complexion and wonderful legs in this, her second year in movies."

COMMENTS:
- In one musical number, directed by Busby Berkeley, Mary, disguised as a Chorus boy in top hat and tails, joins male dancers in a dance routine which she does not know. She ends up falling into a bass drum.
- Grable reportedly acted as the "Dance-in" for Miss Pickford in the long shots.
- In a calculated attempt to play more mature roles, Pickford even studied with Fifi D'Orsay and Maurice Chevalier's wife to learn a French accent.
- The film cost $810,568 but only grossed $426,513. It was the first Mary Pickford film to lose money for United Artists. It had been filmed in 1926, starring Norma Talmadge.

## F6.     Ex-Sweeties

(Educational, Release date: April 1, 1931) (Short), 16 minutes

CREDITS:
Producer, Mack Sennett; director, Marshall Neilan; story and dialogue, John A. Waldron, Earle Rodney, Walter Weems, Ewart Anderson.

CAST:
Harry Gribbon, Marjorie Beebe, Wade Boteler, Betty Boyd,
Frances Dean [Betty Grable].

SYNOPSIS:
Two men (Harry Gribbon and Wade Boteler) chase a pretty woman
(Marjorie Beebe) until another beauty (Betty Boyd) comes
along. However, her gun-toting husband makes the clumsy
Gribbon hastily exit.

REVIEW:
MOTION PICTURE HERALD, 1931: "The lines are not half bad and
the plot idea is fair enough, but the old stuff makes the
short drag too much to be really effective...Slow, but fair
enough entertainment."

COMMENTS:
- Billed as a "Mack Sennett Comedy."
- Betty's first release as "Frances Dean." Reputedly, Betty's
mother insisted she change her name, since Fatty Arbuckle was
her director (working under the name of "William Goodrich" in
her next release) and Mrs. Grable did not want Betty's
association with him to tarnish her career (B13, B151).
Various sources have written conflicting information about
this name change: that she used the name for ten years; that
Samuel Goldwyn suggested it (B197); and that she changed it
for her contract at RKO. She is not billed in any of her RKO
films as "Frances Dean" and it has also been written that she
used it to do outside work, unbeknownst to RKO (B119).

## F7.   Crashing Hollywood

(Educational, Release date: April 5, 1931) (Short), 22
minutes

CREDITS:
Director, William Goodrich; assistant director, Ralph
Nelson; story and dialogue, Ernest Pagano and Jack Townley;
camera, Dwight Warren.

CAST:
Virginia Brooks, Rita Flynn, Phyllis Crane, Eddie Nugent,
Wilbur Mack, Walter Merrill, Frances Dean [Betty Grable].

SYNOPSIS:
A naive woman from Iowa finds comic complications at a fake
"Wild" Hollywood party.

COMMENTS:
-   The second picture in the Educational "Ideal
Comedy/Hollywood Girls" series of short films. A sequel to
Three Hollywood Girls.

## F8.   Palmy Days

(UA, Release date: October 3, 1931) 80 minutes

CREDITS:
Producer, Samuel Goldwyn; director, Edward Sutherland; story and dialogue by Eddie Cantor, Morrie Ryskind, David Freedman; continuity, Keene Thompson; camera, Gregg Toland; editor, Sherman Todd; settings, Richard Day, Willy Pogany; costumes, Alice O'Neil; musical director, Alfred Newman; dances and ensembles, Busby Berkeley.

SONGS:
"BEND DOWN SISTER;" "GOOSE PIMPLES" (deleted) and "DUNK DUNK DUNK" by Harry Akst and Con Conrad
"THERE'S NOTHING TOO GOOD FOR MY BABY" by Eddie Cantor and Bennie Davis
"MY HONEY SAID YES,YES" by Cliff Friend

CAST:
Eddie Cantor (Eddie Simpson); Charlotte Greenwood (Helen Martin); Spencer Charters (A.B.Clark); Barbara Weeks (Joan Clark); George Raft (Joe - The Frog); Paul Page (Steve); Harry Woods (Plug Moynihan); Walter Catlett (Cake Eater), Charles B. Middleton (Yolando); Betty Grable (Goldwyn Girl).

SYNOPSIS:
Eddie Simpson (Eddie Cantor) works for a phoney spiritualist, Professor Yolando (Charles B. Middleton), who plans to rob A. B. Clark (Spencer Charters), the millionaire owner of a large bakery and restaurant, of his employee's $25,000 Christmas bonus. The bakery's physical culturist, Helen (Charlotte Greenwood), is a client of Yolando's, seeking a husband. When Eddie arrives at the Bakery gymnasium, she assumes he is the "True Love" Yolando promised. After an exhausting physical workout with Helen, Eddie escapes to Clark's office. Yolando has also promised Clark an "Efficiency Expert" and Clark hires Eddie on the spot. Clark is delighted with Eddie's "Efficiency" efforts and allows him to see the Christmas Bonus money and where it is kept. When Yolando finds out that Eddie knows the combination to the bakery's safe, he sends his henchmen (George Raft and Harry Woods) to get the information. In a wild chase, Eddie hides the money in a loaf of unbaked dough and masquerades as a girl, even fooling Helen. At a party at the Clark mansion that evening, it is announced that the money is missing and Eddie is accused of stealing it. He and Helen elude the police and rush to the bakery, to find the loaf of bread, followed by Yolando and his henchmen. Another chase and comic fight ensue, but Eddie and Helen retrieve the money and give it to the police, as the crooked gang is led to jail. Back at the Clark mansion, Eddie is forgiven and he realizes that he truly loves Helen after her brave support.

REVIEWS:
PHOTOPLAY, October 1931: "Ten-to-one, this will bring back film musicals in a veritable inundation. It's *that* good! It's mostly Eddie Cantor, of course...and in spite of the fact that the girls present extensive epidermic displays, the fun always manages to remain clean. If they can make musicals like this then there's no reason at all why they shouldn't

come back."

NEW YORK TIMES, 9.21.31.- Mordaunt Hall: "It is quite a good entertainment...There are two or three inconsequential melodies and a great deal to gaze, including pretty damsels from the Pacific Coast and effectively photographed groups of dancers."

COMMENTS:
- The film contains a salacious piece of Berkeley staging: during the song "BEND DOWN, SISTER," the camera explores the cleavage of each beautiful girl as she "Bends Down."
- As one of the most successful films of 1931, Palmy Days made 1.6 million dollars.
- For the first time, the title, "The Goldwyn Girls" is used in the screen credits and promotion for the film.
- Betty, again leading geometric patterns in the chorus, met George Raft on this film and they began a long relationship, which would eventually blossom into love.
- Charles Middleton, portraying a sinister psychic in the film, would go on to "Serial" fame as "Ming, The Mercilous" in Flash Gordon. He broadly performed a self-parody in an hilarious comedy scene with Eddie Cantor, as Cantor physically throws him around, eventually walking on top of him.
- The ads for the film touted: "Mammoth riot of girls, gaiety, spectacle and story."

**F9.    Once A Hero**

(Educational, Release date: November 22, 1931) (Short), 19 minutes

CREDITS:
Director, William Goodrich; story and dialogue, Ernest Pagano, Jack Townley.

CAST:
Emerson Treacy, Jack Shutta, Frances Dean [Betty Grable].

COMMENTS:
- A "Mermaid Comedy."

**F10.   The Greeks Had A Word For Them**

(UA, Release date: February 13, 1932) 77 minutes

CREDITS:
Producer, Samuel Goldwyn; director, Lowell Sherman; screenplay, Sidney Howard; based on the play The Greeks Had a Word For It by Zoe Akins; camera, George Barnes; editor, Stuart Heisler; art director, Richard Day; costumes, Coco Chanel.

CAST:
Madge Evans (Polaire); Joan Blondell (Schatze); Ina Claire (Jean); David Manners (Dey Emery); Lowell Sherman

(Boris Feldman); Phillips Smalley (Justin Emery); Sidney Bracey (Waiter); Betty Grable (Showgirl).

SYNOPSIS:
Polaire (Madge Evans), Schatze (Joan Blondell) and Jean (Ina Claire) are three stylish "Gold diggers," attempting to find wealthy husbands. Jean has no scruples whatsoever, Schatze has a heart-of-gold and Polaire finds true love with a young playboy.

REVIEWS:
VARIETY, 2.9.32: "It's an interesting experiment on the screen in that it's one of the first attempts to put over a smart bit of wit for feature length...The men won't care for it much, but flap and matron will adore its flashy sophistication."

NEW YORK TIMES, 2.4.32: "A riot of fun emerges from the screen shadows. There is beauty, too, lavish settings and good acting."

COMMENTS:
- Originally titled <u>The Greeks Had a Word For It</u>, from Zoe Akins' hit comedy, the Hays Office demanded a title change. This film was also known as <u>Three Broadway Girls</u> and would eventually be remade with Grable as <u>How To Marry a Millionaire</u> in 1953 (F81).
- The role of "Schatze" was orginally offered to stage actress Ina Claire by producer Goldwyn at the Hotel Pierre in New York. He then considered Jean Harlow, but was talked out of it by Frances Marion and Darryl Zanuck. Carole Lombard was finally cast in the role, but as filming began, complained of illness. After two weeks of filming, Lombard was still ill, so filming was temporarily halted. She was replaced by Joan Blondell and filming resumed. Lombard's exact illness was never diagnosed, although it was suspected to be a reaction to the smell of "Turkey." Ina Claire was so angered over being given another role than the one promised her that she paid Goldwyn $10,000 to tear up her contract. Claire said about Lombard: "Nobody believed she was sick. I think she knew it was a lousy movie and she just wanted out."
- Joan Blondell and cameraman George Barnes met on the film, fell in love and she became the fourth of his seven wives.
- Universal made a ten minute comedy short spoof of the film titled: <u>The Greeks Had No Word For Them</u>.
- Ad copy for the film read: "Every man in the world has heard about these three Loreleis who started out as working girls but ended working men!"

VIDEO: <u>Three Broadway Girls</u> - Barr Films (V35)

## F11.  Lady! Please!

(Sennett/Educational, Release date: February 28, 1932)
(Short) 20 minutes

CREDITS:
Director, Del Lord.

CAST:
Frances Dean [Betty Grable].

## F12.   Hollywood Luck

(Educational, Release date: March 13, 1932) (Short), 22 minutes

CREDITS:
Director, William Goodrich; story and dialogue, Ernest Pagano, Jack Townley.

CAST:
Virginia Brooks, Rita Flynn, Frances Dean [Betty Grable], Clarence Nordstrom, Fern Emmett, Addie Mc Phail.

REVIEW:
MOTION PICTURE HERALD, 3.5.32: "This might be the answer to a film-struck maiden's prayers - but it's a comedy. It concerns a practical joke on a film aspirant, in fact, two of them."

COMMENTS:
- One of the "Ideal Comedy" series.

## F13.   The Flirty Sleepwalker

(Educational, Release date: March 27, 1932) (Short) 19 minutes

CREDITS:

Director, Del Lord; dialogue, John A. Waldron, Earle Rodney, Harry Mc Coy, John Grey.

CAST:
Arthur Stone, Wade Boteler, Dorothy Granger, Patsy O'Leary,  Frances Dean [Betty Grable].

SYNOPSIS:
Two brash golf-playing men (Arthur Stone and Wade Boteler) nearly end their friendship when Stone gives Boteler's wife flowers on her birthday and then, accidentally sleep-walks into her boudoir. Boteler finds him and pursues him onto a fire escape. They repent and go to church with their wives.

REVIEW:
MOTION PICTURE HERALD, 4.9.32: "It is hardly new, at best."

## F14.   Hollywood Lights

(Educational, Release date: May 8, 1932) (Short),   20 minutes

CREDITS:
Director, William Goodrich; story and dialogue, Ernest Pagano and Jack Townley; Camera, D. Warren.

CAST:
Rita Flynn, Virginia Brooks, Tut Mace, Frances Dean [Betty Grable].

SYNOPSIS:
The humorous adventures of three women and their hunt for Hollywood jobs as extras to get money for the train fare home. They get work in a Western and end up having to ride a rickety horse home.

REVIEW:
MOTION PICTURE HERALD, 4.30.32: "More than a little slapstick in this comedic effort...only a fair effort."

COMMENTS:
- An "Ideal Comedy."

## F15.   The Age of Consent

(RKO, Release date: August 12, 1932) 100 minutes

CREDITS:
Associate producer, Pandro S. Berman; director, Gregory La Cava; screenplay, Sarah Y. Mason, Francis Cockerell; based on the play Crossroads by Martin Flavin; camera, J. Roy Hunt; editor, Jack Kitchin.

CAST:
Dorothy Wilson (Betty); Richard Cromwell (Michael); Eric Linden (Duke); Arline Judge (Dora); John Halliday (David); Aileen Pringle (Barbara); Reginald Barlow (Swale); Betty Grable (unbilled).

SYNOPSIS:
A college story about two undergraduates (Dorothy Wilson and Richard Cromwell) who become involved in unhappy romances as they search for maturity and true love.

COMMENTS:
- The RKO Story (B84) lists this as an unbilled appearance for Grable at the beginning of her RKO contract.
- Star Dorothy Wilson was a secretary at RKO selected to play the leading role. She made several more films and then married director Lewis R. Foster in 1936, retiring from the screen.

## F16.   Hold 'Em Jail

(RKO, Release date: September 2, 1932) 69 minutes

CREDITS:
Executive producer, David O. Selznick; associate producer, Harry Joe Brown; director, Norman Taurog; screenplay, Walter DeLeon, Eddie Welch and S. J. Perelman; based on the story by Tim Whelan and Lew Lipton; camera, Len Smith; editor, Artie Roberts; art director, Carroll Clark; music director, Max Steiner.

CAST:
Bert Wheeler (Curly Harris); Robert Woolsey (Spider
Robbins); Edna May Oliver (Violet Jones); Robert Armstrong
(Radio Announcer);   Roscoe  Ates  (Slippery  Sam  Brown);
Edgar  Kennedy  (Warden  Jones);  Betty  Grable  (Barbara
Jones); Paul Hurst (Butch); Warren Hymer (Steele); G. Pat
Collins (Whitey); Stanley Blystone (Kravette); John Sheehan
(Mike Maloney); Jed Prouty (Warden Charles Clark); Spencer
Charters (Governor); Monty Banks (Timekeeper); Lee Phelps
(Spike); Ernie Adam, Monte Collins (Referees); Ben Taggart
(Doorman).

SYNOPSIS:
Warden Jones (Edgar Kennedy) loves football and is hoping for
some "New Blood" at the Bidemore State Penitentiary for his
team. Curly (Bert Wheeler) and Spider (Robert Woolsey), a
pair of novelty item salesmen, have been framed for a robbery
and arrive at the penal institution. They are quickly
recruited for the team, with Warden Jones' daughter, Barbara
(Betty Grable) becoming romantically involved with Curly.
Bidemore and the Lynwood "Lifers" play a football game and
with the comic help of Curly and Spider, Warden Jones' team
triumphs. During the hectic game, the comics also manage to
force the tough who framed them to sign a confession proving
their innocence.

REVIEWS:
VARIETY, 7.23.32: "Made sometime ago, but held back until the
approach of a new football season, Wheeler and Woolsey go
through their usual nonsensicalities with a rather doubtful
score...the comedy is laboredly built up with Edna May Oliver
and Betty Grable as the other end of romantic interest with
Miss Oliver required to overact and losing many of her
points."

NEW YORK TIMES, 8.24.32: "In this noisy, fractious offering
Bert Wheeler and Robert Woolsey indulge in their usual
energetic nonsense, and...are not nearly as funny as they
have been in one or two of their other comedies.   Betty
Grable plays the Warden's daughter, who falls in love with
Curly (Wheeler)."

MOTION PICTURE HERALD, 6.25.32: "Betty Grable, a pleasing
eyeful for love interest...You can sell it to everyone. The
kids will eat it up and the grownups will go out raving about
it."

COMMENTS:
- Betty worked for the first time with Wheeler and Woolsey in
their 12th film for RKO. She replaced Dorothy Lee, who
usually played the love interest in the Wheeler and Woolsey
films. Miss Lee had recently been married and spent some time
off the screen. Lee returned with **Hips, Hips Hooray** (RKO
1934), a film which is often mistakenly credited to Grable's
filmography. Wheeler and Woolsey are oddly forgotten today
amidst movie comedy teams (Laurel and Hardy, Abbott and
Costello, Martin and Lewis) although they made twenty three
films together. After successful solo careers, they were

first teamed together by Florenz Ziegfeld in the Broadway hit
Rio Rita (1928). When the property was filmed in 1929 by RKO,
they were brought to Hollywood and signed to a contract. When
Woolsey died in 1938, Wheeler appeared in three more films,
appeared on Broadway, television and nightclubs before his
death in 1968.
- Edna May Oliver, portraying the Warden's prudish spinster
sister, plays Woolsey's bizarre romantic interest. As she
attempts to prove her worldliness to the cigar-stomping
wildman, she declares:"I learned to sing in Paris. I was
there for four years. Of course, I'm not a virtuoso!," to
which he replies: "Not after four years in Paris!"
- The film lost $55,000 for RKO.

## F17.    Over The Counter

(MGM, Release date: November 8, 1932), (Short), 18
minutes, Technicolor

CREDITS:
Producers, Jack Cummings, Harry Rapf; director, Jack
Cummings; story, Stanley Rauh, Edward Dowling.

SONGS:
"CHECK YOUR HUSBANDS"
"PLAYGROUND MAN"

CAST:
Frances Dean [Betty Grable], Sidney Toler, Franklin
Pangborn.

SYNOPSIS:
The son of the owner of a department store has a brilliant
idea to boost sales: While the wives shop, their husbands are
entertained by Chorus girls, leading to comic tiffs with the
jealous wives.

REVIEWS:
MOTION PICTURE HERALD, 2.25.33: "There is light, fast
entertainment in this number of the Colortone Musical Revue
series, with the Technicolor adding much to the brightness of
the piece."

VARIETY, 5.9.33: "...a vast improvement over the average
musical sketch the market offers...A Maypole idea tops the
dance routine atop a circular platform, shot from sides and
above with the men mixing into this for the fun of
it...Numerous short bits around the department store also
designed for comedy purposes."

## F18.    Probation

(Chesterfield, 1932) 60 minutes

CREDITS:
Director, Richard Thorpe; screenplay, Edward T. Lowe; based
on the story by Arthur Hoehl and Lowe; camera, M.A.
Anderson; editor, Richard Thorpe.

CAST:
Sally Blane (Janet Holman); J. Farrell McDonald (Judge Holman); Eddie Phillips (Alan Wells); Clara Kimball Young (Mrs. Humphreys); Betty Grable (Ruth Jarrett); David Rollins (Alec); Mary Jane Irving (Gwen); Matty Kemp (Bert); David Durand (The Kid).

SYNOPSIS:
Janet Holman (Sally Blane), a socialite, is bored with her life and her fiance, Alec (David Rollins). To add a little excitement to her daily routine, she visits her uncle's court session, where Judge Holman (J. Farrell McDonald) sentences Alan (Eddie Phillips), a handsome young man on probation, to serve as Janet's chauffeur in her custody. Romance begins between the duo and the day before her intended wedding, Janet realizes that she truly loves Alan. He happily exchanges his probation for a "Life Sentence" with Janet.

REVIEWS:
VARIETY, 4.12.32: "Too much drawing up and stopping the car before many doors proves a bit wearying to the average fan. Smart cracking dialogue in between and an occasional fist fight, however, serve to minimize this fault."

MOTION PICTURE HERALD, 4.23.32: "Moderately received at a New York neighborhood situation, this independent effort centers its attention upon a rather simple story, which was considered in the main to have been well executed in treatment and satisfactorily performed by the players."

MOTION PICTURE GUIDE, 1987: "Betty Grable makes an appearance in a secondary role, which, ultimately, is all this film is memorable for."

VIDEO: The Worst of Hollywood - Silver Mine Video (V37)

## F19.  The Kid From Spain

(UA, Release date: January 1, 1933) 90 minutes

CREDITS:
Producer, Samuel Goldwyn; director, Leo McCarey; screenplay, William Anthony McGuire, Bert Kalmar, Harry Ruby; camera, Gregg Tolland; editor, Stuart Heisler; costumes, Milo Anderson; music director, Alfred Newman; dance director, Busby Berkeley.

SONGS:
"WHAT A PERFECT COMBINATION" by Bert Kalmar, Harry Ruby, Irving Caesar, Harry Askt
"THE COLLEGE SONG;" "IN THE MOONLIGHT;" "LOOK WHAT YOU'VE DONE" by Bert Kalmar and Harry Ruby

CAST:
Eddie Cantor (Eddie Williams); Lyda Roberti (Rosalie); Robert Young (Ricardo); Ruth Hall (Anita Gomez); John Miljan (Pancho); Noah Beery (Alonzo Gomez); J. Carroll Naish (Pedro); Robert Emmett O'Connor (Crawford); Stanley

Fields (Jose); Paul Porcasi (Border Guard); Sidney Franklin (American Matador); Walter Walker (The Dean); Julian Rivero (Dalmores); Theresa Maxwell Conover (Martha Oliver); Ben Hendricks, Jr. (Red); Grace Poggi (Dance Specialty); Leo Willis (Thief); Jean Allen, Loretta Andrews, Consuelo Baker, Betty Bassett, Lynn Browning, Maxie Cantway, Hazel Craven, Dorothy Rae Coonan, Shirley Chambers, Patricia Farnum, Sara Jane Fulks [Jane Wyman], Betty Grable, Paulette Goddard, Jeannie Gray, Ruth Hale, Pat Harper, Margaret La Marr, Adele Lacey, Bernice Lorimer, Nancy Lynn, Vivian Mathison, Nancy Nash, Edith Roark, Marian Sayers, Renee Whitney, Diana Winslow, Toby Wing (Goldwyn Girls).

SYNOPSIS:
Eddie Williams (Eddie Cantor) and Ricardo (Robert Young) are expelled from college after being caught in the girls' dormitory. While Ricardo is drawing money out of the bank, Eddie gets mixed up in a bank robbery. They escape to Mexico, Ricardo's home, and in a case of mistaken identity, the Border Guard (Paul Porcasi) thinks Eddie is Don Sebastian, a famous Matador. Aside from all of the dangers of bullfighting, Eddie also helps Ricardo with his romance with Anita (Ruth Hall), angering Alonzo Gomez (Noah Beery), a dangerous outlaw. Eddie finds himself romantically involved with Rosalie (Lyda Roberti), Anita's best friend. To escape the American police, Eddie must go into the bullring to prove himself, with the police and the outlaws both watching his comical antics. By sheer luck, he kills the Bull, gets the girl and is given freedom.

REVIEWS:
PHOTOPLAY, January 1933: "Lavish, nonsensical - with the loveliest chorus of girls Hollywood has produced - and topped by an utterly ridiculous fight between Eddie Cantor and a bull, The Kid From Spain is the culmination of musicals on the screen...Here is the season's opportunity to laugh your head off."

VARIETY, 11. 22, 32: "Sub-billed with Lyda Roberti are the Goldwyn girls, a galaxy of lookers who require no lines other than their own physical ones for international comprehension. They are tastefully presented in the now familiar school of Berkeley choreography which is bullish on the overhead camera shots."

COMMENTS:
- Filmed at a cost of $1,400,000, the film earned 2.6 million dollars and was the most popular and financially successful film of 1932, as well as being #4 within the decade.
- Betty is the first face on the screen and the first voice you hear as she awakens and "intros" the film in "THE COLLEGE SONG," a musical number in an all-female dormitory suggestively staged by Busby Berkeley. Other "Goldwyn Girls" include Jane Wyman, Paulette Goddard and Toby Wing. For their efforts in the film, the "Goldwyn Girls" were given gold pins with a bull's head decoration.
- Songwriters Bert Kalmar and Harry Ruby also worked on the

screenplay. They would be the subjects of MGM's 1950 musical biography **Three Little Words**, with Fred Astaire playing Kalmar and Red Skelton as Ruby.
- Specialty dancer Grace Poggi would appear with Betty in the stage show **Tattle Tales** (S5).

## F20.   Cavalcade

(Fox, Release date: January 4, 1933) 109 minutes

CREDITS:
Producer, Winfield Sheehan; director, Frank Lloyd; screenplay, Sonya Levien, Reginald Berkeley; based on the play by Noel Coward; assistant director, William Tummel; camera, Ernest Palmer; editor, Margaret Clancy; art director, William S. Darling; music director, Louis Francesco; dance director, Sammy Lee.

SONG:
"TWENTIETH CENTURY BLUES" by Noel Coward

CAST:
Clive Brook (Robert Marryot); Diana Wynyard (Jane Marryot); Ursula Jeans (Fanny Bridges); Herbert Mundin (Alfred Bridges); Una O'Connor (Ellen Bridges); Merle Tottenham (Annie); Irene Browne (Margaret Harris); Beryl Mercer (Cook); Frank Lawton (Joe Marryot); John Warburton (Edward Marryot); Margaret Lindsay (Edith Harris); Tempe Piggot (Mrs. Snapper); Bill Bevan (George Grainger); Desmond Roberts (Ronnie James); Frank Atkinson (Uncle Dick); Ann Shaw (Mirabelle); Adele Crane (Ada); Stuart Hall (Lt.Edgar); Mary Forbes (Duchess of Churt); Lionel Belmore (Uncle George); C. Montague Shaw (Major Domo); Bonita Granville (Fanny - Age 7 - 12); Sheila MacGill (Edith - at 10); Douglas Scott (Joey - at 8); Dick Henderson Jr. (Edward - at 12); Claude King (Speaker); Pat Somerset (Ringsider); Betty Grable (Girl on couch); Brandon Hurst (Gilbert and Sullivan actor).

SYNOPSIS:
The epic tale of Britishers Jane and Robert Marryot (Diana Wynyard and Clive Brook) and the effect of World events on their lives and family during the three decades between New Year's Eve 1899 and the same eve thirty three years later: the calls to war, the death of Queen Victoria, the knighthood of Robert and the tragic loss of one son on the Titanic and another in World War I.

REVIEWS:
VARIETY, 1.10.33: "Here's a big, brave and beautiful picture. It's pretty certain and road show material...The picture is long enough to cut with ease for regular picture house showings."

NEW YORK TIMES, 1.6.33 - Mordaunt Hall: "It is a most effective and impressive picture that the Fox Studios have produced from Noel Coward's stage panorama."

COMMENTS:
- The property began as a successful stage piece running 405 performances in London before Fox bought it for the screen.
- One of the rare Hollywood-made films with a complete leading cast of British actors and actresses.
- Cavalcade was the number two box office champion in 1933, according to the Motion Picture Herald survey. It broke the record at Radio City Music Hall during its first week, drawing 167,383 admissions and $110,000 at the box office.
- Betty appears in her only Academy Award winning "Best Picture" in a very brief bit. The film has been ignored in most Academy Award retrospectives.

ACADEMY AWARDS: "Best Picture," "Best Direction" (Frank Lloyd), "Best Interior Decoration" (William S. Darling) 1932-'33. Nomination for "Best Actress" (Diana Wynyard) - her screen debut.

VIDEO: Fox Video (V3)

## F21.   Child Of Manhattan

(Columbia, Release date: January 25, 1933) 91 minutes

CREDITS:
Director, Eddie Buzzell; screenplay, Gertrude Purcell; based on the play by Preston Sturges; camera, Ted Tetzlaff.

SONG:
"CHILD OF MANHATTAN" by Elmer Colby and Maurice Abrahams

CAST:
Nancy Carroll (Madeleine McGonegal); John Boles (Paul Vanderkill); Warburton Gamble (Eggleston); Clara Blandick (Aunt Sophie); Jane Darwell (Mrs. McGonegal); Gary Owen (Buddy); Betty Grable (Lucy); Luis Alberni (Bustamente); Jessie Ralph (Aunt Minnie); Charles Jones (Panama Kelly); Tyler Brooke (Dulcey); Betty Kendall (Louise).

SYNOPSIS:
Madeleine (Nancy Carroll) is a dance-hall hostess who falls in love with a handsome millionaire, Paul (John Boles). She becomes pregnant, but the baby dies and believing that Paul only married her out of sympathy, she goes to Mexico to obtain a divorce. There, she decides to marry Panama Kelly (Charles Jones). Paul follows her and saves her from making a mistake and returning to him.

REVIEWS:
VARIETY, 2. 14. 33: "It's hoke, baby shoes and all, plus the Cinderella yarn brought to a 10-cent dance joint."

NEW YORK TIMES, 2.13.33: "Although Child of Manhattan, based on the Preston Sturges play, is a title with dash and spirit, the new picture at the RKO Roxy does nothing new to report on the whirligig of metropolitan life."

COMMENTS:
- Betty's first major career step in feature films, landing a role with a Character name.
- It is her first association with Preston Sturges, at the beginning of his illustrious career. Sadly, she would not personally work with him until the end of his career, in the badly received <u>Beautiful Blonde From Bashful Bend</u> (F75) in 1949, some sixteen years later.

## F22.  Melody Cruise

(RKO, Release date: June 23, 1933) 76 minutes

CREDITS:
Executive Producer, Merian C, Cooper; associate producer, Louis Brock; director, Mark Sandrich; screenplay, Ben Holmes, Sandrich; additional dialogue, Allen Rivkin, R.G. Wolfson; camera, Bert Glennon; editor, Jack Kitchin; art directors, Van Nest Polglase, Carroll Clark; musical director, Max Steiner, ice ballet staged by Dave Gould.

SONGS:
"I MET HER AT A PARTY;" "HE'S NOT THE MARRYING KIND;" "ISN'T THIS A NIGHT FOR LOVE;" "THIS IS THE HOUR" by Val Burton and Will Jason

CAST:
Charlie Ruggles (Pete Wells); Phil Harris (Alan Chandler); Greta Nissen (Elsa Von Rader); Helen Mack (Laurie Marlow); Chick Chandler (Hickey); June Brewster (Zoe); Shirley Chambers (Vera); Florence Roberts (Miss Potts); Marjorie Gateson (Mrs. Wells); Betty Grable (Stewardess).

SYNOPSIS:
Pete (Charlie Ruggles) and Alan (Phil Harris) are two wealthy friends traveling on a steamship. Pete is married and, as a joke, Alan writes a letter to Pete's wife describing all of Pete's girl-chasing, only to be opened on the occasion of confirmed bachelor Alan's wedding. Pete worries the entire trip, as Alan romances Elsa (Greta Nissen), a German beauty who has followed him, and Laurie (Helen Mack), a shy, young schoolteacher who catches Alan's fancy. To complicate matters, two golddiggers, Zoe and Vera (Jane Brewster and Shirley Chambers) have passed out at the "Bon Voyage" party in Pete's room and become "Stowaways" for the entire trip. Pete passes them off as his "nieces," terrified that Hickey (Chick Chandler), the wisecracking Steward, will reveal his indiscretions. Docking in California, Alan decides that Laurie is the one he loves and chases after her. When they plan to marry, Pete's wife, Grace (Marjorie Gateson) opens and reads the letter, finding out the truth about her philandering husband.

REVIEWS:
VARIETY, 6.27.33: "Story and playing lack genuine spontaneity. It's just a well-rehearsed musical trifle, padded out unmercifully...Ruggles wears well, better than the lingeried background of dizzy girls rung in from time to

time."

NEW YORK TIMES, 6.23.3 - Mordaunt Hall: "The rollicking happenings know no bounds...one of the most spectacular episodes depicts a host of men and women skating - dancing on ice."

NEW YORK MIRROR, 6.23.33: "Decorated with pretty girls, punctuated with melodic interludes, its strong points are a very pretty ice-skating ballet and the work of Charles Ruggles."

COMMENTS:
- This film marked the feature length directorial debut of Mark Sandrich, who would receive acclaim with the Astaire/Rogers musicals he directed at RKO.
- Betty appears in one sequence among a group of Cruise Ship stewardesses who eavesdrop at Phil Harris' cabin door on the amorous adventures going on inside.
- One of RKO's most successful films in 1933.

VIDEO: Turner Home Entertainment (V22)

## F23.    What Price Innocence?

(Columbia, Release date: June 23, 1933) 64 minutes

CREDITS:
Director-screenplay, Willard Mack; camera, Joseph A. Valentine; editor, Arthur Hilton.

CAST:
Willard Mack (Dr. Dan Davidge); Minna Gombell (Amy Harper);  Jean Parker (Ruth Harper); Betty Grable (Beverly Bennett); Bryant Washburn (John Harper); Ben Alexander (Tommy Harrow); Beatrice Banyard (Mrs. Bennett); Louise Beavers (Hannah).

SYNOPSIS:
Willard Mack (screenwriter/director and star) portrays Dan Davidge, a kindly doctor who maintains an interest in the children he delivered. One of them, Ruth Harper (Jean Parker), commits suicide when her love affair with an older boy, Tommy Harrow (Ben Alexander), comes to a screeching halt due to her Mother's (Minna Gombell) unwillingness to discuss the facts of life with her.

REVIEWS:
VARIETY, 6.27.33: "...could be categorized as visual education for adolescents, particularly girls, and for parents who are a bit abashed at the thought of initiating their offspring into an understanding of what's what ...nothing unclean or unwholesome about Innocence and exploitation that infers otherwise will be misleading."

NEW YORK TIMES, 6.26.33: "The film is presented with a certain blunt skill and it is produced with a certain

sincerity. But is has none of the subtlety, indirection or
dramatic power to make the theme palatable for the public
screens."

COMMENTS:
- An unusually frank film for its time. Unnoticed by critics
or audiences. A tour-de-force for director, writer and star
Willard Mack, who died the following year at the age of 56.
The multitalented Mack wrote many plays in which he starred.
- Ben Alexander, who portrayed the callous deflowerer, would
find fame as "Officer Frank Smith," Jack Webb's sidekick in
the successful crime television series <u>Dragnet</u> (1952-1959).

## F24.   Sweetheart of Sigma Chi

(Monogram, Release date: November 20, 1933) 73 minutes

CREDITS:
Director, Edwin I. Marin; screenplay, Luther Reed, Albert
De Mond and Frank L. Moss; based on the story by George
Waggner; camera, Gilbert Warrenton; editor, J. Edwin
Robbins; dance direction by Eddie Prinz.

SONGS:
"FRATERNITY WALK" and "IT'S SPRING AGAIN" by George Waggner
and Ed Ward
"FIVE MINUTES MORE" by Jule Styne and Sammy Cahn
"SWEETHEART OF SIGMA CHI" by Byron D. Stokes and F. Dudley
Vernor

CAST:
Mary Carlisle (Vivian); Buster Crabbe (Bob North); Charles
Starrett (Morley); Florence Lake (Dizzy); Eddie Tamblyn
(Coxswain); Sally Starr (Madge); Mary Blackford (Bunny);
Tom Dugan (Trainer); Burr McIntosh (Professor); Major
Goodsell (Coach); Grady Sutton (Pledge); Purnell Pratt
(Doctor); Franklin Parker (House Prexy); Ted Fiorito and
his Orchestra, including Leif Erickson, Betty Grable, Bill
Carey, Muzzy Marcellino, The Three Midshipmen and The Blue
Keys (Themselves).

SYNOPSIS:
Fickle cutie Vivian (Mary Carlisle) is the most popular girl
on Campus, accepting fraternity pins from many beaus. But
when she meets the Captain of the rowing team, Bob North
(Buster Crabbe),the school's most handsome "Jock," she finally
begins to focus her romantic attentions on one man. Morley
(Charles Starrett) competes for Vivian's love, but Bob and
his team win the big race - and Capt. Bob wins Vivian.

REVIEWS:
VARIETY, 11.14.33: "Unlike the average undergraduate theme
there is nothing rough here...Nary a squabble occurs on the
campus or elsewhere. Story doesn't permit any of its students
to be jealous or belligerent, neither are there any
fraternity hazing episodes. For a change, and almost a
novelty, action actually devotes one sequence to the
classroom."

HOLLYWOOD REPORTER, 10.6.55.:"Indie turns out good hotcha yarn...Ted Fiorito and his orchestra are a tuneful asset and the soloists acquit themselves nicely."

NEW YORK TIMES, 11.9.33.- Mordaunt Hall: "The happy-go-lucky students of Rawley, the latest co-educational institution sponsored by the screen, having a proper disdain for work, indulge in a curriculum which consists chiefly of singing, flirting and encouraging their rowing eight."

COMMENTS:
- This film was made while Grable was performing live with the Fiorito Band on the West Coast. Costar Leif Erikson would also go on to a healthy career as a leading man in over seventy films.
- Eddie Tamblyn, playing a Coxswain and involved in the subplot romance with Florence Lake, is Russ Tamblyn's father. A supporting actor in films, he never attained the success of his actor/gymnast son.
- Remade in 1946 by Monogram with Phil Regan and Elyse Knox.

## F25.   Air Tonic

(RKO, Release date: December 22, 1933) (Short), 21 minutes

CREDITS:
Producer, Lou Brock; director, Sam White; story, Joseph A. Fields, Walter Weems; camera, Nick Musuraca; editor, Charles Kimball; recording, Bert Hodges.

SONGS:
"SERENADE OF LOVE"
"DON'T BLAME ME" by Dorothy Fields and Jimmy McHugh
"STAY ON THE RIGHT SIDE OF THE ROAD" by Bloom and Ted Koehler

CAST:
Ted Fiorito and his Orchestra, Betty Grable, Leif Erickson, Will MacClarind, Bill Carey, Muzzy Marcellino, Eddie Borden, Tom Hanks.

SYNOPSIS:
A milkman (Leif Erickson) and a waitress (Betty Grable) dream of becoming a singer and dancer. Over the radio, they hear that Ted Fiorito is holding auditions for hopefuls at the St. Francis Hotel in San Francisco. Arriving after the other auditionees have been dismissed, band member Will Mac Clarind pretends that he is Fiorito and tells them to audition, playing their music either too fast or too slow. Frustrated and disappointed, they start to leave, but Fiorito overhears them talking and takes them back to audition again. With the correct tempos, they prove their talent. Fiorito apologizes and hires them.

COMMENTS:
- When asked what her specialty is, Betty proudly answers: "Fast buck and wing!" She also dances a brief toe-tap,

something she would do again in Old Man Rhythm (1935 - F37).
- In Motion Picture Herald,1.13.34, a movie-theater manager wrote: "Air Tonic - a very, very nifty musical that went over with a bang. Our audience liked it immensely." - W.T. Briggs, Adair Theatre, Adair, Iowa.
- Another film appearance while Grable was with the Fiorito Orchestra.

## F26.   Elmer Steps Out

(Columbia, Release date: February 24, 1934) (Short), 19-20 minutes

CREDITS:
Director, Jules White; screenplay and story, Arthur Ripley, Jac Cluett; Editor, Robert Carlisle.

CAST:
Walter Catlett, Anita Garvin, Arthur Housman, Greta Meyer, Gloria Warner, Betty Grable, James P. Burtis, Marion Lord, Jack Hill, Bert Young, Robert "Bobby" Burns.

SYNOPSIS:
After arguing with his wife, Elmer (Walter Catlett), goes out with his friends. While stopped for speeding,they tell the Police Officer that Elmer is an expectant father. The Officer escorts him home to show him the wife and new baby but instead is introduced to a big Scandinavian servant and an Organ Grinder's monkey. Finally, his wife returns and Elmer finds himself in major trouble.

COMMENTS:
- Remade in 1942 as Three Blonde Mice. The original title was Playful Husbands.

## F27.   Love Detectives

(Columbia, Release date: March 3, 1934) (Short), 2 reels

CREDITS:
Director, Archie Gottler; screenplay, Edward Eliscu, Archie Gottler.

CAST:
Frank Albertson, Betty Grable, Gloria Warner, Armand Kaliz, Red Stanley, Tom Dugan.

SYNOPSIS:
A lovely young girl is pursued by two ardent suitors.

COMMENTS:
- A "Musical Novelty."

## F28.   Business Is A Pleasure

(Warner Brothers/Vitaphone, Release date: April 30, 1934) (Short), 16 minutes, Technicolor

CREDITS:
Director, Eddie Cline; story, Edmund Joseph, Barry Trivers.

CAST:
Teddy Joyce and his Band, Betty Grable.

SYNOPSIS:
Betty is back in a department store setting (see Over The Counter, F17), but instead of chorus girls, an ambitious sales promotions manager tries bands, singers and dancers to lure the customers in.

REVIEW:
VARIETY, 2.6.34: "It's similar to a two-reeler Tunefilm, also in Technicolor, made by Metro a year or so ago...Camera moves all over a department store the sets of which point to money and production background. Coloring a good job, too...the line girls and others go through a series of routines and all pleasing."

## F29.   Susie's Affairs

(Columbia, Release date: May 10, 1934) (Short), 2 reels

CREDITS:
Director and story, Archie Gottler; editor, James Sweeney.

CAST:
Arthur Jarrett, Betty Grable, Lois January, Red Stanley, Gene Sheldon, Thelma White, Marion Byron, Jay Mills.

SYNOPSIS:
Susie (Betty Grable) and her friends pretend to be "High Society," but their working class roots are quickly revealed.

COMMENTS:
- A "Musical Novelty."

## F30.   The Gay Divorcee

(RKO, Release date: October 11, 1934) 107 minutes

CREDITS:
Producer, Pandro S. Berman; director, Mark Sandrich; screenplay, George Marion, Jr., Dorothy Yost and Edward Kaufman; based on the novel and play The Gay Divorce by Dwight Taylor; camera, David Abel; editor, William Hamilton; art directors, Van Nest Polglase and Carroll Clark; costumes, Walter Plunkett; musical director, Max Steiner; music adaptation, Kenneth Webb and Samuel Hoffenstein; dance directors; Dave Gould, Fred Astaire (unbilled); assistant dance director, Hermes Pan.

SONGS:
"NIGHT AND DAY" by Cole Porter
"LOOKING FOR A NEEDLE IN A HAYSTACK" and "THE CONTINENTAL" by Herb Magidson and Con Conrad

"DON'T LET IT BOTHER YOU" and "LET'S K-KNOCK K-KNEES" by Mack Gordon and Harry Revel

CAST:
Fred Astaire (Guy Holder); Ginger Rogers (Mimi Glossop); Alice Brady (Aunt Hortense); Edward Everett Horton (Egbert Fitzgerald); Erik Rhodes (Rodolfo Tonetti); Eric Blore (Waiter); Betty Grable (Hotel Guest); Charles Coleman (Guy's Valet); William Austin (Cyril Glossop); Lillian Miles (Guest); George Davis, Alphonse Martell (French Waiters); E.E. Clive (Chief Customs Inspector); Paul Porcasi (French Headwaiter); Charles Hull (Call Boy at Dock).

SYNOPSIS:
American dancer Guy Holder (Fred Astaire) and lawyer friend Egbert Fitzgerald (Edward Everett Horton) are taking a holiday in Europe. Guy meets American girl Mimi (Ginger Rogers) at the dock in Le Havre, where her Aunt Hortense (Alice Brady) has accidentally locked Mimi's skirt in her trunk. In trying to aid her, Guy tears Mimi's dress and he loans her his raincoat, to be returned in London. In London, Aunt Hortense hires old friend Egbert to obtain a divorce for Mimi. They decide upon hiring a co-respondent and at a beachside resort, Guy mistakenly says the password to Mimi that she is expecting to hear from the hired Gigolo, Rodolfo Tonetti (Eric Rhodes). She believes that Guy is the man who has been hired to spend the night in her hotel room so that she can be caught "in flagrante delicto" by the detectives in the morning. Rodolfo finally arrives at her hotel room and the mistaken identity is straightened out. Guy is determined to spend the night with Mimi and Rodolfo, but the lure of the music downstairs is too strong. He and Mimi sneak out of the hotel room and enjoy "The Continental," the newest dance rage. The next morning, the detectives arrive, Mimi is granted her divorce and Guy proposes marriage.

REVIEWS:
MOTION PICTURE GUIDE, 1987: "Betty Grable does a number with Edward Everett Horton which establishes herself as a force to contend with."

VARIETY, 11.20.34: "Astaire gumshoed into flickers as a dancing straight for Joan Crawford but scaled the heights almost overnight in Flying Down To Rio with Ginger Rogers, his vis-a-vis in Rio, Radio and the team repeats. And how...Blonde kid number-leader in 'K-KNOCK K-NEEZ'(sic) in that Brighton-by-the-sea setting, shows lots of promise."

NEW YORK TIMES, 11.16.34. - Andre Sennwald: "The studio balladists contribute several excellent chansons...the cinema brewmeisters hurl them into the composition of an entirely agreeable photoplay which sings, dances and quips with agility and ease."

COMMENTS:
- The filmization of a major Broadway smash hit, utilizing several of the original Broadway cast members in the film

(Erik Rhodes and Eric Blore). The Hays Office thought that the original title <u>The Gay Divorce</u> was too risqué, so the title was changed. Only one of Cole Porter's original songs from the stage smash was used ("NIGHT AND DAY") as Hollywood continued to tamper with stage successes bringing them to the screen.

- Dave Gould is credited as dance director, but Astaire and Hermes Pan, actually created the choreography. Gould, who would win one of the few Academy Awards for "Dance Direction" for <u>Folies Bergere</u> (1935), was infamous for not being able to perform a single dance step. This was the first of thirteen films Hermes Pan would choreograph for Grable, second only to the eighteen he would make with Fred Astaire.

- Betty performed "LET'S K-NOCK K-NEES" with Edward Everett Horton with vigor and charm. Because of her good work in the film, she was given a contract with RKO and her hair dyed "Quicksilver" blonde.

- The elaborate musical number performed to "THE CONTINENTAL" is seventeen minutes long, a major portion of the film's 107 minute length.

ACADEMY AWARDS: Best Song ("THE CONTINENTAL"). Nominations for Best Picture, interior decoration, sound recording, musical score.

VIDEO: "Nostalgia Merchant" (V10)
RECORDING: EMI and Sountrack (D17). Also "LET'S K-NOCK K-KNEES" can be heard on "Betty Grable" (D1 and D2)

## F31.    Student Tour

(MGM, Release date: October 15, 1934) 85 minutes

CREDITS:
Producer, Monta Bell; director, Charles Reisner; screenplay, Philip Dunne, Ralph Spence; based on a story by George Seaton, Arthur Bloch and Samuel Marx; camera, Joseph A. Valentine; editor, Frank Hull; art director, Cedric Gibbons; music director, Jack Virgil; dance director, Chester Hale.

SONGS:
"A NEW MOON IS OVER MY SHOULDER;" "FROM NOW ON;" "BY THE TAJ MAHAL;" "THE SNAKE DANCE;" "THE CARLO;" "FIGHT 'EM" by Arthur Freed and Nacio Herb Brown
"I JUST SAY IT WITH MUSIC" by Jimmy Durante

CAST:
Jimmy Durante (Hank); Charles Butterworth (Professor "Lippy" Lippincott); Maxine Doyle (Ann); Phil Regan (Bobby); Florine McKinney (Lilith); Douglas Fowley (Mushy); Monte Blue (Jeff); Betty Grable (Cayenne); Fay McKenzie (Mary Lou); Bobby Gordon (Jakie); Mary Loos (Dolores); Pauline Brooks (Peggy); Herman Brix [Bruce Bennett] (Hercules); Nelson Eddy (Himself); Mischa Auer (Sikhi Cop); Arthur Hoyt (Assistant to the Dean); Dave O'Brien, Dale Van Sickle, June Storey, Bryant Washburn, Jr., Joan Arlen, Mary Jane Irving, Maxine Nash, Edna May Jones,

Dixie Dean and Clarice Wood (Students); Helen Chan (Sun Toy), Eddie Hart (Stewart), D. Slickenmeyer (Officer); Mick Copeland (Waiter); Florence and Alvarez (Dance Team).

SYNOPSIS:
Hank (Jimmy Durante) is the trainer of a college rowing team whose members have all flunked a Philosophy exam. They are about to lose their chance to visit England and compete in an important rowing event there when Philosophy professor "Lippy" (Charles Butterworth) agrees to travel with them, tutoring them along the way. He brings his dowdy niece Ann (Maxine Doyle) along and when she removes her glasses, team captain Bobby (Phil Regan) falls madly in love with her. All turns out well for lovers and the team.

REVIEWS:
VARIETY, 10.16.34: "Music, dances, youth, comedy flashes and collegiate romancing are the ingredients here in a musical story mixture that fails to satisfy...Dancing routines are pleasing rather than sensational and include a Geisha in the Singapore locale."

NEW YORK TIMES, 10.31.34: "Shed a tear for Jimmy Durante and Charles Butterworth, who went down with the good ship Student Tour at the Mayfair today...the photoplay does contain two good songs, but otherwise it possesses the sparkle and wit of a performing elephant and the headlong speed of Mr. Stepin Fetchit."

COMMENTS:
- Nelson Eddy does a specialty as himself in the film, just before being teamed with Jeanette MacDonald in Naughty Marietta in 1935 and finding fame.

RECORDING: "THE SNAKE DANCE" on "Betty Grable" (D2)

## F32.    By Your Leave

(RKO, Release date: November 8, 1934) 81 minutes

CREDITS:
Producer, Pandro S. Berman; director, Lloyd Corrigan; screenplay, Allan Scott; based on the play by Gladys Hurlbut, Emma B.C. Wells; camera, Nick Musuraca, Vernon Walker; editor, William Morgan.

CAST:
Frank Morgan (Henry Smith); Genevieve Tobin (Ellen Smith); Neil Hamilton (David McKenzie); Marian Nixon (Andrea); Glenn Anders (Freddy Clark); Gene Lockhart (Skeets); Margaret Hamilton (Whiffen); Betty Grable (Frances Gretchell); Lona Andre (Miss Purcell); Charles Ray (Leonard).

SYNOPSIS:
Henry Smith (Frank Morgan), about to experience a "Mid Life" crisis, convinces his wife, Ellen (Genevieve Tobin), that they should take separate vacations. Henry's vacation turns

out to be a failure as his fantasies of being chased by dozens of beautiful girls do not come true. But, Ellen meets David McKenzie (Neil Hamilton) and they decide to cruise on his yacht, where she becomes attracted to the young man. Henry returns just in time, confessing his deep love for Ellen, never knowing how close he came to losing her.

REVIEWS:
VARIETY, 1.1.35: "Once the customers are in they'll get some laughs and entertainment, but they're not going to be easy to entice because of lack of marquee weight."

### F33.    The Spirit of 1976

(Astor, Release date: February 2, 1935) (Short), 21 minutes

CREDITS:
Producer, Lee Marcus; associate producer, Bert Gilroy; director, Leigh Jason; story, Ernest Pagano, Leigh Jason, Roy Webb; photographed by J. Roy Hunt; editor, John Lockert; musical director, Roy Webb.

SONGS:
"VOTE FOR ELMER GREEN;" "MY FIRST LADY OF THE LAND" by Val Burton and Will Jason.

CAST:
Betty Grable, Walter King.

SYNOPSIS:
Elmer Green (Walter King), a Presidential candidate with a political platform to rid the people of the woes of working, appeals greatly to the citizens of futuristic America in 1976. But, shortly after he is elected, the citizens go on "Strike," as they quickly tire of all play and no work. As his Cabinet members and advisors discuss the political unrest, Green's lady love (Betty Grable) arrives for a luncheon date with the President. When she left her home, her Father and his friends quickly put away the card table and secretly began to work in the garden. When her Father is arrested for working, she pleads with the President to change his tactics. He allows the citizens to return to work and Betty becomes "The First Lady of the Land."

REVIEWS:
VARIETY, 2.20.35: "This is a knockout featurette...It's a mixture of Gilbert and Sullivan and 'Of Thee I Sing'...cute blonde Betty Grable was more than the customary painted figurehead, giving a lubricated and intelligent assist."

COMMENTS:
- Male star Walter King had starred on Broadway in operettas (Countess Maritza, The Dream Girl, Melody, May Wine) as "Walter Woolf" and "Walter Woolf King." The Spirit of 1976 marked his film debut. He also starred in an operetta The Lady in Ermine in 1922, which has no relationship to Grable's That Lady in Ermine in 1948.

## F34.   The Nitwits

(RKO, Release date: June 7, 1935) 81 minutes

CREDITS:
Producer, Lee Marcus; director, George Stevens; screenplay, Fred Guiol and Al Boasberg; based on the story by Stuart Palmer; camera, Edward Cronjager; editor, John Lockert; art director, Van Nest Polglase; musical director, Roy Webb.

SONGS:
"YOU OPENED MY EYES" by L. Wolfe Gilbert and Felix Bernard "MUSIC IN MY HEART;" "THE BLACK WIDOW WILL GET YOU IF YOU DON'T WATCH OUT" by Dorothy Fields and Jimmy McHugh

CAST:
Bert Wheeler (Johnny); Robert Woolsey (Newton); Fred Keating (Darrell); Betty Grable (Mary); Evelyn Brent (Mrs. Lake); Erik Rhodes (Clark); Hale Hamilton (Mr. Lake); Charles Wilson (Captain Jennings); Arthur Aylesworth (Lurch); Willie Best (Sleepy); Lew Kelly (J. Gabriel Hazel); Dorothy Granger (Phyllis); Arthur Treacher (unbilled).

SYNOPSIS:
Johnny (Wheeler) and Newton (Woolsey) have a cigar stand in the "Lake" building, home of a successful music publishing company. Johnny loves Mary (Betty Grable), the secretary of Mr. Lake (Hale Hamilton) who is being blackmailed by "The Black Widow," a villain terrorizing the city. With his wife (Evelyn Brent), he hires the services of a private detective, Darrell (Fred Keating) to protect him. Nevertheless, he is shot and killed, with Mary becoming the prime suspect. To save her, Johnny and Newton play detective and after a slapstick chase in the costume factory in the building, discover that detective Darrell is the real villain.

REVIEWS:
VARIETY, 6.26.35: "This time its a full-grown whodunit, with the Director sticking to the plot and weaving the comedy into the fabric...Comedy pair give their standard performances with Miss Grable a trifle too mechanical."

COMMENTS:
- Betty, with light brown hair, is surprisingly subdued in her performance, allowing Wheeler to have all of the energy and the laughs. She reported to work on the film March 5, 1935, after a personal appearance in Chicago with Wheeler (S9).
- Directed by George Stevens as his fifth film for RKO. He would next direct Katharine Hepburn in Alice Adams and go on to the great successes of Swing Time, Gunga Din, A Place in the Sun, Shane and Giant.
- Arthur Treacher is the comic highlight of this film in an unbilled appearance as a proper Englishman carrying tennis balls, racquets and nets down the stairway. As a "running gag," he and Woolsey continue to become comically tangled.

LASER DISC: Image Entertainment (V24)

## F35.   A Night At The Biltmore Bowl

(RKO, Release date: June 21, 1935) (Short), 17-18 minutes

CREDITS:
Producer, Lee Marcus; director, Alf Goulding; story, Joseph A. Fields; editor, Edward Mann; musical director, Roy Webb.

CAST:
RKO contractees Betty Grable, Joy Hodges, Edgar Kennedy, Lucille Ball, Grady Sutton, Anne Shirley, Preston Foster, Dennis O' Keefe, Bert Wheeler and the Jimmy Grier Orchestra.

SYNOPSIS:
A documentary about nightlife at the Biltmore Hotel supper club in Los Angeles.

## F36.   Drawing Rumors

(RKO, Release date: July 12, 1935) (Short), 17-22 minutes

CREDITS:
Producer, Lee Marcus; director, Ben Holmes; story, Joseph A. Fields; editor, Edward Mann; musical director, Roy Webb.

CAST:
Joey Ray, Betty Grable.

SYNOPSIS:
A nightclub M.C. quits to get married.

## F37.   Old Man Rhythm

(RKO, Release date: August 2, 1935) 75 minutes

CREDITS:
Associate producer, Zion Myers; director, Edward Ludwig; screenplay, Sig Herzig, Ernest Pagano; based on a story by Lewis Gensler, Herzig and Don Hartman; additional dialogue, H. W. Henemann; camera, Nick Musuraca; editor, George Crone; art director, Van Nest Polglase; music director, Roy Webb; song numbers staged by Sam White; dance numbers by Hermes Pan.

SONGS:
"OLD MAN RHYTHM;" "I NEVER SAW A BETTER NIGHT;" THERE'S NOTHING LIKE A COLLEGE EDUCATION;" "BOYS WILL BE BOYS;" "WHEN YOU ARE IN MY ARMS;" "COME THE REVOLUTION BABY" by Johnny Mercer and Lewis Gensler

CAST:
Charles "Buddy" Rogers (Johnny Roberts); George Barbier (John Roberts, Sr.); Barbara Kent (Edith Warren); Grace Bradley (Marian Beecher); Betty Grable (Sylvia); Eric Blore (Phillips); Erik Rhodes (Frank Rochet); John Arledge (Pinky Parker); Johnny Mercer (Colonel); Donald Meek (Paul Parker); Dave Chasen (Andy); Joy Hodges (Lois); Douglas Fowley (Oyster); Evelyn Poe (Honey); Margaret Nearing (Margaret); Ronald Graham (Ronald); Sonny Lamont (Blimp); William Carey (Bill); Lucille Ball, Marian Darling, Jane Hamilton, Maxine Jennings, Kay Sutton (College Girls); Jack Thomas, Erich Von Stroheim, Jr., Carlyle Blackwell, Jr., Bryant Washburn, Jr. and Claude Gillinwater, Jr. (College Boys).

SYNOPSIS:
Johnny (Buddy Rogers) goes to college and his father, John Roberts, Sr.(George Barbier), is suspicious of Johnny's schooltime activities. Dad enrolls in the college, where he sees that gold-digger Marian (Grace Bradley) is after his son and his money. When she is told that the family has lost all of their money in a bad business deal, Marian leaves Johnny. He finds true love with good girl Edith (Barbara Kent).

REVIEWS:
VARIETY, 9.25.35: "In those nabes where they take their illusions less critically this hodge-podge of co-ed romancing and katzenjammer may prove diverting...Cast is top heavy with lookers, while the dancing interludes leave little wanting."

COMMENTS:
- Betty sings the lead in the song "BOYS WILL BE BOYS" with a female quartet, dances an adagio number and surprises with a Toe-Tap number.
- Used as an important publicity ploy for the film, second generation actors Erich Von Stroheim, Jr., Carlyle Blackwell, Jr., Bryant Washburn, Jr. and Claude Gillinwater, Jr., followed their famous fathers' footsteps and were cast as "College Boys." Lucille Ball and composer/lyricist Johnny Mercer also had small roles in the film.

VIDEO: King Video (V25)

## F38.   A Quiet Fourth

(RKO, Release date: August 15, 1935) (Short), 15-16 minutes

CREDITS:
Producer, Lee Marcus; director, Fred Guiol; story, Leslie Goodwins, Jack Townley; editor, Edward Mann.

CAST:
Betty Grable, Edgar Deering.

SYNOPSIS:
The parents of a secretly wed daughter (Grable) plan a Fourth of July picnic to persuade her to marry a rich man. The

picnic goes awry when the real groom shows up and the two men fight over the girl. The girl's bratty little brother adds to the confusion by setting off firecrackers. Furthermore, the parents have laid their picnic on an Army artillery area and when training begins, their "Quiet Fourth" is shattered.

REVIEW:
MOTION PICTURE HERALD, 8.17.35: "Here is an amusing comedy centered around a family on the Fourth of July...Some amusing scenes occur when it is discovered that the army is having maneuvers in that area and the artillery already has commenced firing."

## F39.    Collegiate

(Paramount, Release date: January 9, 1936) 81 minutes

CREDITS:
Producer, Louis D. Lighton; director, Ralph Murphy; screenplay, Walter De Leon, Francis Martin; based on the story "Charm School" by Alice Duer Miller; camera, William Mellor; editor, Doane Harrison; music director, Georgie Stoll; dance director, LeRoy Prinz.

SONGS:
"I FEEL LIKE A FEATHER IN THE BREEZE;" "YOU HIT THE SPOT;" "RHYTHMATIC;" "MY GRANDFATHER'S CLOCK IN THE HALLWAY;" "WHO AM I?;" "GUESS AGAIN;" "WILL I EVER KNOW?;" "LEARN TO BE LOVELY" by Mack Gordon and Harry Revel.

CAST:
Joe Penner (Joe); Jack Oakie (Jerry Craig); Ned Sparks (Scoop Oakland); Frances Langford (Juliet Hay); Betty Grable (Dorothy); Lynne Overman (Sourpuss); Betty Jane Cooper (Dance Instructress); Mack Gordon and Harry Revel (Themselves); Henry Kolker (Mr. MacGregor); Donald Gallagher (Thomas J. Bloodgood); Albert Conti (Headwaiter); Julius Tanning (Detective Browning); Helen Brown (Dance Teacher); Johnny Wrey, Ted Shea, Bob Goodstein, Ruby Shaffer, Jimmy Dime, Jack and Bob Crosby (Chorus Boys); Dorothy Jarvis, Katherine Hankin, Nancy Emery, Irene Bennett, Martha O'Driscoll (Chorus Girls); Edgar Deering (State Trouper); Guy Usher (Lawyer); Marjorie Reynolds (Girl).

SYNOPSIS:
Man-about-town Jerry (Jack Oakie) learns that his Aunt has died and due to a special clause in her will, he becomes the dean of a girl's college. After leaving Broadway, Jerry hires Betty Jane Cooper as a dance teacher in the "Rhythm" class, adding another "R" to the curriculum! When the college funds start to run low, millionaire Joe (Joe Penner) becomes the school's benefactor and saves the day.

REVIEWS:
VARIETY, 1.29.36: "...is fair entertainment. Light, diverting, no socko, but no bore...the rest are bits, save Betty Grable, attractive vis-a-vis to Penner."

NEW YORK TIMES, 1.23.36: "There was a near-riot outside the Paramount at noon yesterday when a crowd, estimated by the police at several hundred and by the management at several thousand, fought to pay their way into the theater to see Collegiate, featuring Joe Penner and a girl's seminary...But it seems manifestly unfair when...producers compel such players as Jack Oakie, Lynne Overman and Ned Sparks, who are comedians, not clowns, to meet Mr. Penner on his own ground and cavort through a picture wearing metaphoric putty noses and swinging metaphoric slapsticks."

COMMENTS:
- Based on Alice Duer Miller's "Charm School," this property had been made before by Paramount in 1921 with Wallace Reid, as Someone To Love in 1928 with Buddy Rogers and in 1929 as Sweetie with Nancy Carroll and would be remade in 1939 as College Swing with Burns and Allen and Grable.
- Martha O' Driscoll and Marjorie Reynolds, two actresses who would have successful film careers as leading ladies, appeared in bits in the film.
- The film advertisements read: "Ya gotta have class! Songs that are the class of '36!"
- Released in Great Britain as The Charm School.

RECORDING: Caliban (D8)

## F40.   Follow The Fleet

(RKO, Release date: February 20, 1936) 110 minutes

CREDITS:
Producer, Pandro S. Berman; director, Mark Sandrich; screenplay, Dwight Taylor; based on the play Shore Leave by Hubert Osborne, Allan Scott; camera, David Abel; editor, Henry Berman; music director, Max Steiner; dance director, Hermes Pan.

SONGS:
"LET'S FACE THE MUSIC AND DANCE;" "LET YOURSELF GO;" "I'M PUTTING ALL MY EGGS IN ONE BASKET;" "GET THEE BEHIND ME SATAN;" "BUT WHERE ARE YOU;" "WE SAW THE SEA;" "I'D RATHER LEAD A BAND" by Irving Berlin.

CAST:
Fred Astaire (Baker); Ginger Rogers (Sherry Martin); Randolph Scott (Bilge Smith); Harriet Hilliard (Connie Martin); Astrid Allwyn (Iris Manning); Ray Mayer (Dopey); Harry Beresford (Captain Hickey); Addison (Jack) Randall (Lt. Williams); Russell Hicks (Jim Nolan); Brooks Benedict (Sullivan); Lucille Ball (Kitty Collins); Betty Grable, Joy Hodges, Jennie Gray (Trio); Tony Martin (Sailor); Maxine Jennings (Hostess); Frank Jenks, Frank Mills, Edward Burns (Sailors); Herbert Rawlkinson (Webber); Jane Hamilton (Waitress).

SYNOPSIS:
Baker (Fred Astaire) is an ex-dancer who has joined the Navy. His former partner, Sherry (Ginger Rogers), now works in a

San Francisco dancehall with her sister, Connie (Harriet Hilliard), where Baker and his pal, Bilge (Randolph Scott), arrive while on leave. Baker and Sherry meet once again at a dance contest and Bilge and Connie are instantly smitten. Baker and Sherry decide to reteam and perform their act in a benefit show to raise money for the restoration of a schooner. The act is a success and they fall once again in love, with Bilge and Connie also becoming a romantic team.

REVIEWS:
VARIETY, 2.26.36: "Astaire once more legs himself into the big time entertainment class...Betty Grable is on and off so quickly its hardly a screen test."

HOLLYWOOD REPORTER, 2.10.36.:"...Betty Grable is in for a helpful bit."

NEW YORK TIMES, 2.22.36: "If you are one of those outlanders who have never seen the screen's premiere dancing team in action, now is a propitious time to complete your education."

COMMENTS:
- Three steps backwards for Betty as she performs as part of a musical trio backing up Ginger Rogers at the dancehall, singing "LET YOURSELF GO." Without any dialogue or featured shots, Betty goes back into the Chorus in this one.
- The script is loosely based on Shore Leave, a 1922 play filmed in 1925, which served as the basis for the 1927 musical Hit The Deck, filmed in 1930 and 1955. The film is unique in the Astaire-Rogers series because of Astaire playing a rare "average Joe" role as an ordinary sailor.
- Tony Martin made his screen debut in the film as a sailor.
- Harriet Hilliard, disguised in a black wig, would go on to show business immortality as the "Harriet" of Ozzie and Harriet and the mother of David and Ricky Nelson.
- Opened at Radio City Music Hall on February 20, 1936.

VIDEO: Turner Home Entertainment (V8)
LASER DISC: Image (V8)
RECORDING: Scarce Rarities, Caliban and Sountrak (D14)

## F41.   Sunkist Stars at Palm Springs

(MGM, Release date: August 6, 1936) (Short), 18 minutes, Technicolor

CREDITS:
Producer, Louis Lewlyn; director, Roy Rolland; dialogue, John Krafft; photography, Aldo Ernini; dances staged by Fanchon.

SONGS:
"WAHOO"
"YOU ARE MY LUCKY STAR;" "BROADWAY MELODY" by Arthur Freed, Nacio Herb Brown
"ALOHA OE" by Queen Liliuokalani
"DIXIE" by D.D. Emmett

CAST:
Edmund Lowe, The Fanchonettes, Lind Hayes and "A Galaxy of Stars": Betty Grable, Jackie Coogan, Frankie Darro, Claire Trevor, Walter Houston, Betty Furness, Frances Langford, Johnny Weismuller, Buster Keaton, The Downey Sisters.

SYNOPSIS:
Prize winning dancers from across the country (the Fanchonettes) are brought to the Biltmore Hotel in Palm Springs for a congratulatory luncheon. Host Edmund Lowe introduces them to the Hollywood stars present, assisted by an oversized microphone (with the voice of "Mike" by Lind Hayes) doing impressions and adding comic comments about the stars.

COMMENTS:
- One in a series of MGM color musical shorts, including Starlit Days At The Lido and Sunday Night At The Trocodero.
- Betty is pulled onscreen in a covered wagon by Jackie Coogan. They lead a "Hoedown" dance number with the Fanchonettes, a leading precision dance troupe of the time who were featured in "Prologues" and Vaudeville presentations in Movie Theatres across the country. Most of the dance numbers take place on a roof top, including a bizarre "Military Medley," with the Fanchonettes in red, white and blue tights performing fencing maneuvers.

## F42.    Don't Turn 'Em Loose

(RKO, Release date: Septmber 18, 1936) 65 minutes

CREDITS:
Producer, Robert Sisk; director, Ben Stoloff; screenplay, Harry Segall, Ferdinand Reyher; based on the story "Homecoming" by Thomas Walsh; camera, Jack MacKenzie; editor, William Morgan.

CAST:
Lewis Stone (Mr. Webster); James Gleason (Daniels); Bruce Cabot (Bat Roberts); Betty Grable (Mildred); Nella Walker (Mrs. Webster); Louise Latimer (Letty); Grace Bradley (Grace); Frank M. Thomas (Attorney Pierce); Maxine Jennings (Mary); Frank Jenks (Pete); Harry Jans (Vic); John Arledge (Walter); Addison Randall (Al); Fern Emmett (Hattie); Arthur Hoyt (Judge Bass); Frenchy Durelle (Deputy Warden); Phillip Morris (Guard); Tommy Graham (Secretary); Gordon Jones (Joe); John Ince (Parole Board Member).

SYNOPSIS:
Mr. Webster (Lewis Stone), a high-school Principal and conscientious member of a state prison parole board, finds out that his own son Bat Roberts (Bruce Cabot), a notorious public enemy, is up for parole. Bat threatens his Father that he will reveal their family connection, so Webster weakens to the blackmail and signs the parole papers. Bat goes on a crime spree with girlfriend/moll Letty (Louise Lattimer) and Mr. Webster realizes his mistake. He shoots his son to prevent him from causing any further grief to the World.

REVIEWS:
VARIETY, 9.30.36: "The manner in which Cabot threatens his father in gangland fashion doesn't ring true...at times Cabot lays on the menace a bit too heavily. Both Miss Latimer and Miss Grable are satisfactory."

NEW YORK TIMES 9.25.36 - Frank S. Nugent: "... if you believe there actually is an underlying social purpose behind its excitements then you should be of a mind today to toss all parole boards before a grand jury on charges of veniality, stupidity and flagrant disregard of law and order."

COMMENTS:
- Grable plays Bruce Cabot's sister in a rare dramatic role.

VIDEO: King Video (V5)

## F43.  Pigskin Parade

(20th Century Fox, Release date: October 23, 1936) 93 minutes

CREDITS:
Producer, Darryl F. Zanuck; associate producer, Bogart Rogers; director, David Butler; screenplay, Harry Tugend, Jack Yellen and William Conselman, based on a story by Arthur Sheekman, Nat Perrin and Mark Kelly; camera, Arthur Miller; editor, Irene Morra; art director, Hans Peters; costumes, Gwen Wakeling;  musical director, David Buttolph; dance director, Jack Haskell.

SONGS:
"IT'S LOVE I'M AFTER;"  "BALBOA;"  "YOU'RE SLIGHTLY TERRIFIC;"  "YOU DO THE DARNDEST THING BABY;"  "T.S.U. ALMA MATER;"  "HOLD THAT BULLDOG" (deleted);  "THE TEXAS TORNADO" by Sidney Mitchell and Lew Pollack
"WOO WOO;"  "DOWN WITH EVERYTHING;"  "FOOTBALL SONG;"  "WE'D RATHER BE IN COLLEGE" by The Yacht Club Boys

CAST:
Stuart Erwin (Amos Dodd); Pasty Kelly (Bessie Winters); Jack Haley (Slug Winters); The Yacht Club Boys (Themselves);  Johnny Downs (Chip Carson); Betty Grable (Laura Watson); Arline Judge (Sally Saxon); Dixie Dunbar (Ginger Jones); Judy Garland (Sairy Dodd); Anthony [Tony] Martin (Tommy Baker); Fred Kohler, Jr. (Biff Bentley); Elisha Cook, Jr. (Herbert Terwilliger Van Dyck); Julius Tannen (Dr. Burke); Pat Flaherty (Referee); Jack Murphy (Usher); Dave Sharp (Messenger Boy); Si Jenks (Baggage Master); Jack Stoney (Policeman); John Dilson (Doctor); Ben Hall (Boy in Stadium); Lynn Bari (Girl in Stadium); Charles Wilson (Yale Coach); Alan Ladd (Student); Edward LeSaint (Judge); Jack Best (Prof. McCormick); Maurice Cass (Prof. Tutwieler); Douglas Wood (Prof. Dutton); Charles Croker (Prof. Pillsbury).

SYNOPSIS:
Yale mistakenly invites Texas State University (instead of

the University of Texas) to play opposite them in an upcoming football game. The faculty of the college in Prairie, Texas, eagerly awaits the arrival of new coach Slug Winters (Jack Haley) and his wife, Bessie (Patsy Kelly), to bring new excitement to the football team. When they hear that they will play against Yale, they assume that it is their new Coach's handiwork. At a Celebration party, Bessie gets drunk and injures Biff Bentley (Fred Kohler, Jr.), the star player. In desperation, she goes to Arkansas to find a replacement with students Chip (Johnny Downs) and Laura (Betty Grable). They accidentally find a country bumpkin, Amos (Stu Erwin), who can really throw a watermelon. He practices tossing the melons to his sister, Sairy (Judy Garland), and after Sairy finds out that she can study music at the school, she convinces Amos to accept their offer of a scholarship. With Amos' talent, the team wins the "Big Game."

REVIEWS:
VARIETY, 11.18.36: "Situations are broad and burlesky, for which may be forgiven the opening shots wherein coeds are shown attending Yale...also in the newcomer category is Judy Garland, about 12 or 13 now, about whom the West Coast has been enthusing as a vocal find...Johnny Downs, juve of much promise in the past, again cements his strong impression ...Betty Grable is an innocuous coed ingenue."

NEW YORK TIMES, 11.14.36 - Frank S. Nugent: "David Butler has directed his pigskin extravaganza at top speed, bridging the chinks in the story with well-timed song and dance interludes, but having the wisdom to keep them well in hand."

COMMENTS:
- Betty's first major role in a film for Twentieth Century Fox, which would become her "Home Studio" in 1940.
- On the only loanout from MGM during her entire career, Judy Garland made her feature film debut and grabbed all of the reviews and attention.
- Tony Martin, billed as "Anthony Martin" portrays the school bandleader and sings "YOU'RE SLIGHTLY TERRIFIC."
- The Yacht Club Boys, performing several songs in the film, are obviously too old to be attending college. A line of dialogue ("He's been in college for seven years") is added to ease the viewer's disbelief.
- Alan Ladd appears silently throughout the film as an extra.
- Stuart Erwin's nomination for an Academy Award must have surprised all of Hollywood. It is a charming performance, but nothing to warrant such praise. One of the rare times a performance in a musical film was noticed by members of the Academy of Motion Pictures Arts and Sciences.
- Released in Great Britain as Harmony Parade.

ACADEMY AWARDS: Nomination for Best Supporting Actor (Stuart Erwin).

RECORDING: Pilgrim and AEI (D33). Also "IT'S LOVE I'M AFTER" heard on "Betty Grable" (D1) and "THE BALBOA" is heard on "Hollywood is on the Air" (D20)

**F44.   This Way, Please**

(Paramount, Release date: October 15, 1937) 70 minutes

CREDITS:
Producer, Mel Shauer; director, Robert Florey; screenplay,
Grant Garrett, Seena Owen and Howard J. Green; based on a
story by Maxwell Shane and Bill Thomas; camera, Harry
Fishbeck; editor, Anne Bauchens; art direction, Hans Drier,
Jack Otterson; costumes, Edith Head; music director, Boris
Morros; dances staged by LeRoy Prinz.

SONGS:
"IS IT LOVE OR IS IT INFATUATION?" by Sam Coslow and
Frederick Hollander
"THIS WAY PLEASE" by Sam Coslow
"DELIGHTED TO MEET YOU" and "WHAT THIS COUNTRY NEEDS IS
VOOM VOOM" by Al Siegal and Sam Coslow
"I'M THE SOUND EFFECTS MAN" by "Jock" and George Gray

CAST:
Charles "Buddy" Rogers (Brad Morgan); Mary Livingstone
(Maxine Barry); Betty Grable (Jane Morrow); Ned Sparks
(Inky Wells); Jim and Marian Jordon (Fibber McGee and
Molly); Porter Hall (S. J. Crawford); Lee Bowman (Stu
Randall); Cecil Cunningham (Miss Eberhardt); Wally Vernon
(Bumps); Romo Vincent (Trumps); Jerry Bergen (Mumps); Rufe
Davis (Sound Effects Man).

SYNOPSIS:
Hollywood Movie Star Brad Morgan (Buddy Rogers) is appearing
at the "Occident" movie theatre as the Master of Ceremonies
for the Vaudeville presentations. Jane Morrow (Betty Grable),
a starstruck young lady, wants to perform in the show but
instead gets a job as an usherette. When Brad finds out that
she is a singer and dancer, he arranges an audition for her.
He is impressed with her talent and although she is attracted
to him, his overly passionate kisses cause her to slap him.
Nevertheless, he asks theater owner S.J. Crawford (Porter
Hall) to hire Jane for the show. Afraid that Jane is yet
another of Brad's many "Flirtations," S.J. fires Jane. In
protest, Brad also quits, leaving the theater without a
headliner. Usherette Maxine Barry (Mary Livingstone)
persuades S.J. to give Jane a chance and after her audition,
he hires her to star. Brad and Jane are reconciled and as a
publicity stunt, they get married at the theater.

REVIEWS:
VARIETY, 9.15.37.: "Nothing in this slowly paced comedy with
music to get excited about. It is neither comic nor
melodious...Betty Grable, whose looks are on the plus side,
applies for a dancing job and is shoved into aisle 3 with a
flashlight...This Way Please suggests its own wisecrack."

NEW YORK TIMES, 10.8.37. - Bosley Crowther: "Mr. Rogers, who
is aged a bit and less exuberant than in the days of his
previous bid for film popularity, is romantically reinforced
by the beautiful Betty Grable...But in spite of the

distracting presense (sic) of Miss Grable, and the laconics of Ned Sparks, as far as we are concerned the star...is the deplorable Rufe Davis and his exhaustive repertoire of imitations."

COMMENTS:
- Shirley Ross, originally slated to play "Jane Morrow," got angry when Mary Livingstone's (Jack Benny's wife) role as Jane's friend was enlarged. She quit and Betty got a good "break." As an obvious boost to Livingstone's film career, she was given "introducing" billing, along with Fibber McGee and Molly to test the box-office power of radio stars.
- As Betty begins her Paramount contract, studio make-up artists describe her hair color as "Pearl Blonde" in press releases. She is gowned in exquisite costumes by Edith Head in the film.
- The ads promised "Gayest Gal and Gag show of the year!"

RECORDING: Medley: "DELIGHTED TO MEET YOU" and "IS IT LOVE OR INFATUATION?" on "Betty Grable" (D2)

## F45.   Thrill Of A Lifetime

(Paramount, Release date: January 1, 1938) 72 minutes

CREDITS:
Producer, Fanchon; director, George Archainbaud; screenplay; Seena Owen, Grant Garret, Paul Gerard Smith; based on a story by Seena Owen and Grant Garrett; camera, William Mellor; editor, Doane Harrison; art directors, Hans Drier, Franz Bachelin; music director, Boris Morros; dance directors, LeRoy Prinz, Carlos Romero.

SONGS:
"KEENO, SCREENO AND YOU;" "I'LL FOLLOW MY BABY;" "THRILL OF A LIFETIME;" "PARIS IN SWING" and "SWEETHEART TIME" by Sam Coslow and Frederick Hollander
"IT'S BEEN A WHOLE YEAR" and "IF WE COULD RUN THE COUNTRY FOR A DAY" by the Yacht Club Boys

CAST:
Judy Canova (Judy Lovelee); Betty Grable (Gwen); Larry "Buster" Crabbe (Don Lansing); Dorothy Lamour (Herself); Johnny Downs (Stanley Jackson); Ben Blue (Skipper); Eleanor Whitney (Betty Jane); Leif Erickson (Howard "Howdy" Nelson); Zeke and Anne Canova (Themselves); Fanchonettes (Specialty Dancers); Howard M. Mitchell (Businessman); Franklin Pangborn (Sam Wattle); Tommy Wonder (Billy); Marie Burton, Paula DeCardo, Norah Gale, Harriette Haddon, Loly Jensen, Gwen Kenyon, Joyce Matthews (the Girls); Billie Daniels, Bill Roberts, Frank Abel, Lee Bennett, Carlya; Blackwell, Jr., Bob Parrish (The Boys), The Yacht Club Beha                                                                gs' (Themselves).

SYNOPSIS:
Gwen (Betty Grable) is a plain-jane secretary in love v her playwright boss, Howard (Leif Erickson). Howard manshow "Camp Romance," a retreat where young people go to find the

"Beautiful legs" award.
- The film's advertisements claimed: "Its full speed ahead in the Grandest Raye Riot! 'Me too' says gorgeous Betty Grable who has a nifty pair of 'sea legs' too!"

**F48. Campus Confessions**

(Paramount, Release date: September 16, 1938) 65 minutes

CREDITS:
Associate producer, William Thomas; director, George Archainbaud; story and screenplay, Lloyd Corrigan and Erwin Gelsey; camera, Henry Sharp; editor, Stuart Gilmore; art directors, Hans Drier and William Flannery; music director, Boris Morros.

CAST:
Betty Grable (Joyce Gilmore); Eleanore Whitney (Susie Quinn); William Henry (Wayne Atterbury, Jr.); Fritz Feld ("Lady Macbeth"); John Arledge (Freddy Fry); Thurston Hall (Wayne Atterbury, Sr.); Roy Gordon (Dean Wilton); Lane Chandler (Coach Parker); Richard Denning (Buck Hogan); Matty Kemp (Ed Riggs); Sumner Getchell ("Blimp" Garrett); Hank Luisetti (Himself).

SYNOPSIS:
A comedy about Sports vs Study, but this time the main topic is basketball. The major contributor to a college, Wayne Atterbury, Sr.(Thurston Hall) hates sports, and when his son, Wayne, Jr. (William Henry), arrives as a freshman at the school, he has a difficult time fitting in. School newspaper reporter Joyce Gilmore (Betty Grable) interviews Wayne, Jr. and he is smitten with her. Trying to win her favor and be accepted by the other students, he works hard at changing his snobbish, anti-sports attitudes, finally inviting the basketball team to hold their Summer Camp at his father's estate, since Dad is out of the country. He becomes the best friend of genuine Sports Star Hank Luisetti and with his natural ability, becomes a star on the basketball team. When School resumes in the Fall, Joyce is pleasantly surprised to find Wayne on the team, helping to lead them onto victory. As the team nears the College Basketball finals, Atterbury,Sr. returns from Europe and tries to prevent the team from playing in "The Big Game." His paternal pride in his son's ability and Joyce's coaxing finally win Dad over to their side as the team wins and Wayne captures Joyce in his arms.

REVIEWS:
VARIETY, 9.14.38: "Paramount parades the all-American basket-baller Hank Luisetti onto the screen in a fast-paced and sparkling collegiate comedy...A well chosen cast is lacking in marquee names, but it performs adequately with William Henry, outstander, showing possibilities of developing strongly ...Yarn, basically, is the same college formula, being done continuously but has refreshing twists and gags new to rah-rah films, plus a fast clip maintained after initial reel."

NEW YORK TIMES, 9.23.38: "Of course the title is felicitous enough, in a certain pulp-magazinish way, and we should like to have seen it justified, particularly since Betty Grable heads the cast."

COMMENTS:
- Betty receives top billing for the first time in a feature length film in this non-musical role.
- The film opens with a statement "This is one of The Movie Quiz $250,000.00 Contest Pictures."
- Real-life basketball star Hank Luisetti does a credible job in his first - and last - movie role.

## F49.   Man About Town

(Paramount, Release date: July 7, 1939) 86 minutes

CREDITS:
Producer, Arthur Hornblow, Jr.; director, Mark Sandrich; screenplay, Morrie Ryskind; based on a story by Ryskind, Allan Scott and Zion Meyers; camera, Ted Tetzlaff; editor, LeRoy Stone; costumes, Edith Head; art directors, Hans Drier and Robert Usher; music director, Victor Young; choreography, Merriel Abbott; dance numbers staged by LeRoy Prinz.

SONGS:
"STRANGE ENCHANTMENT;" "THAT SENTIMENTAL SANDWICH;" "MAN ABOUT TOWN" by Frank Loesser and Frederick Hollander
"FIDGETY JOE" by Frank Loesser and Matty Malneck
"BLUEBIRDS IN THE MOONLIGHT" by Leo Robin and Ralph Rainger

CAST:
Jack Benny (Bob Temple); Dorothy Lamour (Diana Wilson); Edward Arnold (Sir John Arlington); Binnie Barnes (Lady Arlington); Phil Harris (Ted Nash); Eddie Anderson (Rochester); Monty Wooley (Dubois); Isabel Jeans (Madame Dubois); Betty Grable (Susan); E.E. Clive (Hotchkiss); Leonard Mudie (Gibson); Peggy Steward (Mary); Patti Sacks (Jane); Matty Malneck Orchestra, Pina Troupe and the Merriel Abbott Dancers (Themselves).

SYNOPSIS:
Bob Temple (Jack Benny), a Broadway producer in London, tries to woo his singing star, Diana Wilson (Dorothy Lamour), when she and other cast members arrive for their London debut. Diana will not take his amorous notions seriously, as she thinks he is much "Too solid and respectable" for romance. In an attempt to spice up his image, he promises a "Dance Specialty" and a raise to chorine Susan (Betty Grable), if she will pretend to be in love with him, spicing up his Lothario image. He also manufactures phoney romances with Lady Arlington (Binnie Barnes) and Madame Dubois (Isabel Jeans), who just happen to be using Bob to make their husbands jealous. When the outraged spouses go gunning for producer Temple, his Butler, Rochester (Eddie Anderson), saves the day and Bob finally wins the affections of Diana.

REVIEWS:
VARIETY, 6.14.39: "..has its entertaining and laugh moments, but is burdened with several production numbers and three songs that slow things down considerably...Basic story foundation is not too strong. Same goes for most of the song and dance numbers. Exceptions are Rochester's dance turns, and well-routined, snappy and colorful acrobatic number by the Merriel Abbott Dancers...Betty Grable is decorative in brief appearances."

NEW YORK TIMES, 6.29.39 - Frank S. Nugent: "Mark Sandrich, who became a national institution when he made Astaire and Rogers one, has directed it skillfully, weaving in his song, dance and spectacular numbers without suggesting that the story has taken the afternoon off."

COMMENTS:
- In The Paramount Pretties by James Robert Parish (B141), he writes that Betty underwent an appendectomy and Dorothy Lamour inherited the female lead. Another source states that Betty completed one musical number before her operation. Others write that Betty recovered in time to make an appearance in the film. Whatever the truth, she does appear in the film in a minor role. "Appendectomies" are to be a big part of Betty's future career...and mentioned several times over the years. She would soon get her biggest film opportunity when Alice Faye has an emergency "appendectomy" and Grable was rushed from Broadway to Hollywood to star in Down Argentine Way (1940, F42). Grable also was reported to have had several appendicitis operations herself. Printed that while married to Jackie Coogan (1937-'39), she "fainted on the set and rushed to the hospital for an emergency appendectomy" and yet, a Fox press release on April 2, 1943 says that she had her appendix removed in 1942 (B196). There are several references to injuries and operations in newspaper articles printed in 1942 (B105). "Appendectomy" was a polite term employed by film publicists to cover up for less delicate operations in that less-than-enlightened time.
- Betty sings and dances to "FIDGETY JOE" and her energy and appeal are one of the highlights of the film.
- The film's advertisements declared: "That Benny Boy is back...with the hit show of the Summer! The funniest plot...the best songs...the most beautiful girls of the year."

RECORDING: "FIDGETY JOE" is heard on two albums, "Betty Grable", (D1 and D2)

## F50.   Million Dollar Legs

(Paramount, Release date: July 14, 1939) 59 minutes

CREDITS:
Director, Nick Grinde, Edward Dymytyrk (uncredited); screenplay, Lewis Foster, Richard English; based on a story by Lewis Foster; camera, Harry Fischbeck; editor, Stuart Gilmore.

CAST:
Betty Grable (Carol Parker); John Hartley (Greg Melton);
Donald O'Connor (Sticky Boone); Jackie Coogan (Russ
Simpson); Larry "Buster" Crabbe (Coach Baxter); Peter Lind
Hayes (Freddie Fry); Dorothea Kent (Susie Quinn); Richard
Denning (Hunk Jordan); Phillip Warren (Buck Hogan); Edward
Arnold, Jr. (Blimp Garrett); Thurston Hall (Gregory Melton,
Sr.); Roy Gordon (Dean Wixby); Matty Kemp (Ed Riggs);
William Tracy (Egghead Jackson); Joyce Matthews (Bunny);
Russ Clark (Referee); Wallace Rairdan (Crandall); John Hart
(Haldeman); Anthony March (MacDonald); Rob Ireland (Hall);
Roger Laswell (Alden); Si Jenks (Bus Driver); Bill
Conselman, Jr. (Husky Student); Byron Foulger (Mr. Day);
Billy Gilbert (Schultz); Tom Dugan (Man); George Anderson
(President Green); William Holden (Graduate who says "Thank
you.")

SYNOPSIS:
Greg Melton (John Hartley) is the son of the millionaire
benefactor of a college and tries to make it as a college
athlete, without continual financial support from Dad
(Thurston Hall). Freddie Fry (Peter Lind Hayes) comes up with
the bright idea to revive the rowing team, but all of the
equipment is poor and outdated. A "Hot" race track tip about
a horse named "Million Dollar Legs" allows the team and
Greg's girlfriend, Carol (Grable), to place a bet - win - and
buy all new equipment. With the new gear and Greg on the
team, the crew wins the "Big Race."

REVIEWS:
VARIETY, 7.12.39: "Latest collegiate comedy by Paramount is
light and fluffy fare for youthful audiences of high school
and college age. Devoid of marquee strength, picture will
slip in as lower bracketer in the subsequent duals. As
proving ground for Paramount's group of younger contract
stock list, it gives the studio possibilities of various cast
individuals, besides providing the latter with chance to get
before the camera during their apprenticeship. Major fault of
the picture is title misnomer. Tab indicates to audiences
it's a girly leg show - instead, it parades the hefty gams of
college athletes with crew inclinations...Betty Grable and
John Hartley provide mild romantic interest."

COMMENTS:
- Not to be confused with the 1935 Million Dollar Legs made
by Paramount with W.C. Fields and Lyda Roberti.
- Fourteen year old Donald O Connor appears in the film and
William Holden has a one-line bit, before going on to make
Golden Boy - and movie history.
- Betty's second (and final) feature film with real-life
husband Jackie Coogan and the last film on her Paramount
contract.

## F51.  The Day The Bookies Wept

(RKO, Release date: September 15, 1939) 64 minutes

CREDITS:
Producer, Robert Sisk; director, Leslie Goodwin; screenplay, Bert Granet, George Jeske; based on the story "Crazy Over Pigeons" by Daniel Fuchs; camera, Jack MacKenzie; editor, Desmond Marquette; art director, Van Nest Polglase; music director, Arthur Horton.

CAST:
Joe Penner (Ernest Ambrose); Betty Grable (Ina Firpo); Richard Lane (Ramsey Firpo); Tom Kennedy (Pinky Brophy); Thurston Hall (Colonel March); Bernadene Hayes (Margie); Carol Hughes (Patsy March); William Wright (Harry); Prince Alert (The Horse); Emory Parnell (Cop); Vinton Haworth (Taxi Custodian); William "Billy" Newell (Maxie T. Bookmaker); Lloyd Ingraham (Race Track Patron); Paul E. Burns (Race Track Taxi Patron).

SYNOPSIS:
A group of taxi drivers dream of making a killing at the race track. They choose Ernest (Joe Penner) to purchase a horse. He mistakenly buys one with a love of alcohol, named "Hiccup." Just before the "Big Race," the horse drinks a large amount of beer...and it works! The horse wins, Ernest is the hero and his friends all make a fortune.

REVIEWS:
VARIETY, 9.20.39: "This is a very entertaining little comedy starring Joe Penner...the story is well plotted and the dialogue gets the desired results where the action relies on it for laughs...Penner is excellent and times his laughs well, while for able support he has Betty Grable, Richard Lane, Tom Kennedy and Thurston Hall, plus others."

NEW YORK TIMES, 9.14.39 - Frank S. Nugent: "Mr. Penner is superb.  Every time he opens his mouth the script-writers put a good line into it. Or nearly every time; on the off-moments he relies on his adenoids, which are almost as funny."

COMMENTS:
- Grable portrays Joe Penner's girlfriend once again as she comes back to RKO for the last time. Penner, famous for his line "Wanna buy a duck?," died in 1941 at the age of 36, ending a promising career that most probably would have gone onto television success.
- The second of three films in a row with a racetrack theme for Miss Grable, a locale which would become important in her real life.

VIDEO: Blackhawk (V4)

## F52.   Down Argentine Way

> (20th Century Fox, Release date: October 11, 1940) 94 minutes, Technicolor

CREDITS:
Producer, Darryl F. Zanuck; associate producer, Harry Joe Brown; director, Irving Cummings; screenplay, Darrell Ware,

Karl Tunberg; based on a story by Rian James and Ralph Spence; camera, Leon Shamroy, Ray Rennahan; editor, Barbara McLean; art directors, Richard Day, Joseph C. Wright; costumes, Travis Banton; music director, Emil Newman; dances staged by Nick Castle, Geneva Sawyer.

SONGS:
"TWO DREAMS MET;" "DOWN ARGENTINE WAY;" "NENITA;" "SING TO YOUR SENORITA" by Mack Gordon and Harry Warren
"MAMA YO QUIERO" by Al Stillman and Jaraca and Vincente Paiva
"DOIN' THE CONGA" by Gene Rose
"SOUTH AMERICAN WAY" by Al Dubin and Jimmy McHugh

CAST:
Don Ameche (Ricardo Quintana); Betty Grable (Glenda Crawford); Carmen Miranda (Herself); Charlotte Greenwood (Binnie Crawford); J. Carroll Naish (Casiano); Henry Stephenson (Don Diego Quintana); Katherine Aldridge (Helen Carson); Leonid Kinsky (Tito Acuna); Chris-Pin Martin (Esteban); Robert Conway (Jimmy Blake); Bobby Stone (Panchito); Gregory Gaye (Sebastian); Charles Judels (Ambassador); Edward Fielding (Crawford); Edward Conrad (Anastasio); Frank Puglia (Montero); The Nicholas Brothers (Themselves); Thomas and Catherine Dowling (Themselves); Six Hits and a Miss (Themselves); Flores Brothers (Themselves); Bando da Lua (Themselves); Fortunio Bonanova, Armand Kaliz (Hotel Managers).

SYNOPSIS:
As Don Diego (Henry Stephenson) prepares to ship his horses from Buenos Aires to New York for sale, he learns that wealthy Binnie Crawford (Charlotte Greenwood) wishes to have the first bid. He tells son, Ricardo (Don Ameche), that no one with the name of "Crawford" will ever have his prize winning horses. At a New York Horse Show, Ricardo meets Glenda (Betty Grable), as she barters to buy one of the horses. Wooing her, he finds out that she is Binnie's niece, so he turns down her offer. Angrily, she follows him to Argentina with Aunt Binnie to Don Diego's ranch for another bid on the horses. Don Diego finds out there are "Crawfords" on the property and has Binnie thrown off the land. Ricardo convinces Glenda to quickly change her name to "Cunningham" and introduces her to his Father. When the young lovers see "Furioso," one of Don Diego's prize Jumpers, win a race in the Village, they decide to secretly train the horse, hoping to reverse Don Diego's dictum that none of his horses should race. The day of the "Big Race," Don Diego finds out that "Furioso" is going to race and hurries to the track. As Binnie, Glenda and Ricardo all converge on Don Diego, he confesses that Glenda's father had been a schoolmate of his and stolen a girlfriend, hence his aversion to the name: "Crawford." But, since "Furioso" has won the race, all is forgiven and at a gala Fiesta, everyone sings and dances, with Glenda ending up in Ricardo's arms.

REVIEWS:
NEW YORK TIMES, 10.21.40 - Bosley Crowther: "Offhand, we

can't think of anyone more abundantly qualified to serve as ministress (sic) plenipotentiary to the Latin American lands...we can see plenty of her - singing, dancing and wearing clothes of surprising magnificence. We even see her trying to act, which is something less of a pleasure. But hold - what sort of good neighbor would make a remark like that! Pardon us, Miss Grable. Consider it unmade."

VARIETY, 10.9.40: "Carrying advantage of gorgeous Technicolor mounting, with dazzling color throughout in both settings and costumes that keeps constantly reminding the onlooker that it's all a showy revue...Miss Grable is light on vocal abilities, which, however, are overcome by her dances and beauty under the camera."

MOTION PICTURE GUIDE, 1987: "If you're lucky enough to see a mint print of the picture, the Technicolor will bang your eyes out."

COMMENTS:
- Originally titled The South American Way, the film is a remake of the 1938 Fox film Kentucky, in which Loretta Young played Grable's role.
- Betty, with shoulder length light brown hair, finally got the "Big Break" she had been working towards when Alice Faye had an "appendicitis" operation and Grable was handed the leading role. Variety reported (June 12, 1940) that Miss Faye "underwent a major operation day before the picture was slated to roll." Grable left Dubarry Was A Lady (S10) on Broadway and reported for work at Fox on June 24, 1940. The "Appendicitis" story has now been challenged with the rumor that is was actually hemorrhoids which kept Faye out of the film. Miss Faye herself was quoted (B123): "It had been written that I had appendicitis, but it wasn't that. And no, it wasn't an abortion. It was just one of those things." The film was also Grable's first Color feature film.
- This film marked Carmen Miranda's film debut. A recent sensation on Broadway in The Streets of Paris (1939), the Brazilian Bombshell's contract with the Shubert Brothers forbade her to leave New York. Her two musical appearances in the film were filmed during the day at the Fox-Movietone Studios in New York and inserted into the film.
- Planned as part of the Movie Industry's answer to Nelson Rockefeller's "Good Neighbor" policy, the film was nearly banned in Argentina and criticized angrily in Brazil because of its inaccurate depiction of Argentina (B52).
- Don Ameche, using a believable latin accent, begins the casting combination of Betty appearing opposite "Big, dark men" in most of her color musicals. Often, they had moustaches and until Dan Dailey was paired with her in 1947, she was teamed with tall, brunette, often swarthy, leading men to offset her rainbow-hued smallness.
- The film contains a sensational dance routine by the Nicholas Brothers.
- For this film, Betty received the first of many scathing reviews from Bosley Crowther, the leading critic at the New York Times. Throughout the rest of her career, Crowther would pan her acting abilities, while reluctantly having to admit

the power of her natural charms.
- The ads promised "Rhumbas! Congas! Laughter! Love! 8 Grand songs!"

ACADEMY AWARDS: Nominations for Color Cinematography (Leon Shamroy and Ray Rennhan); Best Song ("DOWN ARGENTINE WAY") and Best Interior Decoration - Color (Richard Day and Joseph C. Wright)

VIDEO: Key Video (V6)
LASER DISC:CBS/Fox (V6)
RECORDING: Hollywood Soundstage and Caliban (D13), also "TWO DREAMS MET" on "Hollywood Years of Harry Warren" (D23)

## F53.   Tin Pan Alley

(20th Century Fox, Release date: November 29, 1940) 94 minutes

CREDITS:
Producer, Darryl F. Zanuck; associate producer, Kenneth MacGowan; director, Walter Lang; screenplay, Robert Ellis, Helen Logan; based on a story by Pamela Harris; camera, Leon Shamroy; editor, Walter Thompson; art directors, Richard Day, Joseph C. Wright; costumes, Travis Banton; music director, Alfred Newman; dances staged by Seymour Felix.

SONGS:
"THE SHEIK OF ARABY" by Harry B. Smith, Francis Wheeler and Ted Snyder
"AMERICA I LOVE YOU" by Edgar Leslie and Archie Gottler
"GOODBYE BROADWAY, HELLO FRANCE" by Francis K. Riesner, Benny Davis and Billy Baskette
"K-K-K-KATY" by Geoffrey O'Hara
"MOONLIGHT BAY" by Edward Madden and Percy Wenrich
"HONEYSUCKLE ROSE" by Andy Razaf and Thomas "Fats" Waller
"MOONLIGHT AND ROSES" by Ben Black, Neil Moret and Edwin H. Lemare
"YOU SAY THE SWEETEST THINGS, BABY" by Mack Gordon and Harry Warren

CAST:
Alice Faye (Katie Blane); Betty Grable (Lily Blane); Jack Oakie (Harry Calhoun); John Payne (Skeets Harrington); Allen Jenkins (Sgt. Casey); Esther Ralston (Nora Bayes); Harold and Fayard Nicholas (Dance Specialty); Ben Carter (Boy); John Loder (Reggie Carstair); Elisha Cook, Jr. (Joe Cadd); Fred Keating (Harvey Raymond); Billy Gilbert (Sheik of Araby); Lillian Porter (Telephone Operator); Brian Sisters (Specialty); Robert Brothers (Specialty); Princess Vanessa Ammon (Specialty); Tyler Brooke (Bert Melville); Hal K. Dawson (Hotel Clerk); William B. Davidson (Hotel Manager); Lionel Pape (Lord Stanley); Billy Bevan (Doorman); Dewey Robinson (Dumb Guy); Robert Emmett Keane (Manager); John Sheehan (Announcer); George Watts (Mike Buckner); Jack Roper (Nick Palerno); James Flavin (Sergeant); Franklin Farnum (Man in the audience); Harry

Strang (Doughboy).

SYNOPSIS: New York, 1915, Skeets Harrigan and Harry Calhoun
(John Payne and Jack Oakie) struggle to get their music
publishing business started. Skeets does prize fights,
winning $25 to keep the landlord from locking them out of
their office. They decide that they need someone to "Plug"
their songs. Luckily, Harry knows the beautiful and talented
Blane Sisters, Katie (Faye) and Lily (Grable), and introduces
them to Skeets, who immediately falls in love with Katie. At
dinner,they hear a promising tune performed by the piano
player (Elisha Cook Jr.) and buy his song - Katie putting up
the "Advance." The song becomes a big hit and their music
publishing business becomes "The House of Hits" in "Tin Pan
Alley." Katie joins the company, while Lily goes off to
London to find musical comedy success. All goes well until
Skeets promises Katie that she can introduce a new song at an
upcoming benefit and then allows the famed Broadway star,
Nora Bayes (Esther Ralston), to sing it, instead of Katie.
Hurt and angry, she goes to London to join Lily. The
publishing business fails and Harry and Skeets join the Army,
as World War I has begun. Stationed in England, they both go
AWOL to see the Blane Sisters in their latest success. When
Katie hears that Skeets came backstage to try and see her,
she realizes she is still in love with him. Tracking him down
to the dock where he is about to be shipped off to France,
they reconcile. The film ends with all the principals happily
marching to their latest hit ("K-K-K-KATY") as the War ends
and they are reunited.

REVIEWS:
VARIETY , 11.27.40: "...primed as a successor to Alexander's
Ragtime Band, an extremely profitable grosser of two seasons
back, is substantial entertainment for wide audience appeal
and will click a merry tune at boxoffices...Studio
encountered some headaches along the line. Tyrone Power and
Don Ameche were originally set for the top honors with Alice
Faye, but casting assignments neccesitated shifts of Jack
Oakie and John Payne into the Power-Ameche slots, and
addition of Betty Grable. Switch strengthened, rather than
weakened, the starring combo apparently...Hays office also
stepped in and required extensive cutting of the harem
number...Miss Grable displays her shapeliness in a series of
abbreviated and eyeful costumes, although the camera in other
respects is sometimes none too flattering..."

NEW YORK TIMES, 11.22.40: "...the tearful partings and
reunions of Mr. Payne and Alice Faye, with, if you will
believe it, Betty Grable standing by as a sort of fairy
godmother during the amorous travail...the authors
have...given the Misses Faye and Grable a chance for some
fettlesome wriggling through several big numbers - an
occupation in which they are more adept than acting."

COMMENTS:
- The only joint appearance of Betty and Alice Faye. Although
the fan magazines tried to create a feud between Fox's
reigning musical Queen and the new "Upstart," the ladies

become fast and lifelong friends ("Betty was a great dancer. I loved working with her on Tin Pan Alley. And we became good friends." - B123). Their affection for one another is amply displayed in the film. Because of Grable's strong appeal in Down Argentine Way, a role was written for her into this film. Although given second billing, Betty's role is very small. She portrays the sassy, energetic and independent sister to Faye's trusting, romantic and sensible sibling. It's a shame that the film was not in Technicolor, an obvious economy decision by Fox.

- "THE SHEIK OF ARABY" number was censored by the Hays Office because of the transparent costumes Betty and Alice wore, creating the illusion of nudity. The Nicholas Brothers once again perform a show-stopping routine within the number.

- The "running gag" in the film of Oakie rewriting the song which will eventually become "K-K-K-KATY" occurs every ten minutes. He writes it as "Alaska," "Dixie," "Hawaii," "Australia" and "Ireland" before he luckily falls into the water, starts shivering and yells: "Goodbye K-K-K-Katy" to Faye. A hit is born!

- A song titled: "AMERICA, I LOVE YOU" is given a very elaborate - and bizarre - presentation, with the producers obviously hoping for another "GOD BLESS AMERICA!." First, Alice Faye sings the song (instantly knowing it by heart after glancing at the lead sheet for ten seconds - a skill Grable would acquire in Sweet Rosie O' Grady - F62). Alice is then joined by an instrumental group (the Roberts Brothers), an ear-piercing soprano (Princess Vanessa Ammon), a vocal trio (the Brian Sisters) and finally, by four well-dressed young women playing trumpets! The number concludes with every musician and singer on the Fox lot joining in.

- The musical number "GET OUT AND GET UNDER," about an old-fashioned automobile, was cut from the film.

- In two dance sequences together, Betty's energy level is much higher than Miss Faye's. Although Alice performs some very complicated tap combinations, there is very little energy or action in her arms or upper torso. Betty "sells" and moves like a very hot hoofer...something that June Haver would do to Grable five years later in a similar situation in The Dolly Sisters (F66).

- For the first time at Fox, Betty's name is an important part of the advertising campaign: "Betty Grable - the Down Argentine Way star...more torchy, more dazzling!"

- Remade by Fox in 1950 as I'll Get By with William Lundigan, June Haver and Gloria De Haven (playing Betty's role).

RECORDING: Sountrak and Caliban (D43) also "HONEYSUCKLE ROSE/MOONLIGHT AND ROSES" is heard on "Betty Grable" (D1)

## F54.  Hedda Hopper's Hollywood

(Paramount, 1941) (Short), 10 minutes

CREDITS:
Producer, Herbert Moulton; editor, Duke Goldstone.

SONG:
"THE MOCAMBO" by Phil Loman and Foster Cawley

CAST:
Hedda Hopper, Bill and Jane Hopper, Arlene Judge, Jinx Falkenberg, Kent Rogers, William Farnum, Carole Landis, Evelyn Keyes, Joe E. Brown, Anne Shirley, Mary Pickford, Buddy Rogers, Gene Hersholt, Loretta Young, Kay Kyser, Sam Goldwyn, Phil Loman and his Orchestra, Betty Grable, George Raft, Shirley Ross, Ann Miller, Desi Arnaz.

SYNOPSIS:
One of a series of short films depicting the activities of Hedda Hopper, one of Hollywood's two reigning gossip Queens. This edition features Hedda and silent screen star William Farnum reminiscing over Hedda's early film career at her home. A premiere in Milwaukee of Hedda Hopper's Hollywood is attended by stars. Mary Pickford officiates at a Dedication and Ground Breaking Ceremony for the Motion Picture Relief Fund Home and Hollywood nightlife is depicted at the glamourous Mocambo Nightclub, where Betty is shown entering with George Raft.

VIDEO: Republic Pictures Home Video (V13)

**F55.   Moon Over Miami**

> (20th Century Fox, Release date: July 4, 1941) 91 minutes, Technicolor

CREDITS:
Producer, Harry Joe Brown; director, Walter Lang; screenplay, Vincent Lawrence, Brown Holmes; based on a story by Stephen Powys, adapted by George Seaton and Lynn Starling; camera, Peverell Marley, Leon Shamroy and Allen M. Davey; editor, Walter Thompson; art directors, Richard Day, Wiard B. Inhen; costumes, Travis Banton; music director, Alfred Newman; dances staged by Hermes Pan.

SONGS:
"SOLITARY SEMINOLE;" "LOVELINESS AND LOVE;" "YOU STARTED SOMETHING;" "HURRAY FOR TODAY;" "OH ME OH MI-A-MI;" "I'VE GOT YOU ALL TO MYSELF;" "IS THAT GOOD?;""KINDERGARTEN CONGA (RING AROUND THE ROSIE)" and "WHAT CAN I DO FOR YOU?" by Leo Robin and Ralph Rainger
"MOON OVER MIAMI" by Edgar Leslie and Joe Burke

CAST:
Don Ameche (Phil O' Neil); Betty Grable (Kay); Robert Cummings (Jeff Bolton); Charlotte Greenwood (Aunt Susie); Jack Haley (Jack O'Hara); Carole Landis (Barbara); Cobina Wright, Jr. (Connie); George Lessey (William Bolton); Robert Conway (Lester); Condos Brothers (Themselves); Robert Grieg (Brearly); Minor Watson (Reynolds); Fortunio Bonanova (Mr. Pretto); George Humbert (Boss of Drive-In); Spencer Charters (Postman); Lynn Roberts (Jennie May); Larry McGrath (Bartender); Jack Cole and His Dancers (Specialty); Hermes Pan (Miss Grable's Dance Partner).

SYNOPSIS:
Kay (Grable), her sister Barbara (Carole Landis) and aunt

Susie (Charlotte Greenwood), get a small inheritance and decide to go to Miami to snare a rich husband for Kay, with Barbara posing as her secretary and aunt Susie as her maid. They check into a posh Miami hotel where Kay tries to snag wealthy Jeff (Robert Cummings), but instead is attracted to penniless Phil (Don Ameche). Aunt Susie happily finds romance with Jack (Jack Haley). When Phil finds out about the girls' golddigging plans, he is angered. Barbara, in the meantime, has fallen in love with millionaire Jeff, clearing the way for Kay and Phil to realize their true love. The story ends with all three couples happily committed.

REVIEWS:
VARIETY, 6.18.41: "There's more action, music and comedy in Moon Over Miami than its recent prototypes, with result being satisfactory entertainment on the light and fluffy side... Miss Grable delivers two dance specialties, as do the Condos Brothers...Topliners in the cast work hard and effectively at every turn."

NEW YORK TIMES, 7.5.41: "But if you are content - and we are very content - to be dazzled by Betty Grable and Carole Landis in color, to listen to some saucy tunes warbled with a lilt and to beat time in a couple of swirling production numbers, well, one can think of less pleasant ways of spending a hot Summer's eve."

COMMENTS:
- Breaking with the usual Fox formula of a "Backstage Story," this musical actually integrates the score with the story and dialogue. None of the characters are performers and many of the musical numbers evolve out of the action, rather than a rehearsal or performance situation. Highly praised in the book, Hollywood in the 40's (B76).
- Betty, her hair a dark golden brown in this film, performs an energetic dance number entitled "KINDERGARTEN CONGA" with choreographer Hermes Pan, giving us a glimpse of what her work with Fred Astaire might have been. This is Pan's first on-screen teaming with Grable.
- Jack Cole, eventually to choreograph for Grable, and his dancers, filmed a featured sequence in the number "SOLITARY SEMINOLE." Although given screen credit, Cole's appearance has been edited from the film, with the excuse that the number ran too long. Cole contends that it was removed because his sensual choreography was rated too erotic by the Hays Office (B98).
- First made in 1938 as Three Blind Mice with Loretta Young and Joel McCrea, it was remade by Fox in 1946 as Three Little Girls in Blue with June Haver (playing Betty's Role), Vivian Blaine and Vera-Ellen.
- The Condos Brothers dance with Betty to "YOU STARTED SOMETHING." Nick Condos was later to marry Martha Raye in 1942 and their daughter, Melodye, would figure prominently in a well-publicized battle over control of the ailing Ms. Raye's finances in 1992.

VIDEO: Key Video (V23)
RECORDING: Caliban (D30). "KINDERGARTEN CONGA" is heard on

"Betty Grable" (D1) and "LOVELINESS AND LOVE" on "Thanks For The Memory - The Classic Movie Musicals of Ralph Rainger 1930-'43" (D39)

## F56.     A Yank In The R.A.F.

(20th Century Fox, Release date: October 3, 1941) 98 minutes

CREDITS:
Producer, Darryl F. Zanuck; associate producer, Lou Edelman; director, Henry King; screenplay, Karl Tunberg, Darrel Ware; based on a story by Melville Crossman; camera, Leon Shamroy, Ronald Neame; editor, Barbara McLean; special effects, Fred Sersen, E.H. Hansen; art directors, Richard Day, James Basevi; costumes, Travis Banton; music director, Alfred Newman.

SONGS:
"ANOTHER LITTLE DREAM WON'T DO US ANY HARM" and "HI-YA LOVE" by Leo Robin and Ralph Rainger

CAST:
Tyrone Power (Tim Baker), Betty Grable (Carol); John Sutton (Capt. Morley); Reginald Gardiner (Roger); Donald Stuart (Harry Baker); Morton Lowry (Squadron Leader); Ralph Byrd (Al); Richard Fraser (Thorndyke); Bruce Lester (Richardson); Denis Green (Redmond); Lester Matthews (Group Captain); Frederic Worlock (Canadian Major); Dennis Hoey, Stuart Robinson (Intelligence Officers); Lynn Roberts (Nurse at Boat); Fortunio Bonanova (Headwaiter - Regency); Gladys Cooper (Mrs. Pillby); James Craven (Instructor); Guy Kingsford (Officer); Charles Irwin (Uniform Man); John Meredith (Cadet); Howard Davies (Warden).

SYNOPSIS:
Tim Baker (Tyrone Power) is a cocky American who joins the R.A.F. in England, partly to impress his entertainer girlfriend Carol (Grable). He offends most of his collegues with his smug attitude - treating war as if it were a game. But during one of his bombing raids, when his best friend, Roger (Reginald Gardiner), is killed, he truly realizes the seriousness and horror of the War. When he is given an important mission, he tries to inform Carol. After so many disappointments with his lack of honesty, she refuses to believe him. His mission is a dangerous one and after being shot down over France, he manages to sneak through enemy lines to England, where Carol is waiting for him. His experiences in combat bring maturity and respect.

REVIEWS:
NEW YORK TIMES, 9.27.41 - Bosley Crowther: "...(she) acts as though she knows what she is doing."

VARIETY, 9.10.41: "No more timely production has hit the release channels in several years than this picturization of a topic getting current headline attention and close public interest. Combo of title, subject and Tyrone Power's marquee voltage and general presentation assures hefty grosses and key holdovers ...Miss Grable grooves excellently as the girl who fully realizes Power's inconsistencies, but finally breaks down...She ably delivers a pair of tuneful numbers in night club sequences."

COMMENTS:
- Earning $1,500,000, A Yank in the R.A.F. was rated as one of the five most successful films in 1941.
- The original ending, shown only in previews, had Tyrone Power losing Betty to John Sutton and being killed in action. British authorities were unhappy about this ending, fearing it would hurt potential R.A.F. volunteers, so the ending was changed to let Tyrone live - and go off into the sunset with Betty.
- "When Zanuck tagged Grable for the role, he told her to act her bottom off for Britain" (B133). He also considered sequels about a female American in England (A W.A.F. in the R.A.F.) and an English soldier on the American team (A Tommy in the U.S.A.).

ACADEMY AWARDS: Nomination for Special Effects (Fred Sersen, E.H. Hansen).

RECORDING: "HI-YA LOVE" and "ANOTHER DREAM WON'T DO US ANY HARM" on "Betty Grable" (D1) and "Thanks For The Memory - The Classic Movie Musicals of Ralph Rainger 1930 - '43" (D39)

## F57.   I Wake Up Screaming/Hot Spot

(20th Century Fox, Release date: October 31, 1941) 81 minutes

CREDITS:
Producer, Milton Sperling; director, H. Bruce Humberstone; screenplay, Dwight Taylor; based on the novel by Steve Fisher; camera, Edward Cronjager; editor, Robert Simpson; art directors, Richard Day, Nathan Juran; music, Cyril J. Mockridge.

SONG:
"THE THINGS I LOVE" by Harold Barlow and Lewis Harris

CAST:
Betty Grable (Jill Lynn); Victor Mature (Frankie Christopher); Carole Landis (Vicky Lynn); Laird Cregar (Ed Cornell); William Gargan (Jerry McDonald); Alan Mowbray (Robin Ray); Allyn Joslyn (Larry Evans); Elisha Cook, Jr.(Harry Williams); Chick Chandler, Cyril Ring (Reporters); Morris Ankrum (Asst. District Attorney); Wade Boteler, Ralph Dunn (Detective Partners); Brooks Benedict (Man); Forbes Murray (Mr. Handel); May Beatty (Mrs. Handel).

SYNOPSIS:
Jill (Grable) Lynn's sister Vicky (Carole Landis), an up-and-coming model and media celebrity, is murdered and Vicky's promoter, Frankie (Victor Mature), is the chief suspect.

Detective Ed Cornell (Laird Cregar) tells him that he is determined to pin the crime on him. When Frankie was promoting Vicky, Jill saw him only as an opportunist. But now his true vulnerabilty shows through and they fall in love. She decides to help Frankie escape the Detective's grasp and clear his name. Frankie discovers that Harry Williams (Elisha Cook, Jr.), a quirky switchboard operator at the apartment hotel where the sisters lived, had been in the girl's apartment the afternoon Vicky was murdered. Harry confesses to the crime to Frankie and says that he was told by Det. Cornell to keep his mouth shut so that Frankie would be executed for the crime. Frankie goes to the Detective's apartment, where he discovers a shrine to Vicky, complete with photos and fresh flowers, and forces a confession out of the bereaved Cornell. The neurotic detective fantasized of being Vicky's boyfriend before Frankie glamoured her and started her career. Frankie turns the Detective and Harry in to the police and returns to Jill's waiting arms.

REVIEWS:
VARIETY, 10.22.41: "This picture is first rate entertainment and may be depended upon to do from better than average to very good business. Its femme cast names won't hurt either...Betty Grable is enormously appealing as the sister of the slain girl...The book on which this picture is based is called "I Wake Up Screaming." It sounds like a better title than Hot Spot, but the film need not beg forgiveness."

NEW YORK TIMES, 1.17.42 - Bosley Crowther: "...three of the principal roles are played with virtually no distinction by Betty Grable, Victor Mature and Carole Landis...Incidentally, the picture never does make it clear who it is that wakes up screaming."

COMMENTS:
- An unusually straight role for Grable in this "Film Noir" feature distinguished by an excellent performance by Laird Cregar.
- Released in Great Britain and some sections of the U.S. as Hot Spot, the film was remade in 1953 by Fox as Vicki with Jeanne Crain playing Betty's role. In Vicki, the role of Larry, the columnist, is played by Casey Adams (aka Max Showalter), who would eventually costar with Betty in Hello Dolly (S19). The role of Harry, the murderer, is played in the remake by a very young Aaron Spelling, who would abandon his acting career and become one of Television's most successful producers (Charley's Angels, Dynasty, Beverly Hills 90210, etc.).
- "OVER THE RAINBOW" is used as the film's love theme - an unusual occurence for one studio (Fox) to use another's (MGM) music in its film.
- To give the film audiences a glimpse of Grable in a swimsuit, the screenwriters invented a trip to a New York swimming pool as part of an evening "Out on the Town" with Mature.

VIDEO: Key Video (V18)

## F58.  Song Of The Islands

(20th Century Fox, Release date: March 13, 1942) 75 minutes, Technicolor

CREDITS:
Producer, William LeBaron; director, Walter Lang; screenplay, Joseph Schrank, Robert Pirosh, Robert Ellis, Helen Logan; camera, Ernest Palmer; editor, Robert Simpson; costumes, Gwen Wakeling; music director, Alfred Newman; dances staged by Hermes Pan.

SONGS:
"BLUE SHADOWS AND WHITE GARDENIAS" (deleted); "O'BRIEN HAS GONE HAWAIIAN;" "MALUNA MALALO MAWAENA;" "WHAT'S BUZZIN' COUSIN?;" and "DOWN ON AMI AMI ONI ONI ISLE" by Mack Gordon and Harry Owens
"SING ME A SONG OF THE ISLANDS" by Mack Gordon and Harry Warren
"HAWAIIAN WAR CHANT" by Ralph Freed, Johnny Noble and Prince Leleiohau
"COCKEYED MAYOR OF KAUNAKAKAI" by R. Alex Anderson and Al Stillman

CAST:
Betty Grable (Eileen O'Brien); Victor Mature (Jefferson Harper); Jack Oakie (Rusty); Thomas Mitchell (O'Brien); George Barbier (Harper); Billy Gilbert (Palola's Father); Hilo Hattie (Palola); Lillian Porter (Palola's cousin); Hal K. Dawson (John Rodney); Harry Owens and His Royal Hawaiians (Themselves); Amy Cordone (Specialty); Bruce Wong (House Boy); Alex Pollard (Valet), Harold Lishman (Old Native).

SYNOPSIS:
Eileen O'Brien (Grable) returns home from college to Ami Oni Island, where she is greeted by her father (Thomas Mitchell) and the natives. A ship, carrying Jefferson Harper (Victor Mature) and Rusty (Jack Oakie), lands on the island and Eileen, pretending to be a native girl, escorts them to the Harper Cattle Ranch, owned by Jefferson's father (George Barbier) and run by the super-efficient John Rodney (Hal K. Dawson). For years, Mr. Harper has tried to buy O'Brien's beach property to build a pier so that he can move his cattle easily onto boats. Jefferson and Rusty go to make a deal with O'Brien and they find out that Eileen is not really a islander. Jefferson and Eileen fall in love and Rusty is pursued by the lusty Palola (Hilo Hattie). Rodney phones Mr. Harper in Chicago, warning him that his son has "Gone Native," so Harper arrives on the sleepy island. After much bickering (O'Brien is against progress and Harper thinks only of business), and the sharing of Tropical Spirits, the two men become friends and reach an agreement at the big St. Patrick's Day Luau. Jefferson and Rusty marry and Palola snares the reluctant Rusty.

REVIEWS:
NEW YORK TIMES, 3.12.42: "As a movie, Song of the Islands is

a great bathing suit advertisement...Most of the film seems to have been staged by Hermes Pan, who has given it the character of an interminable production number in which Miss Grable twitches through a grass skirt routine that shouldn't lose her any of her adoring public."

VARIETY, 2.11.42: "Picture displays plenty of eye-and-ear assets. Betty Grable, in abbreviated Hawiian attire, displays a particularly formful figure to hold the interest of the male section, while the athletic Victor Mature will get attention of the female customers. Hilo Hattie scores with a couple of comedy hula dances, and Miss Grable also delivers grass-skirt gyrations with an ensemble assisting."

COMMENTS:
- Seeing the barrel chested Mature, clothed in form fitting sweaters and shirts throughout the film, one is reminded of Groucho Marx's comment at the <u>Samson and Delilah</u> Premiere (1949 - in which Mature costarred with Hedy Lamarr): "I always hate a movie where the male star has bigger boobs than the female star."
- Betty, with golden blonde hair, attacks Hermes Pan's quasi-Hawaiian choreography with zest and energy, making the sight of the blonde, blue-eyed star surrounded by dark tressed and complexioned "Natives" palatable.
- Attendance makes it the most popular film in Army Theaters in March, 1942.

VIDEO: Key Video (V31)
LASER DISC: CBS/FOX (V31)
RECORDING: Caliban (D36) and "SING ME A SONG OF THE ISLANDS" and "DOWN ON AMI AMI ONI ONI ISLE" on "Betty Grable" (D1); "BLUE SHADOWS AND WHITE GARDENIAS" on "Choice Cuts" (D6)

## F59.   Footlight Serenade

(20th Century Fox, Release date: August 1, 1942) 80 minutes

CREDITS:
Producer, William LeBaron; director, Gregory Ratoff; screenplay, Robert Ellis, Helen Logan and Lynn Starling; based on the story "Dynamite" by Fidel LaBarba and Kenneth Earl; camera, Lee Garmes; editor, Robert Simpson; music director, Charles Henderson; dance director, Hermes Pan.

SONGS:
"LIVING HIGH (ON A WESTERN HILL);" "I'LL BE MARCHING TO A LOVE SONG" (deleted); "I'M STILL CRAZY FOR YOU;" "I HEARD THE BIRDIES SING;" "ARE YOU KIDDIN'?;" "EXCEPT FOR YOU" and "LAND ON YOUR FEET" by Leo Robin and Ralph Rainger
"I'M STEPPING OUT WITH A MEMORY TONIGHT" by Herb Magidson and Allie Wrubel

CAST:
John Payne (Bill Smith); Betty Grable (Pat Lambert); Victor Mature (Tommy Lundy); Jane Wyman (Flo LaVerne); James Gleason (Bruce McKay); Phil Silvers (Slap); Cobina

Wright, Jr. (Estelle Evans); June Lang (June); Frank Orth (Doorman); Mantan Moreland (Dresser); Irving Bacon (Porter); Charles Tannen (Stage Manager); George Dobbs (Dance Director); Sheila Ryan (Girl); Frank Coghlan, Jr. (Usher); Harry Barris (Composer); Trudy Marshall (Secretary): Don Wilson (Announcer); John Dilson (Clerk); William "Billy" Newell (Writer); Pat McKee (Pug); Wilbur Mack (Boxing Commissioner); George Holmes (Boy); Russ Clark and Frankie Van (Referees); Bud and Jim Mercer (Dance Specialty); Hermes Pan (Miss Grable's Dance Partner).

SYNOPSIS:
A conceited heavyweight fighter, Tommy Lundy (Mature), takes a role in a Broadway musical and makes a play for its star, Pat Lambert (Grable). She is already married to Bill (John Payne), but has been keeping her marriage a secret for publicity purposes. Pat secures a prizefighting role in the show for Bill and during rehearsals, he resents Tommy's attentions. In the climactic fight scene within the show, Bill pummels Tommy, knocking him out and changing the scenario of the show. When Tommy finds out that the two are married, he relents, allowing the couple romantic peace.

REVIEWS:
VARIETY, 6.8.42: "20th-Fox is apparently attempting to swing Betty Grable into the song-and-dance headline spot, and although picture is a typical backstage number, it gives her several chances to click in both the vocal and terp departments."

NEW YORK TIMES, 9.10.42 - Bosley Crowther: "One has to confess that Mr. Mature gives a performance as a loud, conceited numbskull and that Miss Grable does quite nicely when it comes to tossing her torso around...Now, remember Twentieth Century Fox - your turn's up. You've had your backstage musical for this year. If you expect to try another, you'll have to put some effort into it."

COMMENTS:
- In the musical number "I HEARD THE BIRDIES SING," choreographer Hermes Pan again partners Grable.
- The musical number "I'LL BE MARCHING TO A LOVE SONG" (a number that Hermes Pan was very embarrassed about - B91) was deleted from the film, but salvaged by being placed in All Star Bond Rally, a Fox short released in 1945 (F67).
- Originally titled Strictly Dynamite.

VIDEO: Key Video (V9)
RECORDING: Caliban (D15) and "I HEARD THE BIRDIES SING" on "Betty Grable" (D1), "I'LL BE MARCHING TO A LOVE SONG" on "Cut! - Volume 1" (D10); "I'M STILL CRAZY FOR YOU" and "I HEARD THE BIRDIES SING" on "Thanks For The Memory - The Classic Movie Musicals of Ralph Rainger 1930-'43" (D39)

## F60.   Springtime In The Rockies

(20th Century Fox, Release date: November 6, 1942) 91 minutes, Technicolor

CREDITS:
Producer, Darryl F. Zanuck; director, Irving Cummings;
screenplay, Walter Bullock, Ken Englund; based on a
story by Philip Wylie; adapted by Jacques Thery; camera,
Ernest Palmer; editor, Robert Simpson; art directors,
Richard Day, Joseph C. Wright; costumes, Earl Luick;
music director, Alfred Newman; dance director, Hermes Pan.

SONGS:
"I HAD THE CRAZIEST DREAM;" "POEM SET TO MUSIC;" "PAN-
AMERICAN JUBILEE;" "RUN, LITTLE RAINDROP, RUN;" "CHATTANOOGA
CHOO CHOO" and "I LIKE TO BE LOVED BY YOU" by Mack Gordon
and Harry Warren
"TIC TAC DO MEU CORACAO" BY Vermelho and Silva

CAST:
Betty Grable (Vicky); John Payne (Dan); Carmen Miranda
(Rosita); Cesar Romero (Victor); Charlotte Greenwood,
(Phoebe Gray); Edward Everett Horton (Mc Tavish); Harry
James and his Music Makers (Themselves); Bando De Lua
(Themselves); Frank Orth and Harry Hayden (Bickle and
Brown); Jackie Gleason (Dan's Agent); Trudy Marhsall
(Marilyn); Chick Chandler (Stage Manager); Iron Eyes Cody
(Indian); Bess Flowers (Mrs. Jeepers); Helen Forrest
(Herself).

SYNOPSIS:
Vicky (Grable) and Dan (Payne) are an engaged pair of
entertainers who love each other but continue to have
arguments over Dan's constant flirtations. After their hit
show closes on Broadway, Vicky goes to Lake Louise, where she
has an engagement with her former dancing partner, Victor
(Romero) and Dan follows. Vicky intends to make Dan jealous
by harmlessly firting with Victor. Dan hires Rosita, a
Brazilian secretary (Miranda) to make Vicky jealous. After a
series of comic arguments and misunderstandings, true love
triumphs and all end up with the right romantic interest.

REVIEWS:
VARIETY, 9.23.42: "It's solid entertainment, aiming for hefty
grosses all along the line. Talent list brings together a
slick cast recognized for individual abilities in their
respective lines. Betty Grable, in addition to providing eye
appeal as the femme lead, steps out with several song and
dance numbers of showmanship calibre."

NEW YORK TIMES, 11.12.42: "Pretty as a lollipop and just as
common...a smooth job with faded material...It should be
mentioned that each appearance of bandleader Harry James on
the screen was the signal for frenzied applause."

COMMENTS:
- This successful film made the list of box office leaders in
1942, earning more than $2,000,000. Another Springtime in the
Rockies had been filmed by Republic in 1937, starring Gene
Autry and containing the familiar title song.
- Again, Betty substitutes for Alice Faye, who was pregnant.
- The film's big song hit, "I HAD THE CRAZIEST DREAM" was

sung by Helen Forrest with Harry James and His Music Makers, not Miss Grable. It was however, a chance for Betty and Harry James to work together, after meeting in Chicago in 1940.
- The film was Cesar Romero's second dance assignment on film. He had started in show business as a ballroom dancer, but his dark, romantic looks most often found him cast in dramatic roles. Because Romero successfully partnered Alice Faye in a dance number in Weekend on Havana the previous year, Fox must have felt that he could handle the role as Grable's ex-dancing partner in Rockies and assigned him the role - and a major dance number with her. He reminisced about her patience and sense of fun during the rehearsal and filming of the complicated dance sequence.
- Carmen Miranda performed a classic version of "CHATTANOOGA CHOO CHOO" (last year's hit from Sun Valley Serenade) in Portuguese!
- During filming, Betty reportedly injured herself because of "strenuous dance routines" and had to have an operation (B105).

VIDEO: Key Video (V32)
LASER DISC: CBS/FOX (V32)
RECORDING: Pelican, Hollywood Soundstage, Sandy Hook and Titania (D37) as well as "PAN AMERICANA JUBILEE" on "Hollywood is on the Air" (D20) and "Hollywood Years of Harry Warren, 1930-'57" (D23)

## F61.   Coney Island

> (20th Century Fox, Release date: June 18, 1943) 96 minutes, Technicolor

CREDITS:
Producer, William Perlberg; director, Walter Lang; screenplay, George Seaton; camera, Ernest Palmer; editor, Robert Simpson; art directors, Richard Day, Joseph C. Wright; costumes, Helen Rose; music director, Alfred Newman; musical sequences supervised by Fanchon; dances staged by Hermes Pan.

SONGS:
"TAKE IT FROM THERE;" "BEAUTIFUL CONEY ISLAND;" "MISS LULU FROM LOUISVILLE;" "GET THE MONEY;" "THERE'S DANGER IN A DANCE" and "OLD DEMON RUM" by Leo Robin and Ralph Rainger
"CUDDLE UP A LITTLE CLOSER" by Karl Hoschna and Otto Harbach
"PRETTY BABY" by Gus Kahn, Tony Jackson and Egbert Van Alstyne
"PUT YOUR ARMS AROUND ME HONEY" by Albert Von Tilzer and Junie Mc Creek
"WHO THREW THE OVERALLS IN MRS. MURPHY'S CHOWDER?" by George L. Giefer
"DARKTOWN STRUTTER'S BALL" by Shelton Brooks
"LET ME CALL YOU SWEETHEART" by Beth Slater Whitson and Leo Friedman

CAST:
Betty Grable (Kate Farley); George Montgomery (Eddie

Jackson); Cesar Romero (Joe Rocco); Charles Winninger
(Finnegan); Phil Silvers (Frankie); Matt Briggs
(Hammerstein); Paul Hurst (Louie); Frank Orth (Bartender);
Phyllis Kennedy (Dolly); Carmen D'Antonio (Dancer); Andrew
Tombes (Carter); Harry Seymour (Piano Player); Hal K.
Dawson (Cashier); Bud Williams (Singing Waiter); Alec Craig
(Man); Herbert Ashley, James Lucas, Francis Sayles
(Hecklers); Tom Dugan (Fitch); Trudy Marshall, Claire James
(Girlfriends); Tene Ramey, Gus Reed, Delos Jewkos, George
Grumlick (Singing Waiters); Delos Jewkos, Harry Masters,
Frank Orth, Joe Niemoyer (Quartette); Hermes Pan (Miss
Grable's dancing partner).

SYNOPSIS:
At the turn-of-the-century, rival saloon owners Eddie (George
Montgomery) and Joe (Cesar Romero) pull elaborate schemes on
each other as they battle for having the most successful
business and winning the hand of Kate (Betty Grable), a
brassy entertainer. Eddie, realizing that Kate's raucous song
delivery and gaudy tastes in fashion will keep her in
saloons, teaches her some finesse and she becomes a star for
him and his establishment. Her newfound fame eventually
catches the eye of Hammersmith (Matt Briggs), an important
producer of the day, and she goes on to star on Broadway.
When Joe sees how distraught Eddie is over losing his protege
he gives up his practical jokes and Kate and Eddie marry.

REVIEWS:
NEW YORK TIMES, 6.17.43 - Bosley Crowther: "Twentieth Century
Fox has a formula for high, wide and fancy musical films
which seldom fails to render a tuneful and Technicolorful
show. It calls for a locale and period of glitter and
gaudiness, say, the Barbary Coast in 1900 or Tony Pastor's -
anything that leads to flash. It also calls for some old
songs of a certain nostalgic quality and a pet love triangle
in which a singer - always a lady singer - is involved. It's
a formula which makes for pictures having more basis in fancy
than in fact...She also puts a mean and snakey wiggle into
her dancing (and singing)...And when Miss Grable agitates her
torso, in a Technicolored pink jacket and short mauve skirt,
it is not an exhibition which is likely to lull you to
sleep."

VARIETY, 5.19.43: "The true Coney Island, corny, bawdy and
brash, evidently wasn't deemed sufficiently colorful for
George Seaton, scripter of this film, so he just hung the
title on what amounts to a 95-minute audition of Betty
Grable's legs and chassis - in color...he makes a lady of
Miss Grable, a gaudy singing moll, and she winds up at the
finish as star of a Willie Hammerstein-produced musical at
the Victoria on Broadway. Fact that Willie Hammerstein didn't
produce musicals, and that the Victoria was strictly a
straight Vaudeville theatre, evidently escaped this film's
scenarist...there's no gainsaying Miss Grable's charms for
the male masses, but it's hard to conceive such wild audience
acclaim as occasions every one of her fair singing stints.
She's pretty with a terrific set of gams and other physical
assets - period."

COMMENTS:
- The first of Grable's highly successful "Turn-of-the-Century" musicals, it contains the famous "Camp" scene which was later to be spoofed on The Carol Burnett Show on TV and the popular Billy Barnes Revues onstage, where Betty is handcuffed (both hands and feet!) and leaned against a prop tree, stripped of the feathers and fluff from her costume and told to simply sing "CUDDLE UP A LITTLE CLOSER" by George Montgomery, rather than as an up-tempo, "barrellhouse" piece. As the curtain opens and she begins to hurriedly sing, George, on the keyboard, slows the song down to a ballad. Betty eventually "calms down" and the song is a smash!
- A typical Fox "Formula" film, also made with slight variations as Alexander's Ragtime Band (1938).
- Financial sidelight: the film studios (Fox, in particular), set many of their musicals at the turn-of-the-century so that they could avoid royalty payments for the songs, as most of them had slipped into "Public Domain." Turn-of-the-century theatrical costume designs also allowed them to show as much as possible of their leading ladies.
- Choreographer Hermes Pan once again dances with Betty in "THERE'S DANGER IN A DANCE." By now, she must have started wishing for an on-screen partner to match her song and dance skills. Fanchon is credited as "supervisor of the musical numbers" and her attention to details creates some unique staging. Fanchon had been very helpful to Miss Grable in her early career producing the Hollywood Secrets tour (S10) and the film Thrill of a Lifetime (F44) and this may have been Betty's way of repaying her by having her assigned to her films.

ACADEMY AWARDS: Nomination for Best Musical Score (Alfred Newman).

RECORDING: Caliban (D9) and "CUDDLE UP A LITTLE CLOSER" and "TAKE IT FROM THERE" are heard on "Betty Grable" (D1);"CUDDLE UP A LITTLE CLOSER" on Four Jills In A Jeep (D16);"TAKE IT FROM THERE" and "THERE'S DANGER IN A DANCE" on "Thanks For The Memory - the Classic Movie Musicals of Ralph Rainger, 1930-43" (D39)

## F62.   Sweet Rosie O'Grady

   (20th Century Fox, Release date: October 1, 1943) 74 minutes, Technicolor

   CREDITS:
   Producer, William Perlberg; director, Irving Cummings; screenplay, Ken Englund; based on a story by Frederick Stephani, Walter R. Lipman and Edward Van Emery; camera, Ernest Palmer; editor, Robert Simpson; art directors, James Basevi, Joseph C. Wright; costumes, Rene Hubert; music directors, Alfred Newman, Charles Henderson; musical numbers supervised by Fanchon; dance director, Hermes Pan.

   SONGS:
   "MY HEART TELLS ME;" "THE WISHING WALTZ;" "GET YOUR POLICE GAZETTE;" "MY SAM;" "GOING TO THE COUNTY FAIR" and "WHERE

OH WHERE IS THE GROOM?" by Mack Gordon and Harry Warren
"WAITING AT THE CHURCH" by Fred W. Leigh and Henry E.
Pether
"SWEET ROSIE O'GRADY" by Maude Nugent
"SIDEWALKS OF NEW YORK" by Charles Lawlor and James Blake
"TWO LITTLE GIRLS IN BLUE" by Charles Graham
"LITTLE ANNIE ROONEY" by Michael Nolan
"HEAVEN WILL PROTECT THE WORKING GIRL" by Edgar Smith and
A. Baldwin Sloane

CAST:
Betty Grable (Madeleine Marlow); Robert Young (Sam
Mackeever); Adolph Menjou (Morgan); Reginald Gardiner (Duke
Charles); Virginia Grey (Edna Van Dyke); Phil Regan
(Composer); Sig Rumann (Joe Flugelman); Alan Dinehart
(Arthur Skinner); Hobart Cavanaugh (Clark); Frank Orth
(Cabby); Jonathon Hale (Mr. Fox); Stanley Clements (Danny);
Byron Foulger (Rimplemayer); Lilyan Irene (Gracie); Milton
Parsons (Madison); Hal K. Dawson (Poindexter); George
Chandler (Kelly); Charles Trowbridge (Husband); St.
Brendan's Choir (Themselves); Leo Diamond and His
Solitaires (Themselves); Oliver Blake (White the Artist);
Cyril Ring, Herbert Vigran, Perc Launders
(Photographers); Dorothy Granger (Singer); Mary Gordon,
Connie Leon (Charwomen); Gabriel Canzona (Hurdy Gurdy man
with monkey); Edward Earle, James Metcalfe, Bruce Warren,
John Dilson, Paul Maxey, Sam Wren, Hooper Atchley
(Salesmen); Joe King (Burl ship official); Hermes Pan (Miss
Grable's dance partner).

SYNOPSIS:
Madeleine Marlow (Grable), famous Brooklyn singer and dancer,
wants more than her success in the beer halls of New York in
the early 1900s. She goes to London to perform and tries to
snare Duke Charles (Reginald Gardiner) to camouflage her
humble background. Sam McKeever (Robert Young), an American
Police Gazette reporter on assignment in London falls for
Madeleine. He writes spicy tidbits about her real background
for the Gazette, so that her romance with the Duke will end -
and he can have her for himself. After much bickering and
trickery, the climax arrives when Madeleine turns the tables
by performing a comic number about Sam in her show. After he
gets over the embarrassment of being so publicly parodied,
Madeleine and Sam fall into each other's arms.

REVIEWS:
VARIETY, 9.22.43: "With the b.o. boff of Coney Island fresh
in mind, exhibitors will have plenty to shout about in
heralding this Betty Grable starrer, also a Technicolored
musical primed for super grosses...Betty Grable, already an
exhibitor's fave pinup girl on the marquees, outdoes herself
in the mauve decade decolletage."

NEW YORK TIMES, 10.21.43: "...again offering Miss Betty
Grable of the legs divine in an hour-and-a-half long display
of assorted poses, suitable for pin-up. In luscious
Technicolor that fairly exudes from every square inch of the
screen, Miss Grable flounces about a good deal in some low-

Publicity pose for *Sweet Rosie O'Grady*, 1943.

necked ensembles that resemble nothing so much as an Italian wedding cake.  But the real tours de force come when blue-eyed, platinum-haired Miss Grable sings dreamily in a bathtub with soapsuds up to her glistening shoulders, or later when clad in pink tights she again proves that 20th Century Fox has under contract the legs which since have become immortal."

COMMENTS:
- Grable's second "Period Piece" contains the ludicrous "Hollywood Unreality" scene where Betty, in a bubble bath, is handed the musical lead sheet for "MY HEART TELLS ME," while the composer has her male co-star sing and play it in an adjoining room. After looking at the music for a few seconds, Betty begins singing the song - as if she has known it all of her life!
- "WAITING AT THE CHURCH," the film's opening number, is probably one of the better recreations of a "Gay 90's" stage piece, complete with candles for footlights. Once again, Fanchon supervised the musical numbers, her expertise adding colorful details.
- A charming A Cappella duet of several popular "Gay 90's" songs is performed by Betty and Robert Young in a carriage. Young, not known as a musical performer, sings with great confidence.
- In the number, "THE WISHING WALTZ," choreographer Hermes Pan again partners Betty.
- The story was filmed first by Fox in 1937 as Love is News with Tyrone Power and Loretta Young and then remade again in 1949 as That Wonderful Urge with Power and Gene Tierney.
- Alice Faye was originally announced to do this film but was giving birth to Alice, Jr.
- In 1950, Warner Brothers filmed The Daughter of Rosie O' Grady starring June Haver, capitalizing on the success of the Fox film. Both films were based on popular turn-of-the-century songs which saluted a fictious Irish heroine.
- The colorful ads proclaimed: "Its Sweet Betty Oh Grable in her - and the screen's greatest m-m-musical! Don't you dare miss the Bathtub Scene!"

RECORDING: Titania and Sandy Hook (D38) and "WAITIN' AT THE CHURCH" on "Betty Grable" (D1) and "MY HEART TELLS ME" on "Hollywood on the Air Presents 'The Feminine Touch'" (D21), "Hollywood Stars" (D22), "Hollywood Years of Harry Warren, 1930-'57" (D23), "Those Bombastic Blonde Bombshells" (D40)

### F63.    Four Jills In A Jeep

(20th Century Fox, Release date: April 1, 1944) 89 minutes

CREDITS:
Producer, Irving Starr; director, William A. Seiter; screenplay, Robert Ellis, Helen Logan and Snag Werris; based on the story by Froma Sand and Fred Niblo, Jr.; camera, Peverell Marley; editor, Ray Curtiss; special effects, Fred Sersen; art directors, James Basevi, Albert Hogsett; costumes, Yvonne Wood; musical directors, Emil

Newman, Charles Henderson; dance director, Don Loper.

SONGS:
"CRAZY ME;" "YOU SEND ME;" "HOW BLUE THE NIGHT?;" "HOW MANY
TIMES DO I HAVE TO TELL YOU?;" "OHIO;" "IT'S THE OLD ARMY
TRICK;" "YOU NEVER MISS A TRICK;" "HEIL HEEL HITLER;"
"SNAFU" (deleted) by Harold Adamson and Jimmy Mc Hugh
"CUDDLE UP A LITTLE CLOSER" by Karl Hoschna and Otto
Harbach
"YOU'LL NEVER KNOW;" "I YI YI YI YI I LIKE YOU VERY MUCH"
by Mack Gordon and Harry Warren
"MR. PAGININI" by Sam Coslow
"NO LOVE, NO NOTHING" by Leo Robin and Harry Warren
"OVER THERE" by George M. Cohan
"WHEN THE CAISSONS GO ROLLING ALONG" by Edmund L. Gruber

CAST:
Kay Francis (Herself); Carole Landis (Herself); Martha Raye
(Herself); Mitzi Mayfair (Herself); Jimmy Dorsey and His
Band (Themselves); John Harvey (Ted Warren); Phil Silvers
(Eddie); Dick Haymes (Lt. Dick Ryan); Alice Faye, Betty
Grable, Carmen Miranda (Guest Stars); George Jessel (Master
of Ceremonies); Glenn Langan (Capt. Stewart); Lester
Matthews (Capt. Lloyd); Ralph Byrd (Sergeant); Miles Mander
(Col. Harley); Lester Dorr (Soldier); Paul Harvey
(General); Mary Servoss (Nurse Captain).

SYNOPSIS:
Four film stars (Kay Francis, Carole Landis, Martha Raye and
Mitzi Mayfair - playing themselves) volunteer to make a
U.S.O. tour for the servicemen overseas. Arriving in London,
they are met by Eddie (Phil Silvers), their liaison man.
Garbed in furs and fussy outfits, the jeep ride to the camp
makes them quickly realize that adjusting to military life
will not be easy. More appropriately dressed in fatigues,
Carole meets and falls for a flyer, Capt. Ted Warren (John
Harvey) and Mitzi is reunited with her old show business
partner, Lt. Dick Ryan (Dick Haymes). The girls perform for
the the soldiers and Carole and Ted wed. Their honeymoon,
however, is interrupted when the girls receive papers that
they are to be transferred to North Africa that afternoon. In
North Africa, they must help out at a hospital as well as
sing and dance. An air raid causes them to head for foxholes,
where Mitzi ends up in Dick's arms and Martha finds comfort
and romance with Eddie.

REVIEWS:
NEW YORK TIMES,4.6.44 - Bosley Crowther: "...claptrap saga...
is just a raw piece of capitalization upon a widely
publicized affair...As an authentic record of that journey it
may or may not have its points...As a piece of screen
entertainment it is decidedly impromptu. It gives the painful
impression of having been tossed together in a couple of
hours."

NEW YORK HERALD TRIBUNE - Otis L. Guernsey, Jr.: "Primarily,
its silly actual experiences, its bad acting and production
and its retakes of dead and buried Fox musical numbers make

it one of the dullest bits of entertainment ever."

COMMENTS:
- The film is based on the real life adventures of Martha Raye, Kay Francis, Carole Landis and Mitzi Mayfair's U.S.O. experiences. Miss Landis had written a series of articles for the Saturday Evening Post. Fox optioned the articles and had a story and screenplay written.
- In 1928, Betty Grable had created a vaudeville act with Emylyn Pique, a school chum at the Hollywood Professional School, with Emylyn dancing and Betty playing the saxophone. The act was a flop, but Emylyn went on to change her name to "Mitzi Mayfair" and achieve Broadway success in The Ziegfeld Follies of 1931, Take a Chance (1932 - with Ethel Merman), Calling All Stars (1934 - with Martha Raye) and The Show is On (1936 - with Charles Walters, Grable's song-and-dance partner in Dubarry Was a Lady). Mitzi's only other film credit is Paramount on Parade (1930).
- Betty appears only as a guest star, singing "CUDDLE UP A LITTLE CLOSER," her hit from the previous year's Coney Island. The other guest stars, Alice Faye and Carmen Miranda, were added for boxoffice value.
- Dance director Don Loper was to go on to greater Hollywood success as a costume and fashion designer.
- One song was cut from the film because it was deemed too explicit for the Hays Office, the film censorship Board of the time. The song was called "SNAFU," which the cast thought meant "Situation Normal, All Fouled Up," but the Hays Office knew its military jargon better.
- This film was the feature film debut of popular crooner Dick Haymes, who would appear in four more films with Grable. She was introduced to Haymes at the same time she first met husband-to-be Harry James in Chicago in October, 1940.

RECORDING: Hollywood Soundstage (D16), and the deleted number "SNAFU" on "Choice Cuts" (D6)

**F64.    Pin Up Girl**

> (20th Century Fox, Release date: May 10, 1944) 83 minutes, Technicolor

CREDITS:
Producer, William LeBaron; director, H. Bruce Humberstone; screenplay, Robert Ellis, Helen Logan and Earl Baldwin; based on a story by Libbie LeBlock; camera, Ernest Palmer; art directors, James Basevi, Joseph C. Wright; costumes by Rene Hubert; music directors, Emil Newman, Charles Henderson; musical numbers supervised by Fanchon; dance director, Hermes Pan; military number staged by Alice Sullivan; roller skating number staged by Gae Foster.

SONGS:
"ONCE TOO OFTEN;" "YOU'RE MY LITTLE PIN-UP GIRL;" "YANKEE DOODLE HAYRIDE;" "THE STORY OF THE VERY MERRY WIDOW;" "DON'T CARRY TALES OUT OF SCHOOL;" "TIME ALONE WILL TELL" and "RED ROBINS, BOB WHITES AND BLUE BIRDS" by Mack Gordon and Jimmy Monaco.

CAST:
Betty Grable (Lorry Jones); John Harvey (Tommy Dooley);
Martha Raye (Marian); Joe E. Brown (Eddie); Eugene Pallete
(Barney Briggs); Skating Vanities (Themselves); Dave
Willock (Dud Miller); The Condos Brothers (Themselves);
Charlie Spivak and His Orchestra (Themselves); Dorothea
Kent (Kay); Marcel Dalio (Headwaiter); Roger Clark
(George); Gloria Nord (Roller-Skating Headliner); Irving
Bacon (Window Cleaner); Mantan Moreland (Red Cap); Hermes
Pan and Angela Blue (Specialty Dancers); J. Farrell
MacDonald (Trainman); Lillian Porter (Cigarette Girl); Max
Willenz (Waiter).

SYNOPSIS:
Lorry Jones (Grable), a stenographer and U.S.O. Canteen
volunteer loved by hundreds of military personnel as their
favorite "Pin-Up Girl," is on her way to Washington D.C. for
a new job. She stops in New York and to obtain a table in
Eddie's (Joe E. Brown) swank nightclub, she pretends that she
is the date of Tommy Dooley (John Harvey), acclaimed Navy war
hero. Dooley surprises her when he arrives at the nightclub
and they fall for each other. She lies and tells him that she
is "Miss Lorraine," a Broadway musical star. In D.C., when
Dooley unexpectedly shows up at her office, she slips on
glasses, creates a new hairdo, crosses her eyes and pretends
to be the dowdy "Miss Jones." To help "Miss Lorraine," Dooley
asks Eddie, who has opened a new nightclub in D.C., to sign
her as his new star, which does not make former headliner
Marion (Martha Raye) happy. Of course, "Miss Lorraine" is a
smash! Marion is extemely jealous and  causes trouble when
she invites one of Lorry's ex-boyfriends to the club. In a
credibility-stretching resolution, Dooley  escorts Miss Jones
to the club, where she pops up onto the stage and performs
"Miss Lorraine's" number.

REVIEWS:
VARIETY, 4.19.44: "Betty Grable in Pin Up Girl - a natural.
The title and the star are right and even if the story isn't
they make it right for the b.o. This is one of those escapist
filmusicals which you accept, or else...In Technicolor Miss
Grable is a looker in pastel shades and spades."

NEW YORK TIMES, 5.11.44 - Bosley Crowther: "The Roxy's new
Technicolored film is a spiritless blob of a musical, and a
desecration of a most inviting theme...Miss Grable performs
her obligation in an oddly restricted style...She goes
through the paces of being coy with John Harvey in a manner
not likely to advance her for an Academy Award...It must be
added that this picture comes to the most abrupt and
pointless end you ever saw. Could it be that this is the
musical which really scraped the bottom of the barrel?"

COMMENTS:
- An obvious attempt to cash in on Betty's "Pin Up" photo
success. Not only was the photo used as the artwork behind
the main titles in this film, but it is seen as a newspaper
photo when Joe E. Brown signs her to a nightclub contract.
The photo was also used in many Fox wartime films as an

authentic prop. Even the film's advertisement capitalized on the photo's popularity: "Glorifying the All American Pin Up Girl! Here's the girl in every serviceman's dreams...set to music, set to dancing, set to loving in a musical you'll never forget!" Its a shame that a recreation of the shooting of the photo was not used in a musical number.
- This super-patriotic film contains two of the most bizarre musical numbers in Wartime musical films: a long roller skating number performed by Gloria Nord and the Skating Vanities to "RED ROBINS, BOB WHITES AND BLUE BIRDS" and "THE STORY OF THE VERY MERRY WIDOW," which begins traditionally enough with Grable singing and dancing in a period setting but then, segueing to her leading a "Close Arms" drill with eighty women soldiers. The film ends very abruptly with this number, as John Harvey watches from the wings and she winks at him, signifying that everything will be alright between them.
- Choreographer Hermes Pan, partners Betty in a sexy Apache dance in "ONCE TOO OFTEN." This is his fifth (and last) appearance partnering Miss Grable. Gae Foster, who staged the roller skating number, had a very popular line of dancing girls ("The Gae Foster Girls") in vaudeville, nightclubs and film shorts.
- The Condos Brothers appear with Betty once again, performing two specialty tap dances - one at the top of the film in a U.S.O. canteen where Betty works in Missoula, Missouri...and then mysteriously showing up at the nightclub in New York that she just happens to visit. Nick Condos was married to co-star Martha Raye at the time. Raye plays a strangely unsympathetic role in the film, a highly ambitious man-chaser who causes all of the trouble in the scenario.
- The third of Grable's films with "musical numbers supervised by Fanchon."
- Betty's variety of outlandish period 1940's hairdos for her golden blonde hair is mind-boggling. The pompadours, curls, swirls and up-sweeps are awe-inspiring. It is no wonder that her hair started to thin out in the early 1950's and she had to resort to wearing wigs and falls.

VIDEO: Key Video (V26)
LASER DISC: CBS/FOX (V26)
RECORDING: Caliban (D34)

## F65.    Billy Rose's Diamond Horseshoe

(20th Century Fox, Release date: May 2, 1945) 104 minutes, Technicolor

CREDITS:
Producer, William Perlberg; director, George Seaton; screenplay, Seaton; based on the play The Barker by John Kenyon Nicholson; camera, Ernest Palmer; editor, Robert Simpson; art directors, Lyle Wheeler, Joseph C. Wright; wardrobe supervision, Charles Le Maire; costumes designed by Kay Melson, Rene Hubert, Sascha Brastoff, Bonnie Cashen; music directors, Alfred Newman, Charles Henderson; dance director, Hermes Pan.

SONGS:
"I WISH I KNEW;" "THE MORE I SEE YOU;" "IN ACAPULCO;" "PLAY
ME AN OLD FASHIONED MELODY;" "A NICKEL'S WORTH OF JIVE;"
"MOODY;" "WELCOME TO THE DIAMOND HORSESHOE;" "YOU'LL NEVER
KNOW" and "COOKING UP A SHOW" by Mack Gordon and Harry
Warren
"CARRIE MARY HARRY" by Junie McKee and Albert Von Tilzer
"LET ME CALL YOU SWEETHEART" by Beth Slater Whitson and Leo
Friedman
"SLEEP BABY SLEEP" by S.A. Emery
"SHOO SHOO BABY" by Phil Moore
"ABA DABA HONEYMOON" by Arthur Fields and Walter Donovan
"I'D CLIMB THE HIGHEST MOUNTAIN" by Lew Brown
"MY MELONCHOLY BABY" by George A. Norton and Ernie Bennett

CAST:
Betty Grable (Bonnie Collins); Dick Haymes (Joe Davis,
Jr.); Phil Silvers (Blinky Walker); William Gaxton (Joe
Davis,Sr.); Beatrice Kay (Claire Williams); Carmen
Cavallaro(Himself); Willie Solar (Himself); Margaret Dumont
(Mrs. Standish); Roy Benson (Harper); George Melford (Stage
Doorman); Hal K. Dawson (Carter); Kenny Williams (Dance
Director); Reed Hadley (Intern); Eddie Acuff (Clarinet
Player); Edward Gargan (Stagehand) ; Ruth Rickaby (Wardrobe
Woman); Dorothy Day (Dorothy); Julie London (Girl); Cyril
Ring (Man); Milton Kibbee (Prop Man); Lee Phelps
(Bartender); Virginia Walker (Girl); Bess Flowers (Duchess
of Duke); Charles Coleman (Major Domo); Paul Bakanas (King
Otto IV); Eric Wilton (Sir How Dare You).

SYNOPSIS:
Bonnie (Grable) is the star entertainer at the famous New
York nightclub, where the featured headliner is Joe (William
Gaxton). His son, Joe, Jr.(Dick Haymes), arrives at the club,
announcing that he has quit Medical school. Joe, Sr. is
devastated, for he had promised his dying wife on her death
bed that Joe, Jr. would become a doctor - rather than
struggling as a performer. To keep an eye on his son, he asks
stage manager Blinkie (Phil Silvers) to give the boy a job
backstage. Claire (Beatrice Kay), Joe, Sr's stage partner and
girlfriend, is angered when Joe deserts her to spend all of
his time with his son. She makes a bargain with Bonnie, her
roommate, that she will give her a fur coat if Bonnie will
make the youngster fall in love with her, jilt him and cause
him to go away in defeat. Bonnie agrees and begins a campaign
to make the young man love her. The campaign works, but
Bonnie also falls in love, finally confessing her plot to
Joe. One evening, backstage, Bonnie witnesses him saving the
life of a stagehand and realizes how much medicine means to
him. Against his father's wishes, they marry and after
several months of unemployment, Bonnie convinces him to
return to medical school, supporting him. Blinkie works hard
to reunite everyone at the Diamond Horseshoe and the film
ends with Bonnie, Joe, Sr. and Claire back together again on
the stage - with Doctor Joe singing from the wings.

REVIEWS:
NEW YORK TIMES, 5.3.45 - Bosley Crowther: "...all the

standard ingredients of such fare have been pleasantly combined with a book of more than average life and it all has been directed cheerfully...Betty Grable plays the glamourous cutie with considerable down-to-earthiness, and Dick Haymes is surprisingly natural as the wishful young medico."

VARIETY, 4.11.45: "While Haymes looks a shade too adolescent as Miss Grable's romance interest, which is no unchivalrous reflection on the highly photogenic femme, he overcomes that as the footage progresses. Per usual, Miss Grable handles her song-and-danceology for socko results."

COMMENTS:
- Flamboyant producer and entrepreneur Billy Rose was famous for self-promotion and finding ways to financially benefit from the use of his name. Songs written for most of his shows carried his name as co-lyricist (to share royalties) and the famous New York nightclub he owned contained his name as part of the official title. By contract, Fox was forced to pay $76,000 to use Rose's name as part of the title. This was similar to Mr. Rose's contract for MGM's filmization of Billy Rose's Jumbo (1962) - which led show folks to cynically ask: "Billy's Rose's Jumbo what?"
- This film contains the classic lines delivered by Gaxton backstage after he accuses Grable of trying to upstage him with her legs: "You're in show business for only two reasons and you're standing on both of them. If you ever put on a long dress, you'd starve to death!" Versions of this dialogue are often printed as direct quotes from Grable. If she said them, she was merely repeating George Seaton's screenplay dialogue.
- "ABA DABA HONEYMOON," an old vaudeville song performed during an "Old Fashioned Song Vs. Jive" Medley by Grable and Beatrice Kay, was to go on to become a recording hit when performed by Debbie Reynolds and Carleton Carpenter in Two Weeks With Love five years later at MGM.
- The song "WELCOME TO THE DIAMOND HORSESHOE" has been used as the theme song for the Diamond Horseshoe Saloons at Walt Disney World and Tokyo Disneyland and the Golden Horseshoe Saloon at Disneyland in the "Guiness Book of World Records" long-running Golden/Diamond Horseshoe revues....for over thirty seven years! The show was replaced in America, but the song is still being performed in Japan - in Japanese.

RECORDING: Caliban (D3) and "WELCOME TO THE DIAMOND HORSESHOE" and "IN ACAPULCO" on "Betty Grable" (D1); "I WISH I KNEW" on "Hollywood Years of Harry Warren, 1930-'57" (D23)

## F66.    The Dolly Sisters

(20th Century Fox, Release date: October 5, 1945) 114 minutes, Technicolor

CREDITS:
Producer, George Jessel; director, Irving Cummings; screenplay, John Larkin, Marian Spitzer; camera, Ernest Palmer; editor, Barbara McLean; music directors, Alfred Newman, Charles Henderson; dance director, Seymour Felix.

SONGS:
"GIVE ME THE MOONLIGHT" by Lew Brown and Albert Von Tilzer
"ON THE MISSISSIPPI" by Ballard MacDonald, Arthur Fields and Harry Carroll
"WE HAVE BEEN AROUND" by Mack Gordon and Charles Henderson
"CAROLINA IN THE MORNING" by Gus Kahn and Walter Donaldson
"ARRAH GO ON, I'M GONNA GO BACK TO OREGON" by Joe Young, Sam Lewis and Bert Grant
"DARKTOWN STRUTTER'S BALL" by Shelton Brooks
"THE VAMP" by Byron Gay
"SMILES" by Will Callahan and Lee S. Roberts
"PACK UP YOUR TROUBLES" by Felix Powell and George Asaf
"MADEMOISELLE FROM ARMENTIERES" and "THE SIDEWALKS OF NEW YORK" by James Blake and Charles B. Lawlor
"POWDER, LIPSTICK AND ROUGE" by Mack Gordon and Harry Revel
"I CAN'T BEGIN TO TELL YOU" by Mack Gordon and James V. Monaco
"I'M ALWAYS CHASING RAINBOWS" by Joseph McCarthy and Harry Carroll (based on a melody by Frederic Chopin)

CAST:
Betty Grable (Jenny); John Payne (Harry Fox); June Haver (Rosie); S.Z. Sakall (Uncle Latsie); Reginald Gardiner (Duke); Frank Lattimore (Irving Netcher); Gene Sheldon (Prof. Winnup); Sig Rumann (Tsimmis); Trudy Marshall (Leonore); Collette Lyons (Flo Daly); Evan Thomas (Jenny as a child); Donna Jo Gribble (Rosie as a child); Robert Middlemass (Hammerstein); Paul Hurst (Dowling); Lester Allen (Morrie Keno); Frank Orth (Stage Manager); William Nye (Bartender); Herbert Ashley (Fields); Trudy Berliner (German Actress); Eugene Borden (Chauffeur); Claire Richards (Operator); Andre Charlot (Phillipe); Mae Marsh (Flower Lady); Virginia Brissac (Nun); Frank Ferguson (Reporter); Crauford Kent (Man); J. Farrell MacDonald (Doorman); Albert Petit (Croupier).

SYNOPSIS:
Jenny (Grable) and Rosie (Haver) Dolly are two young Hungarian beauties raised and trained by their uncle (Sakall) for show business careers at the turn of the century. In their struggle for success, they go from small theatres to becoming the toast of two continents in the "Ziegfeld Follies" on Broadway and the "Folies Bergere" in Paris. Along the way, Jenny falls for songwriter Harry Fox (John Payne), but while he is serving in World War I, she becomes involved with a Duke (Gardiner again - see Sweet Rosie O'Grady - F62) in Monte Carlo. While hallucinating over her love for Harry, she suffers a near-fatal automobile crash. Harry rushes to her side for a tearful reconciliation, while Rosie finds true love with Irving (Frank Lattimore).

REVIEWS:
VARIETY, 9.26.45: "... another in the nostalgic cycle. Big box office looms...the Dollys, known for their Raven bobbed coiffures - so here they're glamourous blondes, and their looks-alike is startling...they're certainly a pair of super-glam babes."

NEW YORK TIMES, 11.15.45 - Bosley Crowther: "Feeling, no doubt, that Miss Grable and Miss Haver, decked out in bright costumes, are sufficiently overpowering to knock anybody for a loop, the producers have coyly neglected to put much else in the film."

COMMENTS:
- A highly fictionalized version of the story of two famed Vaudeville performers. The Dolly Sisters were both dark-haired, dark-complexioned Hungarian girls - portrayed in this film by cotton candy blondes Grable and Haver. Jenny Dolly, the character Grable played, committed suicide by hanging in 1941 in Hollywood. Alice Faye was originally slated to appear with Grable, but when she bowed out, the role was given to newcomer June Haver. Producer George Jessel was quoted about the script and casting (B123):"...the many gay things about the Dolly Sisters, such as their numerous love affairs, would not suit the requirements of the strict, silly, strangling censorship of those days. Nevertheless, we came up with an excellent script...Alice, just at the crucial moment, decided to retire. Zanuck suggested that I use another of the Fox contract players, but I wanted June Haver - I had made a secret test of her...When Darryl saw the test, he agreed I was right."
- The movie ads heralded: "Those lovely Dolly Sisters, Those Glamourous Dolly Sisters, Those Scandalous Dolly Sisters. Their lives and loves...in the greatest musical story ever!"
- Contains two of the "Movie Musicals'" most famous (or infamous) numbers created by dance director Seymour Felix: "LIPSTICK, POWDER AND ROUGE" in which outlandish showgirls portray such absurd cosmetics as "Ruby Rouge" and "Libby Lipstick" and "THE DARKTOWN STRUTTER'S BALL" with Betty and June in blackface and showgirls dressed in such racist images as watermelons, dice and playing cards.
- The film broke the attendance records at New York's Roxy Theater, eventually grossing 4 million dollars during its initial release.
- Noel Coward caustically remarked that Fox must have wanted to save money and only hired one lady to play both roles.
- Carol Burnett, an avid fan of Grable's, performed a satire of the film, called "The Doily Sisters," on her television show on March 29, 1972. Miss Burnett played Grable's role with Vicki Lawrence playing Haver. Grable saw the sketch and loved it. She and Burnett had worked together on February 3, 1968 on The Carol Burnett Show (T34), with great success.

ACADEMY AWARDS: Nomination for Best Song "I CAN'T BEGIN TO TELL YOU."

VIDEO: "MAGNIFICENT MOVIE MUSICALS" - Goodtimes (V20 - contains the "Prevue" of the film)

RECORDING: CIF (D12) and "I CAN'T BEGIN TO TELL YOU" on "Golden Moments From The Silver Screen" (D19), "The Hot Canaries" (D24), a single with Harry James (D25), and "The White Cliffs of Dover" (D45)

## F67.   All Star Bond Rally

(20th Century Fox, 1945) (Short), 19 minutes

CREDITS:
Producer, Fanchon; director, Michael Audley; written by Don Quinn; music supervisor, Emil Newman; editor, Stanley Rabjohn.

SONGS:
"I'LL BE MARCHING TO A LOVE SONG" by Leo Robin & Ralph Rainger
"SATURDAY NIGHT IS THE LONELIEST NIGHT OF THE WEEK" by Sammy Cahn and Jule Styne
"THANKS FOR THE MEMORY" by Leo Robin and Ralph Rainger
"BUY, BUY, BUY, BUY A BOND" by Harold Adamson and Jimmy Mc Hugh

CAST:
Bob Hope, Betty Grable, Fibber McGee and Molly, Bing Crosby, Frank Sinatra, Harry James, Harpo Marx and "The Living Pin-Ups" (Linda Darnell, Jeanne Crain, June Haver, Vivian Blaine and Carmen Miranda).

SYNOPSIS:
Produced by 20th Century Fox and the Motion Picture Industry for the Office of War Information, this promotional film for the sale of War Bonds features Bob Hope as the Master of Ceremonies. He first presents Betty Grable, seen in "I'LL BE MARCHING TO A LOVE SONG," deleted from Footlight Serenade. Frank Sinatra and Harry James and His Music Makers perform "SATURDAY NIGHT IS THE LONELIEST NIGHT OF THE WEEK." After some girl-chasing shenanigans, Harpo Marx performs a harp solo. The "Living Pin-Ups" come to life and talk to Servicemen to "THANKS FOR THE MEMORY." The film finishes with Bing Crosby performing "BUY, BUY, BUY, BUY A BOND" and making a "Pitch" to the movie audience to buy War Bonds at the theatre.

REVIEW:
MOTION PICTURE HERALD, 4.21.45: "The film, which has a fabulous cast of box office names, is designed not only for the stimulation of Bond sales but for entertainment as well."

VIDEO: "HOLLYWOOD GOES TO WAR" - Video Images (V15)
RECORDING: "I'LL BE MARCHING TO A LOVE SONG" is heard on "Cut! - Volume 1" (D10)

## F68.   Do You Love Me?

(20th Century Fox, Release date: May 2, 1946) 91 minutes

CREDITS:
Producer, George Jessel; director, Gregory Ratoff; screenplay, Robert Ellis, Helen Logan; based on a story by Bert Granet; camera, Edward Cronjager; editor, Robert Simpson; art directors, Lyle Wheeler, Joseph C. Wright;

musical directors, Emil Newman, Charles Henderson; dance director, Seymour Felix.

SONGS:
"AS IF I DIDN'T HAVE ENOUGH ON MY MIND" by Charles Henderson, Lionel Newman and Harry James
"I DIDN'T MEAN A WORD I SAID" by Harold Adamson and Jimmy Mc Hugh
"MOONLIGHT PROPAGANDA" by Herb Magidson and Matty Malneck
"DO YOU LOVE ME?" by Harry Ruby

CAST:
Maureen O'Hara (Katherine Hilliard); Dick Haymes (Jimmy Hale); Harry James (Barry Clayton); Reginald Gardiner (Herbert Benham); Richard Gaines (Ralph Wainwright); Stanley Prager (Dilly); Harry James Music Makers (Themselves); B. S. Pulley (Taxi Driver); Chick Chandler (Earl Williams); Alma Kruger (Mrs. Crackleton); Almira Sessions (Miss Wayburn); Douglas Wood (Dr. Dunfee); Harlan Briggs (Mr. Higbee); Julia Dean (Mrs. Allen); Harry Hays Morgan (Prof. Allen); Eugene Borden (Headwaiter); Lex Barker (Guest); Harry Seymour (Headwaiter); Sam McDaniel (Bartender); William Frambes (Usher); Betty Grable (Clayton's Admirer); Jesse Graves (Bartender); Evelyn Mulhall (Woman); Esther Brodelet, Jack Barnett, Lillian Porter, Marjorie Jackson (Dancers); Les Clark, Jimmy Cross (Bellhops); Maria Shelton (Miss Fairchild); Kay Connors (Secretary); Jack Scordi and Diane Ascher (Dance Team).

SYNOPSIS:
Katherine (Maureen O'Hara), dean of a music school, goes to New York to hire a symphony conductor. On the train, she meets band leader Barry Clayton (Harry James), who tells her that she is dowdy. Finding that that she really "digs" the Big Band sound, she changes her image completely and falls in love with the band leader and his lead singer, Jimmy (Dick Haymes). Because of her association with popular music, she loses her job, but Barry and "The Boys" present a concert at her school to prove the worth of swing music. She finally makes her romantic choice and it is Jimmy, the singer.

REVIEWS:
VARIETY, 4.17.46: " A thoroughly entertaining musical. A little slow to get rolling but picking up good pace about midway ...It's not a big pic but the cast is good, the color job excellent, and there are a couple of strong tunes...In fact, James proves quite an actor. His poise can't go unnoticed, and in closeups he's particularly at ease."

NEW YORK TIMES, 5.25.46 - E.J.B.: "While not in the first rank of screen musicals, it should provide an hour and a half of divertissement from current problems...With a few more specialty numbers and a little brighter dialogue, this could have been first rate entertainment."

COMMENTS:
- This property was to launch Harry's solo film career. When Betty read the script and found out that Harry loses the girl

to Dick Haymes, she demanded to make a surprise appearance at the end of the film ("Don't worry, chum. A cute blonde's been calling for you. She's waiting outside."), going off with Harry and saving his reputation as a "Ladies' Man." Harry was suprisingly natural in his performance, one of the few Big Band leaders who could say dialogue and portray a character. - Also known as Kitten on the Keys.

**F69.   Hollywood Park**

(20th Century Fox, 1946) (Short) Length unknown

CAST:
Betty Grable, Harry James, Jackie Coogan, George Raft, Mervyn Leroy, Darryl F. Zanuck

SYNOPSIS:
A documentary which reflected the movie world's passion for horse races showing film celebrities attending Hollywood Park, a popular race track in Inglewood, California.

**F70.   The Shocking Miss Pilgrim**

(20th Century Fox, Release date: December 31, 1946) 85 minutes, Technicolor

CREDITS:
Producer, William Perlberg; director-screenplay, George Seaton; based on the story by Ernest and Frederica Maas; camera, Leon Shamroy; editor, Robert Simpson; art directors, James Basevi, Boris Leven; costumes, Orry-Kelly; music director, Alfred Newman; dance director, Hermes Pan.

SONGS:
"AREN'T YOU KINDA GLAD WE DID?;" "BACK BAY POLKA;" "FOR YOU, FOR ME, FOR EVERMORE;" "BUT NOT IN BOSTON;" "STAND UP AND FIGHT;" "CHANGING MY TUNE;" "ONE, TWO, THREE;" "SWEET PACKARD;" "WALTZ ME NO WALTZES;" "DEMON RUM" and "WALTZING IS BETTER SITTING DOWN" by Ira and George Gershwin

CAST:
Betty Grable (Cynthia Pilgrim); Dick Haymes (John Pritchard); Anne Revere (Alice Pritchard); Allyn Joslyn (Leander Woolsey); Gene Lockhart (Saxon); Elizabeth Patterson (Catherine Dennison); Elizabeth Ridgon (Mrs. Pritchard); Arthur Shields (Michael Michael); Charles Kemper (Herbert Jothan); Roy Roberts (Mr. Foster); Tom Moore (Office clerk); Stanley Prager (Lookout in office); Edward Laughton (Quincy); Hal K. Dawson (Peabody); Lillian Bronson (Viola Simmons); Raymond Largay (Mr. Packard); Constance Purdy (Sarah Glidden); Mildred Stone (Miss Nixon); Pierre Watkin (Wendall Paige); Junius Matthews (Mr. Carter); Mary Field, Kay Riley (Teachers); John Sheehan (Vendor); Vic Potel (Speaker); Frank Dawson (Waiter).

SYNOPSIS:
Cynthia Pilgrim (Grable) is a typist (called "Typewriter") for a shipping company in Boston in 1874 who falls in love

with her young boss, John Pritchard (Dick Haymes). She is
also a suffragette and advocate of women's rights.
Conservative John is at first reluctant to agree with her
modern ideas, but finally Cynthia persuades him to understand
the needs for women's equality. He supports her cause and
their romance blooms.

REVIEWS:
VARIETY, 1.1.47: "In stringing some George Gershwin tunes dug
up out of the trunk a few years ago on a slim thread of a
story, the William Perlberg-George Seaton team have gone
about the whimsy in too heavy-handed a manner...Draped in
fabulous Orry-Kelly gowns that belie her $8-a-week salary
...plenty of care has been taken that the Victorian drapings
don't conceal too much of Miss Grable's figure, and the gal
looks tops with a darker shade of blondine than usual. She
also turns in a slightly more subdued thesping job than is
her habit...There isn't much dancing, but the waltzes staged
by Hermes Pan make pleasant interludes. Sum total is a film
that's easy on the eye and ear but not too bright."

NEW YORK TIMES, 2.12.47 - Bosley Crowther: "According to The
Shocking Miss Pilgrim...we have to thank Betty Grable - or
someone who looked just like her - for establishing the
inalienable right of women to be stenographers and thus marry
the boss...There is no more voltage in The Shocking Miss
Pilgrim than in a badly used dry cell."

COMMENTS:
- The film featured a posthumous musical score by George
Gershwin, from previously unheard musical manuscripts. His
brother, Ira, set lyrics to the unused songs.
- The script is one of filmdom's first very conscious
attempts at "Women's Lib" stories. To soften Betty's
"Glamour" image, her hair is tinted a dark brown.
- Longtime Grable friend Robert Osborne confessed that Betty
secretly harbored a lust for two-time costar Dick Haymes.
Haymes, a popular recording star during the 1940's, squired
many of filmdom's most beautiful female stars and married
Rita Hayworth. His drinking addiction and erratic behavior
ended the marriage, as well as most of his romances, but his
appeal made Betty remark years later that she was "Crazy
about him."
- The ads promised: "There's more to 'The Shocking Miss
Pilgrim'...than meets the eye! Shameless? Blameless?
Nameless?"

RECORDING: CIF (D35)

## F71.   Mother Wore Tights

(20th Century Fox, Release date: August 20, 1947)
107 minutes, Technicolor

CREDITS:
Producer, Lamar Trotti; director, Walter Lang; screenplay
by Lamar Trotti; based on the novel by Miriam Young;
camera, Harry Jackson, editor, J. Watson Webb, Jr.;

costumes, Orry Kelly; music directors, Alfred Newman, Charles Henderson; dance directors, Seymour Felix, Kenny Williams.

SONGS:
"YOU DO;" "KOKOMO, INDIANA;" "THERE'S NOTHING LIKE A SONG;" "ROLLING DOWN TO BOWLING GREEN;" "THIS IS MY FAVORITE CITY;" "FARE THEE WELL, DEAR ALMA MATER" by Mack Gordon and Joseph Myrow
"BURLINGTON BERTIE FROM BOW" by William Hargreaves
"TRA-LA-LA-LA" by Mack Gordon and Harry Warren
"SWINGIN' DOWN THE LANE" by Gus Kahn and Isham Jones
"STUMBLING" by Zez Confrey
"LILY OF THE VALLEY" by L. Wolfe Gilbert and Anatole Friedland
"CHOO'N GUM" by Mann Curtis and Vic Muzzy

CAST:
Betty Grable (Myrtle McKinley Burt); Dan Dailey (Frank Burt); Mona Freeman (Iris Burt); Connie Marshall (Mikie Burt); Vanessa Brown (Bessie); Robert Arthur (Bob Clarkman); Sara Allgood (Grandmother McKinley); William Frawley (Mr. Schnieder); Ruth Nelson (Miss Ridgeway); Anabel Shaw (Alice Flemmerhammer); Michael [Stephen] Dunne (Roy Bivens); George Cleveland (Grandfather McKinley); Veda Ann Borg (Rosemary Olcott); Sig Rumann (Papa); Lee Patrick (Lil); Senor Wences with Johnny (Specialty); Maude Eburne (Mrs. Muggins); William Forrest (Mr. Clarkman); Kathleen Lockhart (Mrs. Clarkman); Chick Chandler (Ed); Will Wright (Withers); Frank Orth (Stage Doorman); Harry Cheshire (Minister); Billy Green (1st policeman); David Thursby (2nd Policeman); Tom Stevenson (Hotel clerk); Ann Gowland (Mikie at age 3); Joan Gerians (Baby - one month old); Anne Baxter (Narrator); Kenny Williams (Dance Director); Eula Morgan (Opera Singer); Tom Moore, Harry Seymour (Men); Lee MacGregor (boy); Stephen Kirchner (Myrtle's Dancing partner); Alvin Hammer (Clarence); Brad Slaven, Ted Jordon (Sailors); George Davis (Waiter); Karolyn Grimes (Iris at age 6); Lotte Stein (Mama); Antonio Filauri (Papa Capucci).

SYNOPSIS:
Myrtle and Frank Burt (Grable and Dailey) are a mildly successful song-and-dance team in vaudeville circa 1910, who also manage to raise a family. When their daughters (Mona Freeman and Connie Marshall) reach school age, they are placed in a girls' school, where elder daughter Iris (Freeman) becomes embarrassed at her parent's occupation. As she matures, she realizes the many sacrifices they have made for her and changes her snobbish attitude. In a touching graduation ceremony, she proves her love for her "Show Biz" parents as she sings one of their hit songs in front of all her peers.

REVIEWS:
NEW YORK TIMES, 8.21.47: "...displays the shapely gams of Betty Grable whenever it gets the chance, and it must be said that Miss Grable in Technicolor is balm for the eyes."

VARIETY, 8.29.47: "Marquee values are limited solely to Betty Grable's name, which will not be strong enough to pull this film out of the just-fair b.o.class...Miss Grable and her gams are set off to best advantage, and while her singing and dancing are okay, her emoting is unpersuasive."

COMMENTS:
- In 1947, Betty was the highest paid woman in the United States. In the film, makeup artists attractively aged her and she comfortably played an older woman.
- Despite Variety's gloomy forecast for box office grosses in its review, this was Betty's most successful film to date, grossing $4.5 million dollars at the box office. It was Grable's second film to break attendance records at New York's Roxy Theater, topping the record of The Dolly Sisters.
- With this film, she was finally teamed with a song-and-dance partner, Dan Dailey. When the project was announced, she expected Fred Astaire or James Cagney, both of whom requested larger salaries than the ever budget-watching Zanuck would agree to. After playing many small roles in films, Dan Dailey was finally escalated to star status with this film. Gene Nelson, under contract to Fox to be groomed as a possible partner for Grable or June Haver, met producer Lamar Trotti for the role and was told he looked young enough to play Grable's son. He lost the role to Dailey and his option was dropped by 20th. He was then placed under contract by Warner Brothers, who featured him in their musical films and made him a star.
- Betty, her hair now a golden blonde, performs "BURLINGTON BERTIE FROM BOW" with her famous figure and gams covered by a shabby suit and exhibits her fine talent for mimicry.
- Senor Wences - a popular ventriloquist who used his painted hand as his "Dummy" - was given a featured spot in the film. He later went on to become a frequent guest on The Ed Sullivan Show.

ACADEMY AWARDS: Best Scoring of a Musical Picture, Alfred Newman. Nominations for best color cinematography, best song ("YOU DO")

RECORDING: CIF (D31) and "BURLINGTON BERTIE FROM BOW" and "YOU DO" are heard on "Betty Grable" (D1)

## F72.   Hollywood Bound

(Astor Pictures, 1947) (Short)

SYNOPSIS:
A collection of shorts Betty made under the name of "Frances Dean" for Educational Pictures. Astor also released a similar compilation of Bing Crosby's early shorts.

## F73.   That Lady In Ermine

(20th Century Fox, Release date: August 10, 1948) 89 minutes, Technicolor

CREDITS:
Producer-director, Ernst Lubitsch; co-director, Otto Preminger; screenplay, Samson Raphaelson; based on the operetta This is the Moment by Rudolph Schanzer, Ernest Welisch; camera, Leon Shamroy; editor, Dorothy Spencer; art directors, Lyle Wheeler, J. Russell Spence; costumes, Rene Hubert; music director, Alfred Newman; choreographer, Hermes Pan.

SONGS:
"THIS IS THE MOMENT;" "THE MELODY HAS TO BE RIGHT;" "THERE'S SOMETHING ABOUT MIDNIGHT" (deleted); "THE JESTER'S SONG;" "OOH, WHAT I'LL DO (TO THAT WILD HUNGARIAN)" by Leo Robin and Frederick Hollander
"IT'S ALWAYS A BEAUTIFUL DAY" by Leo Robin and Ernst Lubitsch

CAST:
Betty Grable (Francesca/Angelina); Douglas Fairbanks, Jr. (Colonel/Duke); Cesar Romero (Mario); Walter Abel (Major Horvath/Benvenuto); Reginald Gardiner (Alberto); Harry Davenport (Luigi); Virginia Campbell (Theresa); Whit Bissell (Guilio); Edmund MacDonald (Captain Novak); David Bond (Gabor); Harry Cording, Belle Mitchell, Mary Bear, Jack George, John Parrish, Mayo Newhall (Ancestors); Lester Allen (Jester); Harry Carter, Thayer Roberts, Don Haggerty (Staff officers); Duke York (Sergeant); Francis Pierlot (Priest); Joe Haworth (Soldier); Ray Hyke (Albert's Knight).

SYNOPSIS:
On their nineteenth century wedding night, Mario (Cesar Romero) and Angelina (Grable) realize that their Italian castle is being invaded by Hungarian Hussars, led by the handsome Colonel (Fairbanks). Mario leaves Angelina before their marriage is consummated to join his regiment so that he can take back control of the Castle. In the Ancestral Hall, the paintings of the Royal family come to life with Francesca (also Grable), Angelina's great, great Grandmother, leading the family ghosts to the Castle turrets. She spots the handsome Hungarian Colonel and vows to tame him as she had done in 1561, when she killed an invading Italian Duke (also Fairbanks), dressed in her ermine robes. When the Colonel interrogates Angelina the next morning, he finds that her new husband has deserted her. Mario, disguised as a Gypsy, is captured and imprisoned. The Colonel suggests that Angelina join him for dinner that night, to recreate the ancient Legend. While waiting for her to appear, he falls asleep. In a dream, Francesca appears and they fall in love. The next morning, the Colonel, realizing that it had only been a dream, releases Mario and retreats with his troops from the Castle. Angelina deserts her foolish husband and follows the Colonel, arriving to his embrace.

REVIEWS:
NEW YORK HERALD TRIBUNE - Howard Barnes: "Since Miss Grable treats the whole proceedings as though she were appearing in a straight musical, the fanciful yarn of warriors and fair

ladies gets short shrift."

VARIETY, 7.14.48: "This film is a departure from previous Grable musicals in its absence of any special production numbers...Miss Grable registers strongly in lavish costumes, and handles the musical numbers and dancing chores in usual personable style."

NEW YORK TIMES, 8.25.48 - Bosley Crowther: "Credit Betty Grable with bringing to the title role a certain attractiveness of person which makes the Hussar's dreams entirely plausible. Miss Grable, even wrapped in ermine, looks sharper than most girls in bathing suits and the flashes she gives of territory for which she's noted are few but rewarding, let us say."

COMMENTS:
- After only eight days of filming, famed director Ernst Lubitsch suffered a heart attack and was replaced by Otto Preminger. Grable seemed uncomfortable in such historical surroundings and was not certain how to play the humor. In the "Dream Sequence," which contains the only dancing in the film and allows her to show her famous legs, she and co-star Fairbanks have a wonderful time, playing the humor broadly...perhaps what Lubitsch had in mind but was unable to guide.
- Grable's hairstyle is a fussy cascade of Mary Pickford-type golden curls. She, Fairbanks and Walter Abel all play double roles, with Grable appearing with herself in a special effects sequence.
- Of all of Grable's musical films, this property, originally titled This Is The Moment, has the weakest musical score. Because of her light "Pop" voice and her co-star's complete lack of any vocal talents, composers Robin and Hollander seemed to have been stumped about how to musicalize the period piece.

ACADEMY AWARDS: Nomination for Best Song ("THIS IS THE MOMENT")

RECORDING: "THERE'S SOMETHING ABOUT MIDNIGHT" (deleted) on "Cut! - Volume 3" (D11)

## F74.    When My Baby Smiles At Me

(20th Century Fox, Release date: November 5, 1948) 98 minutes, Technicolor

CREDITS:
Producer, George Jessel; director, Walter Lang; screenplay, Lamar Trotti; based on the play Burlesque by George Manker Watters and Arthur Hopkins; adapted by Elizabeth Rhinehart; camera, Harry Jackson; editor, Barbara McLean; art directors, Lyle Wheeler, Leland Fuller; costumes, Rene Hubert; music director, Alfred Newman; choreographer, Seymour Felix.

SONGS:
"BY THE WAY" and "WHAT DID I DO?" by Josef Myrow and Mack Gordon
"OUI OUI MARIE" by Alfred Bryan, Joseph McCarthy and Fred Fisher
"DON'T BRING LULU" by Billy Rose, Lew Brown and Ray Henderson
"SHOE SHINE BLUES," "BIRTH OF THE BLUES" by Buddy De Sylva, Lew Brown and Ray Henderson
"WHEN MY BABY SMILES AT ME" by Andrew B. Sterling, Ted Lewis and Bill Munro
"THE DAUGHTER OF ROSIE O'GRADY" by M.C. Brice and Walter Donaldson
"SAY SI SI" by Al Stillman and Ernesto Lecuona

CAST:
Betty Grable (Bonny Kane); Dan Dailey (Skid Johnson); Jack Oakie (Bozo); June Havoc (Gussie); Richard Arlen (Harvey); James Gleason (Lefty); Vanita Wade (Bubbles); Kenny Williams (Specialty Dancer); Robert Emmett Keane (Sam Harris); Jean Wallace (Sylvia Marco); Pati Behrs (Woman in Box); Jerry Maren (Midget); George "Beetlepuss" Lewis (Comic); Tom Stevenson (Valet); Sam Bernard (Process Server); Mauritz Hugo (Stage Manager); Frank Scannell (Vendor); J. Farrell MacDonald (Doorman); Les Clark, Harry Seymour (Troupers); Lee MacGregor (Call Boy); Charles Tannen (Intern); Noel Neill, Lu Anne Jones, Joanne Dale and Dorothy Babb (Specialty dancers); Hank Mann (Man); Edward Clark (Box-office man); Charles LaTorre (Tony); Lela Bliss (Woman).

SYNOPSIS:
Bonny (Grable) and Skid (Dailey) are a struggling Vaudeville team during the 1920s, performing in a Burlesque theater with friends Bozo (Jack Oakie) and Gussie (June Havoc). An easy-going, talented man, Skid goes on to become a success on Broadway - but the pressures of his new-found fame cause him to succumb to his love of alcohol. As his career and their marriage begin to fall apart, Bonny divorces him and plans to marry a rancher, Harvey (Richard Arlen). At a party for the newly engaged couple, Skid becomes very drunk and shows his deep love for Bonny, collapsing in a nervous breakdown. He is a broken man and admitted to Bellevue Mental Institution. When Lefty (James Gleason) tries to help his old friend and hires Skid to appear in his re-opened Burlesque theater, he convinces Bonny to help Skid through his rehabilitation. Skid arrives in an alcoholic stupor on Opening Night but Bonny is determined to help him make this much needed "Comeback." They return to the stage as a team - and each other's lives.

REVIEWS:
VARIETY, 11.10.48: "Betty Grable and Dan Dailey function strongly in their star spots, both trouping their roles and handling song and dance with a style that pleases...Miss Grable is more than an eyeful ornament to the story. She's a wow when interpreting a burley queen at work, and shows up well in the story sequences."

NEW YORK TIMES, 11.24.48 - Bosley Crowther: "Betty Grable and Dan Dailey, who are its stars go through the same sort of song-and-dance that they have gone through unnumbered times before. Miss Grable struts and wiggles in her easy, voluptuous way - which may be perennially beguiling but not what you'd call original."

COMMENTS:
- Noel Neill, billed as one of the "Specialty Dancers" and appearing in blackface in "THE BIRTH OF THE BLUES," would find fame as "Lois Lane" in the Superman film serials. Another "Specialty Dancer," Kenny Williams, was also a choreographer for Fox, creating the choreography for Mother Wore Tights (with Seymour Felix), You Were Meant For Me, The Glenn Miller Story and other films.
- Based on the famous play Burlesque, (with Barbara Stanwyck originating Grable's role on the stage) this property had been previously filmed in 1929 as The Dance of Life with Nancy Carroll, and Swing High, Swing Low with Carole Lombard and Dorothy Lamour (Par., 1937). The film was originally announced as being titled Burlesque.
- Dan Dailey's Academy Award nomination for "Best Actor" was scoffed at by several factions in Hollywood at the time. It is one of the rare times that a performer was nominated from a musical, a subject that is still being discussed today by film scholars. He was also given several featured musical numbers in the film without Grable, a new look for Betty's film formula.
- Grable's hair is short and platinum blonde, an attempt by the hairstylists to acknowledge the period (the 1920's) but actually reflecting the hair styles of the late 1940's.
- The ads boasted: "They're Mr. and Mrs. Show Business in the flamboyant story of show people as they really are!" They also promised "Songs your lips will sing" (for the tunes written especially for the film) and "Songs your heart remembers" (for the old musical chestnuts.)

ACADEMY AWARDS: Nominations for Best Actor (Dan Dailey), Best Musical Score (Alfred Newman).

## F75.   The Beautiful Blonde From Bashful Bend

(20th Century Fox, Release date: May 24, 1949) 77 minutes, Technicolor

CREDITS:
Producer-director-screenplay, Preston Sturges; based on a story by Earl Felton; camera, Harry Jackson; editor, Robert Fritch; art directors, Lyle Wheeler, George W. Davis; musical director, Cyril Mockridge.

SONGS:
"BEAUTIFUL BLONDE FROM BASHVILLE BEND" by Don George and Lionel Newman
"EVERYTIME I MEET YOU" by Mack Gordon and Josef Myrow
"IN THE GLOAMING" by Meta Orred and Annie F. Harrison

CAST:
Betty Grable (Freddie Jones/Hilda Swandumper); Cesar
Romero (Blackie Jobero); Rudy Vallee (Charlie Hingleman);
Olga San Juan (Conchita); Sterling Holloway, Danny Jackson
(Basserman Boys); Hugh Herbert (Doctor); El Brendel
(U.S. Marshall); Porter Hall (Judge O'Toole); Margaret
Hamilton (Elvira O'Toole); Emory Parnell (Mr. Hingleman);
Chris-Pin Martin (Joe); J. Farrell MacDonald (Sheriff
Sweetzer); Marie Windsor (LaBelle Bergere); Esther Howard
(Mrs. Smidlap); Chester Conklin (Messenger Boy); Mary
Monica MacDonald (Freddie at age 6); Torben Meyer (Dr.
Schultz); Dewey Robinson (Bartender); Richard Kean (Dr.
Smidlap), Russell Simpson (Grandpa); Snub Pollard (First
Hanger-on); Frank Moran (Hood); Joseph Turkel, George Lynn
(Reporters); James Joseph O'Neil (Patrolman); Len Hendry
(New Yorker); Elmo Lincoln (unbilled).

SYNOPSIS:
High-spirited Freddie Jones (Grable) has been taught to be a
crack shot in the Wild West of the 1890's by her grandfather
(Russell Simpson). When boyfriend Blackie Jobero (Romero)
begins chasing other girls, she shoots at him. Surprisingly,
she misses and hits Judge O'Toole (Porter Hall) in the
derriere. Fleeing justice, she escapes to another town,
posing as schoolmarm "Hilda Swandumper." In this quiet,
little town, meek Charlie Hingleman (Rudy Vallee) becomes
smitten with her. When Blackie shows up to reclaim Freddie -
or get the $1,000 reward for her capture - two of her older
students, the unruly Basserman Boys (Sterling Holloway and
Danny Jackson), are believed to have been killed. Their
Father comes to town for revenge, shoots it up and kidnaps
both of Freddie's suitors. She rescues the men with more
crack sharpshooting and the Basserman Boys turn up after
playing hookey. Returning to justice with Blackie, he begins
flirting at the trial and she goes wild, mistakenly shooting
the Judge once again. The slapstick farce ends as it began,
with Freddie panicking at her mistake.

REVIEWS:
NEW YORK TIMES, 2.12.49 - Bosley Crowther: "One might say
that Betty Grable, as the beautiful blonde, is no great help
since she shows a peculiar reluctance for the rowdy-dow of
knock-down drag-out farce. For one reason or the other, Mr.
Sturges has not got out of her what he got out of Betty
Hutton in The Miracle of Morgan's Creek."

VARIETY, 5.25.49: "Miss Grable is the chief asset as a
western dancehall gal who knows how to handle a gun - and
gets into trouble because of it...cast goes about its
business okay in answering Sturges' demands for burlesquing
of the characters and occasionally makes the coarse humor pay
off."

COMMENTS:
- Former Silent Screen comic greats Snub Pollard, J. Farrell
MacDonald, Elmo Lincoln (the original "Tarzan") and Chester
Conklin make cameo appearances in the film.
- Preston Sturges, once Paramount's "Golden Boy," made his

final film with this misdirected attempt at satire. Betty was very uncomfortable with the film and her role and had nothing good to say about her only experience with Mr. Sturges. In Intrepid Laughter, Preston Sturges and the Movies (B35), the film's failure is attributed to "Handicapped by the lead, Betty Grable, the reigning Fox pinup star and herself in the decline of her career, the problems...owe as much to Sturges' conception of the story and to his script as they do to the deficiencies of his performers."

- In recent viewing of this film, it appears that Screenwriter/Director Sturges must have had a great love of the phrase: "Shut Up!" Nearly every character in the film says it at least twice. Perhaps it was a new "Catch phrase" of the time. Also, it is difficult to imagine Grable giving a broader performance. Her antics border on the grotesque - but one does get the feeling that she did not find any of it particularly humorous.

- Grable was injured during filming when a piece of flesh was torn from her trigger finger as she caught it cocking the Colt revolver used in the film. Elmo Lincoln was also injured on the film when a faulty squib exploded prematurely near his left hand.

- As everyone involved on the film floundered to define its sense of humor, the film's copy tastelessly trumpeted "She's got the biggest six-shooters in the West!"

VIDEO: Key Video (V1)
LASER DISC: CBS/FOX (V1)

## F76.    Wabash Avenue

(20th Century Fox, Release date: March 31, 1950) 92 minutes, Technicolor

CREDITS:
Producer, William Perlberg; director, Henry Koster; screenplay, Charles Lederer, Harry Tugend; camera, Arthur E.Arling editor, Robert Simpson; art directors, Lyle Wheeler, Joseph C. Wright; costumes, Charles LeMaire; musical director, Lionel Newman; choreographer, Billy Daniel.

SONGS:
"WALKING ALONG WITH BILLY;" BABY WON'T YOU SAY YOU LOVE ME;" "WILHELMINA;" "MAY I TEMPT YOU WITH A BIG, RED, ROSY APPLE?;" "CLEAN UP CHICAGO" and "DOWN ON WABASH AVENUE" by Mack Gordon and Josef Myrow
"I'VE BEEN FLOATING DOWN THE OLD GREEN RIVER" by Bert Kalmer and Joe Cooper
"I WISH I COULD SHIMMY LIKE MY SISTER KATE" by Armand J. Piron and Peter Bocage

CAST:
Betty Grable (Ruby Summers); Victor Mature (Andy Clark); Phil Harris (Uncle Mike); Reginald Gardiner (English Eddie); James Barton (Hogan); Barry Kelley (Bouncer); Margaret Hamilton (Tilly Hutch); Jacqueline Dalya (Cleo); Robin Raymond (Jennie); Hal K. Dawson (Healy); Collette

Lyons (Beaulah); Charles Arnt (Carter); Walter Long, Billy
Daniel (Dancers); Marion Marshall (Chorus Girl); Percy
Helton (Ship's Captain); Henry Kulky (Joe); Alexander Pope
(Charlie); Dick Wessel (Electrician); Peggy Leon
(Hairdresser); Bill Phillips (Attendant).

SYNOPSIS:
Andy (Victor Mature) and Mike (Phil Harris) are business
partners in Chicago in 1893 who play tricks on each other as
they try to outdo one another in their quest for the favors
of Ruby (Grable), a brassy entertainer who headlines at
Mike's casino. To make Ruby a successful musical star and
lure her away from his friendly rival's employment, Andy
refines her, with her kicking and screaming the entire way.
The "toning down" pays off and she becomes a big star, making
a name for herself on Broadway and proving Andy's talent as a
producer. Andy and Mike continue competing over her, with the
good natured Mike finally allowing Andy to win Ruby's love.

REVIEWS:
NEW YORK TIMES,4.29.50 - Bosley Crowther, commenting on Miss
Grable's rendition of "I WISH I COULD SHIMMY LIKE MY SISTER
KATE": "This round and voluptuous young lady proceeds to
unlimber herself in a manner her sister, we feel, could not
surpass. And this form of agitation rather sets the style for
the whole show. They never got above the level of the shimmy
in Wabash Avenue."

VARIETY, 4.5.50: "Betty Grable as her fans like her would
seem to point to a smart b.o. future...It's Miss Grable's
picture, viewed strictly from the angle of physical
attractions which she uses to the fullest, but she is abetted
by some strong personalities in the male department."

COMMENTS:
- Originally, the title Wabash Avenue was to be used by Fox
for a biographical film about composer Gus Kahn to star
Betty. Kahn's estate and widow complicated the legalities, so
Fox simply remade Coney Island with the new title to please
the film exhibitors who had been promised a Grable film with
the title. Warner Bros made the life story of Gus Kahn as
I'll See You in My Dreams in 1952 with Danny Thomas and Doris
Day.
- A virtual remake of Grable's own Coney Island (F61) with
the once again famous "Handcuffed and forced to slow the
tempo down" scene as, this time, Victor Mature tries to teach
her some "Class."
- Betty, her hair tinted a white blonde, attacks the role of
a "barrelhouse" performer with great gusto and performs more
suggestive movements in Billy Daniel's choreography, based
partly on popular "Burlesque/Stripper" moves of the period.
The song "WALKING ALONG WITH BILLY" contains some very risque
implications for the time.
- James Barton, a once very popular Broadway performer, would
enjoy a "Comeback" with this film and his 1951 Broadway
success in Paint Your Wagon.

ACADEMY AWARDS: Nomination for best song ("WILHELMINA")

RECORDING: Caliban (D44) and "I WISH I COULD SHIMMY LIKE MY SISTER KATE" on "Betty Grable" (D1), a "MEDLEY" on "Betty Grable" (D2) and "MAY I TEMPT YOU WITH A BIG, RED, ROSY APPLE?" on "Ladies of Burlesque" (D26)

## F77.   My Blue Heaven

(20th Century Fox, Release date: August 23, 1950) 96 minutes, Technicolor

CREDITS:
Producer, Sol C. Siegel; director, Henry Koster, screenplay, Lamar Trotti, Claude Binyon; based on the story "Storks Don't Bring Babies" by S. K. Lauren; camera, Arthur E. Arling; editor, James B. Clark; art directors, Lyle Wheeler, Joseph C. Wright; costumes, Charles LeMaire; musical director, Alfred Newman; choreographers, Billy Daniel, Seymour Felix.

SONGS:
"LIVE HARD, WORK HARD, LOVE HARD;" "THE FRIENDLY ISLANDS;" "IT'S DEDUCTIBLE;" "HALLOWEEN;" "DON'T ROCK THE BOAT DEAR;" "I LOVE A NEW YORKER;" "COSMO COSMETICS" and "WHAT A MAN!" by Ralph Blane and Harold Arlen
"MY BLUE HEAVEN" by George Whiting and Walter Donaldson

CAST:
Betty Grable (Molly Moran); Dan Dailey (Jack Moran); David Wayne (Walter Pringle); Jane Wyatt (Janet Pringle); Mitzi Gaynor (Gloria Adams); Una Merkel (Miss Gilbert); Louise Beavers (Selma); Laura Pierpont (Mrs. Johnson); Don Hicks (Young Man); Irving Fulton (Specialty Dancer); Billy Daniel (Dance Director); Larry Keating (Doctor); Minerva Urecal (Miss Bates); Mae Marsh (Maid); Noel Reyburn (Studio Employee); Phyllis Coates (Woman); Barbara Pepper (Waitress); Myron Healey (Father); Lois Hall (Mother); Frank Remley (Orchestra Leader).

SYNOPSIS:
Molly and Jack Moran (Grable and Dailey) are a pair of highly successful radio stars who desperately want to have a baby, but, after a car accident in which Molly loses the baby she is carrying, they are told she is unable to conceive. They try to adopt, but because of their show business background, are considered bad risks. Finally, they get a baby through devious means, but it is taken away from them. Since Molly has retired, Jack now stars in a successful television show, with newcomer, Gloria Adams (Mitzi Gaynor), flirting with him. Through a kindly head of a home for foundlings, they get another child - their first child is returned to them - and Molly discovers she is pregnant!

REVIEWS:
NEW YORK TIMES, 9.16.50 - Bosley Crowther: "Miss Grable is a better hand at displaying her gams than mumbling baby talk to a succession of bright-eyed infants."

VARIETY, 8.23.50: "Here's a picture that's going to set

thousands of people to buying television sets...The tele shows that Betty Grable and Dan Dailey do in the film as a Mr.-and-Mrs. TV song-and-dance team are so entertaining they're bound to set a lot of yokels wondering why they're not catching this kind of thing at home for free."

COMMENTS:
- One of the first films to acknowledge the presence of TV - the new "Monster" which would threaten the movie business.
- Musical numbers featuring Grable and Dailey from When My Baby Smiles at Me (F74) and Mother Wore Tights (F71) were used for a TV montage sequence.
- The number "LIVE HARD, WORK HARD, LOVE HARD" features Mitzi Gaynor with Dan Dailey - a rarity in films for a newcomer to get a musical number of her own. Betty wanted Mitzi to be featured in the film and even campaigned to get her this exposure.
- Claude Binyon was originally announced as the film's director but Betty wanted Henry Koster. In one of her first battles with Fox executives, she demanded - and got - Koster to direct the movie.
- In one of her musical numbers, Mitzi Gaynor performs an intro to "THE FRIENDLY ISLANDS," a pointed take-off on South Pacific, a gigantic Broadway hit of the time and also the film that Mitzi would finally attain major stardom in.
- Originally titled Storks Don't Bring Babies, the title was not approved by the Johnson Office (the censor of the time).

RECORDING: Titania (D32)

## F78.   Call Me Mister

(20th Century Fox, Release date: January 31, 1951) 95 minutes, Technicolor

CREDITS:
Producer, Fred Kohlmar; director, Lloyd Bacon; screenplay, Albert E. Lewin, Burt Styler; suggested by a revue by Harold Rome and Arnold M. Auerbach; camera, Arthur E. Arling; editor, Louis Loeffler; art directors, Lyle Wheeler, Joseph C. Wright; costumes, Charles LeMaire; musical director, Alfred Newman; dances staged by Busby Berkeley.

SONGS:
"JAPANESE GIRL LIKE AMERICAN BOY;" "LOVE IS BACK IN BUSINESS;" "I JUST CAN'T DO ENOUGH FOR YOU BABY" by Mack Gordon and Sammy Fain
"CALL ME MISTER;" "GOING HOME TRAIN" and "MILITARY LIFE" by Harold Rome
"LAMENT TO THE POTS AND PANS" by Jerry Seelan and Earl K. Brent
"I'M GONNA LOVE THAT GUY" by Frances Ash

CAST:
Betty Grable (Kay Hudson); Dan Dailey (Shep Dooley); Danny Thomas (Stanley); Dale Robertson (Capt. Johnny Comstock); Benay Venuta (Billie Barton); Richard Boone (Mess

Sergeant); Jeffrey Hunter (The Kid); Frank Fontaine
(Sergeant); Harry Von Zell (Gen. Steele); Dave Willock
(Jones); Lou Spencer, Art Stanley, Bob Roberts (Dance Team -
The Dunhills); Bobby Short (Singer); Jerry Paris
(Brown); Ken Christy (Chief of Staff); Dabbs Greer (Aide to
the Colonel); John McGuire (Andy); Harry Lauter, Jack
Kelly, Paul Burke (Soldiers); Geraldine Knapp (Canape
Girl).

SYNOPSIS:
Kay (Grable) is an entertainer performing for the American
troops in Japan during the Korean War where she unexpectedly
runs into her estranged husband, Shep (Dailey). They have
been separated but Shep optimistically hopes for a
reconciliation. Kay is now dating Johnny (Dale Robertson), so
Shep forges a duty assignment paper to assist her with "The
Big Show" that she is trying to produce. During rehearsals,
they spend lots of time together and get to review their
differences. The show is a hit and they fall in love once
again.

REVIEWS:
SATURDAY REVIEW, 2.24.51: "..Betty Grable proves to be the
champion manager of them all, keeping in line the ardent Dan
Dailey with one hand and putting on a G.I. show that out-
Rockefellers Radio City with the other. The Fox version of
Call Me Mister is essentially a vehicle for the
pulchritudinous Miss Grable, and neither script nor camera
overlooked a single angle that might help accentuate her
enduring young charms...which makes Call Me Mister perfect
for the Grable fans."

VARIETY, 1.24.51: "Probably the best is 'JAPANESE GIRL LIKE
AMERICAN BOY' during which Miss Grable works with a Japanese
femme chorus, and scene then segues into a dance with the
Dunhill dance trio of three males. Miss Grable, impersonating
a sailor with the dance trio, does a wow job."

VIDEO REVIEW, October, 1983: "More like Call Me Tired, since
stars Betty Grable and Dan Dailey both appear weary from
having stretched one basic plot over a half-dozen movies."

COMMENTS:
- Call Me Mister a smash 1946 Broadway plotless musical revue
by Harold Rome, was purchased by Fox, re-written with a plot
and only using four of Rome's original tunes.
- Bobby Short, who was to find fame as a recording artist and
posh Hotel performer, appears at the beginning of the number
"GOING HOME TRAIN." The film also marks Danny Thomas' screen
debut.
- Betty, with her hair still white blonde, appears in
"Yellowface" as a Japanese Geisha in the film's opening
number, "JAPANESE GIRL LIKE AMERICAN BOY." She is surrounded
by an Asian female chorus (an unusual - and prophetically
healthy sight) and wears a very odd version of a Japanese
Kimono, complete with cherry blossoms defining where the
nipples would be on their busts! The number segues into a
sensational tap dance section performed by Betty, now dressed

as a sailor, with the Dunhills, a trio of talented young men who were headliners in nightclubs across the country. Grable's best dance work was still being done in the competitive atmosphere of a "Challenge" dance sequence.
- The opulent Finale number "LOVE IS BACK IN BUSINESS" contains many classic Busby Berkeley touches: overhead shots, turntables and wind machines.
- The ad campaign contained some of the funniest copy for any Fox film: "Betty Grable - willing and able! Dan Dailey - dancing so gaily! Danny Thomas - laughter he'll promise! Dale Robertson - he's got love on the run! Benay Venuta - who couldn't be cuta!"

RECORDING: Titania (D5) and "LIKE HE'S NEVER BEEN LOVED BEFORE" and "I JUST CAN'T DO ENOUGH FOR YOU, BABY" on "Classic Movie Musicals of Sammy Fain" (D7)

## F79.   Meet Me After The Show

(20th Century Fox, Release date: August 15, 1951) 86 minutes, Technicolor

CREDITS:
Producer, George Jessel; director, Richard Sale; screenplay, Mary Loos, Richard Sale; based on a story by Erna Lazarus and W. Scott Darling; camera, Arthur E. Arling; editor, J. Watson Webb, Jr.; art directors, Lyle Wheeler, Joseph C. Wright; costumes, Travilla; musical director, Lionel Newman; choreographer, Jack Cole.

SONGS:
"IT'S A HOT NIGHT IN ALASKA;" "NO TALENT JOE;" "I FEEL LIKE DANCING;" "BETTIN' ON A MAN;" "MEET ME AFTER THE SHOW;" LET GO OF MY HEART" by Jule Styne and Leo Robin

CAST:
Betty Grable (Delilah); Macdonald Carey (Jeff); Rory Calhoun (David Hemingway); Eddie Albert (Christopher Leeds); Fred Clark (Tim); Lois Andrews (Gloria Carstairs); Irene Ryan (Tillie); Steve Condos and Jerry Brandow (Dancers); Arthur Walge (Joe); Edwin Max (Charlie); Robert Nash (Barney); Gwen Verdon (Dancer); Max Wagner (Doorman); Al Murphy (Process Server); Rodney Bell (Dr. Wheaton); Harry Antrim (Judge); Lick Cogan (Man); Billy Newell (Stage Manager).

SYNOPSIS:
Delilah (Grable) is a Broadway star who separates from her producer husband, Jeff (Macdonald Carey), because of his constant flirtations. She leaves his show, pretends to have amnesia and returns to her old nightclub job in Miami, where she is courted by a local playboy, David (Rory Calhoun). When she succeeds in driving her husband mad with jealousy, she admits the plot and they are reunited.

REVIEWS:
NEW YORK TIMES, 8.16.51 - Howard Thompson: "Familiarity has yet to breed contempt among the effervescent lady's army of

admirers."

VARIETY, 8.8.51: "A Technicolored, light, bright musical such as this Betty Grable offering should be a good tonic for a flagging box office...Miss Grable gets topflight dance assists from the uncredited terping of Jack Cole, who staged the hoofing, and Gwen Verdon."

PHOTOPLAY, 1951: "A Grable musical and that's that...for the first time in ten years Betty appears in a bathing suit, wrapped, for some reason, in more garments that a Hindu. Male customers should sue."

COMMENTS:
- Choreographer Jack Cole gave Betty more intricate moves and sophisticated musical number construction, pairing her on film with his then-assistant, Gwen Verdon. Cole's jazz based style was entirely new for her, but she worked very hard and the choreographer had nothing but praise for her and her capabilities. Cole himself appears in the film, dancing in silhouette in the number "BETTIN' ON A MAN."
- Irene Ryan, of eventual The Beverly Hillbillies TV fame, portray's Grable's maid. MacDonald Carey, who played Grable's flirtatious husband, would also find great success in television, appearing on Days of Our Lives for over 25 years.
- While performing a lift in one of the musical numbers, dancer Marc Wilder accidentally slipped one of his fingers between her buttocks. As he placed her back down on the floor to continue the number, he feared that she would angrily halt the filming. Instead, she whispered "Let's get married!" and continued.

RECORDING: Caliban (D29)

## F80.    The Farmer Takes A Wife

(20th Century Fox, Release date: June 4, 1953) 80 minutes, Technicolor

CREDITS:
Producer, Frank P. Rosenberg; director, Henry Levin; screenplay, Walter Bullock, Sally Benson, Ann Joseph Fields; based on the novel "Rome Haul" by Walter D. Edmonds and the play by Frank B. Elser, Marc Connelly; camera, Arthur E. Arling; editor, Louis Loeffler; art directors, Lyle Wheeler, Addison Hehr; costumes, Travilla; musical director, Lionel Newman; incidental music, Cyril Mockridge; choreographer, Jack Cole.

SONGS:
"WE'RE IN BUSINESS;" "ON THE ERIE CANAL;" "WE'RE DOING IT FOR THE NATIVES IN JAMAICA;" "WHEN I CLOSE MY DOOR;" "TODAY I LOVE EVERYBODY;" "SOMETHIN' REAL SPECIAL;" "WITH THE SUN WARM UPON ME" and "CAN YOU SPELL SCHENECTADY?" by Harold Arlen and Dorothy Fields

The dream ballet from *The Farmer Takes a Wife*, 1953. The sequence was cut from the final version of the film. From left to right: John Carroll, Dale Robertson, Thelma Ritter, and Betty Grable.

CAST:
Betty Grable (Molly Larkin); Dale Robertson (Daniel Harrow); Thelma Ritter (Lucy Cashdollar); John Carroll (Jotham Klore); Eddie Foy, Jr. (Fortune Friendly); Charlotte Austin (Pearl); Kathleen Crowley (Susanna); Merry Anders (Hannah); Donna Lee Hickey (Eva); Noreen Michaels (Amy); Ruth Hall (Abbie); Mort Mills (Floyd); Gwen Verdon (Abigail); Gordon Nelson (Race Official); Ed Hinton (Boater); Emile Meyer (Cargo Master); Lee Phelps (Bartender); Ted Jordan (Driver).

SYNOPSIS:
Molly Larkin (Grable) works as a cook for Jotham Klore (John Carroll), the toughest captain on the Erie Canal, in 1850. He hires a young farmer, Daniel Harrow (Dale Roberston), who is trying to save money to buy a farm, as a boat hand. Molly tires of Jotham's hard-drinking, two-fisted ways and falls in love with the gentle young farmer as he tells her of his love of the land and shares his future dreams. When a large prize is announced for an upcoming barge race on the Erie Canal, Molly and Daniel find an old boat, renovate it and enter it in the race. With Molly at the helm, they win the prize...and the farmer gets a wife.

REVIEWS:
HOLLYWOOD REPORTER, 4.22.53: "The dance routines are unimaginative...a mediocre musical with so-so entertainment values that will have to be carried most of the way by Miss Grable's marquee strength."

VARIETY, 4.22.53: "Betty Grable, off the screen for sometime, needs a much more auspicious vehicle than this mediocre musical for her return...Miss Grable takes prettily to the Technicolor hues and the period costuming, the latter being rather fancy for a canal boat cook."

NEW YORK TIMES, 6.13.53 - Bosley Crowther: "It is only fair to advise you that you can't see much of Betty Grable's legs in Twentieth Century Fox's new musical...to put it bluntly, you won't see a goldarned thing of them in this hopeless pretense of Oklahoma!"

COMMENTS:
- A remake of a story first filmed in 1935 by Fox with Janet Gaynor (in Grable's role) and Henry Fonda, making his film debut. It is one of Grable's few "Book" musicals (with the songs coming out of the story, rather than having a Show Business setting) and as Bosley Crowther states in his review, is an obvious attempt by the film's creators to make a "Folksy" musical in the style of Oklahoma! and Carousel.
- The film ends with an obviously "Tacked On" Jack Cole staged "Finale," filmed entirely on a soundstage, whereas the rest of the film was shot outdoors. Cole's jazz-oriented dance movements do not work well in the film, but as he was the Dance Director at Fox at the time, he was given the assignment. Gwen Verdon once again dances with Betty, playing a small role.
- A musical dream sequence cut from the film is depicted in

the film's posters.
- As one of filmdom's few glamorous "Good Sports," Betty allowed herself to be dunked, pushed, doused and soaked throughout the film in the various canals. One musical number, "WE'RE IN BUSINESS" takes place almost completely in the water, with Betty easily splashing and frolicking with the kids, dogs and cast members.
- The advertisements tried to build excitement about the film, touting it as "This one is really stacked with greater-than-ever musical fun!" This use of the word "Stacked" may have been a leering acknowledgement of the breast fixated 1950's.

VIDEO: Key Video (V7)
LASER DISC: CBS/FOX (V7)

## F81.   How To Marry A Millionaire

(20th Century Fox, Release date: November 4, 1953) 95 minutes, Technicolor and  Cinemascope

CREDITS:
Producer-screenplay, Nunnally Johnson; director, Jean Negulesco; based on the plays The Greeks Had A Word For It by Zoe Akins and Loco by Katherine Albert, Dale Eunson; camera, Joe MacDonald; editor, Louis Loeffler; art directors, Lyle Wheeler, Leland Fuller; costumes, Charles LeMaire, Travilla; musical directors, Alfred Newman, Cyril Mockridge.

CAST:
Betty Grable (Loco); Marilyn Monroe (Pola); Lauren Bacall (Schatze Page); David Wayne (Freddie Denmark); Rory Calhoun (Eben); Cameron Mitchell (Tom Brookman); Alex D' Arcy (J. Stewart Merrill); Fred Clark (Waldo Brewster); William Powell (J.D. Hanley); George Dunn (Mike the Elevator Man); Harry Carter (Elevator Operator); Tudor Owen (Mr. Otis); Percy Helton (Brenton); Maurice Marsac (Antoine); Emmett Vogan (Man at Bridge); Charlotte Austin, Merry Anders, Ruth Hall, Lida Thomas, Beryl McCutcheon (Models); Richard Shackleton (Bell Boy); Eve Finell (Stewardess); Benny Burt (Reporter).

SYNOPSIS:
Three golddigging girls: Loco, Pola and Schatze (Grable, Monroe and Bacall) pretend to be wealthy in order to snare rich husbands. Loco goes to the mountains for the weekend with Waldo Brewster (Fred Clark), a rich married man, but falls for Eben, a poor forest ranger (Calhoun). Pola falls for Freddie Denmark (David Wayne),the wealthy owner of the apartment they rent and Schatze turns down the proposal of wealthy J. D. Hanley (William Powell) because of her love for Tom Brookman (Cameron Mitchell), who she thinks is poor. In the final tally, both Pola and Schatze have found their millionaire husbands, while Loco has found true love.

REVIEWS:
NEW YORK TIMES,11.11.53 - Bosley Crowther: "Miss Grable, as a

breezy huntress who cuts out a skittish gent, Fred Clark, and shamelessly pursues him right up to his snowbound lodge in Maine, is the funniest of the ladies. And she does work the simple running gag of thinking she is going to an Elk's convention for as much meager jest as it contains. Her off-screen capitulation to a forest ranger, Rory Calhoun, is by far the most sensible and painless bit of feminine behavior in the film."

CUE, 11.14.53 - Jesse Zunser: "Millionaire's Technicolor long shots -- along the skylines of New York and the Rockies -- are breathlessly beautiful and overpowering. The story itself is somewhat less so...The girls work hard."

TIME, 11.23.53.: "Betty Grable, a performer who has always appeared to have just as much above the eyebrows as below, carries off the show..."

COMMENTS:
- Actually the first of Fox's Cinemascope (their new film process) features to be completed, but as Zanuck wanted his own personal production, The Robe, to reap all of the publicity, How To Marry A Millionaire was released as the second Cinemascope film. It obviously was regarded as "Important," as it contains an Overture, showing the huge Fox Orchestra performing "STREET SCENE."
- A remake of Grable's own The Greeks Had A Word For Them (F10), with screenwriter Johnson interpolating material from a play titled Loco for Betty's role and situations.
- She is reputed to have said to the young, frightened Marilyn on the set: "Honey, I've had it. Go get yours. It's your turn now." This note of assurance has been reported to have been said to Dan Dailey on the set of Mother Wore Tights (B151) and to Mitzi Gaynor, on the set of My Blue Heaven. Perhaps Betty, remembering her long personal struggle, said it to every newcomer she worked with.
- In a fashion show sequence, Grable spoofs her famous "Pin Up" pose for a brief second. In the actual film, Grable receives top billing, but in the prevues of coming attractions, she is given second billing, after Marilyn.
- Ranking #5 in 1953, costing $2.5 million and earning $7,300,000 at the box office.
- Named "One of the Ten Worst films of the year" by Harvard Lampoon.
- How To Marry A Millionaire was telecast on September 23, 1961 as the premiere film presented on NBC's Saturday Night at The Movies - the first major television series composed of films released by the major studios after 1948.
- Used as the basis of a syndicated television series in 1957 -'58, starring Barbara Eden, Merry Anders and Lori Nelson. Lori Nelson played Grable's role, renamed "Greta," while Barbara Eden, in the Monroe role, was redubbed "Loco." Merry Anders, who had appeared in the film as a model in the Fashion show sequence, played Bacall's role, renamed "Mike." Lori Nelson left the show in 1958 and was replaced by Lisa Gaye as "Gwen."
- To lure potential moviegoers away from their television screens, and to assure that their new film process did not

duplicate the negative aspects of 3-D, the film's ads promised "The Big-Time, Grand-Time, Great-Time Show of all time in Cinemascope, the new dimensional marvel you see without glasses!"
- Bosley Crowther's first positive review for Miss Grable's work. Had he softened towards her talent - or did he merely dislike the next blonde superstar, Marilyn Monroe, more?

ACADEMY AWARDS: Nomination for Best Costume Design - Color (Charles Le Maire, Travilla)

VIDEO: CBS/FOX (V17)
LASER DISC: CBS/FOX (V17)
RECORDING: Two scenes with Grable, Monroe and Bacall on "Marilyn Monroe - Rare Recordings 1948 - 1962" (D27)

## F82.   Three For the Show

> (Columbia, Release date: January 15, 1955) 93 minutes, Technicolor and Cinemascope

CREDITS:
Producer, Jonie Taps; director; H.C. Potter; assistant director, Earl Bellamy; screenplay, Edward Hope, Leonard Stern; based on the play Too Many Husbands by W. Somerset Maugham; camera, Arthur E. Arling; editor, Viola Lawrence; art director, Walter Holscher; costumes, Jean Louis; musical director, Morris Stoloff; music arranger, George Dunning; choreographer, Jack Cole.

SONGS:
"SOMEONE TO WATCH OVER ME" and "I'VE GOT A CRUSH ON YOU" by Ira and George Gershwin
"HOW COME YOU DO ME LIKE YOU DO?" by Gene Austin and Roy Bergere
"DOWN BOY" by Hoagy Carmichael and Harold Adamson
"WHICH ONE?" by Lester Lee and Ned Washington
"I'VE BEEN KISSED BEFORE" by Bob Russell and Lester Lee
"SWAN LAKE" by Tchaikovsky

CAST:
Betty Grable (Julie); Marge Champion (Gwen Howard); Gower Champion (Vernon Lowndes); Jack Lemmon (Marty Stewart); Myron McCormick (Mike Hudson); Paul Harvey (Colonel Wharton); Robert Bice (Sgt. O'Hallihan); Hal K. Dawson (Theater Treasurer); Charlotte Lawrence (Girl); Willard Waterman (Moderator); Gene Wesson (Reporter); Aileen Carlyle (Mother); Rudy Lee (Boy); Eugene Borden (Costume Designer).

SYNOPSIS:
Broadway star Julie (Grable) suddenly discovers that she has two husbands! Number one, Vernon Lowndes (Gower Champion), is her current co-star and the other, Marty Stewart (Jack Lemmon), was thought to have been killed during the War. When Marty unexpectedly returns to New York, confusion reigns supreme as Julie tries to decide which husband she will keep. Friend and co-star Gwen (Marge Champion) waits patiently,

hoping that Julie will reject Vernon, so that she can have
him for herself. When Julie finally decides to stay married
to Marty, Vernon and Gwen team up, with everyone arm-in-arm
for the cheerful "Finale."

REVIEWS:
VARIETY, 2.16.55: "Elaborately staged comedy tuner in the old
Betty Grable tradition...Mostly this is Betty Grable's
picture, and there's no question that, despite the passing
years, she's still an entertainer with plenty of oomph who
can put a routine over with sock impact."

DANCE MAGAZINE, April 1955 - Arthur Knight: "Jack Cole...had
a hand in the dances for There's No Business Like Show
Business, choreographing Marilyn Monroe's torrid "HEAT WAVE"
routine, although he was not mentioned in the credits. That
explains some of the raised eyebrows at previews of
Columbia's Three For The Show, also a Jack Cole job...Betty
Grable has a number...that seems almost a carbon of la
Monroe's. Cole's imagination has fashioned a more amusing,
more polished and sophisticated routine for the relatively
modest Columbia effort than for the Fox musical. He seems to
work best with small, smartly paced groups moving in sharp
counter-rhythms to each other; and Betty Grable's smiling
acceptance of her own sexiness is in closer accord with
Cole's amusingly sensual patterns than the all-out, unrelaxed
selling of Marilyn Monroe."

5001 NIGHTS AT THE MOVIES,1991 - Pauline Kael: "Betty Grable
started singing and dancing in Hollywood musicals in 1930
(when she was 13), and she was thrown into so many dumb,
garish pictures...that her career ended before she was 40.
This picture was made in her last year in films, and she
shows the comedy style of a buoyant veteran."

COMMENTS:
- Betty "Out Monroe's" Marilyn in the number, "HOW COME YOU
DO ME LIKE YOU DO?," moving her mouth with lip-licking
sensuality and writhing on a hammock in a satin slip - an
obvious take-off on "HEAT WAVE," also choreographed by Cole,
performed by Marilyn in There's No Business Like Show
Business, the previous year, as noted in the Dance Magazine
review quoted above.
- A remake of Too Many Husbands, starring Jean Arthur in
1940, originally titled The Pleasure Is All Mine.
- Given a "C" (Condemned) rating by the Catholic Legion of
Decency because of its lenient attitude toward polygamy, the
film was recut and received a "B" (Some parts morally
objectionable) rating.
- This film marks character actor Hal K. Dawson's eighth
appearance in a Grable film, giving him the distinction of
being the performer who worked most frequently in films with
Betty.
- In another of Jack Cole's bizarre "Dream Ballets,"
performed to Tchaikovsky's "SWAN LAKE," Marge Champion is
featured in a setting similar to Cole's staging of "DIAMONDS
ARE A GIRL'S BEST FRIEND" in Gentlemen Prefer Blondes (1953).
Frustrated at Grable's inability to select a husband,

Champion excels in a dance drama in which she duels with and kills Grable's character, performed by Pat Denise. Marge, Gower and Jack Lemmon all play themselves in the ballet and one wonders why Grable chose not to portray herself. Perhaps her death was deemed unappealing by the creative team or perhaps she felt uncomfortable with the lyrical choreography.

LASER DISC: Pioneer Special Editions (V34)
RECORDING: Mercury (D42)

## F83.   How To Be Very, Very Popular

> (20th Century Fox, Release date: July 15, 1955) 89 minutes, Deluxe Color and Cinemascope

CREDITS:
Producer-director-screenplay, Nunnally Johnson; based on the play She Loves Me Not by Howard Lindsay, from the novel by Edward Hope and Sleep It Off, a play by Lyford Moore and Harlan Thompson; assistant director, Ad Schaumer; camera, Milton Krasner; editor, Louis Loeffler; art directors, Lyle Wheeler, John DeCuir; costumes, Travilla; musical directors, Cyril Mockridge, Lionel Newman; choreography, Paul Godkin; "SHAKE RATTLE AND ROLL" staged by Sonia Shaw.

SONGS:
"HOW TO BE VERY VERY POPULAR" by Jule Styne and Sammy Cahn
"SHAKE, RATTLE AND ROLL" by Charles Calhoun
"BRISTOL BELL" by Lionel Newman and Ken Darby

CAST:
Betty Grable (Stormy Tornado); Sheree North (Curly Flagg); Robert Cummings (Wedgewood); Charles Coburn (Tweed); Tommy Noonan (Eddie); Orson Bean (Toby); Fred Clark (Mr. Marshall); Charlotte Austin (Midge); Alice Pearce (Miss Syl); Rhys Williams (Flagg); Andrew Tombes (Moon); Noel Toy (Cherry Blossom Wang); Emory Parnell (Chief of Police); Harry Carter (Bus Driver); Jesslyn Fax (Music Teacher); Jack Mather (1st policeman); Michael Lally (2nd policeman); Milton Parsons (Mr. X); Harry Seymour (Teacher); Hank Mann (Newsvendor); Leslie Parrish (Girl on Bus).

SYNOPSIS:
Stormy (Grable) and Curly (Sheree North) are strippers who witness the cold-blooded murder of an Asian Stripper in their show. Mr. X (Milton Parsons), the bald-headed murderer, warns them that since they can identify him, they will be next. Their meager savings allow them to escape to a college town to hide from the killer. Taking refuge in a fraternity house, Curly is accidentally hypnotized by Eddie (Tommy Noonan) and told that when she hears the name "Salome," she will begin to dance. Stormy falls for "Perpetual Student" Wedgewood (Robert Cummings) and Curly falls in love with Toby (Orson Bean), a dumb student who flunks every course. At the college Commencement Ceremony, Curly, while pretending to be a graduating student, hears the word "Salomnis" in one of the Graduation speeches and thinking it is her cue "Salome," tears off her cap and gown and begins to dance a torrid rock

and roll number. The killer spots her and starts shooting, but luckily is captured by the police. The girls find safety and happiness with their elder students.

REVIEWS:
VARIETY, 7.20.55: "The wild and wacky doings dreamed up by producer-director-writer Nunnally Johnson are dressed up considerably in eye appeal by having the Misses Grable and North running through most of the footage in costumes appropriate to their strip tease profession. The Cinemascope lensing does justice to the ladies."

NEW YORK TIMES, 7.23.55 - A. H. Weiler: "Sheree North, as the somnambulistic blonde, and Betty Grable, as her equally blonde, wise-cracking partner are a treat to the male eyes...and they handle their dialogue with ease and zest."

WASHINGTON DAILY NEWS, 8.5.55, Bill Majeski: "If you expect to see a standard Betty Grable-type opus...you're going to be disappointed, because it is a funny, entertaining picture."

COMMENTS:
- A remake of Paramount's She Loves Me Not (1934) starring Bing Crosby and Miriam Hopkins in Grable's role.
- Noel Toy, appearing briefly as the murdered "Cherry Blossom Wang," was the star of San Francisco's "Forbidden City," America's most famous all-Asian nightclub show.
- At one point, Marilyn Monroe was announced to co-star in the film with North. Sheree North, Fox's "insurance policy" against Monroe, had started as a dancer and went unnoticed for several years in Hollywood. In 1953, choreographer Robert Alton took her to Broadway, where she scored a huge success in Hazel Flagg. Like Grable (also in an Alton staged show, Dubarry Was A Lady), she was "discovered" and brought back to Hollywood to be a movie star. Her big number, "SHAKE, RATTLE AND ROLL," was one of Hollywood's first attempts to incorporate the new demon "Rock and Roll" into formula musical films. North was to be Fox's last "Blonde waiting in the wings" and as musical films were on the wane, she went on to become an acclaimed actress. Her character name ("Curly Flagg") is an obvious acknowledgement of North's success in Hazel Flagg by Producer/director/screenwriter Johnson.
- Although critics of the time gave it generally good reviews (often mentioning that it was not "typical Grable fare"), audiences did not enjoy seeing their Pin Up Girl as the "Straight Man" to North's larger, comedy role. Grable sings and dances only as a member of a "Hootchy Kootch" Burlesque chorus line and wears one costume throughout the entire film. Sadly, in Betty's final film, she is back in college, where she labored for so many films at Paramount. Viewed today, the slow-moving film is brightened by wonderful performances by Charles Coburn, as Dean of the College; Fred Clark, as Orson Bean's multi-millionaire father and Alice Pearce, as the "House Mother" of the fraternity house.

**F84.    The Love Goddesses**

(AVCO Embassy, 1974) 83 minutes

CREDITS:
Director-screenplay, Saul J. Turrell and Graemme Ferguson; music, Percy Faith; narrated by Carl King.

CAST:
Marlene Dietrich, Hedy Lamarr, Greta Garbo, Jean Harlow, Bette Davis, Theda Bara, Betty Grable, Lana Turner, Marilyn Monroe, Sophia Loren, Brigitte Bardot, Dorothy Lamour, Rita Hayworth.

SYNOPSIS:
A history of the female sex on the screen. Betty appears dancing with Jackie Coogan in College Swing, characterizing "The Girl Next Door" of the 1930's and 40's who couldn't say or do anything related to sex, whereas her physical features exuded sex appeal.

REVIEW:
NEW YORK TIMES, 3.4.65, Howard Thompson: "...suffers mainly from sins of omission, not inclusion. As a definitive, full-blown work the picture sags disjointedly, most probably because of the unavailability of vital chunks of footage."

COMMENTS:
- Grable's largest posthumous film appearance. Clips of her also appear in Marilyn (Fox, 1963); Myra Breckenridge (Fox, 1971); That's Dancing (MGM, 1985) and most of the documentaries about Marilyn Monroe, Fox films and film musicals (see "Television Appearances.")

VIDEO: Embassy Home Entertainment (V19)
LASER DISC: Voyager (V19)

# Television
# Appearances

**T1.   Walter Winchell Show** - (ABC) May 10, 1953 - 15 minutes

REVIEW:
VARIETY,5.13.53: "Another of these 'firsts' occurred Saturday night (10) on ABC-TV's 'Walter Winchell Show.' Celebrity concerned was Betty Grable, a member of Winchell's select studio audience and on whom the camera centered briefly while Winchell plugged her next picture. She smiled pretty, but didn't say a word."

COMMENTS:
- After the film studios got over their initial fear and hatred of the new, popular medium, Television quickly became a marketing tool for Hollywood. Advertised as a "Television Debut," film stars were placed in the audiences of such shows as this and <u>The Ed Sullivan Show</u> to be introduced to the viewers at home and their latest film would be publicized. Always mentioned as Grable's first appearance on the new medium,the quoted review describes her limited participation, promoting <u>The Farmer Takes A Wife</u> (F80).

**T2.   Shower Of Stars** - "That's Hollywood," (CBS) September 30, 1954 - 60 minutes

CREDITS:
Executive Producer, Cecil Barker; producer, Nat Perrin; director, Seymour Berns; associate producer, Miriam Nelson; choreographer, Bob Sidney.

CAST: Betty Grable, Harry James, Mario Lanza, Fred Clark, Marvin Kaplan, Gordon Jenkins and his Orchestra.

CONTENTS:
For Betty's first live musical television appearance, she appeared in "We're Gonna Make an Epic," a comedy sketch with Mario Lanza, Harry James, Marvin Kaplan and Fred Clark. She

then performed "I'M JUST WILD ABOUT HARRY" with James and a chorus of dancers in a turn-of-the-century park scene; "DIGGA, DIGGA DOO" in a Hollywood nightclub and "TEN CENTS A DANCE." With James, she sang "ONE FOR THE ROAD" and "BABY, WON'T YOU PLEASE COME HOME?"

REVIEWS:
VARIETY, 10.6.54: "It isn't everyday that a Betty Grable - Harry James - Mario Lanza talent parlay shows up on video...As for Miss Grable, 20th Fox has done much better by her, both as to choice of production numbers and in her vocal-dancing contribs."

PUBLICATION UNKNOWN, 10.1.54 - Anthony La Camera: "There was one dampening effect from the otherwise welcome shower, however. The singing - most of it, at any rate - was not done 'live.' It was pre-recorded by the performers, who subsequently went through that growing TV pastime, known as lip-synchronization...One can only say that Miss Grable's lip-synchronization was excellent...Blonde Betty, in gowns of soft blue, rich gold and flaming red registered beautifully on the color screens."

COMMENTS:
- CBS-TV helped Chrysler to launch its one-per-month series of big-budgeted musicals in the Thursday night 8:30-9:30 time slot. This show was the premiere of the series which ran from September 30, 1954 to April 17, 1958. Dramas filled the rest of the weekly presentations. Betty and Harry were signed to mutiple appearances on the show, from this first show to the last (T19).
- Grable wore the pleated gold lame dress that Marilyn Monroe would later wear in some of her most famous publicity stills.

RECORDING: "Those Bombastic Blonde Bombshells" (D40)
VIDEO: Classic Television (V29)

**T3.   Shower Of Stars** - "Entertainment on Wheels," (CBS) November 18, 1954 - 60 minutes

CREDITS:
Executive producer, Cecil Barker; producer, Ralph Levy; director, Seymour Berns; writers, Milton Pascal and Morris Freedman; conductor, Lud Gluskin.

CAST:
Betty Grable, Harry James, Ed Wynn, Danny Thomas, Jean Hagen, Sherry Jackson, Rusty Hamer, Groucho Marx, Eddie Mayehoff, Rochelle Hudson, Gil Stratton, Jr., Michael O'Shea, William Bishop, James Dunn and Host, William Lundigan.

SYNOPSIS:
Using transportation as the theme of the show and its comedy sketches and musical numbers, Betty appeared in a Showboat sequence, singing "HER GOLDEN HAIR WAS HANGING DOWN HER BACK" and "CLAP HANDS." She also sang "TOO MARVELOUS" and participated in the Finale, a "Cinderella" spoof with Ed Wynn

and Harry James.

REVIEW:
VARIETY, 11.24.54: "...the Grable gams were shown to better advantage than ever before on T.V. And they're still worth a gander. A word about Miss Grable - she seems a far better singer, dancer and personality on tele than she ever was in pixs, largely because with the spontaneity of tele she gets across a vivaciousness she never displayed in motion pictures."

COMMENTS:
- Betty was scheduled to appear in the February 17, 1955 edition of the Shower of Stars series but was replaced by Shirley MacLaine on the show, titled "That's Life," due to straining her right foot and ankle getting out of bed. Coincidentally, Shirley MacLaine was discovered for films by producer Hal Wallis when she went into The Pajama Game (1954) on Broadway as understudy for its also injured dancing star, Carol Haney.

VIDEO: Video Yesteryear (V30)

**T4.    Shower   Of   Stars** - (CBS) June 9, 1955 - 60 minutes

CREDITS:
Executive producer, Cecil Barker; producer, Nat Perrin; director, Seymour Berns; special musical material by Milton Pascal; choreographer, Gene Nelson.

CAST:
Betty Grable, Edgar Bergen, Dan Dailey, Harry James, Jack Oakie, Tony Martin, Ethel Merman, Red Skelton, Shirley MacLaine, Marilyn Maxwell, Gene Nelson, William Lundigan, David Rose (musical director).

CONTENTS:
Betty appeared with Gene Nelson and Dan Dailey in "SWINGIN' THE MUSES," with Harry James and his band in "JAM SESSION" and with the entire cast in the finale, "THANKS A MILLION."

REVIEW:
VARIETY, 6.15.55: "Also in the song department, but with a bit more stress on the terps, was Betty Grable's "SWINGING THE MUSES." She's still got an eye-filling figger and helps get a weak warbling style and a so-so dance effort across. Tune was a potboiler from the old school."

**T5.    Bob Hope Chevy Show** - (NBC) December 27, 1955 - 60 minutes

CREDITS:
Producer, Jack Hope; director, Jim Jordan, Jr.; musical director, Les Brown.

CAST:
Bob Hope, Betty Grable, James Mason, Joan Rhodes.

COMMENTS:
- Portions of the show were filmed at an air base in Keflavik, Iceland. Betty appeared in the segment filmed in Hollywood.

**T6.    Star Stage** - "Cleopatra Collins,"(NBC) March 9, 1956 - 30 minute anthology series

CREDITS:
Director, Sidney Lanfield; written by Fay and Michael Kanin.

CAST:
Betty Grable (Cleo); Casey Adams [aka "Max Showalter"] Pete); Michael Winkleman (Bobbie); Rick Jason (Pookie); Louise Beavers (Effie); Gordon Mills (Harry); Jack Kruschen (Horace); Leon Tyler (Delivery Boy).

SYNOPSIS:
Cleo Collins (Grable) is a former Miss America who has forgotten her beauty contest past after being married to Pete (Casey Adams) for eight years. Cleo decides to give herself a quiet Birthday celebration until former boyfriends and show-business friends intrude on the simple party, reminding Cleo and Pete of her glamourous past. She has the most trouble convincing her husband that Pookie, the Rajah of Pukhanistir (Rick Jason), is simply an old friend.

REVIEW:
VARIETY 3.14.56: "About all it does is to give Miss Grable latitude to strut her physical magnificence...much was made of La Grable's dramatic debut in TV and with her one can forget her acting albeit well mannered and acceptably pleasing...Miss Grable acts out her part as if the watchers were listening rather than ogling."

COMMENTS:
- A lavish press junket was hosted by Beldon Katleman, owner of the El Rancho Vegas, in which critics and press members were wined, dined, treated to Grable and James' Las Vegas stage debut at the hotel showroom and shown the TV show. They were far more impressed with the nightclub act, however.
- On July 20, 1956, Cleopatra Collins was re-run. The Hollywood Reporter remarked:"Much to Grable's embarrassment."
- Grable's first pairing with Casey Adams, who would appear opposite her in Hello Dolly! (S19), using his real name: Max Showalter.

**T7.    Ford Star Jubilee** - "Twentieth Century", (CBS) April 7, 1956 - 90 minutes

CREDITS:
Producer, Arthur Schwartz; director, Paul Nickell; based on the play by Charles Milholland, Ben Hecht and Charles MacArthur; teleplay by Robert Buckner.

SONG:
"FATAL FASCINATION" by Howard Dietz and Arthur Schwartz

CAST:
Orson Welles (Oscar Jaffe); Betty Grable (Lily Garland);
Keenan Wynn (Owen O'Malley); Ray Collins (Oliver Webb);
Olive Sturgess (Mrs. Lockwood); Gage Clark (Matthew Clark);
Lance Fuller (Stone Martin); Norman Sturgess (Stage
Manager); Roy Glenn (Pullman Porter); Robert Johnson
(Redcap); Steve Terell (Mr. Lockwood).

SYNOPSIS:
It is 1928 and Oscar Jaffe (Welles), a bankrupt theatrical
producer, schemes to sign Lily Garland (Grable), a famous
actress he molded from a dowdy clerk named "Mildred Plotka,"
to an exclusive contract and recover his theatrical fortunes.
Lily has deserted Oscar and the Broadway stage for "Talking
Pictures" in Hollywood, winning an Academy Award for a film
role. On a train moving across the country, Oscar tries to
lure Lily back to his company to save his reputation, his
career and his dignity. After tempestuous arguments and
flamboyant displays of hysteria and ego, Lily finally
succumbs to Oscar's wishes.

REVIEWS:
NEW YORK DAILY NEWS, 4.9.56 - Ben Gross: "She seemed far too
nice and wholesome, much too 'cute' to convince this viewer
that she really was the strong and sinuous siren of the play.
Betty made a good try and gave evidence of hitherto
unsuspected dramatic talent. She should do well in the
portrayal of light comedy characters."

VARIETY, 4.11.56: "Betty Grable showed a part of the brassy
quality that was needed for this role. She suggested the role
rather than fulfilled it."

LOS ANGELES TIMES, Robert E. Lubeck: "Miss Grable, at 39, as
shapely as ever...displayed, on practically any pretext, the
famous Grable legs and she displayed, also, a pretty good
comedy touch."

HOLLYWOOD REPORTER, 4.9.56 - James Powers: "To echo the
thought that must have flashed through a million minds
viewing this debacle, 'If you were Betty Grable, would you be
in love with Orson Welles?' To put it as gently as possible:
Uh-uh. Betty Grable was foolishly miscast."

COMMENTS:
- The property was made as a film with John Barrymore and
Carole Lombard in 1934; seen on Ford Theatre - (CBS) October
7, 1949 with Fredric March as "Oscar" and Lilli Palmer as
"Lily" and eventually turned into On The Twentieth Century, a
Tony award winning musical in 1978 starring John Cullum and
Madeline Kahn.
- When rehearsals for the show began on March 20, 1956 at CBS
in Hollywood, Van Johnson was in the cast as "Owen O' Malley."
He was replaced by Keenan Wynn.

T8.    **The Ed Sullivan Show,** "Toast of the Town", (CBS)
May 13, 1956 - 60 minutes

COMMENTS:
- In a remote telecast from the Beverly Hills Hotel, Grable appeared as one of the "Hollywood Mothers of the Year," selected by the City of Hope. Hollywood Reporter columnist Mike Connolly introduced Betty, June Allyson, Ann Blyth, Rosemary Clooney, Deborah Kerr and Betty Hutton, who did a promotion for the medical facility.

**T9.   Bob Hope Show** - "The Road To Hollywood", (NBC) June 17, 1956 - 90 minutes

CREDITS:
Producer, Jack Hope; director, Jack Shea; writers, Lester White, John Rapp, Mort Lachman, Bill Larkin, Jerry Marx.

CAST:
Bob Hope, Betty Grable, Dorothy Lamour, Marilyn Maxwell, Jane Russell, Ed Sullivan, Steve Allen and George Sanders.

SYNOPSIS:
A comedy special created to promote Hope's latest film (That Certain Age). Grable appeared in a comedy skit with Hope and the "Finale" with Lamour, Maxwell and Russell, singing "TAKING A CHANCE ON HOPE," a musical parody by Sammy Cahn.

REVIEW:
HOLLYWOOD REPORTER, 6.18.56: "How could it miss with Dorothy Lamour, Betty Grable, Jane Russell and Marilyn Maxwell? Those fortunate enough to have color sets couldn't have helped but be impressed."

**T10.   Do You Trust Your Wife?** - (CBS) 1956 - 30 minutes

CREDITS:
Producer, Don Fedderson; director, James Morgan; writers, Seaman Jacobs, Si Rose and George Tibbles.

CAST:
Host, Edgar Bergen.

**T11.   Dinah Shore Chevy Show** - (NBC) November 2, 1956 - 60 minutes

CREDITS:
Producer-director, Bob Banner; written by Bob Wells and Johnny Bradford; choreography by Nick Castle.

CAST:
Dinah Shore, Betty Grable, Hildegarde, Jaye P. Morgan, Hal March.

CONTENTS:
Miss Grable appeared in a "Chicago Fire" sequence, sang and danced to "SINGIN' IN THE RAIN" and participated in a Speakeasy episode.

REVIEW:
VARIETY, 11.7.56: "Miss Shore's hired help included Betty
Grable, Hildegarde and Jaye P. Morgan, and each gave the
impression of working with ease and charm."

**T12.    KTLA'S 10th Anniversary** - (KTLA, Los Angeles),
January 22, 1957 - 120 minutes

CAST:
172 stars, including Betty Grable and Harry James.

**T13.    Bob Hope Chevy Show** - (NBC) January 25, 1957 -
60 minutes

CREDITS:
Producers, Jack Shea and Bob Hope; director, Jack Hope;
writers, Mort Lachman, Bill Larkin, Lester White, John
Rapp, Charles Lee; choreographer, Jack Baker; musical
director, Les Brown.

CAST:
Bob Hope, Betty Grable, Eddie Fisher, Dan Rowan, Dick
Martin, Harry James, Jack Kirkwood.

CONTENTS:
Billed as "Bob's Special Guest," Betty performed "GET HAPPY"
with ten dancers and also appeared as "Marsha Mantrap" in a
comedy sketch spoofing the "Faust" legend with Harry James
portraying a trumpet blowing Devil.

VIDEO: "Bob Hope 5 Hour Marathon" - Shokus Video (V2)

**T14.    The Ed Sullivan Show,** "Toast of the Town" -
(CBS), September 22, 1957 - 60 minutes

CREDITS:
Producers, Marlo Lewis and Ed Sullivan; director-
choreographer, John Wray.

CAST:
Betty Grable, Harry James, George Raft, Jo Stafford, Carol
Channing, Alfred Apaka, Jay Nemeth, Jack Dempsey.

CONTENTS:
In the popular Sunday night variety program, Betty sang "PUT
YOUR ARMS AROUND ME" from Coney Island.

REVIEW:
VARIETY, 9.26.57: "Ed Sullivan had a really big show - really
big - on his first of a series of two from Hollywood...Betty
Grable pantomimed a song with a lot of production around her,
and George Raft, in a filmed version of a bolero with the
late Carole Lombard, reprised a dance he did in the old Texas
Guinan days...These perennials pack a lot of entertainment as
well as name and sometimes curiosity value, but principally
they contributed to a well-stacked and fast-moving show."

## T15.    The Eddie Fisher Show - (NBC) October 29, 1957, 60 minutes

CAST:
Eddie Fisher, Betty Grable, George Gobel, Mary Kaye Trio, Elaine Dunn, the Buddy Bregman Orchestra.

CONTENTS:
Grable performed songs from <u>Guys and Dolls</u>, after obtaining special permission from composer Frank Loesser.

## T16.    The Lucille Ball-Desi Arnaz Comedy Hour - "Lucy Wins a Race Horse", (CBS) - February 3, 1958, 60 minutes

CREDITS:
Executive producer, Desi Arnaz; producer, Bert Granet; associate producer, Jack Aldworth; director, Jerry Thorpe; assistant director, Jay Sandrich; writers, Madelyn Martin, Bob Carroll, Jr., Bob Schiller, Bob Weiskopf; director of photography, Sid Hickox; editor, Dann Cahn; choreography, Jack Baker.

SONG:
"THE BAYAMO" by Arthur Hamilton

CAST:
Lucille Ball, Desi Arnaz, Betty Grable, Harry James, Vivian Vance (Ethel Mertz); William Frawley (Fred Mertz).

SYNOPSIS:
Lucy wins a horse ("Whirling Jet") for Little Ricky and when Desi tells her that Betty and Harry have informed him how expensive it is to keep a horse, she tries to hide it in the house. While Betty and Harry are rehearsing their nightclub appearance for Ricky's club at the house, the horse is discovered. When Desi insists that they get rid of the horse, Lucy, Betty and Ethel enter him in a race, with Fred's help, as he is hopelessly enamoured of Betty. The horse loves Lucy and will only run for her, so Lucy also enters the race. They win, but are disqualified due to their comic shenanigans. Ricky relents and allows litte Ricky to keep the horse.

REVIEW:
VARIETY, 2.5.58: "It's getting more difficult to 'love Lucy'...for this outing show called on Betty Grable and Harry James to build the situation. Their contribution was virtually meaningless except when Miss Grable showed off her gams in a terp sequence to Arthur Hamilton's 'THE BAYAMO.' Trumpeter Harry James got off some hot licks on this one, too."

COMMENTS:
- Reunited after many years with former co-RKO contractee Lucille Ball and former swain Desi, Betty sizzles in a song-and-dance with Desi and Harry. The James' comedic contributions were kept to a minimum, however, as Lucy's every move and facial expression was captured in close-up,

while her co-stars were relegated to the background.
- Robert Osborne remembers that Lucille Ball often said:
"Betty Grable is the funniest woman in the World. We always
tried to figure out a way to do a TV series for her. The
camera simply went into her personna." Unfortunately, the
perfect vehicle was never found.
- In a CBS press release for the show, dated January 14,
1958, "THE BAYAMO" is touted as a new song and dance and
described by its composer, Arthur Hamilton as "Somewhere
between a samba and a rhumba." Hamilton also composed the hit
song "CRY ME A RIVER."

**T17.    The Jerry Lewis Show** - (NBC) February 18, 1958 -
60 minutes

CREDITS:
Producer, Ernest Glucksman; director, Jack Shea; writers,
Harry Crane and Jerry Davis.

CAST:
Jerry Lewis, Betty Grable, Sophie Tucker, Hans Conreid.

COMMENTS:
The show was broadcast from the Sands Hotel in Las Vegas.

REVIEW:
VARIETY, 2.26.58: "Miss Grable, in fluffy frock and hiding
her shapely stems, romped through a production number with
Lewis and three dancers stumbling around to whoop up a few
laughs...For the takeout he romanced a mop made to resemble
the object of his affections. Lewis could have trimmed it for
perhaps another orbing of Miss Grable."

**T18.    The 30th Annual Academy Awards Show** -
(NBC), March 26, 1958 - 120 minutes

CONTENTS:
Betty performed "THE LULLABY OF BROADWAY" with Harry James
during a medley of Academy Award winning songs which was the
telecast's "Opening Number," with Mae West, Rock Hudson, Bob
Hope, Shirley Maclaine, Rhonda Fleming, Marge and Gower
Champion, Tony Martin, Russ Tamblyn, Eddie Fisher, Janet
Leigh, Tommy Sands, Shirley Jones, Sheree North, Anita
Ekberg, Van Johnson and Jimmie Rodgers.

RECORDING: "THE LULLABY OF BROADWAY" on "Betty Grable" (D1
and D2)

**T19.    Shower Of Stars** - (CBS) April 17, 1958 - 60
minutes

CREDITS:
Producer, Cecil Barker; director, Seymour Berns; writers,
Hugh Wedlock, Howard Snyder; choreographer, Jack Boyle.

CAST:
Jack Benny, Betty Grable, John Raitt, Janis Paige, Eddie
"Rochester" Anderson, Don Wilson, Dennis Day, Mary

Livingstone, Barbara Nichols, Mel Blanc.

CONTENTS:
- Nanette Fabray was originally scheduled to sing "A LITTLE GIRL FROM LITTLE ROCK" from Gentlemen Prefer Blondes with Grable, but had an accident. She was replaced by Janis Paige. The show was televised from the Moulin Rouge nightclub in Hollywood. Grable also sang a Calypso song and "WHAT DID I DO?," plus participating in a "Hillbilly Sketch" with Benny. This was the last show of the series.

REVIEW:
HOLLYWOOD REPORTER, 4.21.58 - Hank Grant: "Guest star Betty Grable also made this her best TV showing to date...It's a tribute to Benny that he can shine as the star even though he generously steps back to all others full play."

RECORDING: "LITLE GIRL FROM LITTLE ROCK" is heard on "Betty Grable" (D2)

**T20.   Bob Hope Buick Show** - (NBC) November 21, 1958 - 60 minutes

CREDITS:
Producer, Jack Hope; director, Bob Henry; writers, Lester White, John Rapp, Mort Lachman, Bill Larkin, Charles Lee, Norman Sullivan; art director, Jay Kraus; choreographer, Jack Baker.

CAST:
Bob Hope, Betty Grable, Gloria Swanson, Wally Cox, Randy Sparks.

REVIEW:
VARIETY, 11.26.58: "Betty Grable, with a considerable show of glamourous underpinning, scampered and sang...To most at the sets Miss Grable skimmed down to tights is enough of visual pleasure to salvage any deficits. Her skit with Hope, about two busy stars trying to find time to see each other, was only mildy diverting."

**T21.   Dinah Shore Chevy Show** - (NBC) March 8, 1959 - 60 minutes

CREDITS:
Producer, Henry Jaffe; director, Bob Banner; costume designer, Ray Aghayan; choreographer, Tony Charmoli.

CAST:
Dinah Shore, Betty Grable, Tony Randall, Ella Fitzgerald.

**T22.   Dinah Shore Chevy Show** - (NBC) November 22, 1959 - 60 minutes

CAST:
Dinah Shore, Betty Grable, Jackie Cooper, Inbal Ballet Company.

**T23.     Dinah Shore Chevy Show** - (NBC) April 3, 1960 -
60 minutes

CAST:
Dinah Shore, Betty Grable, Vic Damone, The Weire Brothers,
Desi Arnaz, Jr., Richard Keith ("Little Ricky" on I Love
Lucy.)

**T24.     Ford Star Time** - (NBC) June 7, 1960 - 60 minutes.

CREDITS:
Producer, Mac Benoff; director, Greg Garrison; writers, Mac
Benoff and William Burns; choreographer, Hermes Pan.

CAST:
George Burns, Jack Benny, Betty Grable, Bobby Darin, Polly
Bergen, the Hermes Pan Dancers.

REVIEW:
Variety, 6.15.60: "Miss Grable scored with a sexy rendition
of the now dated number 'I REFUSE TO ROCK AND ROLL,' as she
slowly stripped to essentials, revealing a still ship shape
and game gams."

HOLLYWOOD REPORTER, 6.9.60 - Hank Grant:" This was a 'no
strain' effort on the part of George Burns and though the
overall hour had no particular peaks of excitement, neither
did it have any valleys...Betty Grable projected plenty of
personality on a song-and-dance...with the Pan dancers."

COMMENTS:
- The show, taped at the CBS studios in Hollywood on May 20
and 21, 1960, won the Arbitron viewer's rating for its time
slot (8:30 - 9:30 p.m.)

RECORDING: "I REFUSE TO ROCK AND ROLL" on "Betty Grable" (D2)

**T25.     Perry Como's Kraft Music Hall** - (NBC)
December 14, 1960, 60 minutes

CAST:
Perry Como, Betty Grable, Harry James, the Peter Gennaro
Dancers, Mitchell Ayres Orchestra.

CONTENTS:
Betty sang "ARTIFICIAL FLOWERS" from Tenderloin and joined
Perry Como and Harry James in a "Medley" of "MUSIC MAKERS;"
"I'VE HEARD THAT SONG BEFORE;" "I HAD THE CRAZIEST DREAM;"
"JAMES SESSION;" "YOU MADE ME LOVE YOU" and "CIRIBIRIBIN."

RECORDING: "ARTIFICIAL FLOWERS," MEDLEY on "Betty Grable"
(D2)

**T26.     Andy Williams Show** - (NBC) November 8, 1962 - 60
minutes

CAST:
Andy Williams, Betty Grable, Danny Kaye, The Osmond Brothers, The New Christy Minstrels, Lawrence Welk.

RECORDING: "NIGHT LIFE" on "Betty Grable" (D2)

**T27.   The Hollywood Palace** - (ABC) October 24, 1964   - 60 minutes

CREDITS:
Executive producer, Nick Vanoff; producer, William O Harback; director, Grey Lockwood; staged by Marc Breaux and Dee Dee Wood.

CAST:
Betty Grable (Hostess), Harry James, Dan Dailey, Diahann Carroll, the Smothers Brothers, Les Surfs, Alcenty.

**T28.   The Hollywood Palace** - (ABC) December 26, 1964 - 60 minutes

CAST:
Van Johnson (Host); Sergio Franchi, Betty Grable, Jackie Mason, Paul Gilbert, Jamboaz, Mimi Zerbini, Bal Caron Trio.

RECORDING: "YA GOTTA GIVE THE PEOPLE HOKE" with Johnson and Franchi on "Those Bombastic Blonde Bombshells" (D40)

**T29.   What's My Line?** - (CBS) August 29, 1965 - 30 minutes

CREDITS:
Producers, Mark Goodson, Bill Todman.

CAST:
John Daly (Host); Panelists: Arlene Francis, Dorothy Kilgallen, Bennett Cerf; Betty Grable ("Mystery Guest").

**T30.   The Tonight Show starring Johnny Carson** - (NBC) June 15, 1965 - 90 minutes

CREDITS:
Producer, Fred De Cordova; director, Bob Quinn; musical director, Carl "Doc" Severinsen.

**T31.   Password** - (CBS), exact airdate unknown, 1967 - 30 minutes

CREDITS:
Executive producer, Frank Wayne; producers, Mark Goodson, Bill Todman.

CAST:
Allen Ludden (Host), Betty Grable (guest contestant).

**T32.   What's My Line?** - (CBS) June 18, 1967 - 30 minutes

COMMENTS:
Once again, Grable was the "Mystery Guest."

**T33.    Carol Burnett Show** - (CBS) February 12, 1968 -
60 minutes

CREDITS:
Producer, Joe Hamilton; director, Clark Jones; writers,
Arnie Rosen, Mike Marmer, Buzz Kohan, Bill Angelis; costume
designer, Bob Mackie; musical director, Harry Zimmerman,
choreographer, Ernest Flatt.

CAST:
Carol Burnett, Betty Grable, Martha Raye, Harvey Korman,
Lyle Waggoner, Vicki Lawrence, the Ernest Flatt Dancers.

CONTENTS:
Betty performed "HELLO DOLLY" with the Ernest Flatt Dancers.
In "Amnesia" (a soap opera satire), Betty played an amnesia
victim. Lyle Waggoner, Martha Raye, Harvey Korman and Betty
participated in a "Pretty Legs" contest, with Harvey Korman
voted the "winner" by the audience. In the finale, "THAT OLD
GANG OF MINE," Betty, Martha and Carol portrayed gun molls of
the 1930's.

RECORDING: "HELLO DOLLY" on "Betty Grable" (D1) and "Those
Sensational Swinging Sirens of the Silver Screen" (D41)

**T34.    The Hollywood Squares** - (NBC) September 8 - 12,
1969 - 30 minutes

CAST:
Peter Marshall (Host); Betty Grable, Harvey Korman, Gail
Fisher, Cesar Romero, Sally Ann Howes, Sandy Baron (guest
panelists).

**T35.    The Name Droppers** - (NBC) October 6 - 10, 1969,
30 minutes

CREDITS:
Producer, Art Alisi; director, Jerome Shaw

CAST:
Al Lohman, Roger Barkely (cohosts); Betty Grable (guest
panelist); Kenny Williams (announcer).

**T36.    The Hollywood Squares** - (NBC) October 13 - 17,
1969 - 30 minutes

CAST:
Peter Marshall (Host); Betty Grable, Vincent Price, Anne
Baxter, Jackie Vernon, Ed Ames (guest panelists); Paul
Lynde, George Gobel, Vincent Price (regular panelists).

**T37.    The Hollywood Squares** - (NBC) November 17 - 21,
1969 - 30 minutes

CAST:
Peter Marshall (Host); Betty Grable, Jim Backus, Lloyd Haynes, Alan Sues, Ruta Lee, Dick Patterson (guest panelists).

**T38.    The Hollywood Squares** - (NBC) March 23 - 27, 1970, 30 minutes

CAST:
Peter Marshall (Host); Betty Grable, Jackie Vernon, Ed Platt, Sally Ann Howes, Jack Carter (guest panelists).

**T39.    Geritol Vitamin Commercial** - 1971

COMMENTS:
- Grable filmed two highly successful commercials, as well as print ads for the vitamins targeted at senior citizens.

**T40.    The Merv Griffin Show** - (CBS) May 14, 1971 - 90 minutes

CAST:
Merv Griffin (Host); Betty Grable, Buddy Greco (guests).

COMMENTS:
- The show was broadcast from Caesar's Palace in Las Vegas.

**T41.    Those Fabulous Fordies** - (NBC) February 29, 1972 - 60 minutes

CREDITS:
Producers, Digby Wolfe, Bob Wynn; director, Bob Wynn; written by Digby Wolfe; costumes, Ret Turner.

CAST:
Tennessee Ernie Ford, Betty Grable, Maureen O'Hara, Frank Gorshin, Dick Haymes.

CONTENTS:
A music and comedy tribute to the 1940's, with Betty singing "THE MORE I SEE YOU" from Billy Rose's Diamond Horseshoe with Dick Haymes and performing a dance number to "STEPPING OUT WITH MY BABY."

REVIEW:
VARIETY, 4.8.72: "She looked great and flashed her famous gams in a sprightly terp number from Mother Wore Tights (sic) - as good now as it was then."

DAILY NEWS, 4.1.72.- Kay Gardella: "..and there was the off-key singer, Betty Grable. At 56, she's still a real knockout ...She can't sing, but she sure looks terrific - what an ad for Geritol, which she plugged during the commercials."

**T42.    44th Annual Academy Awards Show** - (NBC) April 10, 1972 - 120 minutes

CREDITS:
Producer, Howard W. Koch; executive producer, Robert Finkel; director, Marty Passetta; special musical material, Billy Barnes; choreographer, Ron Field.

COMMENTS:
- Betty's last public appearance as co-presenter with Dick Haymes for "Best Original Dramatic Score" (Summer of '42) and "Best Scoring: Adaptation and Original Song Score" (Fiddler on the Roof). The ceremony was held at the Dorothy Chandler Pavilion in Los Angeles and Charles Chaplin received a special Academy Award.

**T43.   Fred Astaire Salutes the Fox Musicals** -
20th Century Fox (syndicated), October 24, 1974 - 60 minutes

CREDITS:
Producer, Alan P. Sloan; director, Marc Breaux; written by Draper Lewis.

CONTENTS:
A compilation of musical numbers from Fox films, hosted by Fred Astaire (who only made one film for 20th Century Fox - Daddy Long Legs, 1955), Betty appears in "NO TALENT JOE" from Meet Me After The Show; "THE BALBOA" with Johnny Downs, Patsy Kelly and Judy Garland from Pigskin Parade; newsreel footage from Fox Movietone News putting her leg into cement and posterity at the ceremony at Grauman's Chinese Theatre; and with June Haver, singing and dancing to "THE SIDEWALKS OF NEW YORK" from The Dolly Sisters.

**T44.   That's Hollywood** - 20th Century Fox
Television/ABC 1976-1982 (Syndicated) - 30 minutes

CREDITS:
Executive Producer, Jack Haley, Jr.; producer and writer, Draper Lewis; narrator, Tom Bosley.

SYNOPSIS:
A weekly documentary about the films and stars of Twentieth Century Fox. Betty was featured in the installments: "The Fox Ladies," "The Musicals" and "The Blondes."

**T45.   Gotta Dance, Gotta Sing** - (HBO) 1981 - 60 minutes

CREDITS:
Executive producer, Ellen Krass; producer, Daniel Helfgott; creative director, Thomas Royal.

SYNOPSIS:
Betty appears in the classic "Give her some class" scene from Coney Island and performing "DARKTOWN STRUTTER'S BALL" with June Haver from The Dolly Sisters .

Video: RKO (V12)

Betty Grable and the female chorus perform "Night Life" on *The Andy Williams Show*, November 8, 1962. Collection of Bob Izoz.

# Radio Appearances

In researching Grable's radio work, it becomes obvious that she must have done many 20th Century Fox Presents - radio "Commercials" for Fox films; and Command Performances, the radio programs created for Servicemen during World War II. The author was unable to locate "Logs" for either series to verify her appearances. There are also several radio performances on her recordings (see "Discography") that the author was unable to identify or verify the programs and/or air dates.

**R1.** **Odeon Theater** - Live Broadcast - December 25, 1926

COMMENTS:
First radio appearance at the age of seven with Jack Haley and Frank Fay, playing a musical instrument.

**R2.** **20th Century Fox Presents** - Pigskin Parade - exact date unknown, 1936

   CAST:
   Judy Garland, Johnny Downs, Betty Grable.

RECORDING: "IT'S LOVE I'M AFTER" is heard on "Betty Grable" (D1) and "THE BALBOA" on "Hollywood Is On The Air" (D20)

**R3.** **Song Time** - (CBS) July 17, 1937 - 15 minutes

   CREDITS:
   Producer-director, George Zachary.

   CAST:
   John Payne, Betty Grable.

CONTENTS:
"Series of programs to promote young singers. One male singer and one female singer on each show" (CBS press release).

COMMENTS:
- Grable was featured with John Payne on every Saturday show which originated from the West Coast in this series, broadcast from July 12, 1937 to February 25, 1938. With an air time of 6:45 - 7:00 p.m. nightly, other talents featured were Ray Heatherton (father of Joey Heatherton), Jack Shannon, Ruth Carhart, Patti Chapin, Doris Kerr, Lorraine Grimm and Harry Cool.

**R4.**   **Song Time** - (CBS) July 31, 1937 - 15 minutes

   CAST:
   John Payne, Betty Grable.

**R5.**   **Song Time** - (CBS) August 7, 1937 - 15 minutes

   CAST:
   John Payne, Betty Grable.

**R6.**   **Song Time** - (CBS) August 14, 1937 - 15 minutes

   CAST:
   John Payne, Betty Grable.

**R7.**   **Song Time** - (CBS) August 21, 1937 - 15 minutes

   CAST:
   John Payne, Betty Grable.

**R8.**   **Song Time** - (CBS) September 4, 1937 - 15 minutes

   CAST:
   John Payne, Betty Grable, Tom Hanlon (announcer).

**R9.**   **Song Time** - (CBS) September 11, 1937 - 15 minutes

   CAST:
   Betty Grable, John Payne.

**R10.**   **Song Time** - (CBS) September 18, 1937 - 15 minutes

   CAST:
   Betty Grable, John Payne, Maurie Webster (announcer).

**R11.**   **Song Time** - (CBS) September 25, 1937 - 15 minutes

   CAST:
   Betty Grable, John Payne.

**R12.**   **Hollywood Showcase** - (CBS) October 3, 1937 - 30 minutes

   CREDITS:
   Producer, Charles Vanda.

   CAST:
   Lud Gluskin and his Orchestra, Betty Grable, Harry Simeone

Chorus.

CONTENTS:
"Variety program which offers the newest in filmland's music, song and drama. Outstanding personalities, promising young players and new talent are presented" (CBS press release).

**R13.**   **Song Time** - (CBS) October 7, 1937 - 15 minutes

   CAST:
   Betty Grable, John Payne.

**R14.**   **Song Time** - (CBS) October 15, 1937 - 15 minutes

   CAST:
   Betty Grable, John Payne.

**R15.**   **Song Time** - (CBS) October 22, 1937 - 15 minutes

   CAST:
   Betty Grable, John Payne.

**R16.**   **Song Time** - (CBS) October 29, 1937 - 15 minutes

   CAST:
   Betty Grable, John Payne.

**R17.**   **Song Time** - (CBS) November 5, 1937 - 15 minutes

   CAST:
   Betty Grable, John Payne.

**R18.**   **Hollywood Showcase** - (CBS) November 7, 1937 - 30 minutes

   CREDITS:
   Producer, Charles Vanda.

   CAST:
   Lud Gluskin and his Orchestra, Betty Grable, Johnny Downs, Larry "Buster" Crabbe, Eleanor Whitney, Harry Simeone chorus.

CONTENTS:
Preview scenes and songs from Thrill of a Lifetime.

RECORDING: "SWEETHEART TIME" on "Those Bombastic Blonde Bomshells" (D40)

**R19.**   **Song Time** - (CBS) November 12, 1937 - 15 minutes

   CAST:
   Betty Grable, John Payne.

**R20.**   **Song Time** - (CBS) November 19, 1937 - 15 minutes

CAST:
Betty Grable, Jackie Coogan, John Payne.

COMMENTS:
- Betty and Jackie talked about their upcoming wedding.

**R21.   Song Time** - (CBS) November 26, 1937 - 15 minutes

CAST:
Betty Grable, John Payne.

**R22.   Song Time** - (CBS) December 3, 1937 - 15 minutes

CAST:
Betty Grable, John Payne.

**R23.   Song Time** - (CBS) December 24, 1937 - 15 minutes

CAST:
Betty Grable, John Payne.

**R24.   Song Time** - (CBS) December 31, 1937 - 15 minutes

CAST:
Betty Grable, John Payne.

**R25.   Song Time** - (CBS) January 7, 1938 - 15 minutes

CAST:
Betty Grable, Johnny Downs.

**R26.   Song Time** - (CBS) January 14, 1938 - 15 minutes

CAST:
Betty Grable, John Payne.

**R27.   Song Time** - (CBS) February 4, 1938 - 15 minutes

CAST:
Betty Grable, John Payne.

**R28.   Song Time** - (CBS) February 11, 1938 - 15 minutes

CAST:
Betty Grable, John Payne.

**R29.   Song Time** - (CBS) February 18, 1938 - 15 minutes

CAST:
Betty Grable, John Payne.

**R30.   Song Time** - (CBS) February 25, 1938 - 15 minutes

CAST:
Betty Grable, John Payne.

**R31.    Royal Gelatin Hour**, - <u>South of Wilshire</u>, (NBC) March 3, 1938 - 60 minutes

**R32.    Cantor's Camel Caravan** - (CBS) May 16, 1938 - 30 minutes

CREDITS:
Producer, Eddie Cantor; director, Vic Knight (with Eddie Cantor).

CAST:
Eddie Cantor, Hattie Noel, Bert Gordon, Jackie Coogan, Betty Grable, Walter Woolf King (announcer).

COMMENTS:
- This weekly programmed originated from New York until May 16, 1938, when Betty and Jackie Coogan guested on its first West Coast broadcast.

**R33.    Bob Hope Show** - (NBC) April 11, 1939 - 30 minutes

CAST:
Bob Hope, Betty Grable, Jackie Coogan.

**R34.    The Kate Smith Hour** - <u>Tin Pan Alley</u>, (CBS) November 22, 1940 - 55 minutes

CREDITS:
Producer, Ted Collins.

CAST:
Alice Faye (Katie); Betty Grable (Lily); John Payne (Skeets); Jack Oakie (Harry).

COMMENTS:
- A full page ad in <u>Variety</u> promised:"...the greatest radio show in the history of radio showmanship! Alice Faye...Betty Grable...and the other <u>Tin Pan Alley</u> stars...taking over the entire Kate Smith Hour!"

**R35.    Screen Guild Theater** - <u>Altar Bound</u>, (CBS) February 23, 1941 - 30 minutes

CREDITS:
Director, Roger Pryor; play by M.M. Musselman, Kenneth Earle, adapted by Sam Perrin.

CAST:
Bob Hope, Bing Crosby, Betty Grable.

COMMENTS:
- Bing Crosby introduced the song "FRENESI" on the program.

**R36.    Screen Guild Theatre** - <u>The Perfect Speciman</u>, (CBS) November 30, 1941  - 30 minutes

CREDITS:
Director, Roger Pryor; written/adapted by Charles
Tazewell and Helen Deutsch.

CAST:
Melvyn Douglas (Gerald Wicks); Betty Grable (Mona Evans);
Dame May Whitty (Grandma Wicks); Roger Pryor (Master of
Ceremonies).

SYNOPSIS:
Gerald Wicks (Douglas), a wealthy young man who is about to
become the director of the Wicks Enterprise, lives a very
sheltered life, watched over by Grandma Wicks (Whitty.) In an
automobile accident, he meets Mona (Grable) who teaches him
about romance and life.

**R37.   The Edgar Bergen and Charlie Mc Carthy
Show** - (NBC), January 11, 1942 - 30 minutes

CAST:
Edgar Bergen, Charlie Mc Carthy, Betty Grable, George Raft.

CONTENTS:
Betty and George Raft performed the skit "Punctured
Junction."

**R38.   The Kate Smith Hour** - Love is Like a Pearl,
(CBS) February 6, 1942  - 60 minutes

CAST:
Betty Grable, Jack Oakie, Lou Holtz.

**R39.   Screen Guild Theatre** - Love is News, (CBS)
February 22, 1942 - 30 minutes

CREDITS:
Director, Roger Pryor; musical director, Oscar Bradley.

CAST:
Kay Kyser (Steve Leyton); Betty Grable (Tony Gateson);
James Gleason (Marty Canavan); Roger Pryor (M.C.).

SYNOPSIS:
Steve Leyton (Kyser), an ambitious reporter, is trying to get
an exclusive interview with the publicity-shy heiress, Tony
Gateson (Grable). When Steve tricks Tony into an interview,
she retaliates by telling other reporters that she and Steve
are engaged to be married. Fired by his boss, Canavan (James
Gleason) and comically chased by Tony, Steve finally succumbs
to a real romance.

**R40.   Lady Esther Screen Guild Players** - A Yank
in the RAF (CBS) October 26, 1942 - 30 minutes

CREDITS:
Producer-director Bill Lawrence; writer-adapter, Bill
Hampton.

CAST:
Tyrone Power (Tim); Betty Grable (Carol); John Sutton (Capt. Morley).

COMMENTS:
- Advertised as Tyrone Power's final appearance on <u>Screen Guild Players</u> before he joined the U.S. Marines.

**R41.   Command Performance, U.S.A.** - exact airdate
unknown - 30 minutes

CAST:
Betty Grable (M.C.); Danny Kaye, Gregory Ratoff and Carmen Miranda.

**R42.   Silver Theatre** - <u>A Little Journey</u>, - (CBS)
November 21, 1943 - 30 minutes

CREDITS:
Director, Preston Foster; written by Rachel Crothers; music composed by Felix Mills.

CAST:
Betty Grable (Julie Rutherford).

SYNOPSIS:
As heiress Julie Rutherford (Grable) has lost her fortune, she manages to live well by being the "Guest" at various friend's homes. When she hears that her brother has been killed in the War, she decides that life is worthless. Aboard a train, she meets a condemned murderer and when the train is involved in a wreck, the murderer teaches the bitter young girl the meaning of life.

**R43.   Lux Radio Theatre** - <u>Springtime in the Rockies</u>,
(CBS), May 22, 1944 - 60 minutes

CAST:
Dick Powell (Dan); Betty Grable (Vicky); Carmen Miranda (Rosita); Edgar Barrier (Mc Tavish); Louis Silver (Conductor).

COMMENTS:
- On April 17, 1944, LUX presented <u>Coney Island</u>, with Dorothy Lamour playing Betty's role, Alan Ladd and Chester Morris.

RECORDING: "PAN AMERICANA JUBILEE" is heard on "Hollywood Is On The Air" (D20)

**R44.   The Burns and Allen Show** - (CBS) May 30,
1944 - 30 minutes

CAST:
George Burns, Gracie Allen, Betty Grable.

**R45.   Stage Door Canteen** - CBS, June 23, 1944, 30
minutes

CAST:
Walter Abel, Paula Stone, Betty Grable.

COMMENTS:
- This is one of Grable's rare radio appearances from the East Coast. She was probably there with Harry James while he played one of his band engagements.

**R46.  Hollywood Star Time** - Diamond Horseshoe - (CBS) April 14, 1946 - 60 minutes

CAST:
Betty Grable (Bonnie); Frank Lattimore (Joe Davis, Jr.).

**R47.  Lady Esther Screen Guild Theatre** - The Perfect Specimen - (CBS) April 22, 1946 - 30 minutes

CAST:
Betty Grable (Mona Evans); Jack Carson (Gerald Wicks); Dame May Whitty (Grandma Wicks).

COMMENTS:
- A repeat of a script she had done five years earlier (R36), with Jack Carson replacing Melvyn Douglas.

**R48.  Lux Radio Theater** - Coney Island (CBS) September 30, 1946 - 60 minutes

CREDITS:
Producer-director, William Keighley; musical director, Lou Silvers.

CAST:
Betty Grable (Kate Farley); Victor Mature (Eddie Jackson); Barry Sullivan (Joe Rocco).

**R49.  Camel Screen Guild Players** - The Shocking Miss Pilgrim (CBS) October 27, 1947 - 30 minutes

CREDITS:
Director, Bill Lawrence; music director, Wilbur Hatch.

CAST:
Betty Grable (Cynthia Pilgrim); Tony Martin (John).

**R50.  Lux Radio Theater** - Mother Wore Tights (CBS) February 2, 1948 - 60 minutes

CAST:
Betty Grable (Myrtle); Dan Dailey (Frank); Vanessa Brown (Narrator).

**R51.  Philco Radio Time** - (ABC) January 5, 1949 - 30 minutes

CAST:
Bing Crosby, Betty Grable, Harry James, John Scott Trotter

and his Orchestra.

CONTENTS:
In Crosby's 87th program for sponsor Philco, Betty participated in "The Horse Sale Sketch" with Bing, Harry and John Scott Trotter and then sang "WHAT DID I DO?" from When My Baby Smiles At Me.

RECORDING: "WHAT DID I DO?" on "Betty Grable" (D2)

**R52.    Suspense** - The Copper Tea Strainer (NBC) April 21, 1949 - 30 minutes

CREDITS:
Producer-director, Anton M.Leder; writer, John C. Copeland; music composed by Lucien Morewick; conductor, Lud Gluskin.

CAST:
Betty Grable (Jeanne Dunn); Raymond Burr (Detective).

SYNOPSIS:
Jeanne (Grable) is an hysterical young girl being questioned by a Detective (Burr) about a death. Thinking that it must be her ailing, meddling Mother's death, Jeanne confesses that when her whining Mother objected to her new romance, she plotted to kill her with an overdose of a prescribed medicine in her daily tea. The Detective, however, finally reveals to the frightened girl that her boyfriend, Ted, is the victim. He accidentally drank the poison meant for the Mother, served from the lethal copper tea strainer.

COMMENTS:
- In a near-monologue, Grable enacts an unusually dramatic role. Portraying a young girl who is hounded by a crippled Mother who resents having to give up her dreams of success in the entertainment world, Grable possibly found some subtext from her own life and relationship with her mother, Lillian.

**R53.    Lux Radio Theater** - When My Baby Smiles At Me, (CBS), April 25, 1949 - 60 minutes

CAST:
Betty Grable (Bonny); Dan Dailey (Skid).

**R54.    Lux Radio Theater** - Mother Wore Tights (CBS) November 11, 1949 - 60 minutes

CAST:
Betty Grable (Myrtle); Dan Dailey (Frank).

COMMENTS:
- Mother Wore Tights was repeated for the third time on the Lux Radio Theatre on January 4, 1951 with Dan Dailey and Mitzi Gaynor, doing Grable's role.

**R55.    Camel Screen Guild Players** - The Shocking Miss Pilgrim, (CBS) April 27, 1950 - 30 minutes

CAST:
Betty Grable (Cynthia Pilgrim); Dennis Morgan (John).

**R56.   Screen Director's Playhouse** - <u>When My Baby
Smiles At Me</u>, (NBC) May 5, 1950 - 30 minutes

CREDITS:
Director, Walter Lang.

CAST:
Betty Grable (Bonny); Dan Dailey (Skid).

**R57.   Lux Radio Theatre** - <u>Wabash Avenue</u> (CBS)
November 13, 1950 - 60 minutes

CAST:
Betty Grable (Ruby); Victor Mature (Andy); Gerald Mohr
(Uncle Mike).

RECORDING: <u>Wabash Avenue</u> "MEDLEY" on "Betty Grable" (D2)

**R58.   Lux Radio Theatre** - <u>My Blue Heaven</u> (CBS)
February 25, 1952 - 60 minutes

CAST:
Betty Grable (Molly Moran); Dan Dailey (Jack Moran).

# Stage Appearances

Betty Grable's stage appearances were varied and extensive for someone primarily regarded as a film actress. She enjoyed performing in front of live audiences and spent many years in live theater work. Her "Nightclub" appearances are listed in a section of their own.

**S1.**     **Odeon Annual Christmas Show** - Odeon Theater, St. Louis, 1922 or 1923

COMMENTS:
- Each year, Mary Institute, the exclusive school Betty attended, held an annual Holiday Show. Celebrities such as Jack Haley, Bert Wheeler, Frank Fay and Jane Froman would appear as the "M.C." Grable reminisced about making her Odeon debut, in toe shoes, as a piece of coral, "Dressed in pink" (B120).

**S2.**     **Missouri Theater**, St. Louis - 1924

COMMENTS:
- In one of many of the "Amateur Night" contests young Betty participated in, she won the Charleston contest. Bert Wheeler, of the comedy team "Wheeler and Woolsey," was the "M. C." This was to be the beginning of a long association with the team.

**S3.**     **Ambassador Theater**, St. Louis - 1928

COMMENTS:
- Twelve year old Betty danced in the chorus of a vaudeville show starring fourteen year old Ginger Rogers and Ed Lowry.

**S4.**     **Hillstreet Theater**, Los Angeles - 1931 (2 week run)

COMMENTS:
- Betty danced in the chorus of a musical revue featuring Paul Ash and his Orchestra. Years later, she would often tell

the story about auditioning for the show as one of her "most embarrassing moments." (B195).

## S5.     Tattle Tales - "A Sophisticated Musical Revue"

Pre-Broadway tour:
Lobero Theater, Santa Barbara, December 26 - 27, 1932
Belasco Theater, Los Angeles, December 29 - January 25, 1933
The Hollywood Playhouse, January 27 - February 30, 1933
Curran Theater, San Francisco, April, 1933
Broadway:
Opened at the Broadhurst Theater on June 1, 1933 - closing in 28 days.

CREDITS:
Pre-Broadway Tour:
Producer, Felix Young; directors, Richie Craig, Jr.,Barry Trivers; sketches by Benny Rubin, Frank Fay, Howard Jackson, Barry Trivers, Richie Craig, Jr.; musical numbers staged by LeRoy Prinz; music director, Arthur Kay; orchestrations, Howard Jackson; set designer, Charles Dahl.

Broadway:
Producer, Frank Fay; directors, John Lonergan, Frank Fay; book by Nick Copeland and Frank Fay; choreographers, LeRoy Prinz, Danny Dare and John Lonergan; costumes, Elizabeth Zook; music director, Arnold Johnson; orchestrations, Howard Jackson; set designer, Martin.

SONGS:
(Pre-Broadway Tour)
"THE COURT OF LOUIS XV" by Howard Jackson
"PERCY WITH PERSERVERANCE" by Eddie Ward, George Waggoner
"I'LL TAKE AN OPTION ON YOU" by Ralph Rainger, Leo Robin
"HE PASSED ME BY" by Ralph Rainger, Leo Robin
"CHAINS" by Howard Jackson, Leo Robin
"BREAKING UP A RHYTHM" by Eddie Ward, George Waggoner
"WALKING IN THE WIND" by Harry Akst, Leo Robin
"EXTRA MAN" by Harry Akst, Edward Eliscu
"YOU'VE GOT TO DO BETTER THAN THAT" by Harry Akst, Edward Eliscu
"ECHO" by Harry Akst, Edward Eliscu
"THE FIRST SPRING DAY" by Howard Jackson, Edward Eliscu
"BLAME IT ON LOVE" by Eddie Ward, Edward Eliscu

(Broadway)
"ANOTHER CASE OF THE BLUES" by Richard Myers, Johnny Mercer
"BREAKING UP A RHYTHM" by Edward Ward, George Waggoner
"THE COURT OF LOUIS XIV" by Howard Jackson
"THE FIRST SPRING DAY" by Howard Jackson, Edward Eliscu
"HANG UP YOUR HAT ON BROADWAY" by Edward Ward, George Waggoner, Grossman, Silverstein
"HARLEM LULLABY" by Willard Robinson
"HASTA MANANA (SO THIS HAVANA)" by Howard Jackson
"HERE WE ARE TOGETHER" by Edward Walsh, Frank Fay, William Walsh
"I'LL TAKE AN OPTION ON YOU" by Ralph Rainger, Leo Robin

"JIG SAW JAMBOREE" by Eddie Bienbryer, William Walsh
"JUST A SENTIMENTAL TUNE" by Louis Alter, Max and Nathaniel Lief
"PERCY WITH PERSEVERANCE" by Edward Ward, George Waggoner
"SING AMERICAN TUNES #1" by Harry Akst, Edward Eliscu
"SING AMERICAN TUNES #2" by Edward Ward, Frank Fay, William Walsh
"YOU'VE GOT TO DO BETTER THAN THAT" by Harry Akst, Edward Eliscu

CAST:
Pre-Broadway Tour:
Frank Fay, Janet Reade, Guy Robertson, Paal & Leif Rocky, Betty Grable, Charles Kaley, Ruth Gillette, Miller & Mack, Florence Robinson, Olin Howard, Dorothy Douglas, Don Cumming, Lucille Day, Nick Copeland, Adele Cutler, Three Blue Blazes, Charlotte Neste, Luis Arnold, The Callahans, George Mayo, "Poggi" and "The Tattle Tales" (female Chorus).
In San Francisco, Barbara Stanwyck joined the show.

Broadway:
Frank Fay, Barbara Stanwyck, Lillian Reynolds, James Mack, Nick Copeland, John Dryer, Don Cummings, Ray Mayer, Betty Doree, Beuvell and Miss Tova, Evelyn Page, Edith Adams, Jerry Archer, Dorothy Dell, Mary Barnett, Les Clark, Helen Eades, William Hargrave, Jane Morgan, Betty Nylander, Eddie Byrnbrian.

REVIEWS:
Tour:
VARIETY,1.3.33: "This is the best west-coast revue presented in the past five years. Unstinted in costuming and scenery, it is strong in every department except the most important - humor...Betty Grable is cute in her first number, but becomes monotonous in the second."

LOS ANGELES, 1.7.33 - Florence Hayden, Source unknown: "I would emphasize my gratitude to...Betty Grable, about whom, were I of appropriate gender and age I could be all H. and B. Above all, I'm thankful for my wild, unrestrained laughter which was 'just what I wanted.'"

LOS ANGELES EXAMINER, 1.6.33 - Edwin Schallert: "You can count on being entertained by '<u>Tattle Tales</u>.' In fact, here is the best show of its kind that has been staged here in several seasons, made so because it has plenty of clever people...included Betty Grable...and others."

Broadway:
VARIETY, 6.6.33: "In the sticks show gathered considerable money. That's where it belongs."

COMMENTS:
- At the auditions, Betty and Lillian reminded Frank Fay of their appearance together at the Odeon Theater (S1).
- Often erroneously printed that she appeared in the show under the name of "Frances Dean," Betty, fifth billed,

appeared under her real name and was featured in the show, as playbills of the period verify. She sang "I'LL TAKE AN OPTION ON YOU" with Charles Kaley; "WALKING IN THE WIND," also with Kaley and "YOU'VE GOT TO DO BETTER THAN THAT" with Florence Robinson and sixteen "Tattle Tales."
- Ted Fiorito saw Betty in the show in San Francisco and hired her to sing with his band. The show continued to New York without Betty.
- The show was reportedly financed by Barbara Stanwyck, who was Frank Fay's wife and trying desperately to make his career and their marriage work out. Unfortunately, Fay's drinking not only jeopardized the show, but also the marriage. Fay continued to walk out on the show during its West Coast tryout tour. To bolster box office receipts, Stanwyck appeared in the show, performing dramatic scenes.
- From American Musical Theatre by Gerald Bordman (B17): "...and the season concluded with a single June entry. Tattle Tales had begun life as a Hollywood revue assembled by the witty compere, Frank Fay...it had suffered through a troubled career even in Los Angeles with both Fay and Stanwyck out of the cast for various reasons. It offered New York nothing it had not seen beter done and, with the hottest summer recorded ...the show discreetly departed after a month."
- Paal and Leif Rocky, androgynous dancing male twins, had made a sensation in Paris in French Revues and were brought back to America to appear in the show. Betty did not dance with them in the show, but reportedly appeared at the Christie Hotel in Hollywood with them during the show's run (N2).

## S6.    Ted Fiorito Orchestra - 1933-34

St. Francis Hotel, San Francisco, March 13 - June 1, 1933 (Grable joined the band approximately May 15)
Miramar Hotel, Santa Monica - exact date unknown
Municipal Auditorium, San Diego, June 21, 1933 (one night)
Loew's State Theatre, Los Angeles, June 22 - July 12
Long Beach, Santa Monica - exact dates unknown
St. Francis Hotel, San Francisco, September 12 - October 28, 1933 (the band "doubled" during this engagement at various theaters)
Warfield Theatre, San Francisco, September 1 - 12, 1933
Fox Theatre, San Francisco, September 30 - October 28, 1933
Ambassador Hotel, November 12 - December 24, 1933 (taking a "leave of absence" from the St. Francis Hotel)
St. Francis Hotel, January 1 - 14, 1934
Ambassador Hotel, Los Angeles, January 15 - March 4, 1934
St. Francis Hotel, San Francisco, March 6 - 17, 1934
Ambassador Hotel, Los Angeles, March 19 - June 3, 1934
(Grable left the band sometime during this engagement, being replaced by June Marlow)

CAST:
Ted Fiorito, Leif Erickson, Muzzy Marcelino, Betty Grable, Bill Carey, Fiorito Debutantes, thirteen band members.

REVIEWS:
VARIETY, 6.27.33: "Taking the stage for half an hour, the Ted Fiorito band clicks with the same brand of music that has made them the Coast's fav radio and dance music dispensers...Betty Grable supplies the femme solo work and does a neat tap at the windup." (Loew's State, L.A. appearance).

VARIETY, 9.5.33: "Betty Grable, cute blonde, chants coupla numbers, and Bill Carey does several hot tunes." (Warfield, S.F. appearance).

VARIETY, 10.10.33: "Here's an odd one. A stage show without a stage. And well done and liked, at that...Fiorito conducts while residing at the piano, bringing on the cute Betty Grable for several numbers, Leif Erickson, who baritones to plenty of applause." (Fox, S.F. appearance).

COMMENTS:
- After seeing Betty in <u>Tattle Tales</u> (S5), Fiorito asked her to join his band. She reportedly said:"There's just one thing you ought to know. I can't sing." Fiorito answered with "Who is going to notice?"(B166). She replaced Vera Van in May, 1933. Miss Van went to New York to sing with Bert Lown's Band. Coincidentally, June Haver also sang with the Fiorito Band several years later.
- Betty joined the Band in May and during July and August, appeared with them in the films <u>Sweetheart of Sigma Chi</u> (F24) and <u>Air Tonic</u> (F25).
- The tour itinerary alternated between hotel and vaudeville appearances, often with the group "doubling." The St. Francis Hotel in San Francisco was Fiorito's "homebase." He was given a extended leave of absence from November 12 - December 24th when the hotel enlarged the dance/showroom to accomodate the large crowds he drew. He moved his band to the Coconut Grove at the Ambassador Hotel in Los Angeles during this time.
- Fiorito was also doing weekly radio broadcasts for MJB Coffee from San Francisco and Grable probably appeared on the show, but the author was unable to verify these dates.
- The bandleader's name is alternately spelled "Fiorito", "Fio-Rito" and "Fio Rito" in ads for personal appearances and films. The author has chosen "Fiorito."

## S7.    Hal Grayson Band

Biltmore Hotel, Los Angeles, February 19 - March 2, 1934

COMMENTS:
While Fiorito and his troupe were filming <u>20,000 Sweethearts</u> for Warner Brothers, Betty briefly joined Grayson's band.

## S8.    Jay Whidden Orchestra

Mark Hopkins Hotel, San Francisco; Miramar Hotel, Santa Monica; Biltmore Hotel, Los Angeles - exact dates unknown, Fall, 1934

COMMENTS:
This appearance is mentioned in several books and newspaper articles, but the author was unable to find verifying information. As the Fiorito, Grayson and Whidden bands all played the same venues on the West Coast, it is conjectured that Grable perhaps subbed for another singer, or made brief appearances with the Whidden Orchestra between film assignments. The world of "Big Bands" was a small one and vocalists and instrumentalists often moved from band to band for short appearances. In one of her later 20th Century Fox press releases, Grable herself had this to say about her appearances with the Whidden Band in reference to the lack of interest RKO was showing in her:" I gave 'em the absence-makes-the-heart-grow-fonder routine once more, this time with the Jay Whidden Orchestra, playing San Francisco, and once again, history repeated itself." She was called to report back to RKO for film work.

## S9.   Vaudeville

Palace Theater, Chicago, January 25 - 31, 1935

CAST:
Bert Wheeler, Harry Jans, Betty Grable, Virginia Bacon, Dormonde Brothers, Slim Timblin, Annie, Judy and Zeke.

CONTENTS:
A bill of several variety acts, concluding with Wheeler, Jans and Grable perfoming nineteen minutes of comedy, songs and dances.

REVIEWS:
VARIETY, 1.29.35, listed under "New Acts": "With a full load of showmanship and a dose of capable vaude material, this shapes as a variety act of consequence from every angle ...Wheeler sings and dances; so does the eye-filling Miss Grable, Jans towers over the two of 'em, handling the foil excellently. All in all it's an all-round vaudeville act that will smack 'em anywhere."

COMMENTS:
- Harry Jans, who usually worked with partner Harold Whalen, temporarily teamed up with Bert Wheeler for this one week personal appearance. After the run, Wheeler and Betty returned to Hollywood (and Woolsey) to begin filming The Nitwits (F34).

## S10.   Hollywood Secrets - vaudeville unit, December 20, 1935 - April 2, 1936

Itinerary:
Loew's Century Theater, Baltimore, December 20, 1935
Loew's Fox Theater, Washington,D.C., December 27
Location unverified, January 3, 1936
Keith's Theater, Boston, January 10
Palace Theater, Cincinatti, January 17
Michigan Theater, Detroit, January 24
Uptown Theater, Chicago, January 31

RKO Shubert, Cincinatti, February 2
Oriental Theater, Chicago, February 9
Mainstreet Theater, Kansas City, February 21
Ambassador Theater, St. Louis, February 28
RKO Palace Theater, Cleveland, March 6
Rochester, New York (theater unknown), March 13
Keith Theater, Syracuse, March 20
Roxy Theater, New York, March 27

CREDITS:
Producers, Fanchon and Marco; sketch written by Warren
Wilson.

CAST:
Jackie Coogan, Betty Grable, Dick Winslow, Walter Mc Grail,
Josephine Dix, Warren Wilson (M.C.), Chiquita, California
Collegians.

SYNOPSIS:
A musical revue with songs, dance numbers, featured
instrumental numbers and a lengthy comedy sketch about making
films in Hollywood - complete with camera, boom, mixing panel
and kleig lights in which Coogan and Grable portrayed film
stars trying to remember their lines amidst technical
troubles.

REVIEW:
VARIETY, 12.25.35: "Very nifty show all around, and so far
removed from usual sort of entertainment provided by units
that it looks like biz. Has names in Jackie Coogan and Betty
Grable; swell production, and highly novel presentation and
idea...Miss Grable bowls 'em over, having looks and hoofing
ability, plus aptitude for singing a fair number. She and
Coogan pair up for some hoofing during which she sadly
outtrots him...unit carries...complete setup for staging
'Hollywood openings' in front of the the theatres
played...about a half car of scenery, and three stagehands
tour with show."

MOTION PICTURE DAILY, 12.23.35.:"The unit, with the aid of
camera and studio paraphernalia (sic), shows how films are
produced, how dubbing is handled and the use of the
playback."

COMMENTS:
- Using movie set props from the "Motion Picture Hall of Fame
Show" at the 1935 "California Pacific International
Exposition" which opened May 29 in San Diego, producers
Fanchon and Marco created an unique touring unit. The show
was offered to theaters for $4,500 per week. These shows were
called "Flesh Shows" in the industry, referring to the "live"
aspect.
- In Variety's "Picture Grosses" section of January 1, 1936,
the show's success was headlined: "Coogan, Grable with
'Wilderness' $26,500 in Wash" referring to their "swell"
grosses appearing in conjunction with the MGM film Ah,
Wilderness at the Fox Theater in Washington. They also drew
$9,000 over the house average at the Century in Baltimore.

Betty Grable and Jackie Coogan in a publicity pose for their 1935-36 vaudeville tour of *Hollywood Secrets*. Photo from Los Angeles Examiner.

- During their appearance in St. Louis, <u>Variety</u> reported (3.4.36): "Probably only house to benefit from big sale was Ambassador when Coogan and Grable were made stars of an extensive newspaper campaign and radio-hookup. This being her home town, newspapers opened up generously and with all department stores carrying boxes about Betty and her fiance, it looked like one of the best advertising tie-ups any house in this burg has had for years...Her St. Louis friends will help house to a $16,000 week. Good."
- For their appearance at New York's prestigious Roxy, they took out a full-page ad in <u>Variety</u>, proclaiming them as "Hollywood's Sweetest Sweethearts" in "14th week of a limited personal appearance tour.(Miss Grable...through courtesy RKO studios.)" The appearance was deemed responsible for the $28,000 week's receipts.
- After New York, Coogan and Grable returned to film work in Hollywood, but the <u>Hollywood Secrets</u> unit continued to tour with the California Collegians, Warren Wilson, Chiquita and Dawn O' Day taking Betty's place, while <u>Variety</u> erroneously reported that "unit was headed until recently by Jackie Coogan and Toby Wing."

**S11.    Vaudeville,** Treasure Island Music Hall, San Francisco Golden Gate Exposition, July 21 - 28, 1939

CAST:
Jack Haley, Betty Grable, Rubinoff, Alec Templeton.

COMMENTS:
- To promote this appearance, appealing photos of Grable were printed and they caught Darryl F. Zanuck's eye. He signed her to a contract at 20th Century Fox (B19).
- They did three shows daily and the appearance was booked through MCA.
- On January 11, 1939, <u>Variety</u> had reported that Bobby Sanford was preparing his Hollywood Restaurant's (a failing New York nightclub) floor show for presentation houses on the vaudeville circuit. "Deal on with Betty Grable to head the unit." This tour never materialized.
- In a review of "New Acts" on June 29, 1939, when Jackie Coogan appeared at the State Theater in New York with Bob Hope, <u>Variety</u> said: "...and there was a comedy long-distance call from Betty Grable (Mrs. Jackie) asking what 'The Kid' did with the $5 she gave him last week."

**S12.    Vaudeville,** "Grable - Rochester" Unit, August 4 - October 5, 1939

Itinerary:
Warner Earle Theater, Washington D.C., August 4, 1939
Steel Pier, Atlantic City, August 11
Hippodrome Theater, Baltimore, August 18
Warner Earle Theater, Philadelphia, August 25
State Theater, Hartford, September 1
Coronada Theater, Rockford, September 11
Palace Theater, South Bend, September 13
Palace Theater, Cleveland, September 15
RKO Shubert Theater, Cincinatti, September 22

Chicago Theater, Chicago, September 29

CAST:
Eddie ("Rochester") Anderson, Betty Grable, Frankie Masters Orchestra, Lane and Ward, Trado Bros., Marion Francis, Frank Gaby (Steel Pier), Leighton Noble Orchestra (Phil.), Bud Hughes Co., Holland and Hart (Chi.), Art Jarrett(Chi.)

REVIEW:
VARIETY,8.9.39 - Craig: "This is not only sock entertainment, but it's hot for the marquee and will be for some time wherever Rochester (Eddie Anderson) has scored in Man About Town (Par.) and so long as the Betty Grable - Jackie Coogan romance makes news. Both play up to their current fame fully in their performance...First of two big moments come with entrance of Miss Grable in plain white crepe gown, striking tan and load of honey hair. She goes right into 'IT'S ALL YOURS' followed by 'DON'T WORRY 'BOUT ME' sung sentimentally and then hot. Biz about 'meeting the boys in the band' is followed by 'here's how they do it in Hallywood' stuff, in which she mauls Masters (Band leader - author). Finishes vocalizing 'THE LADY IN LOVE' with skirts up for strut-and-bumps exit. She has to repeat three times."

COMMENTS:
- On June 20, 1939 Variety reported that MCA was offering a "Radio" vaudeville unit with Phil Harris, Betty Grable and Rochester to sell at $8,500 per week. Phil Harris did not join the uni and it went out as the "Betty Grable-Eddie ("Rochester") Anderson" unit. Also in Variety, on October 11, 1939, under the headline "Vaude's Many Film Names," an article stated that Hollywood's economy was creating a stage boom with such stars  as Constance Bennett, Martha Raye, Joe E. Brown, Dick Powell, Chester Morris, Claire Trevor, Bela Lugosi, Stuart Erwin, Ann Sheridan, Mary Wilson, Dead End Kids and Freddie Bartholomew appearing throughout the country in the fall of 1939 at movie theaters and attracting big box office.
- In the "Picture Grosses" section of Variety during this tour, Betty made headlines with "Grable-Rochester Build 'Glamour' to $23,500...Marquee names add up...for a first week since return of flesh attractions" (8.30.39 - show appeared with the film Glamour Girls); "Grable-Rochester Boost 'Hawaiaiian' To 16G in Cleve" (9.19.39 - referring to the live unit appearing with Hawaiian Nights);"'Fraud'-Grable-Roch. Head for Big $17,000 "(9.25.39 - the film was The Magnificent Fraud) and "Bette's 2d Plus Grable's Big $44,000" (10.4.39 - referring to Old Maid starring Bette Davis in its second week at the theater, boosted by the box-office appeal of Grable and Company).
- This was to be a very active period for Miss Grable, moving from personal appearances into rehearsals for Dubarry Was A Lady. From her appearance at the SF Exposition with Jack Haley, the signing of her contract with Fox, the tour with "Rochester," her divorce from Coogan and being asked to join Dubarry, it all happened within four months.

## S13.    Dubarry Was A Lady

Tryout Tour:
Shubert Theatre, New Haven - November 9, 1939
Boston - November 13, 1939
Forrest Theatre, Philadelphia - November 27, 1939
Broadway:
46th Street Theatre - opened December 6, 1939 and ran 408
performances. (Grable left the show in June, 1940)

CREDITS:
Presented by B.G. DeSylva; directed by Edgar MacGregor;
book by Herbert Fields and B.G. DeSylva; choreographed by
Robert Alton; settings and costumes; Raoul Pene DuBois;
musical director, Gene Salzer; orchestrations, Hans
Spialek; music and lyrics by Cole Porter.

Musical Numbers:
Act One:
"OPENING" - Ensemble
"EV'RY DAY A HOLIDAY" - Harry, Alice, Ensemble
"IT AIN'T ETIQUETTE" - Louis and Vi
"WHEN LOVE BECKONED" - May
"COME ON IN" - May and Ensemble
"DANCE" - Alice and Harry
"DREAM SONG" - Male Quartet (Douglas Hawkins, Peter
Holliday, Robert Herring, Carl Nicholas)
"MESDAMES ET MESSIEURS" - Chorus Ladies
"GAVOTTE" - Alisande and Ensemble
"BUT IN THE MORNING, NO!" - Du Barry and King Louis
"DO I LOVE YOU" - Du Barry and Alexandre
"DO I LOVE YOU" REPRISE - Du Barry and Zamore
"DANSE VICTOIRE" - Johnny Barnes
"DANSE EROTIQUE" - Audrey Palmer and Men
"DUBARRY WAS A LADY" - Entire Company

Act Two:
"DANSE TZIGANE" - Alisande, Roy Ross, Jack Stanton and
Ballet
"GIVE HIM THE OO-LA-LA" - Du Barry
"WELL, DID YOU EVAH!" - Alisande and Captain
"DANSE" - Audrey Palmer, Jack Stanton, Roy Ross
"IT WAS WRITTEN IN THE STARS" - Alexandre
"L'APRES MIDI D'UN BOEUF" - Zamore and the Dauphin
"KATIE WENT TO HAITI" - May and Company
"KATIE WENT TO HAITI" REPRISE - May and Alex
"FRIENDSHIP" - May and Louis
"FINALE" - Entire Cast

CAST:
Bert Lahr (Louis Blore/His Royal Majesty, The King of
France); Ethel Merman (May Daly/Mme. La Comtesse Du Barry);
Benny Baker (Charley/The Dauphin of France); Betty Grable
(Alice Barton/Mmme. La Marquise Alisande DeVernay); Charles
Walters (Harry Norton/Capt. of the King's Guard); Jean
Morehead (Vi Hennessey/Mme. La Duchesse De Villarde);
Ronald Graham (Alex Barton/Alexandre); Hugh Cameron (Bill
Kelly/Le Duc De Choiseul); Harold Cromer (Florian/Zamore);

Jack Stanton (Rene); Roy Ross (Pierre).

SYNOPSIS:
May Daly (Ethel Merman) is a nightclub singer at the Club
Petite, where Louis Blore (Bert Lahr), the washroom attendant
at the Club, is smitten with the brassy headliner. When Louis
wins the Irish Sweepstakes, he hopes that his new-found
wealth will help him win May's favors. He accidentally takes
a powerful "Mickey Finn," intended instead for newspaper
columnist and romantic rival Alex Barton (Ronald Graham), and
dreams that he is King Louis XV in an extended dream
sequence. May appears as the Countess Dubarry and the rest of
the denizens of the New York nightclub materialize as various
members of the Court. With the show moving back and forth
from the opulent Royal French Court to the glittering 1930's
nightclub setting, the slim plot offers many opportunities
for spectacle, comedy, song and dance before Louis wins May.

REVIEWS:
VARIETY, 11.15.39 - Bone. "Plays Out of Town" - Reviewed
during the New Haven run: "Of the featured Betty Grable -
Phil Regan pair, the former does the better job, pleasing
with looks, dancing and warmth from the acting
angle...There's nothing for Hollywood in Dubarry except
possibly an idea; any film adaptation would require
practially a complete rewriting for a Hays office nod."

NEW YORK TIMES, 12.7.39. - Brooks Atkinson: "The performers
supply more pleasure than the authors and composer. Betty
Grable and Charles Walters, who would also be featured in a
free society, dance and sing with remarkable dash...Betty
Grable who is best known to us as a movie actress makes in
this musical her legitimate stage debut. She is a clever
dancer and can sing a song. She proves that she has something
else besides a pretty face."

DAILY MIRROR, 12.8.39 - Walter Winchell: "...there is Betty
Grable's vivacious hoofing and pretty face and figure to make
up for the draggy story. Miss Grable's numerous appearances
do so much to relieve matters".

NEW YORK HERALD TRIBUNE, 12.7.39 - Richard Watt Jr.: "Miss
Betty Grable, the movie girl, is pictorially helpful, which
is no doubt all that is necessary for her to be in this
particular case."

SOURCE AND DATE UNKNOWN - Sidney Whipple: "Mr. De Sylva has
brought Miss Betty Grable from the Coast...incidentally, Miss
Grable was not what I expected and feared. She was actually
good, despite Hollywood training."

VARIETY, 12. 13. 39 - Ibee.: "Betty Grable is something of a
revelation as a new soubrette. It is her first time on
Broadway, but she performs like a thoroughbred. Not so blonde
as pictured, Miss Grable is a lovely little trick who knows
her stuff in both songs and dances...Miss Grable has appeared
in vaude units, but it is probably the careful training as a
kid that stands her in good stead now."

COMMENTS:
- Betty, fourth billed, performed "WELL, DID YOU EVAH?" with Charles Walters, who went on to become a successful film choreographer and director. The song was finally put onto the screen in High Society (1956), performed by Bing Crosby and Frank Sinatra and directed by Walters. Walters had replaced Johnny Barnes in the role as the show reached New York. Barnes remained with the show in a smaller dance role.
- Betty made the cover of Life magazine (12.11.39) because of her sensational appearance in the show. In the accompanying article, they wrote: "Betty Grable, 22, takes her first bow as a musical-comedy actress in Du Barry Was A Lady. She sings a little, dances some, and is the best-looking thing in the show."
- Betty left the show in June 1940 to begin filming Down Argentine Way (F52) and was succeeded by Ruth Bond. When the show toured, Betty's role was played by Frances Williams.
- Cole Porter paid Betty the ultimate compliment by using her name in the lyrics of "LET'S NOT TALK ABOUT LOVE" from Let's Face It, 1941 and in "CHERRY PIES OUGHT TO BE YOU" from Out of This World, 1950.
- The show was purchased by MGM and as Hollywood was determined to do at that time, nearly completely rewritten with a new musical score and Lucille Ball playing Merman's role, Red Skelton in Lahr's role and Virginia O'Brien (huh?) playing Grable's.
- Phil Regan was replaced after New Haven by Ronald Graham when it was discovered that Regan's voice, usually miked in Vaudeville, did not carry in the theatre. He was paid $6,000.
- Adele Jergens and Janis Carter, two lovely blonde ladies who would go on to film careers at Columbia, were also in the cast.

**S14. Vaudeville** - Chicago Theater, October 25 - November 8, 1940

CAST:
Betty Grable, Ken Murray, Milton Charleston, Park and Clifford, Betty Atkinson.

COMMENTS:
- This vaudeville bill appeared in conjunction with the prestigious premiere of Cecil B. De Mille's North West Mounted Police at the historic Chicago Theatre. Held over for two weeks, it was a "Balaban and Katz" revue. Direct from her success in Down Argentine Way, which was playing at another first-run theater in the city, Grable is billed as "Screen and Broadway's darling of tantalizing delight!" Murray and Grable followed Laurel and Hardy's personal appearance at the theater.
- Harry James opened at the "Panther Room" in the College Inn in Chicago on October 18 and it is here where Betty first met Harry. Victor Mature had taken her there for dinner, where she also met band vocalist Dick Haymes (B207). Carmen Miranda was appearing at the Chez Paree nightclub also at the same time.

**S15.   Act with Harry James** - Chicago Theater, November 27 - December 3, 1953; Michigan Theatre, Detroit, December 5 - 11, 1953.

CREDITS:
Staged & choreographed by Billy Daniel; costumes, Travilla.

CAST:
Betty Grable, Harry James, Billy Daniel, the Harry James Music Makers featuring Buddy Rich, Tommy Gumina, Lewis and Van, a dancing-singing group of three boys and two girls.

REVIEWS:
CHICAGO AMERICAN, date unknown - Sam Lesner: "The film critics agreed that Betty stole the show from Marilyn Monroe and Lauren Bacall in...How To Marry a Millionaire ...but on the Chicago's stage Mr. and Mrs. James compliment each other with such theatrical finesse that a logical sequel to Betty's Cinemascopic debut could be 'How To Marry a Bandleader and Stay Happy.' In person James and Betty are offering the smoothest and best balanced one hour stage show we have seen here in many a season."

DETROIT FREE PRESS, date unknown: "There's only one thing wrong - it's too short. From the first note of the famous band leader's trumpet to the colorful finale, the audience applauded for more."

COMMENTS:
- Billed as "First time together on any stage," the duo reportedly earned $45,000 for their Chicago Theater appearance.
- Louella Parsons covered the Opening of the show and was quoted in Dorothy Manners' syndicated November 28, 1953 column: "Betty is strictly sensational. The line waiting to go into the Chicago Theater for the first show at 10 a.m. extended around the block. If she was nervous, as she told me she was, she didn't show it."
- The act was staged by Billy Daniel, who had choreographed Grable's film Wabash Avenue (F76) and became a close friend of the actress. He appeared onstage in several dance sequences with Betty (B166). Betty performed "HONEY MAN" from Wabash Avenue as part of the show.
- At the Chicago Theater, the live stage show alternated with screenings of MGM's Half A Hero with Red Skelton, Jean Hagen and Polly Bergen.

**S16.   Guys And Dolls**

Arabian Room, Dunes Hotel, Las Vegas; opened December 21, 1962 - June, 1963
Coconut Grove Playhouse, Miami, May 5 - 26, 1964

CREDITS:
Producer, Sammy Lewis; director, Ed Greenberg; choreographer, Roy Wilson; book by Jo Swerling and Abe Burrows; based on "The Idyll of Miss Sarah Brown," a short

story by Damon Runyon; music and lyrics by Frank Loesser.

Musical Numbers:
Act One
"FUGUE FOR TINHORNS" - Nicely-Nicely, Benny, Rusty Charlie
"FOLLOW THE FOLD" - Sarah, Arvide, Calvin, Agatha, Priscilla
"THE OLDEST ESTABLISHED" - Nathan, Nicely-Nicely, Benny, Ensemble
"I'LL KNOW" - Sarah and Sky
"A BUSHEL AND A PECK" - Adelaide and the Hot Box Girls
"ADELAIDE'S LAMENT" - Adelaide
"GUYS AND DOLLS" - Nicely-Nicely, Benny
"HAVANA" - Ensemble
"IF I WERE A BELL" - Sarah
"MY TIME OF DAY" - Sky

Act Two
"TAKE BACK YOUR MINK" - Adelaide and the Hot Box Girls
"ADELAIDE'S LAMENT" (Reprise) - Adelaide
"MORE I CANNOT WISH YOU" - Arvide
"THE CRAP GAME DANCE" - Male Ensemble
"LUCK BE A LADY" - Sky and Crap Shooters
"SUE ME" - Nathan and Adelaide
"SIT DOWN, YOU'RE ROCKIN' THE BOAT" - Nicely-Nicely and Ensemble
"FOLLOW THE FOLD" (Reprise) - Mission Meeting Group
"MARRY THE MAN TODAY" - Sarah and Adelaide
"GUYS AND DOLLS" (Reprise) - Entire Company

CAST:
Betty Grable (Miss Adelaide); Dan Dailey (Sky Masterson); Lola Fisher (Sarah Brown); Alan Gale (Nathan Detroit); James Maloney (Arvide Abernathy); Slapsie Maxie Rosebloom (Big Jule); Jack De Lon (Nicely-Nicely Johnson); Eddie Hanley (Harry the Horse); Robert Lamont (Angie the Ox); Jerry Mann (Benny Southstreet); Rudy Vejar (Rusty Charlie); Robert Gallegher (Lt. Brannigan); Robert Piper (Calvin); Nancy Helm (Agatha); Ingeborg Kjeldsen (General Cartwright); Bill Reddie and His Orchestra (Dunes engagement).

SYNOPSIS:
A romantic fable populated by Damon Runyon's fanciful New York characters, the plot revolves around two love stories. Gambler Sky Masterson (Dan Dailey) uncharacteristically falls in love with prim Salvation Army worker, Sarah Brown (Lola Fisher) after he vows he can win any girl with a large bet with his cronies. Miss Adelaide (Grable), the star of the "Hot Box" nightclub, has been engaged to Nathan Detroit (Alan Gale) for fourteen years - without any date for the altar. In a series of comic plot complications as Nathan tries to find a spot for his large floating Crap Game and Sarah tries to win Sky's "Soul" - but loses her heart, the two couples eventually join for a "Double Wedding" at the show's conclusion.

REVIEWS:
LOS ANGELES TIMES, 12.24.62 - John L. Scott: "Dailey, who has performed the role of Masterson previously, fits it nicely. His singing and dancing talents serve him well and he looks the part. Miss Grable handles Adelaide, who has been engaged for 14 years to Nathan Detroit and is looking for marriage action, very creditably...Guys and Dolls in for an indefinite engagement should keep the Arabian Room filled. It's still a most happy music show."

LAS VEGAS SUN, 12. 30. 62: "And what casting. Everyone was perfect...The usually blase first night audience stood on their feet en masse and demanded a repeat."

VARIETY, 12. 24. 62 - Duke: "Betty Grable has come out of a two-year semi-retirement and tackled something she's never done - a starring role on the musical comedy stage, and she's a delightful success...She plays the part as if it were written for her...After the preem, casino execs were laying bets that she would be offered a role on Broadway."

COMMENTS:
- Guys and Dolls opened on Broadway in 1950 and became one of the classics of the American musical theater. A perfect blending of story, song and dance, the show enhanced the careers of the original creative team, composer Frank Loesser, writer/director Abe Burrows and choreographer Michael Kidd. In 1992, a revival of the show became Broadway's hottest ticket, making a major star out of Faith Prince, who played Grable's role.
- The role of "Miss Adelaide" was a perfect stage vehicle for Grable - allowing her to do the things she did best and meeting all of her fan's expectations. The role is funny, vulnerable and loveable, allowing Grable to perform four comic songs, as well as a strip tease in "TAKE BACK YOUR MINK." This number alone must have been the production's highpoint as Grable stripped down to reveal her still-beautiful figure and famed legs. Grable's role was originally performed on the stage and screen by Vivian Blaine, whose appearance in the hit gave her career new acclaim. Betty was to play the role of "Miss Adelaide" onstage throughout the next six years in various productions.
- In 1953, a newspaper columnist had written about casting for the film version of the show: "Bill Goetz and the Music Corporation of America were cooking up the biggest deal that's ever been put together here, and if it doesn't bring gold to the box office, nothing will. For 'Guys and Dolls' they want Clark Gable as the hero; Bob Hope in the Sam Levene part; Betty Grable as the Brooklynese blonde; Jane Russell for the Salvation Army lassie, and Tony Martin - for good measure. There isn't a banker in the world that wouldn't back this set-up."

**S17.   Guys And Dolls** - Melodyland, Anaheim, September 1963

CREDITS:
Producers, Sammy Lewis and Danny Dare; associate producer,

David Shelley; director, David Tihmar; choreographer, Jack
Beaber; music director, Boris Kogan; scenery designed by
Hal Shafer.

CAST:
Betty Grable (Miss Adelaide); Hugh O'Brian (Sky Masterson);
Mary Ann Mobley (Sarah Brown); Lew Parker (Nathan Detriot);
Ben Lessy (Harry the Horse); Eddie Hanley, Tiger Joe Marsh;
Dale Malone (Nicely-Nicely Johnson); William Fackiner
(Arvide Abernathy); Ida Mae MacKenzie (General Cartwright).

REVIEW:
ANAHEIM BULLETIN, 9.25.63 - Larry Swindell: "Betty Grable is
there, too. She of the magnificent lower extremities (the
rest of her is merely excellent; and yes, she still looks
like a million dollars), who rewrote the box office history
of Hollywood with a Technicolored quill...Despite her Goldwyn
Girl training and all those magnitudinous 20th Century Fox
production numbers, America's Betty has never qualified as
either a singer or dancer of high rank. But she is something
else: an Entity. Her stage display is conditioned by a
knowing approximation of self, and keeps a time-nourished
illlusion intact for the happy audience."

COMMENTS:
- Melodyland, a theater-in-the-round across the street from
Disneyland, was one of Southern California's four major
venues to attempt to bring live theater to Southern
California during the 1960's. Because of its proximity to
Hollywood, they presented such film stars as Betty Hutton and
Harve Presnell in Annie Get Your Gun, Jane Powell in The
Unsinkable Molly Brown and Betty in two shows. The "Boom"
quickly died however and the theater now is owned and
operated by a Christian Church.

**S18.    High Button Shoes** - Melodyland Theater, Anaheim,
September 29 - October 11, 1964

CREDITS:
Producers, Sammy Lee and Danny Dare; director, David
Tihmar; scenery, Hal Shafer; choreography, Zoya Leporska;
book by George Abbott and Phil Silvers (uncredited), based
on the novel "The Sisters Liked Them Handsome" by Stephen
Longstreet; music and lyrics by Jule Styne and Sammy Cahn.

Musical Numbers:
Act One:
"HE TRIED TO MAKE A DOLLAR" - Male Quartet
"CAN'T YOU JUST SEE YOURSELF IN LOVE WITH ME?" - Hubert &
Fran
"THERE'S NOTHING LIKE A MODEL 'T'" - Harrison, Sara
Longstreet, Fran, Henry Longstreet, Stevie, Chorus
"NEXT TO TEXAS, I LOVE YOU" - Hubert and Fran
"SECURITY" - Sara and Fran
"BIRD WATCHER'S SONG" - Sara and Singing Girls
"GET AWAY FOR A DAY IN THE COUNTRY" - Henry, Stevie, Chorus
"A SUMMER INCIDENT" - Dancing Corps
"PAPA, WON'T YOU DANCE WITH ME?" - Sara & Henry

"CAN'T YOU JUST SEE YOURSELF IN LOVE WITH ME?"(Reprise) - Harrison and Fran
"FINALETTO" - Entire Company

Act Two:
"ON A SUNDAY BY THE SEA" - The Singing Chorus
"THE MACK SENNETT BALLET" - Entire Company
"YOU'RE MY GIRL" - Hubert & Fran
"I STILL GET JEALOUS" - Sara & Henry
"YOU'RE MY BOY" - Harrison and Mr. Pontdue
"NOBODY EVER DIED FOR DEAR OLD RUTGERS" - Harrison, Hubert and Singing Boys
"CASTLE WALK/HE TRIED TO MAKE A DOLLAR" - Entire Company

CAST:
Dan Dailey (Harrison Floy); Betty Grable (Sara Longstreet); Glenn Turnbull (Henry Longstreet); John Craig (Hubert "Oggle" Ogglethorpe); Ben Lessy (Mr. Pontdue); Martha Stewart (Fran); Florence Sundstrum (Nancy); Colyer Dupont (Stevie Longstreet).

SYNOPSIS:
In 1913, in New Brunswick, New Jersey, con-man Harrison Floy (Dan Dailey) talks the Longstreet family (Grable, Glenn Turnbull, Martha Stewart and Colyer Dupont) into selling some valueless property. Floy takes the profits and runs off to Atlantic City with side-kick Mr. Pontdue (Ben Lessy) and the Longstreets in hot pursuit. After losing and regaining the money, Floy finally loses it for good by betting on the wrong team in a football game.

REVIEWS:
ANAHEIM BULLETIN, 10.2.64. - Larry Swindell: "'High Button Shoes' needs more than Dandy Dailey...Betty Grable pays a return visit to Melodyland, and a less happy one...She does not hinder the proceedings, but she's of no great help either...Miss Grable is so-so from start to finish, and her trademark charms are literally under wraps in this production...Mr. Dailey is a diamond very much in the rough...a corking good perfomance, but its effect is diluted by a book that is just not working anymore...Let us hope that Melodyland will soon lure Mr. Dailey back to appear in some other musical. Any other musical."

LOS ANGELES TIMES, 10.2.64 - Kevin Thomas: "The lovely Miss Grable sings the best song "PAPA, WON'T YOU DANCE WITH ME?" As enchanting an entertainer as ever, she nowadays performs only occasionally, so her presence in this musical, which is ideally suited to her personality, is a special treat."

SANTA ANA REGISTER, 10.1.64 - Ann Terrill: "'High Button Shoes' down at the heel...Betty Grable's role as Sara Longstreet was not one would call a prominent one."

COMMENTS:
- The show was a moderate success when it opened on Broadway in 1947, mostly due to the brilliant input of choreographer Jerome Robbins. His famed "MACK SENNETT BALLET" was recreated

and included in <u>Jerome Robbins' Broadway</u>.
- Grable's role was originally played by Nanette Fabray on
Broadway. Much to the expectent fan's surprise, her character
is not romantically involved with Dailey's, so their time
together onstage was limited. She did, however, perform two
of the show's most popular musical numbers: "I STILL GET
JEALOUS" and "PAPA, WON'T YOU DANCE WITH ME?" Despite
Grable's weak reviews, the role of "Sara Longstreet" was
sufficient enough to display Fabray's charms to wonderful
reviews. The show was done as a TV special on November 24,
1957 with Don Ameche, Hal March and Fabray, repeating her
stage success, for NBC.

## S19.   Hello Dolly!

First Tour:
Tivoli Theatre, Chattanooga, Tennessee, November 3 - 7,
1965
Knoxville Auditorium, Knoxville, Tennessee, November 9 -
13, 1965
Louisville, Kentucky (Theater and date unknown)
Columbus, Ohio (Theater and date unknown)
St. Paul, Minnesota (Theater and date unknown)
Omaha, Nebraska (Theater and date unknown)
Auditorium Theater, Denver, Colorado, December 15 - 20,
1965

Las Vegas Engagement:
December 23, 1965 - September, 1966, Riviera Hotel

Second Tour:
San Antonio, Texas (Theater and dates unknown)
Will Rogers Memorial Auditorium, Fort Worth, Texas,
September 27 - October 1, 1966
Municipal Auditorium, Kansas City, Missouri, October 3 - 8,
1966
Shubert Theatre, Chicago, Illinois, October 10 - December
10, 1966 (Replacing Eve Arden and her company)
Morris Civic Auditorium, South Bend, Indiana, December 13 -
17, 1966
Fort Wayne, Indiana, December 20 - 25, 1966
Municipal Auditorium, Columbus, Ohio (Dates unknown)
Charlotte, North Carolina (Theater and dates unknown)
Masonic Temple, Scranton, Prennsylvania, January 10 - 14,
1967
Morris A. Mechanic Theatre, Baltimore, Maryland, January 16 -
February 4, 1967
The Playhouse, Wilmington, Delaware, February 6 - 10, 1967

Broadway Engagement:
St. James Theater, New York, June 12 - November 6, 1967

Additional appearances:
Atlanta and Toledo, Ohio, 1971 - replacing Pearl Bailey.

CREDITS:
Producer, David Merrick, directed and choreographed by
Gower Champion; assistant to the director, Lucia Victor;

dance assistant, Lowell Purvis; book by Michael Stewart; based on the play The Matchmaker by Thorton Wilder; scenery, Oliver Smith; costumes, Freddy Wittop; music and lyrics by Jerry Herman (unless noted otherwise).

Musical Numbers:
Act One
"I PUT MY HAND IN" - Dolly and Company
"IT TAKES A WOMAN" - Vandergelder
"PUT ON YOUR SUNDAY CLOTHES" - Cornelius, Barnaby, Dolly, Ambrose, Ermengarde, The People of Yonkers
"RIBBONS DOWN MY BACK" - Mrs. Malloy
"MOTHER HOOD" - Dolly, Vandergelder, Mrs. Malloy, Minnie Fay, Cornelius, Barnaby
"DANCING" - Dolly, Cornelius, Barnaby, Minnie Fay, Mrs. Malloy, Dancers
"BEFORE THE PARADE PASSES BY" (by Charles Strouse and Lee Adams) - Dolly, Vandergelder and Company

Act Two
"ELEGANCE" - Mrs. Malloy, Cornelius, Minnie Fay, Barnaby
"THE WAITER'S GALLOP" - Rudolph and Waiters
"HELLO, DOLLY!" - Dolly, Rudolph, Waiters and Cooks
"IT ONLY TAKES A MOMENT" - Cornelius, Mrs. Malloy, Prisoners and Policemen
"SO LONG DEARIE" - Dolly and Vandergelder
"HELLO, DOLLY!" (Reprise) - Dolly and Vandergelder
"FINALE" - Entire Company

CAST:
(Tour and Las Vegas): Betty Grable (Dolly Levi); Max Showalter (Horace Vandergelder); Billie Hayes/Harriet Lynn (Minnie Fay); Arthur Bartow/Peter Walker (Cornelius Hackl); June Helmers (Irene Malloy); Danny Lockin (Barnaby Tucker); Judy Jenson/Beverlee Weir (Ermingarde); Richard Hermany/Philip Carlson (Ambrose Kemper); Patricia Sauers/Judy Drake (Ernestina); Robert Hocknell (Rudolph).

(New York): Betty Grable (Dolly Levi); Max Showalter (Horace Vandergelder); Alix Elias/Leland Palmer (Minnie Fay); Will McKenzie/Richard Hernay (Cornelius Hackl); June Helmers (Irene Malloy); John Mineo/Harvey Evans (Barnaby Tucker); Alice Playten/Andrea Bell (Ermingarde); Richard Hermany/David Evans (Ambrose Kemper); Patricia Sauers (Ernestina); Dan Marriman (Rudolph).

SYNOPSIS:
Dolly Levi (Grable), a bothersome widowed "Matchmaker" in turn-of-the-century New York, is trying to find a suitable mate for pompous Yonkers merchant, Horace Vandergelder (Max Showalter). She also takes on as clients Cornelius (Bartow/Walker) and Barnaby (Danny Lockin), Vandergelder's young clerks, who have run away to New York City for adventure. After many comic plot complications, Dolly realizes that Vandergelder is the man she needs in her life and makes her own "Match."

REVIEWS:
First Tour:
THE CHATTANOOGA TIMES, 11.4.65 - Louise McCamy: "The audience lost its heart to Miss Grable's adorable Dolly. She gave the part such authenticity, such sweetness and such gallantry under the funny surface - and she was exquisite to watch - nobody was satisfied with merely six curtain calls she took."

THE DENVER POST, 12.16.65 - Del Carnes: "The show's star, of course, is Betty Grable...A younger generation watching her command of the stage will have no difficulty understanding why she was the sweetheart of World War II. She is still a sweetheart and I adore her profusely."

Las Vegas engagement:
LOS ANGELES TIMES, 12.29.65 - John L. Scott: "As Dolly Gallagher Levi, who sets her cap for the pompous Horace Vandergelder (Max Showalter), Miss Grable came on strong although somewhat handicapped at the press opening by an ailing throat. She gave a spirited perfomance and for the most part avoided a carbon copy impression of the original Dolly, Carol Channing."

Second tour:
CHICAGO'S AMERICA, 10.11.66 - Roger Dettmer: "...leans upon its leading lady, and Miss Grable - in spite of a cold that inhibited her singing last night - carried on famously...Miss Grable is much more than a tradition, she's a trouper, and...a damn' fine Dolly. Not, perhaps, the wistful widow of Librettist Michael Stewart's soliloquies, but you can't have everything. And don't need it."

WILMINGTON EVENING JOURNAL, 2.7.67 - Philip Crosland: "Grable's legs star in 'Hello Dolly'... last night seemed to be suffering from a cold or hoarseness, is unable to project above the orchestra and background chorus enough to assert command over the stage."

Broadway:
NEW YORK TIMES, 6.14.67 - Vincent Canby: "There was hardly a dry eye in the house as the audience, according to the lyrics, welcomed her back where she belongs...At fifty, Miss Grable looks great. The dimples in the Pretty Girl are intact. The outlines of the Pretty Girl figure have filled in a bit - those appendages that Dad used to call gams are still magnificent from the occasional glimpses we get beneath the turn-of-the-century gowns...Miss Grable's Dolly Levi lacks a certain free-wheeling wackiness and the kind of incredible dominating self-assurance that would make the farce as funny as it is frantic. Thus the high comic moments of this version are left almost entirely to the subsidiary characters...When, however, the widowed matchmaker sets her cap for the merchant of Yonkers and tells us something about herself in Mr. Herman's 'BEFORE THE PARADE PASSES BY,' she adds a most appealing dimension to the show. This quality is Miss Grable's principal contribution."

NEW YORK POST, 6.14.67: "Betty Grable was the best received

'Dolly' of them all."

VARIETY, 6.14.67: "Betty Grable is Broadway's fourth Dolly, but perhaps it's second only after Carol Channing in quality of performance. She is an artful mugger, a seductive hoofer and a limited but effectively husky-voiced singer. What she lacks in expertise, she recoups in presence."

COMMENTS:
- In <u>Betty Grable,The Reluctant Movie Queen</u> (B207), the author writes that Betty was only one of many contenders for the role of "Dolly Levi." A supposed stroke of luck happened when she went to the Riviera Hotel in Las Vegas to see Eddie Fisher perform and he introduced her from the audience, asking: "How would you people like to see Betty Grable right here in 'Hello Dolly'?" The ovation was so overwhelming that the Riviera Hotel management cast their vote for Betty.
- Betty inherited the chorus of the Mary Martin company of the show, which had played Vietnam. She rehearsed for several weeks in New York and then joined the company in Chattanooga, Tennesee. Grable performed the show in a bright red wig.
- The show has a varied and long life as a theatrical property. In 1835, author John Oxenford wrote <u>A Day Well Spent</u>, which was reworked by Viennese author Johann Nestroy as <u>Einen Jux Will er Sich Machen</u> (<u>He Wants to Have a Lark</u>) in 1841. American author Thornton Wilder turned the plot into <u>The Merchant of Yonkers</u> in 1938 and seventeen years later rewrote it as <u>The Matchmaker</u>. This version had a successful Broadway run in 1955 starring Ruth Gordon and was filmed by Paramount in 1958, starring Shirley Booth, Shirley Maclaine and Anthony Perkins. The musical version opened on Broadway in 1964, starring Carol Channing and was filmed by Twentieth Century Fox in 1969. Grable's agent, Kevin Pines, campaigned to interest 20th Century Fox in teaming Grable with Dan Dailey for the film. Barbra Streisand was cast in the role.
- After the rigors of her Las Vegas engagement (two shows per night, seven days a week for nine months) her throat and voice weakened. Most reviews after Las Vegas mention that she was "suffering" from an opening night cold or laryngitis. Many performers have claimed "Vegas Throat" (a combination of the dryness in the Nevada air and the strong air-conditioning used in all of the hotels), but Betty's condition was possibly a combination of vocal overwork, arid atmosphere, her smoking and the disease which would finally claim her.
- For the Las Vegas engagement, the show was trimmed by 35 minutes to create a "tab" version which could be presented twice nightly. Initially booked at the Riviera Hotel for 16 weeks, the show was extended to a nine month run.
- While Grable was rehearsing, Harvey Church, who had appeared in her nightclub act, visited rehearsals and overheard Lucia Victor (Gower Champion's assistant) remark: "Once this broad gets into the part, she will be the best "Dolly" of them all. Channing is a caricature, Ginger Rogers mugs - but Grable has the heart!"
- When the show opened at the St. James Theater in New York, Betty, following Martha Raye in the title role, returned triumphantly to Broadway after an absence of twenty eight years.

Betty Grable and Max Showalter in *Hello Dolly!* at the Riviera Hotel, Las Vegas. Collection of Bob Izoz.

## S20.   Guys and Dolls

Westbury Music Fair, Westbury, Long Island, June 18 - 23, 1968

Shady Grove Music Fair, June 25 - 30, 1968
Honolulu Concert Hall, July 23 - August 4, 1968

CREDITS:
Producer, Herb Rogers; director, Jack Sydow; choreographer, Larry Stevens.

CAST:
Westbury and Shady Grove: Betty Grable (Miss Adelaide); Joey Adams (Nathan Detroit); Norwood Smith (Sky Masterson); Louise O'Brien (Sarah Brown); Tom Pedi (Harry the Horse); Johnny Brown (Benny Southstreet); Ronn Carroll (Nicely-Nicely Johnson).

Honolulu: Betty Grable (Miss Adelaide); Danny Dayton (Nathan Detroit); Seth Riggs (Sky Masterson); Rosemary Rainer (Sara Brown); Jim Demarest (Nicely-Nicely Johnson).

REVIEWS:
SOURCE AND DATE UNKNOWN - Leo Seligsohn (Westbury Music Fair version): "To say that the years melted away as Miss Grable sang and danced would be a slight exaggeration. Yet, she still has a nice legs and a bouncy way about her. The big moment came when, in the number "TAKE BACK YOUR MINK," she whipped off her furs, and, wearing the kind of black, frilly little thing she has worn in umpty-um movies, did a swinging song-and dance routine. She got the long, loud applause that the middle aged reserve for old troupers. Miss Grable's voice was a bit husky but pleasant..."

SOURCE AND DATE UNKNOWN - Hank Mc Cann (Westbury Fair version): "Yes, Betty Grable looked fine...slim, active and propelled on the famous legs that can easily be compared with the best anywhere. She put pep in her role and she has mastered the idiom of the Damon Runyon chorus queen."

HONOLULU STAR-BULLETIN, 7.24.68 - Phil Mayer: "An admirably tacky, expertly wise-cracking performance by gaunt Danny Dayton...and Betty Grable's beautiful legs were the best thing in 'Guys and Dolls' when it opened last night ...Unfortunately, Miss Grable seemed hoarse."

## S21.   Belle Starr

Tryout:
(under the title The Piecefull Palace) Alhambra Theatre, Glasgow, Scotland, April 1 - 21, 1969
Palace Theatre, London, April 30, 1969 - 16   performances

CREDITS:
Producers, Jerry Schafer, Rory Calhoun, Clarke Reynolds; director, Jerry Schafer; book by Warren Douglas; music director and vocal arranger, Maurice Arnold; musical

staging and choreography by Jack Card; fight scenes staged by Dick Shane; lighting; Michael Nothern; set designer, Peter Proud; costumes, David Crowther; music by Steve Allen; lyrics by Steve Allen, Warren Douglas and Jerry Schafer.

Musical Numbers
Act One:
"STORY SONG"- Sloane, Malone, Lucas, Rowdy Joe, San Francisco Sam
"BELLE" - Belle Starr and Company
"HAPPY BIRTHDAY TO VEGAS"- Belle Starr and Company
"WE'RE GONNA MAKE HISTORY"- Belle Starr and Company
"THE GUNFIGHTER'S BALLAD"- Billy the Kid
"A LADY DON'T DO"- Belle Starr, Calamity Jane and Company
"A LADY DON'T DO(Reprise)" - Saloon Girls

Act Two:
"LADYLIKE LADY LIKE ME" - The Company
"IT TAKES ONE TO KNOW ONE"- Belle Starr and Company
"DIRTY, ROTTEN, VICIOUS, NASTY GUYS"- Killer Malone, L.D. Sloane, Turkey Lucas, San Francisco Sam, Rowdy Joe
"DANCE POLKA"- The Company
"GEE, YOU'RE PRETTY" - Billy The Kid and Company
"I'M A LADY"- Calamity Jane and Boys
"THE BIGGEST PAIR OF 38'S IN TOWN" - Belle Starr and Company
"NEVER HAD THIS FEELING BEFORE" - Jesse James
"FINALE" - Entire Company

CAST:
Betty Grable (Belle Starr); Valerie Walsh (Calamity Jane); Ray Chiarella (Jesse James); Blayne Barrington (Billy the Kid); Michael Hawkins (Killer Malone); Thick Wilson (Ned Buntine); Terry Williams (Boliver Shagnasty); Frank Blanch (Joker); Keith Galloway (P.U. Luie); Mostyn Evans (Sheriff J.J. Sarno); Angela Rider (Big Buttes); Ron Eagleton (Luscious); Maggie Vickers (Flea); Tina Scott (Charity); Georgia Gee (Dumb Nora); Tammy Filhart (Cowboy Maggie); Delia Sainsbury (Rotary Rosie); Peter Honri (Professor); Ross Petty (Skeeter); Walter Cartier (Bat); Sally Mates (Lady Jane); Mike Rowlatt (L.D. Sloane); Richard Manuel (Turkey Lucas); Marc Urquhart (San Francisco Sam); John Alexander (Rowdy Joe); Malcom Cheeseman (Odie Thudpucker); Yolanda Callaghan (Lulu).

SYNOPSIS:
Belle Starr (Grable) is the owner and operator of the "Piecefull Palace," a rough-and-tumble saloon and house of prostitution in Las Vegas, Nevada in 1869. The Sheriff (Mostyn Evans) declares amnesty amongst the battling gunfighters and invites all of the local ruffians to celebrate the first birthday of the town. Billy the Kid (Blayne Barrington) and Jesse James (Ray Chiarella) vie for Belle's favors, while Calamity Jane (Valerie Walsh) adds humor with her tomboy ways and when Billy The Kid realizes her charms, she changes into a lady. The "Bad Guys," led by Killer Malone (Michael Hawkins) eventually start a huge

fight, which ends with the Saloon burning to the ground. The citizens all join together and rebuild "The Palace."

REVIEWS:
GLASGOW DAILY RECORD, 4.2.69. - Ruth Wishart: "They stood and clapped and they cheered at Glasgow's Alhambra last night. Not just for Betty Grable the superstar who cried a little as she thanked them...The show itself is the rootinest tootinest package of mock-Western madness...Betty Grable is a revelation. I saw the lady rehearsing in London, and to be honest the drab surroundings and daytime gear did nothing much for her. Fully made-up and clad in revealing black velvet that they didn't buy in any sale, she looks sensational...Her low husky voice is more than sexy enough...She is on-stage virtually non-stop and doesn't put an elegantly-turned ankle wrong."

GLASGOW EVENING TIMES, 4.2.69 - Jack House: "Betty Grable can't act for toffee, and she can't sing either. But she has personality and beautiful legs. That's maybe enough."

SCOTTISH DAILY EXPRESS, 4.2.69 - Mamie Crichton: "Flowers and curtain calls, storms of applause and the floods of nostalgia made Glasgow's salute to Betty Grable last night 'the highlight of her whole career.' These words in her short speech, charged with emotion, came after the rollicking premiere of The Piecefull Palace - one more glamourous night in the history of the Alhambra, soon to disappear."

VARIETY 4.23.69 -   Gord.: "Betty Grable, on her European stage bow, comes over with all the attractive now-how of the longtime trouper...had the oldsters among her admirers applauding and even younger ones who were moppets when she was a star standing in their seats to give her an ovation."

EVENING STANDARD, 5.2.69: "..a weak voice that not even the microphones could aggrandize, a timid wiggle masquerading as voluptuousness and the wholesome appeal of Miss Vanilla Ice Cream of 1936."

DAILY MAIL, 5.2.69 - Barry Norman: "Excruciating rubbish, wonderfully bad...her famous legs are well matched, pretty and able to dance effortlessly for several seconds at a time."

COMMENTS:
- Originally titled The Piecefull Palace for its tryout in Glasgow, Scotland, the show gave Grable the reason to visit Europe for the first time. While the reviews were mostly lethal, the audiences adored her, giving her six curtain calls on Opening Night in London. Betty's "profile" in the souvenier program included: "Betty's only regret about coming to Europe is parting from her black Tibetan terrier, Kato, who is in quarantine at the moment." Grable adored her pets.
- The choreography by Jack Card and spectacular stage settings by Peter Proud and special effects (ie. the burning to the ground of the Saloon) received the best press notices of all. Damned by some of the reviewers for being smutty, the

show was perhaps ahead of its time in terms of sexual honesty and humor. Audiences and critics possibly did not want to see Grable associated with something they felt was "off-color." The song "THE BIGGEST PAIR OF 38'S IN TOWN" might have been inspired by the salacious ad copy for <u>Beautiful Blonde From Bashful Bend:</u> "She's got the biggest six-shooters in town!"
- When close friend Bob Isoz visited London to see the show, he remarked about the colorful costumes. Betty admitted that she had designed most of them herself, although did not receive credit.
- Ginger Rogers was also appearing on the West End in <u>Mame</u> at the time.
- A bootleg audio tape exists of the show recorded from backstage. In it, Grable sounds very husky and hoarse.

## S22.    Born Yesterday

Stock tour schedule for the Summer of 1970:
Little Theatre, Sullivan, Illinois - May 19(three weeks)
Kenley Star Theatre, Wichita, Kansas - June 9
Canal Fulton Summer Theatre, Canal Fulton, Ohio - June 16 (two weeks)
Candlewood Theatre, Fairfield, Conn. - June 30
Pocono Playhouse, Mountainhome, Penn. - July 6
Famous Artist Playhouse, Syracuse, N.Y.- July 13
Town and Country Playhouse, Rochester, N.Y. - July 20
Ivoryton Playhouse, Ivoryton, Conn.- July 27
Falmouth Playhouse, Falmouth, Mass. - August 3
Lakewood Playhouse, Skowhegan, Maine - August 10
Gilford Playhouse, Gilford, New Hampshire - August 17
Hyde Park Playhouse, Hyde Park, N.Y. - August 24
Playhouse on the Mall, Paramus, N.J. - September 1
Tappan Zee Playhouse, Nyack, N.Y. - September 7

CREDITS and CAST:
Unverified, other than play written by Garson Kanin and Grable played the role of "Billie Dawn."

SYNOPSIS:
Junk tycoon Harry Brock has hired Paul Verall to tutor his malaprop-dropping mistress Billie Dawn (Grable). Brock is embarrassed by Billie's lack of knowledge as he attempts to get questionable Government support for his wheelings and dealings in Washington. Verrall is actually a writer who plans to expose Brock's shady operations. As Billie gains knowledge, she also gains power, falling in love with her teacher and helping to expose her tyrannical "Sponsor" - finally triumphantly squelching him with the brains she always had, but was never required to use.

COMMENTS:
- The play by Garson Kanin opened on Broadway February 4, 1946 and ran for 1,642 performances. Jean Arthur originally had the role of "Billie Dawn" and Judy Holliday was her understudy. When Arthur withdrew from the play, Holliday got the role - and Broadway immortality. The property was purchased by Columbia Studios for its reigning queen, Rita Hayworth, but she married Aly Kahn and relocated in Europe.

Dozens of actresses were announced and tested for the role, with Columbia mogul Harry Cohn finally relenting and giving the role to Holliday, teaming her with William Holden and Broderick Crawford. She won an Oscar for "Best Actress" in 1950 for the role. Her successful film and stage career was halted when she died prematurely at the age of 43 in 1965. The property was refilmed in 1992 by Disney with Melanie Griffith and Don Johnson.
- The role of "Billie Dawn" is a close kin to "Miss Adelaide" in Guys and Dolls. Both of the ladies are ditzy, terminally blonde chorus girls with comically irritating vocal patterns whose street smarts allow them to triumph and capture great audience sympathy.
- Betty was also announced as the star of Plaza Suite by Neil Simon, to tour the Midwest in 1971, produced by Bill Dempsey and Roy Franklin of Theatre Projects Co. For unknown reasons, the project did not happen with Miss Grable.

### S23.    This  Is  Show  Business  - St. Louis Municipal Opera, August 30 - September 5, 1971

CREDITS:
Producer, Edward M. Greenberg; orchestra director, Anton Coppola; musical coordinator, Harper MacKay; staging, Scott Salmon; choreographic consultant, Ted Cappy; sets and lighting, C. Murasaki.

CAST:
Betty Grable, Dorothy Lamour, Don Ameche, Chita Rivera, Dennis Day, Rudy Vallee, Eileen Schauler, Nolan Van Way, Gilbert Price, Avind Harum, Municipal Opera Singing and Dancing Ensemble.

SYNOPSIS:
"A passing parade of stage and filmusical highlights through the years..." (from the program).

COMMENTS:
- A final, triumphant return to her hometown. In 1991, she was posthumously inducted into the "Muny Hall of Fame" (M9).

### S24.    BORN YESTERDAY

1972 and 1973 appearances:
Chicago and Mill Run Playhouse, September, 1972 (Exact dates unknown)
Alhambra Dinner Theatre, Jacksonville, Florida, January 24 - March 23, 1973

CREDITS:
Alhambra Dinner Theatre: Director, George Ballis; set design by Ham Waddell; play written by Garson Kanin.

CAST:
Mill Run: Betty Grable (Billie Dawn); Ray Rayner (Harry Brock); Dick Valentine (Paul Verrall); Bob Thompson (Ed Devry); Art Kassul (Senator Norval Hedges); Virginia Lee Gilbert (Mrs. Hedges/Helen); Robert Ruth (Eddie Brock);

Haskell Gordon (Hotel Manager).

Alhambra Dinner Theatre: Betty Grable (Billie Dawn); Art
Kassul (Harry Brock); Jess Osuna (Paul Verall); Matt Conley
(Ed Devry); Lee H. Doyle (Senator Norval Hedges); Duchess
Tomasello (Mrs. Hedges/Helen); Pat Cronin (Eddie Brock).

REVIEW:
SOURCE AND DATE UNKNOWN - Elaine Fallon (Mill Run
engagement): "Whether you're too young to remember Betty
Grable as THE Pin-Up Girl of World War II or whether you're
too old to ever forget her, you'll enjoy '<u>Born Yesterday</u>'
which opened at the Mill Run Playhouse...As Bille Dawn, the
tart turned smart, she captures the same aura of not-so-dumb
blonde that the late Judy Holliday originated. Her comedy is
great - and so is that figure!...The audience had its share
of stars among them on opening night too. Jackie Coogan
...was...applauding his one-time wife."

COMMENTS:
- Grable vainly performed in the comedy in various locations,
although her illness made it very difficult for her. The run
at the Alhambra Dinner Theatre was extended many times, due
to its success.
- She also planned to star in <u>No, No Nanette</u> in Australia in
1972, but her illness prevented her. Cyd Charisse replaced
her in the company.

Betty Grable and Dan Daily in a publicity photo for their Las Vegas engagement in *Guys and Dolls*, 1963. Collection of Bob Izoz.

# Nightclub Appearances

The author has created a separate listing for Grable's nightclub appearances, as they were abundant and highly successful. As her film career ended, she appeared consistently in cabarets from 1956 to 1961, enjoying the adulation of fans and live audiences after nearly sixteen years behind the unresponding camera. This body of work also allowed a major change of address for her and her family, leaving Hollywood and settling in Las Vegas. The evolution of a nightclub act is complicated, so many of the cast members, contents and creative personnel were difficult to verify. Even those who worked with her had memory lapses trying to recall the changes, transitions and appearance dates and locales.

**N1.** **The Golden Gate**, St. Louis, 1931 or 1932

Donn Arden remembers seeing young Betty perform at a club in St. Louis. Announced as "Direct from films and on her way to Broadway," Arden related that she really "worked the room," singing "GET HAPPY" and easily moving from table to table, charming the customers. Since this was during Prohibition, the club was a "Speakeasy." Judging from Grable's work schedule at the time, this was probably in 1932, just prior to Tattle Tales (S5), hence the mention of "Broadway." Mr. Arden's memory is impeccable.

**N2.** **Christie Hotel,** Hollywood, 1932

Harriet Parsons, the daughter of Hollywood gossip columnist Louella Parsons, related a story about this appearance in Spero Pastos' biography of Grable (B151). She stated that the first time she ever saw Grable was in a song and dance act with the Rocky Twins at the hotel, obviously during the run of Tattle Tales (S5), in which she worked with the twins. The Christie Hotel is still standing at 6724 Hollywood Blvd., now owned and occupied by the Scientology religious group.

**N3.** **El Rancho Vegas** - February 16 - March 14, 1956

CREDITS:
Staged and choreographed by Jack Cole.

CAST:
Betty Grable, Harry James, Buddy Rich, Jack Costanzo, Mr. Ballantine (featured comic), Buddy Bryan, Bill Skipper, Ted Fiorito and His Orchestra, The Harry James Music Makers, The El Rancho Cover Girls.

CONTENTS:
"I WISH I COULD SHIMMY LIKE MY SISTER KATE" (Opening); "I DON'T WANT TO WALK WITHOUT YOU;" "CUDDLE UP A LITTLE CLOSER".

REVIEW:
LAS VEGAS SUN, "Vegas Daze and Nites",2.20.56 - Ralph Pearl: "Grable doesn't even wait for the curtains to come to a complete halt before she's out there center stage shimmying like somebody's sister named Kate...Betty returns to bring down the drapes and most of the house with a highly undressed bit of terpsichore."

HOLLYWOOD REPORTER, 2.17.56 - Les Devor: "Atmosphere could well be the one word to describe the El Rancho Vegas Opening of the Betty Grable and Harry James show. Betty Grable's first Las Vegas stage entrance was heralded by four male dancers who carried her on after a few minutes of warm-up terp. The grand entrance was effected by means of a huge jewel box, from which were extended BG's famous gams. As the big box came to rest and the lid was lifted, the luscious Miss Grable came into view."

COMMENTS:
- Betty and Harry were contracted by the El Rancho Vegas from 1956-1960 to perform ten weeks per year. This act also played Harrah's Tahoe.
- In the ad in the Las Vegas Sun for the World Premiere of the act, Betty is billed as "The Most Glamourous Personality the Motion Picture Industry Has Ever Produced."
- During the run, Mike Connolly's "Rambling Reporter" in the Hollywood Reporter noted: "Grable and James bought two percent of El Rancho Vegas" (March 7, 1956).
- On their closing day, March 15, 1956, Betty and Harry were sued by the El Rancho Vegas for $53,000 ($48,000 in salary advances and hotel rent from January 11 - March 15th.) They were paid $12,750 weekly but had used four bedrooms and five cottages housing Lillian, family, two managers, band members and guests during the rehearsal and performance period (B111).

**N4.**    **Desert Inn**, Las Vegas - December 31, 1957 - January 30, 1958

CREDITS:
Conceived, created and produced by Donn Arden.

CAST:
Betty Grable, Dave Barry (featured comic); Art Johnson

(production singer); Donn Arden Dancers (production dancers); "The Boys" (Ray Baxter, Ken Chertok, John Drexel, Jim Hodge); Carlton Hays Orchestra.

CONTENTS:
Appearing in a luxurious fur wrap, Betty sang an "Opening Medley":"JUST IN TIME," "THE LADY'S IN LOVE WITH YOU;" "THERE HE GOES, HE'S MINE;""I'M JUST LUCKY I GUESS;" and "ALL THE WAY" before she began performing tunes from her films. Each section was introduced by her singing "Producers." Songs: "CUDDLE UP A LITTLE CLOSER;" "CHICAGO;" "I'M IN LOVE WITH YOU, HONEY;" "SWEET ROSIE O'GRADY;" "EVERYBODY LOVES MY BABY;" "PUT YOUR ARMS AROUND ME, HONEY;" "K-K-K-KATIE;" "CAROLINA IN THE MORNIN';" "AIN'T SHE SWEET?;" "YES SIR, THAT'S MY BABY;" "JA DA;" "YES, WE HAVE NO BANANAS" and "KATIE WENT TO HAITI."

REVIEWS:
LAS VEGAS SUN, 1.4.58: "The first ten minutes of Betty Grable's new song and dance act at the Desert Inn had me biting at my finger nails like a guy who'll eat anything. Ten minutes and Betty had yet to show her world famous gams. And just when it got to a point where I could stand it no longer, Betty came out in a scanty thingamajig, her famous gams revealed for one and all to see."

HOLLYWOOD REPORTER, 1.2.58 - J.H.: "...a warm welcome to Betty Grable who appeared for the first time in a long time without trumpet man husband Harry James. Miss Grable ran the gauntlet of scenes from her technicolored musical splashes of a decade ago."

COMMENTS:
- This solo act was conceived, produced and staged by acclaimed "Nightclub Master," Donn Arden. Not remembering that they had attended grammar school together in St. Louis, Grable came to him in 1957 for his help. He related that she had no ideas of her own about what she should perform and was completely pliable and cooperative. The act was structured so that she appeared at her glamourous best in the "Opening;" segued into a humorous piece of special material ("I'M JUST LUCKY I GUESS") which she performed as a mock-striptease; changed to a very quiet moment on a stool while she sang "ALL THE WAY" and then moved into the "Film Hit Medley" which closed the show. The act was conceived so that Grable always appeared with a featured comic, a special Arden production number, a featured female who could perform The Dolly Sisters songs with her and a group of four male dancers.
- This act also played the Auto Show in Memphis, Tennessee and Puerto Rico.

**N5.    Moulin Rouge**, Hollywood, March 20 - April 2, 1958

CAST:
Betty Grable, "The Grable Grabbers" (Ray Baxter, Ken Chertok, John Drexel, Jim Hodge), Flo Walters, Donn Arden dancers, Toni Dalli.

REVIEW:
LOS ANGELES HERALD EXAMINER, 3.21.58 - Harold Hildebrand: "Don't be surprised if 20th Century Fox remakes some of the Betty Grable musicals - starring Betty Grable. That is, if any of the studio executives take in her current engagement at the Moulin Rouge...Betty has lost none of the warm girlish charm for which she is so well remembered. Unpretentious, without affectation or chi-chi, she projects the familiar Grable effervescence."

HOLLYWOOD REPORTER, 3.21.58 - Hank Grant: "One thing certain, Betty Grable's a sharp showman. Hers is a tightly knit 30-minute act, smartly designed so necessary for the huge confines of the Moulin Rouge."

HOLLYWOOD REPORTER 3.31.58 - "Rambling Reporter" by Mike Connolly: "Oh that Betty Grable - she had the weekend Moulin Rougers smackdab in her pretty palm singing the Oscar-winning "ALL THE WAY"...Betty's seven new costume changes all reveal her real-gone gorgeous gams, for which let us give thanks."

COMMENTS:
- The act was titled "Memories" and was presented as part of the regularly scheduled Donn Arden production.

**N6.    Desert Inn**, Las Vegas, June 5 - 10, 1958

   CAST:
   Betty Grable, Flo Walters, Art Johnson, "The Grable Grabbers" (Ray Baxter, Ken Chertok, John Drexel, Jim Hodge).

REVIEW:
HOLLYWOOD REPORTER, 6.9.58 - Howard Brandy: "Betty Grable rates the pounding ovation the packed house gave her breezy 30-minute turn opening night. She completely captivates the tablers."

COMMENTS:
- She only played at the Desert Inn June 5-10, 1958, so that she and Harry could attend daughter Vickie's graduation from her Catholic high school.

**N7.    Cal Neva Lodge**, Lake Tahoe, July 4 - 24, 1958,

   CAST:
   Betty Grable, Flo Walters, Art Johnson, "The Grable Grabbers" (Ray Baxter, Ken Chertok, John Drexel, Jim Hodge), the Cal Neva Lovelies.

**N8.    Desert Inn**, Las Vegas, September 29 - October 8, 1958

   CAST:
   Betty Grable, Flo Walters, Art Johnson, "The Grable Grabbers" (Jim Hodge, Bobby Navarro, John Drexel, Harry Nafel).

REVIEW:
VARIETY, 10.4.58 - Duke: "Miss Grable admits early in the session that she doubts if anyone came to hear her sing, but her shortcomings in that department are over-balanced by her personality, her fancy footwork, and the fact, let's face it, that's she's Betty Grable."

## N9.    Latin   Quarter, Miami, January 22 - February 11,1959

CAST:
Betty Grable, Holger and Dolores, Jay Lawrence (featured comic), the Del Rubio Triplets, "Legs" Diamond, Tommy Wonder, Don Dellair, John Juliano, "The Grable Grabbers" (Jim Hodge, Bobby Navarro, John Drexel, Harry Nafel).

REVIEWS:
MIAMI BEACH SUN, 1.23.59 - Paul M. Bruun: "Miss Grable came to town and completely captured it all by herself...Betty Grable Came, Saw and Conquered, applauded by all, criticized by none."

THE MIAMI NEWS, 1.23.59 - Herb Kelly: "Betty Grable stood with a bouquet of roses in her arms and tears of happiness streaming down her cheeks, bewildered by the wild ovation she got at the close of her act on opening night at the Latin Quarter."

## N10.   Latin Quarter, New York, April 2 - 29, 1959

CAST:
Betty Grable, Dominique (featured magician); The Schaller Brothers (trampoline artists); Joyce Roberts, Pony Sherrell, "The Grable Grabbers" (Dean Campbell, Gene Hardy, Jim Hodge, John Drexel), Joe Lombardi Orchestra.

REVIEWS:
VARIETY, 4.8.59.- Trau.: "Self-effacing, agreeably simple and charming, she doesn't have to do much more than caper where dance is indicated or spout some lyrics that pass for thrushing...In medley, reprise-from-pix, Bumpsy-Daisy and Cuddle-Up routines, Grable & Co. have themselves a ball."

TIME, "Ham and Legs", 4.13.59: "..for a packed house on her opening in New York, it was the night the old nostalgia burned down...The kids down from prep school for Easter vacation were puzzled by this heroine of another generation...at 42 or thereabouts, Betty still has the legs everyone remembers - almost."

COMMENTS:
- It was publicized that costumes for the show cost $47,000.
- During this appearance at the Latin Quarter in New York, long-time fan Bob Isoz finally got to meet his idol. After the show, he went to the backstage entrance, but the Security Guard refused to allow him to go any further. He told Bob to write a note, which was taken to the dressing room. In a few minutes, one of the backstage staff appeared and the Security

Guard exclaimed:"My God, she'll see you!" Bob was escorted to the dressing room, where Grable, disheveled after her performance and dressed in her pink dressing gown with her hair in rollers, warmly greeted the young man. The many years of his sincere fan letters had made a great impression on her and for the next fourteen years, they remained close friends.
- The act was supposed to play the Tropicana Hotel in Las Vegas beginning June 24, 1959, but Grable cancelled, due to disagreements with management about who was to pay the people in her act. She was making $25,000 per week at the time for the act.

**N11.   Flamingo**, Las Vegas - September 10 - October 8, 1959

CREDITS:
Staged by Barry Ashton.

CAST:
Betty Grable, Harvey Stone (featured comic); Dick Humphreys, "Company" (Roberta Tennes, Joanne Patrick, Kim Hayward, Harvey Church), the Flamingoettes, Jack Cathcart Orchestra.

CONTENTS:
"I STILL GET A THRILL OUT OF YOU" - Opening, "I LOVE A NEW YORKER;" "CIRIBIRIBIN," "CUDDLE UP A LITTLE CLOSER;" "WHAT HAPPENED TO THE OLD SONGS?;" "KOKOMO, INDIANA;" "BETTIN' ON A MAN;" "I'LL REMEMBER YOU;" "BILLY;" "WOMAN WITHOUT A MAN;" "BIG DADDY."

REVIEWS:
HOLLYWOOD REPORTER,9.14.59 - Gene Tuttle: "Betty Grable toplines a bill which not only is fine entertainment - it can be seen by the entire family."

LAS VEGAS SUN, 9.12.59 - Ralph Pearl: "Unfortunately Betty's new song and dance act isn't as good as her old act was. It's too choppy and overly burdened with 'original material' which tends to give her act that artificial look."

COMMENTS:
- This act, which was a completely new one created by Barry Ashton, featured two men, two women and a male song-and-dance partner. The first one was Dick Humphreys and then, Bobby Van - who had achieved fame in the 1953 MGM films (Kiss Me Kate, Small Town Girl). He starred on Broadway in No, No Nanette (1971), as the TV host of Make Me Laugh (1979) and then met an untimely death in 1980 at the age of fifty.
- Fluff Le Coque, long time associate of Donn Arden, appeared in the act under the name of "Fluff Charlton." She remembers Grable as being great fun and very willing to spend most of her time with the "Kids" in the act. She related that Betty and Harry always travelled separately when the act moved locations because of their fear of a plane crash and its possible effect on their daughters.
- The act was booked in Australia, but when the bond did not arrive, Grable cancelled - one week before the scheduled

departure. She did not trust "foreign producers" and did not want to get the company stranded in Australia without money. Australian cast member Harvey Church was very disappointed not to visit his home.

- During this Flamingo engagement, Harry James and His music Makers were appearing at the hotel, in the Swingin' Stage Bar Lounge.

- The reference in the <u>Hollywood Reporter</u> review: "it can be seen by the entire family" refers to the controversy in Las Vegas regarding nude shows. Donn Arden's "Lido De Paris" had just opened to great acclaim at the Stardust Hotel and Vegas conservatives feared that all of the shows would follow suit with nudity.

**N12.**    **Mapes Showroom**, Reno - October 9 - 29, 1959

CAST:
Betty Grable, Lenny Gale (featured comic); Dick Humphreys, the Company (Mary Doyle, Chris Miller, Harvey Church, Kim Hayward), Jack Melick's Orchestra.

REVIEWS:
VARIETY, 10.14.59. - Long: "Miss Grable steps from a large ornate picture frame as the opening curtain parts, and the costume is designed to give an uncensored view of her famed gams. From the first moment on, she has full attention."

**N13.**    **Deauville Hotel**, Miami Beach - February 27 - March 25, 1960

CAST:
Betty Grable, Dick Shawn (featured comic), Dick Humphreys, the Company (Mary Doyle, Chris Miller, Steve Preston, Harvey Church), Henry Levine Orchestra.

REVIEWS:
VARIETY, 2.28.60: "It's a miniature musicomedy all the way...she...with invaluable aid of Dick Humphries (sic), who could be termed her partner in full sense of the act-word, displays a renewed flair for hoofery."

MIAMI BEACH SUN, 2.28.60 - Paul M. Bruun: "She has a much smarter and improved act over the one she presented last season at the Palm Island Latin Quarter...At the risk of being repitious, this is one of the best revues ever presented on a local night club stage."

**N14.**    **El Rancho Vegas**, Las Vegas - April 8 - 27, 1960

CAST:
Betty Grable, Dick Shawn (featured comic); Bobby Van, the Company (Fluff Charlton, Harvey Church, Steve Preston), Billy Daniel Dancers (production number).

CONTENTS:
"LET ME ENTERTAIN YOU;" "JUST IN TIME;" "KOKOMO, INDIANA;" "CUDDLE UP A LITTLE CLOSER;" "I'M IN THE MARKET FOR YOU;" "HONEY IN THE HONEYCOMB;" "BILLY;" "BETTIN' ON A MAN;"

"SILVER DOLLAR."

REVIEW:
VARIETY, 4.6.60 - Duke: "Betty Grable bounced back into the Opera House here with a new...package which incorporates some of the best material of her past Vegastints, plus some new material which makes the turn solid nitery fare."

HOLLYWOOD REPORTER, 4.11.60 - "Wheeling Around Las Vegas" by Colin McKinlay: "Betty Grable is playing to SRO crowds at the El Rancho Vegas where she teams with comic Dick Shawn. La Grable dispels any notion that she's slowing up as she rips through 28 action-packed minutes filled with songs and sillies. Her troupe of 10 includes Bobby Van, with whom she dances and sings some film numbers for which she is famous."

## N15.   **Municipal Auditorium**, Lubbock, Texas - April, 29 - 31, 1960

CAST:
Betty Grable, Bobby Van, the Company (Fluff Charlton, Harvey Church, Steve Preston), Harry James and His Music Makers, Peter Palmer, Mark IV, Bob Mc Fadden (M.C.).

COMMENTS:
- The company was appearing at the El Rancho Vegas. They closed, performed for three days in Texas (Wed-Fri), and then flew back to Vegas to open on Saturday night (B169).

REVIEWS:
AVALANCHE-JOURNAL, date unknown - Jack Sheridan: "The show is really an incredible performance in many aspects...The show moves with speed and color and is ideal springtime entertainment...She shares the stage with her husband, Texan Harry James, and this is the only the fourth time that happy occurrence has happened in the country."

## N16.   **El Rancho Vegas** - June 8 - July 14, 1960

CAST:
Betty Grable, George De Witt (featured comic); Bobby Van, the Company (Fluff Charlton, Harvey Church, Steve Preston).

REVIEWS:
VARIETY, 6.8.60: Jose: "Although not an artiste, Miss Grable is a good entertainer. Her songs and routines show arduous practice and rehearsal sessions...She works for applause and she gets it."

HOLLYWOOD REPORTER, 6.13.60 - Colin McKinley: "Harry James probably got the best laugh of the evening when he joined his wife onstage, carrying a newspaper advertisement announcing his own opening in the Flamingo lounge."

COMMENTS:
- They were appearing at the El Rancho Vegas when the hotel caught fire on July 15, 1960. Betty and several of the dancers were staying in bungalows on the hotel property and

they watched the hotel burn to the ground. Betty lost all of her costumes, musical arrangements and show props. Harvey Church reminisced that Grable usually went out with the dancers to eat after the show, because she did not want her stomach to be full before the show. On the evening of the fire, Harry James was in Las Vegas, so Grable ate with him, telling the dancers that they could go on by themselves.

**N17.    Sahara**, Las Vegas - October 4 - 18, 1960

CAST:
Betty Grable, Dick Humphreys, the Company (Joyce Roberts, Shirley Kirkes, Buddy Bryan, Richard Allan), Les Charlivels.

REVIEW:
VARIETY, 10.6.60 - Duke: "Betty Grable, in for a special two-week stint in the Congo Room, fronts a fresh, lively romp that tops all her previous efforts on the strip...Miss Grable admits early in the session that she doubts if anyone came to hear her sing, but her shortcomings in that department are over-balanced by her personality, fancy footwork, and the fact, let's face it, that she's Betty Grable."

**N18.    Flamingo** - February 16 - March 16, 1961

CREDITS:
Staged by Billy Daniel.

CAST:
Betty Grable, Dick Shawn (featured comic); Dick Humphreys, "The Grable Grabbers" (Joyce Roberts, Judy Chapman, Steve Preston, Lance Avant), the Flamingoettes, Nat Brandwynne Orchestra.

REVIEW:
HOLLYWOOD REPORTER, 2.20.61 - Colin Mc Kinlay: "Miss Grable was sporting a husky voice opening night, and showed tremendous courage by appearing in an identical outfit along with two scantily-clad young dancing girls."

COMMENTS:
- Billy Daniel was now being credited with staging and choreography for the act, although it was probably a combination of the work of Donn Arden, Barry Ashton and perhaps even some of Jack Cole's original work from her 1956 debut act. Harvey Church recollected that Daniel, a good friend of Grable's from their film work together, was often around during her nightclub appearances.
- This was the last published report of Grable's nightclub appearances that the author was able to locate.

An autographed photo for a fan, circa 1945. Collection of Nancy Thompson.

# Videography

Betty Grable is well represented on Video - although in so many of her minor films. In 1989, Fox released "The Betty Grable Collection" of eight films on Key Video, but it was an odd selection. Most of Grable's most memorable and successful films have not yet been released on video (Mother Wore Tights, Coney Island, Wabash Avenue, The Dolly Sisters, Sweet Rosie O'Grady, etc.) which makes one wonder just who is selecting titles for video release from Fox's neglected treasure trove of Technicolored musicals.

V1.  Beautiful Blonde From Bashful Bend - Key Video #1727
     Laser Disc: CBS Fox #1808-80 (w/ The Farmer Takes a Wife)

V2.  Bob Hope 5 Hour Marathon - Shokus Video #416 B-V

V3.  Cavalcade - Fox Video #1809

V4.  Day The Bookies Wept,The - Blackhawk #0759

V5.  Don't Turn 'Em Loose - King Video

V6.  Down Argentine Way - Key Video #1718
     Laser Disc: CBS/FOX #1741-80 (w/ Pin Up Girl.)

V7.  Farmer Takes a Wife,The - Key Video #1724
     Laser Disc: CBS Fox # 1808-80 (w/ The Beautiful Blonde From Bashful Bend)

V8.  Follow The Fleet - Turner Home Entertainment #2038 and Nostalgia Merchant #NM8013
     Laser Disc: Image #ID8293TU

V9.  Footlight Serenade - Key Video #1719

V10. Gay Divorcee,The - The Nostalgia Merchant #NM 8015
     Laser Disc: Image #ID8303TU

V11. Going Hollywood - The War Years - Warner Home Video

#35070

V12.   Gotta Dance, Gotta Sing - RKO #1010

V13.   Hedda Hopper's Hollywood - Republic Pictures Home
Video #5025

V14.   Hold 'Em Jail - Republic Pictures Home Video #0739

V15.   Hollywood Goes to War - Video Images #801 (Contains
All Star Bond Rally - Fox, 1945)

V16.   Hollywood Home Movies - Maljack Production #2059

V17.   How To Marry A Milionaire - CBS/Fox #1023
Laser Disc: CBS/Fox# 1023-80

V18.   I Wake Up Screaming - Key Video # 1720

V19.   Love Goddesses,The - Embassy Home Entertainment #6002
Laser Disc: Voyager #V10241

V20.   Magnificent Movie Musicals - Goodtimes Video #8094
(contains the "Prevue of Coming Attractions" of The
Dolly Sisters.)

V21.   March Of Time - Showbiz in the War Years - Embassy
Home Entertainment #1762

V22.   Melody Cruise - Turner Home Entertainment #6089

V23.   Moon Over Miami - Key Video #1725

V24.   Nitwits,The - Laser Disc: Image Ent. #107058TU

V25.   Old Man Rhythm - King Video

V26.   Pin Up Girl - Key Video #1721
Laser Disc: CBS/FOX #1741-80 (w/ Down Argentine Way)

V27.   Saturday Night at the Movies - Media Home Ent. #3001

V28.   Showbiz Goes To War - Video Late Show #220-1020

V29.   Shower Of Stars - Volume 1 - Classic Television

V30.   Shower of Stars - Volume 5 - Classic Television

V31.   Song Of The Islands - Key Video #1722
Laser Disc: CBS/FOX #1742-80 (w/ Springtime In The
Rockies)

V32.   Springtime In The Rockies - Key Video #1723
Laser Disc: CBS/FOX #1742-80 (w/Song Of The Islands)

V33.   Strictly G.I. - (contains All Star Bond Rally)

V34.   Three For The Show - Laser Disc: Pioneer #PSE91-15

**V35.**   <u>Three Broadway Girls</u> - (new title for <u>Greeks Had A Word For Them, The</u>) - Barr Films #HMO 176V

**V36.**   <u>Whoopee</u> - Embassy #3076 and HBO #90748

**V37.**   <u>Worst of Hollywood, The, Volume 3</u> - (contains <u>Probation</u>) - Silver Mine Video #610

# Discography

(b/w = backed with; ST = sound track recording; R = radio broadcast; TV = television broadcast). Most listings are long playing records. Grable is heard on few Compact Discs (CD) as of this writing her film soundtracks have not been released on the new format.

D1.   **Betty Grable** (Screen Star Series Curtain Calls 100/5, Scarce Rarities 5501, Sandy Hook 2014) (ST,R,TV)

Contents:
"COWBOY NUMBER" from Whoopee
"LET'S K-NOCK K-NEES" from The Gay Divorcee with Edward Everett Horton
"IT'S LOVE I'M AFTER" from Pigskin Parade with Johnny Downs, Judy Garland (Radio, Twentieth Century Fox Presents, 1936)
"FIDGETY JOE" from Man About Town
"HONEYSUCKLE ROSE/MOONLIGHT AND ROSES" from Tin Pan Alley
"KINDERGARTEN CONGA" from Moon Over Miami
"HI-YA LOVE" and "ANOTHER DREAM WON'T DO US ANY HARM" from A Yank in the R.A.F.
"SING ME A SONG OF THE ISLANDS" and "DOWN ON AMI AMI ONI ONI ISLE" from Song of the Islands with Hilo Hattie
"I HEARD THE BIRDIES SING" from Footlight Serenade
"WAITIN' AT THE CHURCH" from Sweet Rosie O' Grady
"CUDDLE UP A LITTLE CLOSER" and "TAKE IT FROM THERE" from Coney Island
"WELCOME TO THE DIAMOND HORSESHOE" and "ACAPULCO" from Billy Rose's Diamond Horseshoe
"BURLINGTON BERTIE FROM BOW" and "YOU DO" from Mother Wore Tights
"I WISH I COULD SHIMMY LIKE MY SISTER KATE" from Wabash Avenue
"LULLABY OF BROADWAY" with Harry James (TV, Academy Awards Show, 1958)
"HELLO DOLLY!" (TV, Carol Burnett Show, 1968)

**D2.**   **Betty Grable, 1934-60** (Star-Tone 219) (ST, R & TV)
Contents:
"THE SNAKE DANCE" from Student Tour (Rehearsal Radio check)
"LET'S K-NOCK K-NEES" from The Gay Divorcee (Radio performance, 1934)
Medley: "DELIGHTED TO MEET YOU," "IS IT LOVE OR INFATUATION?" from This Way Please (Radio performance, 1937)
"FIDGETY JOE" from Man About Town (Radio, 1939)
"I CAN'T BEGIN TO TELL YOU" with Harry James, 1945
"ARTIFICIAL FLOWERS" (TV, Perry Como Kraft Music Hall 1960)
Medley: "MUSIC MAKERS," "I'VE HEARD THAT SONG BEFORE," "I HAD THE CRAZIEST DREAM," "JAMES SESSION," "YOU MADE ME LOVE YOU," "CIRIBIRIBIN" with Perry Como and Harry James ( TV, Perry Como Kraft Music Hall, 1960)
"LITTLE GIRL FROM LITTLE ROCK" with Janis Paige (TV, Shower of Stars, 1958)
Wabash Avenue Medley: "I WISH I COULD SHIMMY LIKE MY SISTER KATE," "BABY, WON'T YOU SAY YOU LOVE ME?," "WILHELMINA," "MAY I TEMPT YOU WITH A BIG, RED ROSY APPLE?" (Radio, Lux Radio Theater, 1950)
"DOIN' THE TANGO" (TV, Bob Hope Chevy Show, 1955)
"NIGHT LIFE" (TV, Andy Williams Show, 1962)
"LULLABY OF BROADWAY" with Harry James (TV, Academy Awards Show, 1958)
"I REFUSE TO ROCK AND ROLL" (TV, Ford Star Time, 1960)
"WHAT DID I DO?" intro by Bing Crosby (Radio, Philco Radio Time, 1949)

**D3.**   **Billy Rose's Diamond Horseshoe** (backed with Doris Day Soundtrack Songs)(Caliban 6028) (ST)

Contents:
"MAIN TITLES" - Orchestra
"GAL IN KALAMAZOO" - Band
"WELCOME TO THE DIAMOND HORSESHOE" - Female Chorus
"COOKING UP A SHOW" - William Gaxton, Chorus
"WELCOME TO THE DIAMOND HORSESHOE" (Reprise) - Betty Grable, Chorus
"IN ACAPULCO" - Betty, Chorus
"MY MELANCHOLY BABY" - Dick Haymes
"I WISH I KNEW" - Dick Haymes
"FUR COAT DREAM" - Betty, Margaret Dumont, Chorus
"THE MORE I SEE YOU" - Dick Haymes
"CARRIE MARY HARRY" - Beatrice Kaye, William Gaxton
MEDLEY: "PLAY ME AN OLD FASHIONED MELODY" - Kaye, Gaxton; "A NICKEL'S WORTH OF JIVE" - Betty, "LET ME CALL YOU SWEETHEART" - Beatrice Kaye; "YOU'LL NEVER KNOW" - Betty; "SLEEP, BABY, SLEEP" - Kaye; "SHOO SHOO BABY" - Chorus; "ABA DABA HONEYMOON" - Willie Solar
"I WISH I KNEW" (Reprise) - Dick Haymes
"IN ACAPULCO" (Reprise) - Carmen Cavallaro
"I WISH I KNEW" (Reprise) - Betty
"COOKING UP A SHOW" (Reprise) - Betty, Gaxton
"THE MORE I SEE YOU" FINALE - Entire Cast

**D4.**   **Calling All Stars** (Star-Tone 203) (ST)

Betty sings "SWEETHEART TIME" with Buster Crabbe from <u>Thrill of a Lifetime</u>.

**D5.**   **Call Me Mister** (backed with <u>Starlift</u>) (Titania 510) (ST)

Contents:
"MAIN TITLES" - Orchestra, Chorus
"JAPANESE GIRL LIKE AMERICAN BOY" - Betty, Female Chorus
"I'M GONNA LOVE THAT GUY" - Betty, G.I.s
"LAMENT TO THE POTS AND PANS" - Danny Thomas
"GOING HOME TRAIN" - Bobby Short, Male Chorus
"I JUST CAN'T DO ENOUGH FOR YOU, BABY" - Betty, Dan Dailey
"CALL ME MISTER" - Betty, Dan Dailey, Chorus
"MILITARY LIFE" - Danny Thomas
"LOVE IS BACK IN BUSINESS" - Betty, Dan, Danny, Benay Venuta, Chorus

**D6.**   **Choice Cuts** - Vol 1 (500/1) (ST)

In this collection of musical numbers deleted from films, Betty sings "BLUE SHADOWS AND WHITE GARDENIAS" from <u>Song of the Islands</u> with Ben Gage (dubbing for Victor Mature). Also of Grable interest on the album is "SNAFU," cut from <u>Four Jills and a Jeep</u>, sung by Martha Raye, Carole Landis and Mitzi Mayfair.

**D7.**   **Classic Movie Musicals of Sammy Fain** (JJA 19842) (ST)

Betty sings "I'M GONNA LOVE THAT GUY" and "I JUST CAN'T DO ENOUGH FOR YOU, BABY" with Dan Dailey from <u>Call Me Mister</u>.

**D8.**   **Collegiate** (b/w <u>Flirtation Walk</u>, <u>She Loves Me Not</u> and <u>Here Is My Heart</u>) (Caliban 6042) (ST)

Contents:
"MAIN TITLES" - Orchestra
MY GRANDFATHER'S CLOCK IN THE HALLWAY" - Jack Oakie, Chorus
"FOR HE'S A JOLLY GOOD FELLOW" - Chorus
"WHO AM I?" - Joe Penner
"YOU HIT THE SPOT" - Frances Langford, Jack Oakie
"LEARN TO BE LOVELY" - Jack Oakie, Betty Jane Cooper
"I FEEL LIKE A FEATHER IN THE BREEZE" - Female Chorus
"RHYTHMATIC" - Betty Grable, Jack Oakie
"YOU HIT THE SPOT" (Reprise) - Frances Langford, Betty Grable, Jack Oakie, Joe Penner, Ned Sparks, Chorus
"END TITLES" - Orchestra

**D9.**   **Coney Island** (b/w <u>Moon Over Miami</u>) (Caliban 6001) (ST)

Contents:
"CONEY ISLAND MONTAGE" - Chorus
"PUT YOUR ARMS AROUND ME, HONEY" - Betty and Girls
"WHO THREW THE OVERALLS IN MRS. MURPHY'S CHOWDER?" -
Charles Winninger
"EGYPTIAN DANCE/IN MY HAREM" - Phil Silvers, Girls
"WHEN IRISH EYES ARE SMILING" - Betty, Chorus
"CUDDLE UP A LITTLE CLOSER" - Betty
"WINTER, WINTER/PRETTY BABY" - Betty, Chorus
"MISS LULU FROM LOUISVILLE" - Betty, Chorus
"TAKE IT FROM THERE" - Betty, Chorus
"DARKTOWN STRUTTER'S BALL" - Instrumental
"BEAUTIFUL CONEY ISLAND" - Betty, George Montgomery,
Chorus
"TAKE IT FROM THERE" (Reprise) - Betty
"THERE'S DANGER IN A DANCE" - Betty, Chorus
"TAKE IT FROM THERE" Finale - Betty

D10.   **Cut!** - Volume 1 (Out Take OTF - 1)(ST)

Betty sings "I'LL BE MARCHING TO A LOVE SONG" from
Footlight Serenade.

D11.   **Cut!** - Volume 3 (Out Take OTF - 3) (ST)

Betty sings "THERE'S SOMETHING ABOUT MIDNIGHT" from
That Lady in Ermine.

D12.   **The Dolly Sisters** (CIF 3010) (ST)

Contents:
"OPENING AND MAIN TITLES" - Orchestra
"VAMP" - Betty and June Haver
"I CAN'T BEGIN TO TELL YOU" - John Payne
"GIVE ME THE MOONLIGHT" - Betty and John Payne
"WE'VE BEEN AROUND"/"CAROLINA IN THE MORNING" - Betty
and June Haver
"DON'T BE TOO OLD FASHIONED"/"LIPSTICK, POWDER AND
ROUGE" -  Betty and June Haver
"I'M ALWAYS CHASING RAINBOWS" - John Payne
"DARKTOWN STRUTTERS BALL" - Betty and June Haver
"I CAN'T BEGIN TO TELL YOU" (Reprise) - Betty
"ARRAH GO ON, I'M GONNA GO BACK TO OREGON"/"SMILES" -
Male Chorus
"I'M ALWAYS CHASING RAINBOWS"/"ARRAH GO ON, I'M GONNA
GO BACK TO OREGON"/"I CAN'T BEGIN TO TELL YOU" - John
Payne
"HINDUSTAN" - Instrumental
"THE SIDEWALKS OF NEW YORK" - Betty and June Haver
"I'M ALWAYS CHASING RAINBOWS" (Reprise) - John Payne
"I CAN'T BEGIN TO TELL YOU" Finale - Betty, June
Haver, John Payne

D13.   **Down Argentine Way**   (b/w Springtime In The Rockies)
(Hollywood Soundstage 5013),(b/w Tin Pan Alley)
(Caliban 6003) (ST)

Contents:
"MAIN TITLES: DOWN ARGENTINE WAY" - Chorus
"SOUTH AMERICAN WAY" - Carmen Miranda, Bando Da Lua
"DOWN ARGENTINE WAY" - Don Ameche, Betty Grable,
Chorus
MUSICAL MONTAGE - Chorus
"DOWN ARGENTINE WAY" (Reprise) - Harold Nicholas,
Chorus
"NENITA" - Leonid Kinsky, Trio
"DOIN' THE CONGA" - Instrumental
"MAMA EU QUERO" - Carmen Miranda, Bando Da Lua
"BOMBU, BOMBU" - Carmen Miranda, Banda Da Lua
"FIESTA TIME" - Instrumental
"SING FOR YOUR SENORITA" - Charlotte Greenwood, Chorus
"TWO DREAMS MET" - Tito Guizar, Betty, Don Ameche,
Chorus
"MAMA EU QUERO" (Reprise) - Instrumental
FINALE: "DOWN ARGENTINE WAY" - J. Carroll Naish,
Chris Pin Martin, Nicholas Brothers
"SING TO YOUR SENORITA" - Charlotte Greenwood, Chorus
"DOWN ARGENTINE WAY" - Henry Stephenson, Leonid
Kinsky, Charlotte Greenwood, Chorus
"TWO DREAMS MET" - Betty, Ameche, Chorus
END CREDITS - Orchestra

D14.    **Follow The Fleet** (b/w A Damsel In Distress, Scarce
Rarities SR-5505; Caliban 6024 - b/w The Joker is
Wild and Sountrak STK-118) (ST)

Betty sings "LET YOURSELF GO" with Ginger Rogers,
Jennie Gray & Joy Hodges.

D15.    **Footlight Serenade** (b/w Rose of Washington Square)
(Caliban 6002) (ST)

Contents:
"MAIN TITLES" - Orchestra
"EXCEPT WITH YOU" - Cobina Wright Jr.
"ARE YOU KIDDIN'?" - Betty Grable
"I'M STILL CRAZY FOR YOU" - Betty, John Payne
"LAND ON YOUR FEET" - Orchestra
"I HEARD THE BIRDIES SING" - Betty, Female Chorus
"I'LL BE MARCHING TO A LOVE SONG" - Betty, Victor
Mature, John Payne, Chorus
"END TITLES" - Orchestra

D16.    **Four Jills In A Jeep** (Hollywood Soundstage 407)
(ST)

Betty sings "CUDDLE UP A LITTLE CLOSER" from Coney
Island.

D17.    **The Gay Divorcee** (EMI 101, Sountrak 105) (ST)

Betty sings "LET'S K-NOCK K-NEES" with Edward Everett
Horton.

D18.    **The Gershwins in Hollywood** (JJA 19773) (ST)

Betty sings "I'VE GOT A CRUSH ON YOU" with Jack Lemmon from <u>Three For The Show</u>.

D19.   **Golden Moments From The Silver Screen** (Harmony H 30549) (ST)

Betty sings "I CAN'T BEGIN TO TELL YOU" from <u>The Dolly Sisters</u>.

D20.   **Hollywood Is On The Air** (Radiola 1718) (R)

Betty sings "PAN AMERICANA JUBILEE" from <u>Springtime in the Rockies</u> and "THE BALBOA" from <u>Pigskin Parade</u> on this album featuring radio programs of the 1930's and 1940's promoting musical films of the era.

D21.   **Hollywood On The Air Presents "The Feminine Touch"** (Star-Tone Records ST-205) (R)

Betty sings "MY HEART TELLS ME" from <u>Sweet Rosie O' Grady</u> (Radio, 1943).

D22.   **Hollywood Stars** (Accord 129011 - CD) (R)

Betty sings "MY HEART TELLS ME" from <u>Sweet Rosie O' Grady</u> (Radio, 1943).

D23.   **Hollywood Years of Harry Warren, 1930-57, The** (JJA 19791) (ST)

Betty sings "TWO DREAMS MET" with Don Ameche from <u>Down Argentine Way</u>; "PAN AMERICANA JUBILEE" with John Payne, Carmen Miranda and Cesar Romero from <u>Springtime In The Rockies</u>; "MY HEART TELLS ME" with Phil Regan from <u>Sweet Rosie O' Grady</u>; "I WISH I KNEW" from <u>Billy Rose's Diamond Horseshoe</u> .

D24.   **Hot Canaries, The** (CL 2534)

Betty sings "I CAN'T BEGIN TO TELL YOU" from <u>The Dolly Sisters</u> in this CD recording of songstresses Peggy Lee, Doris Day, Rosemary Clooney and Kitty Kallen.

D25.   **I Can't Begin To Tell You** - with Harry James (Columbia, 1945)

Due to studio restrictions, Betty was not allowed to make recordings. She however, did make this one single with Harry James, under the pseudonym of "Ruth Haag" (her and Harry's middle names).

D26.   **Ladies Of Burlesque** (Legends 1000/2) (ST)

Betty sings "MAY I TEMPT YOU WITH A BIG, RED ROSY APPLE?" from <u>Wabash Avenue</u>.

D27.   **Marilyn Monroe - Rare Recordings 1948-1962** (Sandy Hook #2103) (ST)

Betty is heard in two scenes with Marilyn Monroe and Lauren Bacall from How To Marry A Millionaire (F81).

D28.  **Marx Brothers, The - Three Hours, Fifty-Nine Minutes, Fifty One Seconds With** (Murray Hill 931680) (R)

Grable performs a comedy sketch on a radio program with Grouch Marx, airdate unknown.

D29.  **Meet Me After The Show** (b/w Painting The Clouds With Sunshine) (Caliban  6012) (ST)

Contents:
"MEET ME AFTER THE SHOW" - Betty, Chorus
"BETTIN' ON A MAN" - Betty, Male Chorus
"OH ME OH MI-AMI" - Chorus
"IT'S A HOT NIGHT IN ALASKA" - Betty, Male Chorus
"EVERYDAY WILL BE A DAY IN MAY" - MacDonald Carey
"NO TALENT JOE" - Betty, Gwen Verdon, Chorus
"I FEEL LIKE DANCING" - Betty, Gwen Verdon
"END TITLES" - Orchestra

D30.  **Moon Over Miami** (b/w Coney Island) (Caliban 6001) (ST)

Contents:
"MAIN TITLES" - Orchestra
"WHAT CAN I DO FOR YOU?" - Betty, Carole Landis
"OH ME OH MI-AMI" - Betty, Carole Landis, Charlotte Greenwood
"YOU STARTED SOMETHING" - Betty, Robert Cummings
"I'VE GOT YOU ALL TO MYSELF" - Don Ameche
"IS THAT GOOD?" - Jack Haley, Charlotte Greenwood
"LOVELINESS AND LOVE" - Betty, Don Ameche
"KINDERGARTEN CONGA" - Betty, Chorus
"SOLITARY SEMINOLE" - Chorus
"FINALE" - Entire Cast

D31.  **Mother Wore Tights** (b/w The Shocking Miss Pilgrim) (CIF 3008) (ST)

Contents:
"MAIN TITLES" - Orchestra
"BERLINGTON BERTIE FROM BOW" - Dan Dailey
"YOU DO" - Dan Dailey, girls
"BERLINGTON BERTIE FROM BOW" (Reprise) - Betty
"THIS IS MY FAVORITE CITY" - Betty, Dan Dailey
"YOU DO" (Reprise) - Betty, Chorus
"KOKOMO, INDIANA" - Betty, Chorus
"TRA-LA-LA" - Betty, Dan Dailey, Mona Freeman
"SWINGING DOWN THE LANE"/"STUMBLING" - Mona Freeman, Lee Patrick, Chick Chandler
"THERE'S NOTHING LIKE A SONG/KOKOMO, INDIANA/ROLLING DOWN BOWLING GREEN" - Betty, Dan Dailey
"FARE-THEE-WELL-DEAR ALMA MATER" - Chorus

**D32.**  **My Blue Heaven** (b/w <u>You Were Meant for Me</u>) (Titania 503) (ST)

Contents:
"MY BLUE HEAVEN" - Betty, Dan Dailey
"IT'S DEDUCTIBLE" - Betty, Dan Dailey
"WHAT A MAN" - David Wayne
"HALLOWEEN" - Betty, Dan Dailey, David Wayne
"COSMO COSMETICS INTRO" - Mitzi Gaynor
"I LOVE A NEW YORKER" - Betty, Dan Dailey
"MY BLUE HEAVEN" - Instrumental
"LIVE HARD, WORK HARD, LOVE HARD" - Betty, Dan Dailey, Mitzi Gaynor
"COSMO COSMETICS INTRO" - Mitzi Gaynor
"THE FRIENDLY ISLANDS" - Betty, Dan Dailey, Chorus

**D33.**  **Pigskin Parade** (b/w <u>Everybody Sing</u>) (Pilgrim 4000 & AEI 2108) (ST)

Betty sings "THE BALBOA" with Judy Garland, Johnny Downs, Dixie Dunbar, The Yacht Club Boys, Patsy Kelly, Jack Haley and Chorus.

**D34. Pin Up Girl**( b/w <u>Song Of The Islands</u>) (Caliban 6009) (ST)

Contents:
"YOU'RE MY LITTLE PIN UP GIRL" - Betty, Chorus
"TIME ALONE WILL TELL" - Charley Spivak Orchestra and Chorus
"RED ROBINS, BOB WHITES AND BLUE BIRDS" - Martha Raye, Chorus
"DON'T CARRY TALES OUT OF SCHOOL" - Betty, Chorus
"YANKEE DOODLE HAYRIDE" - Martha Raye
"ONCE TOO OFTEN" - Betty, Charley Spivak Orchestra
"DON'T CARRY TALES OUT OF SCHOOL" (Reprise) - Betty, Chorus
"THE STORY OF THE VERY MERRY WIDOW" - Betty
"CLOSE ORDER DRILL FINALE" - Betty

**D35.**  **The Shocking Miss Pilgrim** (b/w <u>Mother Wore Tights</u>) (CIF 3008) (ST)

Contents:
"MAIN TITLES" - Orchestra
"SWEET PACKARD" - Chorus
"CHANGING MY TUNE" - Betty
"STAND UP AND FIGHT" - Chorus
"AREN'T YOU KIND OF GLAD WE DID?" - Betty, Dick Haymes
"CHANGING MY TUNE" (Reprise) - Betty
"BACK BAY POLKA (BUT NOT IN BOSTON)" - Betty, Allyn Joslyn, Charles Kemper
"ONE, TWO, THREE" - Dick Haymes
"WALTZING IS BETTER SITTING DOWN" - Dick Haymes
"WALTZ ME NO WALTZES" - Betty
"FOR YOU, FOR ME, FOR EVERMORE" - Betty, Dick Haymes
"FOR YOU, FOR ME, FOR EVERMORE"(Reprise) - Dick Haymes
"FINALE" - Betty, Dick Haymes

**D36.**   **Song Of The Islands** (b/w <u>Pin Up Girl</u>) (Caliban 6009) (ST)

Contents:
"MAIN TITLES" - Orchestra
"HAWAIIAN WAR CHANT" - Chorus
"SING ME A SONG OF THE ISLANDS" - Betty, Chorus
"DOWN ON AMI AMI ONI ONI ISLE" - Betty, Hilo Hattie, Chorus
"HOME ON THE RANGE" - Jack Oakie
"MALUNA, MALALO, MAWAENA" - Chorus
"WHAT'S BUZZIN' COUSIN?" - Jack Oakie
"THE COCK-EYED MAYOR OF KAUNAKAKAI" - Hilo Hattie
"DOWN ON AMI AMI ONI ONI ISLE"/"O'BRIEN HAS GONE HAWAIIAN" - Betty, Chorus
"FINALE" - Grable, Chorus

**D37.**   **Springtime In The Rockies** (b/w <u>Sweet Rosie O' Grady</u>, (Pelican 128 & Hollywood Soundstage 5013)(b/w <u>Down Argentine Way</u> (Sandy Hook SH 2090 & Titania 507) (ST)

Contents:
"MAIN TITLES" - Orchestra
"RUN, LITTLE RAINDROP, RUN" - Betty, John Payne
"CIRIBIRIBIN" - Harry James Orchestra
"I HAD THE CRAZIEST DREAM" - Helen Forrest, Harry James Orchestra
"YOU MADE ME LOVE YOU" - Harry James Orchestra
"RUN, LITTLE RAINDROP, RUN" (Reprise) - Orchestra
"CHATTANOOGA CHOO CHOO" - Carmen Miranda, Bando da Lua
"LATIN DANCE" - Orchestra
"TIC TAC DO MEU CARACOA" - Carmen Miranda, Bando da Lua
"PAN AMERICANA JUBILEE" - Betty, John Payne, Charlotte Greenwood, Edward Everett Horton, Carmen Miranda

**D38.**   **Sweet Rosie O' Grady** (b/w <u>Springtime In The Rockies</u>) (Titania 507 & Sandy Hook SH 2090) (ST)

Contents:
"WHERE OH WHERE IS THE GROOM?"/"WAITING AT THE CHURCH" - Betty, Chorus
"MY HEART TELLS ME" - Phil Regan, Betty
"SWEET ROSIE O' GRADY" - Leo Diamond and His Solitaires
"THE WISHING WALTZ" - Phil Regan, Chorus
"MY HEART TELLS ME" - Betty
"TWO LITTLE GIRLS IN BLUE"/"HEAVEN WILL PROTECT THE WORKING GIRL"/"LITTLE ANNIE ROONEY"/"SWEET ROSIE O' GRADY" - Betty, Robert Young
"GET YOUR POLICE GAZETTE"/"SWEET ROSIE O' GRADY" - Chorus
"PRESS INTERVIEW"/"SWEET ROSIE O' GRADY" - Betty, Chorus
"GOING TO THE COUNTRY FAIR"/"MY SAM" - Betty, Chorus

**D39.**   **Thanks  For  The  Memory  -  The  Classic  Movie
Musicals  of  Ralph  Rainger  1930-'43**  (JJA  1981
(ST)

Betty sings:
"LOVELINESS AND LOVE" with Don Ameche from <u>Moon Over
Miami</u>; "HI-YA LOVE" and "ANOTHER DREAM WON'T DO US ANY
HARM" from <u>A Yank in the R.A.F.</u>; "I'M STILL CRAZY FOR
YOU" with John Payne and "I HEARD THE BIRDIES SING"
from <u>Footlight Serenade</u>; "TAKE IT FROM THERE" and
"THERE'S DANGER IN THE DANCE" from  <u>Coney Island</u>

**D40.**   **Those  Bombastic  Blonde  Bombshells** - (Wallysrite
Records BGM42) CD (ST,TV)

Betty Sings:
"DOIN' THE TANGO" (TV, <u>Bob Hope Chevy Show</u>, 1955)
"YA GOTTA GIVE THE PEOPLE HOKE" with Van Johnson,
Sergio Franchi (TV, <u>Hollywood Palace</u>, 1964)
"DIGGA DIGGA DO" (TV, <u>Shower of Stars</u>, 1954)
"THE BAND PLAYED ON"/"I'M JUST WILD ABOUT HARRY" with
Harry James (TV, <u>Shower of Stars</u>, 1954)
"ONE FOR MY BABY" (TV, <u>Shower of Stars</u>, 1954<u>)</u>
"BABY, WON'T YOU PLEASE COME HOME?" with Harry James
(TV, <u>Shower of Stars</u>, 1954)
"MY HEART TELLS ME" (<u>Sweet Rosie O' Grady)</u>
"SWEETHEART TIME" with Buster Crabbe and Chorus
(<u>Thrill of a Lifetime</u>)

**D41.**   **Those  Sensational  Swinging  Sirens  Of  The  Silver
Screen** (Vintage Jazz Classics JVC #1002-2) CD  (TV)

Betty sings "HELLO DOLLY!" (TV, <u>Carol Burnett Show</u>,
1968).

**D42.**   **Three For The Show** (10" Mercury MG-25204) (ST)

Contents:
"OVERTURE" - Orchestra
"WHICH ONE?" - Betty and Marge Champion
MEDLEY: "SOMEONE TO WATCH OVER ME"/"SWAN LAKE BALLET" -
Marge Champion
"I'VE GOT A CRUSH ON YOU" - Betty and Jack Lemmon
"DOWN BOY" - Betty and Jud Conlon Singers
"SOMEONE TO WATCH OVER ME" - Instrumental
"HOW COME YOU DO ME LIKE YOU DO? - Betty, Chorus
"FINALE - I'VE GOT A CRUSH ON YOU" - Betty,Jack
Lemmon, Marge and Gower Champion

-  Ironically,  this  is  the  only  "Official"  Soundtrack
recording Miss Grable is heard on. All the rest of the albums
listed are classified as "Bootleg" or illegal copies of
television transmissions of her films or tapes. During her
film career, 20th Century Fox did not have a recording
company, as MGM did, so her soundtracks were never released
on  records.  Luckily,  during  the  1960's  and  1970's,
enterprising film fans began releasing many film soundtracks
on  these  so-called  "Bootleg"  albums  -  although  poor  in

quality, they are a boon to fans and collectors. Without them, much of the film musical history would be "lost." It's a sad statement about the lack of interest Hollywood has always had in itself.

**D43.**    **Tin Pan Alley** (Sountrak STK 110); (Caliban #6003)
(b/w Down Argentine Way)    (ST)

Contents:
"MAIN TITLES" - Orchestra
"K-K-K-KATIE - DIXIE" - Jack Oakie, John Payne
"K-K-K-KATIE - HAWAII" - Betty, Alice Faye
"YOU SAY THE SWEETEST THINGS" - Alice Faye, John Payne, Jack Oakie, Chorus
"ON MOONLIGHT BAY" - Alice Faye
MEDLEY: "HONEYSUCKLE ROSE"/"MOONLIGHT AND ROSES" - Betty, Chorus
"AMERICA, I LOVE YOU" - Alice Faye, Princess Vanessa Ammon, Roberts Bros, Brian Sisters, John Payne, Chorus
"GOODBYE BROADWAY, HELLO FRANCE" - Jack Oakie
"ARABIAN SONG" - Chorus
"SHIEK OF ARABY" - Betty, Alice Faye, Billy Gilbert
"FINALE: K-K-K-KATIE" - Betty, Jack Oakie, Alice Faye, John Payne, John Loder, Chorus

**D44.**    **Wabash Avenue**    (b/w Sing, Baby, Sing) (Caliban 6029)
(ST)

Contents:
"MAIN TITLES" - Orchestra
"DOWN ON WABASH AVENUE" - Female Chorus
"I WISH I COULD SHIMMY LIKE MY SISTER KATE" - Betty
"ON THE GOOD SHIP ROCK AND RYE" - James Barton, Chorus
"HONEY MAN" - Betty
"ARE YOU FROM DIXIE?" - Female Chorus and dialogue with Victor Mature and Phil Harris
"MAY I TEMPT YOU WITH A BIG, RED ROSY APPLE?" - Betty, Female Chorus
"BABY, WON'T YOU SAY YOU LOVE ME?" - Betty
"I REMEMBER YOU"/"BILLY" - Betty, Chorus
"WILHELMINA" - Betty, Male Chorus
"BABY, WON'T YOU SAY YOU LOVE ME?" (Reprise) - Victor Mature and Betty

**D45.**    **The White Cliffs Of Dover** (MCA Records WCK/MSD2-35199) CD

Betty sings "I CAN'T BEGIN TO TELL YOU" with Harry James from The Dolly Sisters. This "single" recording may also be found on many compilation albums and CDs (Big Band collections, the hits of Harry James, songs of the 1940's, etc.).

A publicity still which became the advertisement art for *Beautiful Blonde From Bashful Bend*, Twentieth Century Fox, 1949.

# Collectibles

Grable continues to be one of the most collectible stars. Recently, the classic Varga poster from <u>Moon Over Miami</u> sold for $4,400 at auction and a 1-sheet from <u>Hollywood Bound</u> was offered for $800. All of the collectibles listed are currently available from memorabilia shops or companies.

C1.    **BOOKS** -
"Betty Grable and The House With The Iron Shutters" - Whitman, 1943

C2.    **COLORING BOOKS** -
Whitman Publishing Co. 1947
Merrill Publishing Co. #1501

C3.    **DOLLS** - Plaster of paris carnival doll in <u>Down Argentine Way</u> costume, 1940

C4.    **LOBBY CARDS**
From all of her films

C5.    **MAGAZINES** - Magazines generally are priced: 1930's - $50; 1940's - $30; 1950's - $20; 1960's - $10; 1970's - $5.

<u>Cinema</u> -
Volume 5, No. 2 - Cover and "Every Man's Capsule Guide To The Pin-up"

<u>Cinemonde</u> (French) -
January 31, 1949 - Cover

<u>Cine Revue</u> (French) -
March 14, 1947 - Cover and Article
May 6, 1949 - Cover and Article
November 25, 1949 - Cover and Article
October 12, 1951 - Cover and Article

<u>Colliers</u> -
May 17, 1941 - "Out on Two Limbs"

<u>Esquire</u> -
December 1943 - "Manual of Arms (And Legs)"

<u>Film Fan Monthly</u> -
July/August 1973 - "Remembering Betty Grable"

<u>Filmland</u>
July, 1951 - "'Why Worry?' Says Betty Grable"

<u>Films and Filming</u> (British) -
October 1971 - Cover

<u>Films in Review</u> -
August/September 1973 - Article by Jay Gorney

<u>Hit Parader</u> -
May 1949 - Cover
April 1951 - Cover and Article

<u>Hollywood Family Album</u> -
July 1950 - "The James': Only Betty And Harry Could
Make It Work"
July 1951 - "Harry and The Sleeping Beauties"
1953 - "You Can't Ration Love" and "The Horse-Happy
Harry Jameses: Even The Kids Pick The Ponies!"

<u>Hollywood Studio Magazine - Then and Now</u> -
August 1986 - Cover and "She Lived A Lot"
October 1987 - Color Poster
January 1988 - "Alice Faye and The Fox Blondes"
March 1988 - "Betty Grable Superstar!"
August 1989 - Cover with Marilyn Monroe and photos

<u>Life</u> -
December 11, 1939 - Cover and article on <u>Dubarry Was A
Lady</u>
November 4, 1940 - "The New Hollywood"
November 25, 1940 - "Old Songs Make 'Tin Pan Alley'
Tuneful"
September, 1941 - "A Yank in the R.A.F." - Movie of
the Week
December 28, 1942 - "High-Speed Camera Goes To
Hollywood"
June 7, 1943 - "Her Legs a Hollywood Landmark"
March 27, 1944 - "Charted Grable" article and photos
May 8, 1944 - "Grable's Baby"
March 19, 1945 - "Grable's Baby is 1"
September 8, 1947 - "Grable Grabs the Greenbacks"

<u>Look</u> -
August 16, 1949 - Cover and "Betty Grable, Her Legs
Are Her Fortune"
June 30, 1950 - Cover with Monroe, Bacall in <u>How To
Marry A Millionaire</u>

<u>Modern Screen</u> -
January 1941 - "Confessions of a Campus Cutie"
August 1941 - Article about romance with George Raft

August 1942 - Cover
November 1942 - Cover
October 1943 - Cover and "The Love Story of Betty Grable and Harry James", "Betty Grable"
March 1945 - "A High Kick and a Hot Lick"
March 1948 - Cover
June 1948 - Cover
December 1948 - Cover
September 1949 - Cover and "I'm Still Wild About Harry"
February 1950 - "I Don't Run Betty's Life"
July 1950 - Cover
August 1951 - Cover and "Is Grable Quitting?"
April 1952 - Cover
December 1952 - Cover
July 1953 - "The Quiet Happiness"
August 1953 - Cover
March 1954 - "Miss Grable Steps Out"
September 1954 - "There is Nothing Like A Dame"
October 1956 - "Betty Grable, The Fun I Have With My Daughters"
August 1957 - Cover

Motion Picture -
July 1941 - Cover
October 1943 - Cover
May 1946 - "Betty Grable; Pin-Up Girl"
October 1947 - Cover
June 1949 - Cover
August 1950 - Cover and "Call Her Betty James - What is Betty Grable Really Like?"
October 1951 - "There Is No Betty Grable"
February 1953 - "Is Grable Jealous of Monroe?"
September 1953 - "Love Affair"

Movie Classics -
December 1973 - Cover and "The Girl With the Million Dollar Legs"

Movie Fan -
May 1952 - Cover

Movieland -
May 1943 - Cover and "Close-Up of Betty Grable"
June 1943 - "The Heartbreak Behind the Betty Grable - George Raft Parting"
September 1943 - "The Exclusive Story of the Betty Grable - Harry James Marriage"
June 1944 - "The Night Betty's Baby Was Born"
September 1945 - "If I Had A Second Chance"
May 1947 - Cover and "Betty At Her Best"
June 1948 - "This Is Myself"
February 1949 - "'G' Is For Gorgeous Glamorous Grable"
June 1950 - "I'm No Career Girl"
September 1950 - Cover
April 1951 - Cover
August 1951 - "Daughter Knows Best"
May 1952 - "Is the Grable Feud Hotter Than Ever?"

August 1953 - "Why They Thought Grable Was Through"

Movie Life -
July 1941 - "Doin' the 'Sit Down' Strike"
May 1950 - Cover
January 1954 - "The Movie Life of Betty Grable"

Movie Play -
September 1952 - Cover

Movies -
September 1943 - "Hollywood Said It Couldn't Happen"
January 1945 - "Hot Trumpeter"

Movie Songs -
May 1946 - Cover

Movie Stars -
June 1944 - "Pin Up Girl Junior"

Movie Stars Parade -
August 1943 - Cover and "Vote For Queen of the Pin-Up Girls"
January 1945 - "Christmas is Every Day"
September 1946 - Cover
April 1948 - Cover and "Illusion in Lace"
April 1949 - Cover and article
March 1950 - Cover and "I Danced My Way To Fame"
February 1953 - "Betty Grable Fights Back"
July 1955 - "She's Shy"

Movie Story -
October 1940 - Down Argentine Way
January 1941 - Tin Pan Alley
October 1941 - Cover and A Yank in the R.A.F.
December 1943 - Cover and Pin-Up Girl
October 1947 - Mother Wore Tights
January 1949 - Cover and When My Baby Smiles At Me
July 1949 - Cover and The Beautiful Blonde From Bashful Bend
October 1950 - Cover and My Blue Heaven

Newsweek -
June 16, 1952 - Cover with John Wayne
July 16, 1973 - Obituary

Nostalgia Illustrated -
January 1975 - Cover and "A Tribute To The Most Famous Pin-Up of Them All"

Photoplay -
August 1932 - "The New Shady Dames of the Screen"
May 1941 - "How I Keep My Figure"
May 1942 - "What Makes Betty Run?"
June 1943 - Cover and "The Champ Betty Grable"
August 1943 - "What About Betty Grable and Harry James?"
May 1944 - "Introducing Miss James"

December 1944 - Cover and "Grab Bag on Grable"
March 1945 - "The Enchanted Couple"
October 1945 - "Betty Grable's Secret Date"
May 1946 - "If You Were The Ranch Guest of Betty Grable"
August 1946 - "Its A Joke, Son"
November 1946 - Cover and "Its Like This with Harry and Me"
April 1947 - "It's The Darndest Thing"
January 1948 - "They'll Remember Mama"
April 1948 - Cover and "Rules For Wives"
January 1949 - "Her Divided Heart"
April 1949 - Cover and "Beautiful Blonde From Calabasas Ranch"
September 1949 - "Blonde Bonanza"
November 1950 - "Your Photoplay Photo-Plays"
April 1951 - Pin Up
May 1951 - "Does Mother Know Best?"
June 1951 - Cover and "Betty Talks To Horses"
July 1952 - Cover and "Betty Takes a Bow"
February 1953 - "Betty's Other Life"
July 1953 - "Nice Goin', Mrs. James"
November 1955 - "Two Women and a Dream"
September 1972 - "The Queen of Hearts"
October 1973 - "The Men in Her Life Remember Betty Grable"
March 1977 - "Photoplay Back Then - Harry and Me"

Picture Show (British) -
Summer Special 1938 - Cover
February 22, 1941 - Cover
January 3, 1942 - Cover
January 29, 1944 - Cover
June 14, 1947 - Cover
August 13, 1949 - Cover
April 29, 1950 - Cover
December 8, 1951 - Cover
June 27, 1953 - Cover
December 3, 1955 - Cover

Picturegoer (British) -
December 13, 1941 - Cover
March 6, 1943 - Cover
December 9, 1944 - Cover
July 9, 1949 - Cover
December 8, 1951 - Cover
March 12, 1956 - Cover

Picture Show (British) -
June 14, 1947 - Cover with Dick Haymes

Plays and Players (British) -
1969 - Belle Starr

Rona Barrett's Hollywood -
November, 1973 - "She Shined Even in Darkness"

<u>Saturday Evening Post</u> -
April 10, 1948 - "The Role I Liked Best"
April 15, 1950 - "The World's Most Popular Blonde"
October 9, 1954 - Portrait

<u>Screen Album</u> -
Spring 1944 - Cover
Winter 1953 - Cover

<u>Screen Facts</u> -
1964, #4 - Bio by Gene Ringgold

<u>Screen and TV Guide</u> -
June 1949 - "The Beautiful Blonde From Beverly Hills"

<u>Screen Guide</u> -
September 1948 - "My Wife, Betty"
November 1948 - Cover
September 1950 - "Betty Grable"
October 1950 - Cover
March 1951 - Cover and "Mother Is a Glamour Girl"

<u>Screenland</u> -
August 1942 - Cover and "Betty, Behave!"
January 1950 - "Tinsel and Tears"
January 1954 - "Is Betty Velvet or Gingham?"

<u>Screenland and T.V. Time</u> -
September 1953 - Cover

<u>Screenland Plus T.V. Land</u> -
May 1954 - Cover

<u>Screen Romance</u> -
July 1943 - Cover
July 1944 - Cover and <u>Sweet Rosie O' Grady</u> photo story

<u>Screen Star</u> -
February 1945 - "Jotting on James"

<u>Screen Stars</u> -
July 1947 - "The Startling Truth About Betty Grable"
August 1951  - Cover and "Betty Grable's Revealing Story"

<u>Screen Stories</u> -
September 1948 - <u>That Lady in Ermine</u>
May 1950 - <u>Wabash Avenue</u>
April 1951 - <u>Call Me Mister</u>
November 1951 - <u>Meet Me After The Show</u>
March 1953 - <u>The Farmer Takes a Wife</u>
November 1953 - <u>How To Marry A Millionaire</u>
February 1955 - <u>Three For The Show</u>

<u>Silver Screen</u> -
August 1940 - "Grable Makes Good Again"
July 1941 - "The Boys All Go For Betty"

November 1942 - "Are Women Natural Born Feudists?"
December 1942 - "Betty's Tour of the Army Camps"
May 1946 - "Betty and The Simple Life"
December 1947 - "Betty Grable As a Mother"
May 1950 - "I'm Sorry About Those Rumors"
August 1950 - Cover
March 1951 - Cover
July 1951 - "Off-Screen Betty"
August 1952 - "Why I Got Tired of It All"

Song Hits -
December 1940 - Photos and lyrics from Down Argentine Way
February 1941 - Cover
August 1941 - Photos and lyrics from Moon Over Miami
April 1942 - Photos, synopsis and lyrics from Song of The Islands
December 1943 - Cover
April 1944 - Photos, synopsis and lyrics from Pin Up Girl

Television and Screen Guide -
October 1951 - "The Truth About the Grable Rumors"

Time -
August 23, 1948 - Cover and "Living The Daydream"
April 13, 1959 - "Ham and Legs"
July 16, 1973 - Obituary

C6.    **PAPER DOLLS** -
Whitman Co. 1941 #989
Whitman Co. 1943 #976
Merrill Co, Publishers, 1951 #1558

C7.    **PIN UP COLLECTION** -
Footlight Serenade: Betty depicted by artists Petty, Earl Moran, Varga, Bradshaw Crandall and McClelland Barclay.

C8.    **POSTERS**
From all of her films

C9.    **PRESS BOOKS** -
Mother Wore Tights

C10.    **SOUVENIR ITEMS** -
Dubarry Was A Lady - Program
Hello Dolly - Riviera Hotel, Las Vegas: Program, Post Cards - Schubert Theater, New York: Program

C11.    **WINDOW CARD** -
Footlight Serenade

C12.    **SHEET MUSIC**
Sheet music with Grable's photo on the cover:

Beautiful Blonde From Bashful Bend - "BEAUTIFUL BLOND FROM BASHFUL BEND;" "EVERY TIME I MEET YOU" - Leo

Feist, Inc.

Billy Rose's Diamond Horseshoe - "IN ACAPULCO;" "I WISH I KNEW;" "THE MINK LAMENT;" "THE MORE I SEE YOU;" "NICKEL'S WORTH OF JIVE;" "PLAY ME AN OLD FASHIONED MELODY" - Bregman, Vocco and Conn, Inc.

Call Me Mister - "I JUST CAN'T DO ENOUGH FOR YOU BABY;" "JAPANESE GIRL LIKE AMERICAN BOY;" "LOVE IS BACK IN BUSINESS" - Miller Music Corp.

Collegiate - "GUESS AGAIN;" "I FEEL LIKE A FEATHER IN THE BREEZE;" "LEARN TO BE LOVELY;" "MY GRANDFATHER'S CLOCK IN THE HALLWAY;" "RHYTHMATIC;" "WHO AM I;" "WILL I EVER KNOW?;" "YOU HIT THE SPOT" - Famous

College Swing - "COLLEGE SWING;" "HOW'JA LIKE TO LOVE ME?;" "I FALL IN LOVE WITH YOU EVERY DAY;" "MOMENTS LIKE THIS;" "WHAT A RHUMBA DOES TO ROMANCE;" "WHAT DID ROMEO SAY TO JULIET?;" "YOU'RE A NATURAL" - Famous

Coney Island - "BEAUTIFUL CONEY ISLAND;" "MISS LULU FROM LOUISVILLE;" "TAKE IT FROM THERE;" "THERE'S DANGER IN A DANCE" - Miller Music Corp.
"CUDDLE UP A LITTLE CLOSER" - Witmark
"PUT YOUR ARMS AROUND ME HONEY" - Broadway
"WHO THREW THE OVERALLS IN MISTRESS MURPHY'S CHOWDER?" - Marks

The Dolly Sisters - "DARKTOWN STRUTTER'S BALL;" "THE VAMP" - Leo Feist, Inc.
"I CAN'T BEGIN TO TELL YOU" - Bregman, Vocco and Conn, Inc.
I'M ALWAYS CHASING RAINBOWS" - Miller Music Corp.

Down Argentine Way - "DOWN ARGENTINE WAY;" "NENITA;" "SING TO YOUR SENORITA;" " TWO DREAMS MET" - Miller Music Corp.
"MAMA YO QUIERO (I WANT MY MAMA)" - Robbins

The Farmer Takes A Wife - "CAN YOU SPELL SCHENECTADY?;" "ON THE ERIE CANAL;" "SOMETHIN' REAL SPECIAL;" "TODAY I LOVE EVERYBODY;" "WE'RE DOING IT FOR THE NATIVES OF JAMAICA;" "WE'RE IN BUSINESS;" "WHEN I CLOSE THE DOOR;" "WITH THE SUN WARM UPON MY FACE" - Harwin

Footlight Serenade - "I'LL BE MARCHING TO A LOVE SONG;" "I'M STILL YOU CRAZY FOR YOU" - Robbins Music Corp.

Give Me A Sailor - "IT DOESN'T MAKE SENSE;" "A LITTLE KISS AT TWILIGHT;" "THE U.S.A. AND YOU;" "WHAT GOES ON HERE IN MY HEART?" - Paramount

How To Be Very Very Popular - "HOW TO BE VERY VERY POPULAR" - Miller Music Corp.

How To Marry A Millionaire - "NEW YORK" - Simon

I Wake Up Screaming - "THE THINGS I LOVE" - Campbell

Moon Over Miami - "IS THAT GOOD?;" "I'VE GOT YOU ALL
TO MYSELF;" "KINDERGARTEN CONGA;" "LOVELINESS AND
LOVE;" "MIAMI;" "SOLITARY SEMINOLE;" "YOU STARTED
SOMETHING" - Robbins Music Corp.

Mother Wore Tights - "FARE THEE WELL, DEAR ALMA
MATER;" "KOKOMO, INDIANA;" "ON A LITTLE TWO SEAT
TANDEM;" "THERE'S NOTHING LIKE A SONG;" "THIS IS MY
FAVORITE CITY;" "TRA LA LA LA;" "YOU DO" - Bregman,
Vocco and Conn, Inc.

My Blue Heaven - "MY BLUE HEAVEN" - Leo Feist, Inc.
"DON'T ROCK THE BOAT DEAR;" "THE FRIENDLY ISLANDS;"
"HALLOWEEN;" "I LOVE A NEW YORKER;" "IT'S DEDUCTIBLE;"
"LIVE HARD, WORK HARD, LOVE HARD" - Morris

The Nitwits - "MUSIC IN MY HEART;" "YOU OPENED MY
EYES" - Irving Berlin

Pin Up Girl - "DON'T CARRY TALES OUT OF SCHOOL;" "ONCE
TOO OFTEN;" "RED ROBINS, BOB WHITES AND BLUEBIRDS;"
"THE STORY OF THE VERY MERRY WIDOW;" "THIS IS IT;"
"TIME ALONE WILL TELL;" "YANKEE DOODLE HAYRIDE;"
"YOU'RE MY LITTLE PIN UP GIRL" - Bregman, Vocco and
Conn, Inc.

The Shocking Miss Pilgrim - "AREN'T YOU KIND OF GLAD
WE DID?;" "THE BACK BAY POLKA;" "CHANGING MY TUNE;"
"FOR YOU, FOR ME, FOREVERMORE;" "ONE, TWO, THREE" -
Gershwin Publishing Corp.

Song of The Islands - "BLUE SHADOWS AND WHITE
GARDENIAS;" "DOWN ON AMI AM ONI ONI ISLE;" "MALUNA,
MALALO, MAWAENA;" "O'BRIEN HAS GONE HAWAIIAN;" "SING
ME A SONG OF THE ISLANDS;" "WHAT'S BUZZIN' COUSIN?" -
Bregman, Vocco and Conn, Inc.
"SONG OF THE ISLANDS" - Marks

Springtime In The Rockies - "I HAD THE CRAZIEST
DREAM;" "I LIKE TO BE LOVED BY YOU;" "PAN AMERICANA
JUBILEE;" "A POEM SET TO MUSIC"  - Bregman, Vocco and
Conn, Inc.
"O TIC TAC DO MEU CORACAO" - Southern
"RUN, LITTLE RAINDROP, RUN" - Leo Feist, Inc.
"YOU MADE ME LOVE YOU" - BMI

Sweet Rosie O'Grady - "GET YOUR POLICE GAZETTE;"
"GOIN' TO THE COUNTY FAIR;" "MY HEART TELLS ME;" "MY
SAM;" "WHERE, OH WHERE IS THE GROOM?;" "THE WISHING
WALTZ" - Bregman, Vocco and Conn, Inc.
"SWEET ROSIE O' GRADY" - Mills
 "WAITIN' AT THE CHURCH" - Harms

That Lady in Ermine - "THE MELODY HAS TO BE RIGHT;" "OOH! WHAT I'LL DO;" "THERE'S SOMETHING ABOUT MIDNIGHT;" "THIS IS THE MOMENT" - Miller Music Corp.

This Way Please - "DELIGHTED TO MEET YOU;" "LOVE OR INFATUATION?;" "THIS WAY PLEASE;" "VOOM VOOM" - Popular

Three For The Show - "DOWN BOY;" "HOW COME YOU DO ME LIKE YOU DO?" - Mills Music Co.

Thrill of a Lifetime - "PARIS IN SWING" - Famous "SWEETHEART TIME;" "THRILL OF A LIFETIME" - Marlo

Tin Pan Alley - "AMERICA, I LOVE YOU;" "K-K-K-KATY;" "THE SHIEK OF ARABY" - Mills Music Co. "YOU SAY THE SWEETEST THINGS, BABY" - Leo Feist, Inc.

Wabash Avenue - "BILLY;" "I'VE BEEN FLOATING DOWN THE OLD GREEN RIVER" - Mills Music Co. "BABY, WON'T SAY YOU LOVE ME;" "WILHELMINA" - Leo Fiest, Inc. "I WISH I COULD SHIMMY LIKE ME SISTER KATE" - Vogel

When My Baby Smiles At Me - "BY THE WAY" - Bregman, Vocco and Conn, Inc. "OUI OUI MARIE" - Fisher "WHAT DID I DO?" - Triangle "WHEN MY BABY SMILES AT ME" - Von Tilzer

A Yank in the R.A.F. - "ANOTHER DREAM WON'T DO US ANY HARM;" "HI YA LOVE" - Robbins

# Miscellaneous

**M1.**    **Hollywood Walk of Fame Star** at 6527 Hollywood Blvd.

**M2.**    **Right leg, hand prints and Autograph** in Grauman's (now "Mann's") Chinese Theater on Hollywood Blvd. The Ceremony was held February 15, 1943. The cement space alloted to Grable is tinted gray and is inscribed "Thanks Sid." It also includes the date, her signature, imprints of both hands and right leg (with "My Leg" and an arrow pointing to the leg written above it), as well as "USA," "USN" and "USMC" - referring to the Army, Navy and Marine Corps.

**M3.**    **Funeral** at All Saints Episcopal Church, Beverly Hills

**M4.**    **Buried** at Inglewood Memorial Park, 720 E. Florence Ave, in the Golden West Mausoleum - "The Sanctuary of Dawn."

**M5.**    **Residential addresses:**

| | |
|---|---|
| 1916 - | 3955 Lafayette St., South St. Louis |
| 1920 - | Forest Park Hotel, Lindle Ave., St. Louis |
| 1929 - | Canterbury Apartments, Yucca and Cherokee, Hollywood |
| 1930 - | 1848 N. Grammercy Place, Hollywood |
| 1933 - | Knickerbocker Hotel, 1714 Ivar St., Hollywood |
| 1937 - | Montana Street, Brentwood (with Jackie Coogan) |
| | 250 Chadbourne, Brentwood (Conn and Lillian's home) |
| 1939 - | Essex House, New York (while doing <u>Dubarry Was A Lady</u>) |
| 1940 - | 1280 Stone Canyon, Beverly Hills |
| 1943 - | Corner of Coldwater Canyon and Heather, Beverly Hills |
| 1944 - | "Baby J" Ranch, Calabasas, California |
| 1945 - | 275 Rodeo Drive, Beverly Hills - (Lillian's home) |

Sherry Netherlands Hotel, New York (during a long engagement of Harry James' band)
600 Doheny Road, Beverly Hills

1954 -   North Beverly Drive, Beverly Hills
1957 -   38 Country Club Lane, the Desert Inn Golf Course, Las Vegas
1968 -   164 Tropicana Road, Las Vegas

**M6.   Vital Statistics** - (1942):
Height - 5'4"
Bust - 34 1/2"
Waist - 24"
Hips - 36"
Neck - 13 1/2"
Headsize - 22 1/2
Weight - 112 lbs.
Wrist - 6"
Thigh - 20"
Calf - 12 1/2"
Ankle - 7 1/2"
Upper Arm - 10 1/4"
Shoe Size - 4 C
Glove Size - 6

**M7.   Products she advertised:**
Piel's Beer, Maybelline, Motorola, Hollywood Rapid Dry Curler, Lux, Geritol, Westmore Foundation Cream, Dentyne Chewing Gum, Chesterfield Cigarettes, Royal Crown Cola

**M8.   Films she was offered or announced to appear in:**
Campus Dormitory (never filmed) - 1939
The Gang's All Here (also called The Girls He Left Behind - replaced by Alice Faye)- 1942
Weekend in Havana (replaced by Alice Faye) - 1942
My Gal Sal (Alice Faye was pregnant, so the script was reshaped for Irene Dunne. Dunne was busy for the next one and a half years, so it was offered to Mae West. Grable was then announced, but because of her busy schedule, the role eventually went to Rita Hayworth, borrowed from Columbia) - 1942
Something For The Boys (replaced by Vivian Blaine) - 1943
Greenwich Village (Grable was pregnant with Jessica, so, she was replaced by Vivian Blaine) - 1944
Doll Face (replaced by Vivian Blaine) - 1944
Kiki (a remake of the earlier Mary Pickford film she appeared in the chorus of - never filmed) - 1944
Nob Hill (replaced by Vivian Blaine) - 1945
The Razor's Edge (replaced by Anne Baxter) - 1945
Where Do We Go From Here? (with Bob Hope - replaced by June Haver and Fred Mac Murray) - 1945
No Wedding Ring (with Richard Green and Thomas Mitchell - replaced by Jeanne Crain and the film was retitled An Apartment For Peggy) - 1946
Look For The Silver Lining (replaced by June Haver) - 1949

The Pleasure is All Mine (on loanout to Columbia, which she refused. It was then announced that Rita Hayworth would take the role. The film was never made) - 1953
The Girl Next Door (originally titled Father Does A Strip - replaced by June Haver) - 1953
Pickup on South Street (originally titled Blaze Of Glory - replaced by Jean Peters) - 1953
Gentlemen Prefer Blondes (replaced by Marilyn Monroe) - 1953
Guys and Dolls (replaced by Vivian Blaine) - 1955
Love Me Or Leave Me (replaced by Doris Day) - 1955
Teenage Rebel (replaced by Ginger Rogers) - 1956
Please Don't Eat The Daisies (replaced by Doris Day) - 1960

M9.   **Awards and Honors:**

1. Hollywood Artists and Chamber of Commerce declare her "America's Ideal Girl."

2. Top Ten Box Office Stars - 1942 (#8), 1943 (#1), 1944 (#4), 1945 (#5), 1946 (#9), 1947 (#2), 1948 (#2), 1949 (#7), 1950 (#4), 1951 (#3) - The 1940's were dubbed "The Bing Crosby-Betty Grable Years" by the Quigley Poll of Box Office Stars.

3. Voted "Worst Performer" by Harvard Lampoon, 1941. She laughingly agrees.

4. Voted "Foot Locker Queen" - U.S. Army Air Corps at Westover Field, Chicopee Falls, Mass. - October 8, 1941. Lana Turner was the "Runner-up."

5. Had a British Royal Air Force Squadron named after her, 1941.

6. Named "Sweetheart of Camp Joseph T. Robinson" - Army training center near Little Rock, Arkansas, 1941.

7. Photoplay and Movie Mirror magazines name her "The Best Figure in Hollywood," 1941.

8. Named Honorary Lieutenent Colonel by General T. Kennedy of Fort Bragg, South Carolina, September, 1942.

9. The record for jitterbugging with 300 "cut-ins" within one hour at the Hollywood Canteen, 1942.

10. Her right leg and hands are imprinted in the cement at Grauman's Chinese Theatre in Hollywood for posterity, February 15, 1943.

11. The Hollywood studio record for 90,000 fan letters in one year, 1944.

12. The "Sour Apple" from the Hollywood Women's Press Club for being one of Hollywood's most uncooperative stars, 1947.

13. A cast was made of her legs in April, 1948, for an exhibit at the California Museum of Modern Art.

14. On November 14, 1949, she was named "Dance Week Queen" by the National Ballroom Operator's Association.

15. Named one of the "Hollywood Mothers of the Year" by the City of Hope's sponsoring panel, along with June Allyson, Ann Blyth, Rosemary Clooney, Betty Hutton and Deborah Kerr, March 1956.

16. Inducted into the "Muny Hall of Fame" at the St. Louis Municipal Theatre Association on May 10, 1991 as one of the artists who have "Touched the Muny in some special way."

**M10.   Songs associated with Miss Grable:**

1. "LET'S K-NOCK K-NEES" (Gay Divorcee)
2. "SING ME A SONG OF THE ISLANDS" (Song of the Islands)
3. "CUDDLE UP A LITTLE CLOSER" (Coney Island)
4. "TAKE IT FROM THERE" (Coney Island)
5. "I CAN'T BEGIN TO TELL YOU" (The Dolly Sisters)
6. "YOU DO" (Mother Wore Tights)
7. "KOKOMO INDIANA" (Mother Wore Tights)
8. "BABY, WON'T YOU SAY YOU LOVE ME?" (Wabash Avenue)
9. "MY HEART TELLS ME" (Sweet Rosie O'Grady)

**M11.   Songs which mention Miss Grable:**

1. "LET'S NOT TALK ABOUT LOVE" (Cole Porter, 1941 - from Let's Face It.)
2. "CHERRY PIES OUGHT TO BE YOU" (Cole Porter, 1950 - from Out of This World)
4. "THE FORTIES" (Billy Barnes, 1960 - from The Billy Barnes Revue)
3. "BETTY GRABLE" (Neil Sedaka and Howard Greenfield, 1974)

# Bibliography

Betty Grable is mentioned in nearly every book about the major film stars and history of films. Listed are books and articles which contain extensive or unique material on Miss Grable and her career.

**B1.** Agan, Patrick. <u>The Decline and Fall of The Love Goddesses</u>. Los Angeles, Pinnacle Books, 1979. pp. 36 64.

Well-researched full chapter bio with filmography and photos. Her relationship with Bob Remick is detailed, with a quote from Grable to writer Bridget Walsh:" Yes, he's younger...a lot younger. But he's so much more mature than some forty-five-year-old men I've known. Age is all relative. He's very good for me. He's a Libra and doesn't have a nerve in his body. I've never heard him lose his temper. Sure it's very flattering to have a younger man interested in you. But though Bob says he absolutely adores me he's not stupid about it. No, there's no marriage planned. My God, I'm a two-time loser...And why should Bob and I want to marry? Our relationship is great the way it is. It's great to have a man to lean on." Remick is now happily married with a family.

**B2.** Arce, Hector. <u>The Secret Life Of Tyrone Power</u>, New York, William Morrow, 1979. pp. 144-147, 161.

In a discussion of Tyrone Power making <u>A Yank in the R.A.F.</u> with Grable, this biography of Power contains director Henry King's comment about Grable: "I've been directing pictures for twenty-seven years and have seen many stars come and go, and I feel certain that Betty Grable has talents for straight dramas. Give her three dramatic roles in a row and she will surprise Hollywood. She can do what Ginger Rogers, Myrna Loy, Joan Crawford, and many other stars who began as dancers have done."

**B3.** Ardmore, Jane. "The Men In Her Life Remember Her," <u>Photoplay</u>, October 1973. pp.50-51, 74-74.

Fan magazine article written after Grable's death with quotes from the important men in her life - George Raft: "The happiest moments I ever had were when I was going with her;" Jackie Coogan: "We always remained friends. She had too great a sense of humor to have any enemies - marvelous sense of humor;" Dan Dailey: "She was one of the few women I've ever known who had the ability to be friends;" Hugh O'Brian: "I can think of nothing more fun than to keep right on playing 'Guys and Dolls' with her in whatever Valhalla it is to which good troupers go;" Harry James: "If she were here, I could tell you a hundred memories. We had a wonderful life."

**B4.**   Arnold, Maxine. "Betty Takes A Bow," Photoplay, July 1952.

After being suspended by Fox, Betty returned to show business with an appearance on the radio in Lux Radio Theatre's presentation of My Blue Heaven. The article describes her nervousness and her explanation that she had returned to the business for her Mother, Lillian, and her fans. In a discussion of how she had helped up-and-coming co-stars like June Haver, Dan Dailey, Dick Haymes and Dale Robertson, it tells of her insistence on Mitzi Gaynor getting a featured dance number in My Blue Heaven: "'There's so much dancing in the picture, anyway, a lot of ballet work, and I haven't done ballet for a long time - why not let Mitzi Gaynor do that one?,' she suggested." The article ends with a description of the standing ovation she received from the radio studio audience for her tearful "comeback."

**B5.**   Aylesworth, Thomas G. History of Movie Musicals, New York, Gallery Books, 1984.

Lavishly illustrated, brief biography, descriptions of many of her films and abbreviated filmography. In pages 113-116, Grable's career and films are described in the chapter "The War Years."

**B6.**   Barbour, Alan G. Saturday Afternoon At The Movies, New York, Bonanza Books, 1986. pp. 340-343, 349.

Contains three previously published books: "Days of Thrills and Adventure;" "A Thousand and One Delights" and "The Thrill of it All." In chapter 12 of "A Thousand and One Delights," titled "The Horn of Plenty," Grable's films of the Forties are viewed as "Saturday Matinee Fare," with Coney Island being discussed as one of the more enjoyable musicals of the period. Photos of The Dolly Sisters and the advertisement from Sweet Rosie O'Grady.

**B7.**   Basinger, Jeanine. "Betty Grable 1916-1973," New York Times, July 15, 1973.

A very human and loving tribute to Grable after her death, written by this film historian who has written several profiles of the actress. Primarily focusing on Grable's modesty, honesty and devotion to her fans, the article includes this touching statement: "As film buff Eric Spilker told me when we first learned of her illness, 'I don't want to face a world without Betty Grable.'"

**B8.**    Baskette, Kirtley. "A High Kick and Hot Lick," <u>Modern Screen</u>, March 1945. pp.44-47, 79-84.

Interesting Fan magazine article with many unusual anecdotes. In describing Betty's wartime endeavors, the author writes about her Army Camp tour in the Carolinas; making a special recording for a blinded soldier who had written: "I guess I won't ever be seeing you again, Betty, and that's not so good. But the last picture I saw you in was '<u>Coney Island</u>' and I'll always remember you like you were in that," and inviting a Marine to her house for dinner after he gave her a creased pin-up photo with a hole in the center: "My Bud...always carried this one over his heart - and when they got him, that's where they got him." When she gave birth to daughter, Victoria, the same night as the Academy Award presentation, she said: "I'd rather have what I got than what Jennifer Jones got!" The article also describes her on-going support for other performers and friends: June Haver, Vivian Blaine, choreographers Hermes Pan and Kenny Williams, dance-in Angie Blue and Fox commissary waitress Bobbie Coleman.

**B9.**    Basten, Fred E. <u>Glorious Technicolor</u>, Cranbury, N.J., A.S.Barnes, 1980. pp. 9, 105-108, 11, 118, 125.

Brief up-beat biography, several photos and movie ads. In the forward, the author states: "Try to imagine <u>Gone With The Wind</u> without Technicolor. Or <u>Fantasia</u>. Or <u>Ben-Hur</u>. Or Betty Grable. Without Technicolor, those special movie memories, old and new, would not be the same." It also states that Grable made twenty-two Technicolor features.

**B10.**    Beck, Marilyn. "Hollywood Hotline," <u>The Star-Ledger</u>, December 1, 1986.

Syndicated columnist Beck writes that the screen rights to <u>Pin Up: The Tragedy of Betty Grable</u> were purchased by producer Howard Koch for Paramount. It describes the book as: "...another <u>Mommie Dearest</u> tale of child abuse - for '<u>Pin Up</u>' makes the late actress out as a drinker who mistreated her daughters."

**B11.**    Bergen, Ronald. <u>The United Artists Story</u>, New York Crown Publishers, 1986. pp. 44, 50, 55.

In this history of the studio, there are brief synopses, cast and credits of Grable's films for United Artists: <u>Whoopee</u>, <u>The Greeks Had A Word For Them</u> and <u>The Kid From Spain</u>

**B12.**    Bergen, Ronald. <u>Glamourous Musicals</u>, London, Octopus Books, 1984. pp. 19, 20, 40, 89-92.

Brief bio and several photos. In describing Betty and the formula for her films, the British author colorfully writes: "This butter blonde with the peaches and cream complexion, full rose-red lips and beautiful long legs made a vivid

impression. There followed over a dozen absurd, musical
frolics with Betty at their centre. Positively Houdini-like
in their escapism, they were set either in the Gay 90's,
exotic locales or wonderland holiday resorts...If Mae West in
proxy saved many an airman from drowning, then the army
marched metaphorically on Betty's legs."

**B13.**   Biery, Ruth. "The New Shady Dames Of The Screen,"
   <u>Photoplay</u>,  August, 1932.

In this article about how all of the starlets of the period
were changing their make-up, there is a photo of Grable as
"Frances Dean" and describes her as a newcomer "making her
first picture for Educational," under the influence of Garbo.
As it does not mention RKO, this is information which adds
credence to the theory that Betty changed her name because of
the affiliation with Roscoe "Fatty" Arbuckle.

**B14.**   Blevins, Bonnie. "Dolly Cast Receives Praise For
   Candidness," <u>Chattanooga News-Free Press</u>, November,
   1965.

Newspaper article comprised of interviews with the cast of
<u>Hello Dolly</u> after the completion of their appearance in
Chattanooga. It talks about Grable's throat troubles which
plagued her constantly: "Miss Grable, herself, in the age-old
tradition of 'appease the press' accepted a call and talked
freely of a throat condition which had developed because of
the backstage heat and the constant opening of doors for prop
entries; however, her performances were not hindered. Betty
Grable - a genuinely warm and natural lady."

**B15.**   Bloom, Ken. <u>American Song, The Complete Musical
   Theatre Companion</u>, New   York,   Facts   on   File
   Publication, 1985. pp. 59-60, 172, 727.

Complete cast and credits of <u>Tattle Tales</u>, <u>Dubarry Was A Lady</u>
and <u>Belle Starr</u>.

**B16.**   Boller, Paul F. Jr & Davis, Ronald L., <u>Hollywood
   Anecdotes</u>, New York, Ballantine Books, 1988. pp. 93,
   102, 107, 136, 237.

Amusing yarns about Grable from co-workers Benay Venuta,
Douglas Fairbanks, Jr., Walter Abel (quoted on pages 17-19)
and <u>Dubarry Was a Lady</u> costar Charles Walters: "She invented
the word barrelhouse...the dirtiest-mouth dame I've ever
known. But on her it was adorable."

**B17.**   Bordman, Gerald. <u>American Musical Theatre</u>, New York,
   Oxford University Press, 1978. pp. 483, 518.

Notations about <u>Tattle Tales</u> and <u>Dubarry Was a Lady</u> .

**B18.**   Brand, Harry. <u>Twentieth Century Fox Press Release</u>,
   August 1, 1940.

A studio press release which tells about Grable's songwriting efforts. While in New York performing in Dubarry Was a Lady, she wrote both music and lyrics for two songs: "ALLURE" and "I"M NOT WORRIED," which were published by Irving Berlin Company in New York.

**B19.**   Brand, Harry. Twentieth Century Fox Press Release, September 19, 1940.

Studio article which purports Grable's stardom in Down Argentine Way is due to "an unknown news photographer in San Francisco," who took a picture of Grable during a personal appearance tour in the city, which caught Darryl Zanuck's attention. He quickly signed her to a contract at Fox and allowed her to go to New York to appear in Dubarry Was a Lady. "...if it hadn't been for that photographer in San Francisco,' Betty mused, 'I don't think I would have either this role or this contract. In fact, I might have been a has-been at 23.'"

**B20.**   Brand, Harry. Twentieth Century Fox Press Release, May 15, 1941.

Brand, publicity director for Fox, released this publicity article in which Grable names the men she would like to dance with. Labelled "Exclusive in your territory," the article is particulary interesting as she names the leading male dancers of the time. In order of preference, they are: Fred Astaire - "since he's the country's number one male dancer and excels in 'broken rhythm' (a contemporary description of syncopated tap dancing - author);'" George Raft for the tango; Hermes Pan, her dance director on Moon Over Miami, because he is "the most versatile of all dancers," Cesar Romero for the Rhumba; George Murphy for fox-trots; Charles Boyer - "not because he's primarily a dancer...but merely because doing Vienesse Waltzes with Boyer would be an unparalleled thrill;" Paul Draper -   "he excels in the adaptability of his rhythms;" Mickey Rooney for jive and swing; Jack Cole for his "bizarre dancing" and Frank Veloz (of the famous dance team of Veloz and Yolanda): "for all around ballroom dancing."

**B21.**   Burton, Jack. The Blue Book Of Hollywood Musicals, New York, Century House, 1953.

Detailed musical credits from all of Grable's films: songs, composers.

**B22.**   Cassini, Oleg. In My Own Fashion, New York, Simon and Schuster, 1987. pp. 111, 113, 139, 176, 192.

The truth behind the Fashion Designer's well-publicized "Romance" with Grable. He writes that they merely enjoyed each other's company at nightclubs, dancing, etc.: "She was one of the three or four best dancers I've ever met, which was all we had in common, really. She loved to dance and so did I, and we did - very publicly, very obviously, very well - at Ciro's. Beyond that, she was a simple hamburger-and-milkshake type of girl, not very sophisticated but very sweet and very pretty."

**B23.**   Chierichetti, David. <u>Hollywood Costume Design</u>, New York, Harmony Books, 1976. pp. 109-111, 120-122, 126, 128.

Details, photos and comments (mostly negative) from costume designers Charles LeMaire, Orry Kelly, Rene Hubert and Bill Travilla.

**B24.**   Churchill, Douglas W. "A Helping Hand From Hollywood," <u>New York Times</u>, October 25, 1936.

Newspaper article describing how RKO-Radio Studios was offering its contract talent to little theatre and stock companies around America to use for live theatrical appearances. Two reasons are cited: to stimulate theatre box office with the Movie Star names and to gain experience for the film players, with the actors sharing box office profits. Grable is listed as one of the available contract players, along with Lucille Ball, Preston Foster, Van Heflin, Ann Shirley and Erik Rhodes.

**B25.**   Cohen, Daniel. <u>Musicals</u>, Greenwich, Conn., Bison Books, 1984. pp. 22-23, 34-38, 64.

Miniscule bio and commentary about her place in War Time musicals, with photos. Summing up her appeal, the author writes: "Like many a star, Betty was lucky enough to be in the right place at the right time for her particular gifts. She had a beaming toothpaste ad smile which came across in color. She wasn't so beautiful or so exotic that you worshipped her from afar. Rather she had a bland amiability. She was a good-looking but basically ordinary girl that GI Joe might meet in a small town diner or find working in a war plant in a big city. She was nice. You felt you had a chance if you could just get to know her. Well, a boy can dream, can't he?"

**B26.**   Cohen, Daniel & Cohen, Susan. <u>Screen Goddesses</u>, London, Tiger Books, 1984. pp. 46-51, 96.

Ample bio, excellent photos and filmography. In evaluating her appeal, the authors write: "There was always a wholesomeness about Betty which never turned treacly, and a vulgarity that added spice to the family fare she appeared in. That meant the Hay's Office and the women's club were happy with her, yet the boys at the front were free to find her sexy."

**B27.**   Crawley, Tony. <u>Screen Dreams - The Hollywood Pin Up</u>, New York, Delilah Communications, Inc. 1982. pp. 22, 37, 50, 126, 132.

Five unusual pin up photos of Miss Grable from 1930 to 1951 in this light-hearted pictorial of Film cheesecake.

**B28.**   Cronin, Steve. "Is Grable Quitting?," <u>Modern Screen</u>, August, 1951. pp.46, 74 - 75.

When Grable was placed on suspension by Fox, this fan magazine article mentions that the studio was experiencing a box-office drop and had also announced a 50% reduction in all major salaries. Grable is quoted as having said: "When I get out of the top 10 box-office attractions - I'll get out of the business." In 1951, she is listed as the number three woman in the survey, following June Allyson and Claudette Colbert and the author theorizes "She may want to step aside before she catches her first glimpse of that famous skid."

**B29.**    Cross, Robin. <u>2000 Movies, The 1940's</u>, New York, Arlington House, 1985.

Brief synopsis and photo from all of Grable's 1940's films, plus boxoffice status by year.

**B30.**    Cross, Robin. <u>2000 Movies, The 1950's</u>, New York, Arlington House, 1988.

Brief synopsis and photo from all of Grable's 1950's films with boxoffice status by year.

**B31.**    Crown, Lawrence. <u>Marilyn At Twentieth Century Fox</u>, London,Comet Books,1987. pp.22-23,100-101,104,110-111.

Description of Grable's friendship with Marilyn Monroe during the making of <u>How To Marry A Millionaire</u> with photos from the film.

**B32.**    Dana, Joyce. "Million-$-Betty Dances With Tears In Her Eyes," <u>Boston Sunday Advertiser Pictorial Review</u>, April 4, 1943.

Syndicated article concentrating on how Betty still loved George Raft, although he could not obtain a divorce from his wife. It chronicles all of the ladies who hoped Raft would marry: Virginia Peine, Norma Shearer, Mary Brian, Marjorie King and Bonnie Poe (who sued him for $25,000 for allegedly breaking her heart). When asked about her feelings for Harry James, Betty stated: "That is what you call an erroneous Hollywood rumor. I knew Harry long before he was famous. I think I was his first fan. We both love music and are crazy about hearing new tunes. So I went out with him once - of all places - to the Palladium, where you have as much privacy as a goldfish in a glass bowl. If I had been in love with Harry and he with me, we would have gone to some quiet place and sat in a corner, and not to the Palladium, where everyone we know goes to dance." Author's note: She married Harry James three months later.

**B33.**    Deere, Dorothy. "If You Were The Ranch Guest of Betty Grable," <u>Photoplay</u>, May, 1944. pp. 46-49, 106-108.

A fan magazine description of a visit to the "Baby J" ranch in Calabasas: "The small white ranch house, which Betty and Harry wouldn't trade for any mansion they've ever owned, is set in the midst of sixty-some acres in the sparsely settled district of Calabasas, California - thirty miles from the studio as a station wagon flies, which makes it strictly a once-a-week treat for its owners." The article describes the author being driven out to the ranch by "gay, slim-ish 'Mom' Lillian Grable," as Betty must also film on Saturdays. They are greeted by "Pop Grable, who is the ranch manager" at his "small caretaker's house close to the gate." The meager ranch house and the family life are described, as well as the cows, chickens and horses being raised on the ranch. A very different view of a glamourous Movie Star's life.

**B34.**   De Thuin, Richard. <u>Movie Memorabilia</u>, New York, House Of Collectibles, 1990. pp. 75, 76, 175, 267, 271, 272, 275, 292, 318.

Descriptions and prices on Grable memorabilia (autographed photos, magazines, movie posters and lobby cards) in this comprehensive volume on the highly competitive world of movie memorabilia collectibles.

**B35.**   Dickos, Andrew. <u>Intrepid Laughter, Preston Sturges and the Movies</u>, Metuchen, New Jersey, 1985. pp. 46, 48, 127-129.

A complete chapter on <u>The Beautiful Blonde From Bashful Bend</u> with photos, credits and critique in this detailed book about the life and work of filmmaker Sturges.

**B36.**   Dorian, Bob. <u>Bob Dorian's Movie Classics</u>, Holbrook, Mass. Bob Adams Inc., 1990. pp. 46-47, 62-63, 178-179.

Synopsis, cast list, photos and interesting anecdotes on <u>The Dolly Sisters</u>, <u>The Gay Divorcee</u> and <u>Springtime in The Rockies</u>.

**B37.**   Eames, John Douglas. <u>The Paramount Story</u>, New York, Crown Publishers, 1985. pp. 122, 125, 128, 134, 136, 143 - 144.

Photos and brief paragraphs on all of Grable's films at Paramount during the 1930's: <u>Collegiate</u>, <u>Thrill of a Lifetime</u>, <u>This Way, Please</u>, <u>College Swing</u>, <u>Campus Confessions</u>, <u>Man About Town</u> and <u>Million Dollar Legs</u>.

**B38.**   Eames, John Douglas. <u>The MGM Story</u>, New York, Crown Publishers, 1975. pp. 100, 185, 187, 206, 240, 277.

Minute synopsis, partial cast and staff credits for Grable's MGM film in this encyclopedia of MGM: <u>Student Tour</u>, plus mentions of her boxoffice status throughout the years. Unfortunately, there is no mention of the shorts she made for the studio (<u>Sunkist Stars at Palm Springs</u>, <u>Over The Counter</u>).

**B39.**   Eels, George. <u>Cole Porter, The Life That Late He Led</u>, New York, G.P. Putnam's Sons, 1967. pp. 211-212, 293.

Contains the details of Betty's discovery by agent Louis Shurr and producer Buddy de Sylva, which led to her being cast in Porter's <u>DuBarry Was a Lady</u>. It describes how Betty's

original dancing partner was replaced by Charles Walters:
"...and the ovation the Grable-Walters combination received
the first time they appeared together proved Shurr's hunch
was correct."

**B40.**    Engstead, John. <u>Star Shots</u>, New York, E.P. Dutton,
1978. pp. 11, 210.

Brief profile and narrative of the famed Hollywood
photographer Engstead having a photo session with Grable at
the end of her career: "She wore no makeup and had none with
her, although at this point in her career she needed a little
help. I found some makeup and lashes, and she left their
application completely to me. It was difficult to believe
that after all these years Betty had never learned to fix her
face - or would trust the job to me." One rare "Candid" photo
of Betty, Jackie Coogan and Engstead in 1935 - but none from
the session mentioned.

**B41.**    Erfurt Musser, Cynthia. <u>Classic Celebrity Cut-Outs</u>,
Cumberland, Md, Hobby House Press, Inc., 1988.

Chapter on Grable and the Whitman paperdoll book published in
1943. Includes a brief bio as well as photos of the cut-out
book, the two paper dolls and multiple costumes.

**B42.**    Feret, Bill. <u>Lure Of The Tropix</u>, New York, Proteus
Books, 1984. pp. 143 - 148.

In this photo packed light-hearted tribute to "Tropic
Temptresses," there are humourous photos of Grable as a
"Native" in <u>Song of the Islands</u> and <u>My Blue Heaven</u>, plus a
description of Jack Cole's choreographic work in <u>Three For
the Show</u>: "Jack brought his dance splendors of the East with
him for a hilarious satire of Betty's plight in a dream
sequence entitled 'DOWN BOY,' in which, as the harem queen
she is unable to decide which of her harem is to be her
favorite. For the number 'HOW COME YOU DO ME LIKE YOU DO?'
Jack fashioned a torrid, tropic extravaganza for Grable, that
may well very be one of her finest dances ever filmed."

**B43.**    Finler, Joel W. <u>The Hollywood Story</u>, New York, Crown
Publishers, Inc. 1988.

Grable's reign at Twentieth Century Fox is well documented in
the chapter about the studio, with graphs, grosses and
photos. It makes an interesting observation about Grable's
rise to fame: "She had appeared at just the right time for
Fox, picking up in 1940 more or less where Shirley Temple had
left off. A link was provided by Charlotte Greenwood who
played Shirley's mother in her *last* Fox film, <u>Young People</u>, in
1940, then was cast as Betty's lively aunt in her *first*
starring vehicle."

**B44.**    Fowler, Dan. "Betty Grable, Her Legs Are Her Fortune,"
<u>Look Magazine</u>, August 16, 1949.

A profile of the star written during the height of her

success, describing her career and personal life. When their mutual love for horses is discussed, Betty reveals that she and Harry would love to retire from Show Business and only raise horses: "That's where the money is - in the race horse business." When Harry celebrated a birthday in 1948, Betty gifted him with a brood mare from Louis B. Mayer's ranch, "Merry Soul," costing $35,000. Capping the article with a paragraph about her famous legs, the writer states: "Last year, a London photographer, Larry Gordon, selected Betty's right and Marlene Dietrich's left leg as 'the only two perfect legs in the world.' Betty was hurt.'What's the matter with my left leg?' Offhand, the question defies an answer."

**B45.**   Fox-Sheinwold, Patricia. Gone But Not Forgotten, New York, Bell Publishing Co., 1981. pp. 146 - 152.

Full bio chapter with many excellent photos.

**B46.**   Frank, Gerold. Judy, New York, Harper and Row, 1975. pp. 84, 143, 146, 216.

Detailed description of the Artie Shaw-Lana Turner-Judy Garland romantic escapade, primarily from Garland's point of view.

**B47.**   Frank, Rusty E. Tap, New York, William Morrow and Co., 1990.

Grable's rightful place in film tap-dancing history is notated in this unique book with a list of her films which contained exceptional tap-dancing.

**B48.**   Friedrich, Otto. City of Nets, New York, Harper and Row, 1986. pp. 108, 179, 180.

Several interesting mentions of Grable in this illuminating "Portrait of Hollywood in the 1940's" which describes important forces in the film industry during a very turbulent decade.

**B49.**   Gabor, Mark. The Pin-Up, A Modest History, New York, Universe Books, 1972. pp. 31, 77, 135, Color Plate 4, D-39.

Within this photo volume on the history of the Pin Up photo and girlie magazines, Betty's famous pose is printed and its appeal explained thusly: "The classic pose - the one-piece bathing suit, high heels and delicate ankle bracelet - seemed to say:'Follow me home, boys, I'm what you're fighting for.'"

**B50.**   Geist, Kenneth L. Pictures Will Talk, New York, Charles Scribner's Sons, 1978. pp. 49, 138, 256.

In this detailed biography of Joseph L. Mankiewicz, it is revealed that Mankiewicz, as the director of Guys and Dolls, held out to use Vivian Blaine in the film as "Adelaide" "despite Goldwyn's preference for Betty Grable as a bigger movie name."

**B51.**    Gill, Ted. "Betty Grable Has Nice Eyes Also," <u>St. Paul
Pioneer Press</u>, April 14, 1942.

Newspaper article based on Grable's wish "...that for a
change she could make a motion picture with all her clothes
on." Interviewed on the set of <u>Footlight Serenade</u> (being
filmed as <u>Strictly Dynamite</u> at the time of the interview)
Betty shows the author her scanty dance costumes and director
Gregory Ratoff admits that he added eight sequences in the
film where she could appear in various stages of undress. The
article concludes with her dancing until she wears a blister
on her foot, a piece of "business" then written into the
script.

**B52.**    Gil-Montero, Martha. <u>Brazilian Bombshell, The
Biography of Carmen Miranda</u>, New York, Donald I. Fine,
Inc, 1989. pp 96-97, 127, 131, 134, 136-137, 142, 153-
154, 187.

In this full length biography of co-star Carmen Miranda,
Grable is colorfully included in the angry report by the
Assistant Commercial Attache to the American Embassy in
Buenos Aires' objections to <u>Down Argentine Way</u>: "Carmen
Miranda, a Brazilian star, sings in Portugese a Tin Pan Alley
rhumba called 'DOWN ARGENTINE WAY,' which speaks of tangos
and rhumbas being played beneath a pampas moon...Betty Grable
does a conga with bumps...The Nicholas Brothers do a tap
dance...and add to the Argentine impression that all Yankees
think they are Indians or Africans. A colored person is seen
in Buenos Aires as often as a Hindu in Los Angeles."

**B53.**    Gorney, Jeffrey. "Betty Grable," <u>Films In Review</u>,
August-September, 1973, Vol. XXIV No. 7.  pp. 385-401.

Lengthy article about Grable's life and film career, with
many photos and facts, which quotes Samuel Goldwyn as saying:
"I had that girl under contract once; why didn't I do
something with her?" Also states that after her
disappointment with Preston Sturges and <u>The Beautiful Blonde
From Bashful Bend</u>, Betty's demands started getting stronger
at Fox. When Claude Binyon was signed to direct <u>My Blue
Heaven</u>, Betty demanded - and got - Henry Koster instead.

**B54.**    Grable, Betty. "From the Cradle to the Grable,"
<u>Hollywood Reporter</u>, October 1937.

In discussing her career in films, Betty humorously writes:
"They took my nursing bottle away from me and ushered me into
Producer Goldywn's sanctum and he dandled me on his knee,
then and there. I was just turning thirteen. I guess I was
fourteen or so when I began singing with Ted Fiorito's
orchestra, just killing time, so to speak. And I have never
played a child part in my life." She writes about spending
eight years in Hollywood, making public appearances
everywhere and trying to get ahead and the thrill of seeing
her name in lights for the first time with <u>This Way Please</u>.
She ends the article with these prophetic lines: "Wait until
I can pick and choose the cornerstone I have to lay, and

until they say,'You wanna dame to meet the train when Whoozis gets it? You want Grable? Sorry, you can't have Betty - she's taking a nap and we can't disturb her, ever, when she takes a nap."

**B55.**    Grable, Betty. "How I Keep My Figure," Photoplay, May 1941.

After being selected as "The Best Figure in Hollywood" by Photoplay panel members artists Paul Hesse, Dr. Mary Halton, Billy Rose and designer Irene, Betty wrote this article listing her health, exercise and beauty tips. For losing weight, she highly recommends dancing lessons - of any sort. She suggests eating three meals each day, but never taking "Seconds": "Always leave the table just a little hungry." Golf, bowling and keeping a daily eye on what your scales and your clothes tell you are also recommended.

**B56.**    Grable, Betty. Untitled, Twentieth Century Fox Press Release, 1941.

Humorous article purportedly written by Miss Grable about the trials and tribulations of filmmaking. The article begins: "For the last three days Tyrone Power and I have been trying to kiss" and tells how during the making of A Yank In The R.A.F., she and Mr. Power are hounded by 300 crew members, the censor, setting suns, screeching crows, airplanes, bees and other insects as they attempt to film a love scene. "If you make love in pictures, you must have patience."

**B57.**    Grable, Betty."Betty Grable Writes Her Own Story Of Her Early Life In St. Louis... And Admits She Walks In Her  Sleep,"  St. Louis Daily Globe Democrat, September 7, 1942.

Grable reminisces about her childhood in St. Louis' schools, her addresses and her early show business appearances at the Odeon Theater. She also mentions her favorite teacher (Mrs. Minton) and her best friend (Ruth Herms Skinner). Much is made of her sleep-walking habits: "Even now I have to be constantly watched at night and my windows must be opened only from the top. I have been to doctors, but they haven't been able to advance any cure. At one time we tried putting pans of ice-cold water around my bed and another remedy was chaining me to the bed by one leg...I'd still like to know a cure and if anyone knows one I would be extremely grateful if they would pass it on to me."

**B58.**    Grable, Betty. "The Role I Liked Best," Saturday Evening Post, April 10, 1948.

Grable writes that the part of "Kate Farley" in Coney Island has been her favorite. She mentions enjoying the period setting and the musical selections. Despite the fact that she had to reduce her waistline to seventeen inches for the costumes, she states: "My own part was thoroughly satisfying. Kate was a spirited girl at all times, and occasionally she was a hellcat."

**B59.**    Grable, Betty. "The Quiet Happiness," <u>Modern Screen</u>,
July, 1953. pp. 60-61, 66-67.

Discussing her religious beliefs, Grable writes about being
an Episcopalian since the age of five and her spiritual
attitudes. She talks about Lillian: "My Mother's great
ambition to be a singer was never fulfilled. I was
indifferent about a career yet I got one...thrust upon me
practically." About her daughter, Victoria: "When my elder
daughter, Vicki, wanted to take ballet I agreed. When she got
over the notion, I forgot about it too." She also mentions
becoming satisfied with her life and career and in 1948
hearing an erroneous radio broadcast that she had been killed
coming back from the race track, which shocked her out of the
complacency she was feeling about her life.

**B60.**    Grable, Mrs. Lillian, as told to Jane Kessner,
"Daughter Knows Best," <u>Movieland</u>, August 1951. pp 30-
33, 81.

In a fan-magazine "as Told to" story, Lillian recounts how
Betty got into the movies with her dancing talents. Mixing
"Stage Mother" and "Press Agent Hyperbole," Lillian recounts:
"I must confess that at that time my big dream was to see
Betty become a ballet dancer. However, I didn't believe in
forcing her to do anything she didn't like and Betty was not
what you call ambitious. She liked the kind of dancing she
was doing in pictures and that was that." Regarding <u>Dubarry
Was a Lady</u>, Lillian recalls: "Betty's part was brief, her
costumes weren't right, and neither was her partner. One
night as I was watching a rehearsal, an agent asked me:
'What's wrong with Betty? She doesn't seem to have her usual
zip.' I explained that she was disappointed in her
microscopic role. 'Why didn't she say so!' he cried. That was
just the last 'Mothering' I ever had to do. Betty's part was
enlarged, the whole show was changed and Betty was a smash
hit." The interview took place while Betty was filming <u>Meet
Me After The Show</u> and Lillian raves about choreographer Jack
Cole and his assistant, Gwynn (sic) Verdon. Discussing
Betty's suspension from Fox, Lillian is quoted as saying:
"Last year she had to sacrifice her precious six weeks with
Harry and the children at Del Mar, and she considers this
brief respite from picture making a 'must.'" She then
describes how Betty had to fight for her vacation that year,
going on suspension and the wonderful six weeks the James
family enjoys at Del Mar, playing on the beach in the
mornings and spending the afternoons at the racetrack.

**B61.**    Graham, Sheilah. "Still No. 1 Pin-Up Girl," <u>St. Louis
Globe</u>, November 5, 1943.

After the Betty Grable-Harry James wedding, this article
reports that Betty's popularity had not been hurt by the
merger. Betty chronicles their relationship: "We met in
Chicago ...I was doing two weeks of personal appearances and
Harry was playing in a hotel with his orchestra. I admired

him because I've followed bands all my life. But when we met
all he said was: 'Hello, howdy do'...The next time we met was
a year ago when he was in the same picture with me...We said
'Howdy do' again and that's all. I was going with George Raft
at the time. We really got to know each other two months ago
at the Hollywood Canteen...He went there every day to play
for the boys and I went there on Mondays to dance with them.
We had six dates before he went to New York. In the nine
weeks that we didn't see each other I had a telephone call, a
letter and a telegram every day!"

**B62.**    Green, Stanley. Encyclopaedia Of The Musical Film, New
         York, Oxford University Press, 1981.

Brief bio, filmography, synopsis of several of her films,
their Academy Award nominations and comments about some of
the songs she sang.

**B63.**    Green, Stanley. The Broadway Musical - A Picture Quiz
         Book, New York, Dover Publications, 1977. pp. 31, 92.

Interesting photos of Grable in Dubarry Was a Lady and Hello
Dolly.

**B64.**    Green, Stanley. Broadway Musicals, Show By Show,
         Milwaukee, Hal Leonard Books, 1987. p 109.

One page devoted to cast, credits, synopsis and information
about Dubarry Was a Lady.

**B65.**    Green, Stanley. Hollywood Musicals - Year By Year,
         Milwaukee, Hal Leonard, 1990.

Credits and brief comments about Whoopee!, The Gay Divorcee,
Follow the Fleet, Down Argentine Way, Tin Pan Alley, Moon
Over Miami, Springtime in the Rockies, The Dolly Sisters,
Coney Island, Sweet Rosie O'Grady, The Shocking Miss Pilgrim
and Mother Wore Tights; valuable director, composer/lyricist
and choreographer indexes.

**B66.**    Green, Stanley. Ring Bells! Sing Songs! Broadway
         Musicals of the 1930's, New Rochelle, N.Y., 1971. pp.
         81, 176, 188-190, 276, 367.

Descriptions, cast and credits of Tattle Tales and Dubarry
Was a Lady in this unique book detailing an important decade
in the evolution of the American musical.

**B67.**    Green, Stanley & Goldblatt, Burt. Starring Fred
         Astaire, New York, Dodd, Mead & Co. 1973. pp. 69-73,
         79, 119, 121, 124, 130.

Photos and information about Grable's participation in The
Gay Divorcee and Follow The Fleet in this excellent book,
which lavishly covers the career of Fred Astaire. It states
that the song "LET'S K-NOCK K-NEES," sung and danced in the
film by Grable and Edward Everett Horton, was originally

intended for <u>The Ziegfeld Follies of 1931</u>, but was cut during tryouts.

**B68.**    Griffith, Richard. <u>The Talkies</u>, New York, Dover Publications, 1971. pp. 218-219, 328.

This interesting volume of reprinted pages from <u>Photoplay</u> Magazine 1928-1940 contains a reprint of the August 1932 article, "The New Shady Dames of the Screen" by Ruth Biery (B13).

**B69.**    Guild, Leo. <u>Zanuck, Hollywood's Last Tycoon</u>, Los Angeles, Holloway House Publishing, 1970. pp. 72, 149, 155.

Description of Grable's importance to Darryl F. Zanuck and 20th Century Fox and her subsequent fall from favor when Marilyn Monroe arrived at the studio in this photo-filled paperback biography.

**B70.**    Gussow, Mel. <u>Don't Say Yes Until I Finish Talking</u>, New York, Doubleday and Co. 1971. pp. 92, 95-96, 132, 139, 152.

This biography of Fox studio head Darryl F. Zanuck contains Zanuck's diasppointment with Preston Sturges' direction of Betty in <u>The Beautiful Blonde From Bashful Bend</u>: "'He crucified her in it!,' remembered Zanuck. 'We previewed it in Pomona and I walked around the block ten times. God, I didn't know what to do!'"

**B71.**    Halliwell, Leslie. <u>Halliwell's Film Guide</u>, London, Granada, 1977.

Descriptions and critique of 33 of Grable's films in this mammoth guide to 8,000 English language films. The snippy criticisms are often witty: Re.<u>Down Argentine Way</u> - James Agate: "I dislike Technicolor in which all pinks resemble raspberry sauce, reds turn to sealing wax, blues shriek of the washtub and yellows become suet pudding."

**B72.**    Heffernan, Harold. "Grable And Shadow in Tap-Dancing Tiff," <u>The Detroit News</u>, June 11, 1942.

A newspaper article about the Shadow Boxing number in <u>Footlight Serenade</u>. A film was made of Miss Grable performing the "Shadow" role and then projected onto a screen behind her, so that she could dance with herself. She credits George Raft with teaching her boxing moves. Because there was no sound recording of the sequence, she talked throughout filming of the entire number: "That darned shadow (pant, pant) I'll fix you...Upstage me, will you?...(huff, puff) ...Hey, stay where you're supposed to...Oh, gosh." She sums up her feelings about the hard work with: "But I don't want to hear any more about this 'me and my shadow' just being pals stuff. My shadow is just a pain in the, er, neck to me!"

**B73**.    Heide, Robert & Gilman, John. <u>Starstruck, The</u>
<u>Wonderful World Of Movie Memorabilia</u>, Garden City,
N.Y., Doubleday & Co., 1986. pp. 164-171.

Biography and excellent photos of sheet music, lobby cards,
posters and movie magazine covers featuring Grable.

**B74**.    Heimann, Jim. <u>Out With The Stars</u>, New York, Abbeville
Press, 1985. pp. 155, 161, 173, 194, 212, 220.

Various mentions of Grable's active participation and
important social position in Hollywood Nightlife and the
Hollywood Canteen during the 1940's in this elegant tribute
to the nightclubs of the "Golden Era."

**B75**.    Hemming, Roy, <u>The Melody Lingers On</u>, New York,
Newmarket Press, 1986.

Biographical info, synopses, discographies and comments on
Grable's films and songs in relationship to composers Irving
Berlin, George Gershwin, Jimmy Mc Hugh, Cole Porter, Ralph
Rainger, Harry Warren and Jule Styne. Writing about the
Rainger and Robin scores for both <u>Footlight Serenade</u> and
<u>Coney Island</u>, the author notes that neither films scored any
"Hit Parade" songs hits because of the radio ban at the time
on any songwriters affiliated with ASCAP (the American
Society of Composers, Authors and Publishers). The networks
and ASCAP could not come to an agreement about royalty
payments, so the songs simply received no air play.

**B76**.    Higham, Charles & Greenberg, Joel. <u>Hollywood in the</u>
<u>Forties</u>, New York, A.S. Barnes, 1968. pp. 10, 159,
171, 177, 179-180.

Mentions of Grable's fame and musicals. In its synopsis and
raves of <u>Moon Over Miami</u>, the authors write: "Perhaps the
most striking feature of the film is how much it is ahead of
its time, pre-dating <u>On The Town</u>, which in many ways
resembles its use of free dancing through sets and
locations...The songs flow naturally out of the action,
expertly wedded to the dialogue."

**B77**.    Hirschhorn, Clive, <u>The Hollywood Musical</u>, New York,
Crown Publishers, Inc. 1981.

Synopses, song titles, composers, partial cast lists and
photos from all of Grable's musical films in this definitive
volume on film musicals.

**B78**.    Hirschhorn, Clive. <u>The Columbia Story</u>, New York, Crown
Publishers, 1990. pp. 43, 47, 210.

Synopses, brief cast and staff credits of Grable's three
Columbia films: <u>Child of Manhattan</u>; <u>What Price Innocence?</u> and
<u>Three For The Show</u> in this encyclopedia of the films of the
studio.

**B79**.    <u>Hollywood Citizen News</u>. "Harry James, Betty Grable Get

Divorce," October 8, 1965.

"The public wasn't invited, there was no music and the script was secret when the marriage of Betty Grable and Harry James reached the ending so familiar to film folk: divorce." The newspaper article goes on to tell that charging "extreme cruelty" and "mental cruelty," Betty was given a decree by Nevada Clark County District Court Judge John Mowbray after twenty two years of marriage. "Her attorney, Carl J. Christensen, said the settlement was amicable and that 'both parties would remain friends.' He said there would be no statements from Miss Grable or James."

**B80.**    Hopper, Hedda. "Second Baby Girl Born To Betty Grable," <u>Los Angeles Times</u>, May 21, 1947.

In Hopper's tongue-in-cheek report of Betty and Harry's second daughter's birth, she writes: "Jesse James came to town yesterday, in a new version. For the recent arrival is not a gunman wanted by a dozen sheriffs. Instead, she's a brand new baby girl in the Harry James family." Jessica weighed 6 pounds, 14 ounces and was delivered in a Caesarean operation by Dr. George S. Harris.

**B81.**    Howe, Herb. "Beautiful Blonde From Calabasas Ranch," <u>Photoplay</u>, April 1949. pp. 58-59, 92.

Grable's humility and dedication to her career is juxtaposed with descriptions of her home life with Harry and their two daughters. In discussing her willingness to go along with 20th Century Fox's decision as to scripts and directors, she is quoted: "If I just once showed a spark of ambition it would be the crowning joy of Mother's life." Her daughters showed no interest in their Mother's career until they saw her in a cowgirl outfit in <u>Beautiful Blonde From Bashful Bend</u>. Her worldwide appeal is described thusly: "Her appeal is boundless. It embraces all climes, races and cuisines. Cannibals on New Guinea unanimously chose her the girl they would like to have for lunch, according to a visiting GI who took their poll and missed their pot."

**B82.**    Hutchinson, Tom. <u>Screen Goddesses</u>, New York, Exeter Books, 1984. pp. 87 & 178.

In a brief profile entitled "A Pin-Up Goddess," in this primarily pictorial history of film beauties, Grable is described in this interesting analogy: "...she seemed utterly and completely like one of those band-singers so popular in the 1930s and 1940s - girls who stood languidly in front of an orchestra, caressing a microphone and giving forth with a number. She needed that kind of background; her body might have been its own orchestration to others, but as a satisfactory cinematic artist she needed that extension of smooth saxophones and silken strings." The book also includes a section on "Gimmicks" where Betty is quoted regarding her "Million Dollar Legs" as being a publicity stunt dreamed up by a new publicist when she was 17 or 18: "So their phoney contest took place and I was given the cup. But once they'd taken the pictures the cup went back. Then they had my legs sculptured, but all I wanted was that cup!"

**B83.**   Jarvis, Douglas. <u>Encyclopedia of Film Stars</u>, New York, Gallery Books, 1985. pages 64-65.

Brief biography and photos, plus comments from Dan Dailey about his friendship with Grable.

**B84.**   Jewell, Richard B. and Harbin, Vernon. <u>The RKO Story</u>, London, Octopus Books, 1982. pp. 50-51, 64, 77-78, 84, 87, 92, 98, 134.

Synopses, partial cast and staff credits for Betty's RKO films in this encyclopedia of RKO: <u>Hold 'Em Jail</u>; <u>Melody Cruise</u>; <u>The Gay Divorcee</u>; <u>By Your Leave</u>; <u>The Nitwits</u>; <u>Old Man Rhythm</u>; <u>Follow The Fleet</u>; <u>Don't Turn 'Em Loose</u>; <u>The Day The Bookies Wept</u> plus original information about Betty making an unbilled appearance in the 1932 college drama <u>The Age of Consent</u>.

**B85.**   Johnson, Grady. "Maid For Musicals," <u>New York Times</u>, April 30, 1950.

Newspaper profile about Grable's decision to make only musicals, after the failure of <u>That Lady in Ermine</u> and <u>Beautiful Blonde From Bashful Bend</u>. "When the director of the latter film, Preston Sturges, was quoted as saying in an expansive mood that her legs have 'stood in the way of her career,' Miss Grable observed that he must be off his rocker. Said she:'My legs made me.'"

**B86.**   Johnson, Dorris & Leventhal, Ellen. <u>The Letters of Nunnally Johnson</u>, New York, Alfred A. Knopf, 1981. pp. 105-106.

Very detailed reminiscences about the filming of <u>How To Marry a Millionaire</u> in the personal letters of producer, director and screenwriter Johnson: "Betty Grable was quite capable of delivering a line very well. She's a very good comedienne."

**B87.**   Jones, Jack. "Hollywood's Stars From Past Attend Betty Grable Funeral," <u>Los Angeles Times</u>, July 6, 1973.

A rather maudlin recounting of Betty's funeral: "Outside the church, a crowd of aging fans and curious young people stood in the sun for glimpses of the famous, finding that some of them had changed too much to be easily recognizable." The article reports that Harry James attended, sitting with his daughters and Betty's sister, Marjorie, avoiding photographers. "As the casket was taken from the church, a gray haired woman among the spectators delivered a eulogy of her own:'I enjoyed every one of her movies.'"

**B88.**   Katz, Ephraim. <u>The Film Encyclopedia</u>, New York, Perigee Books, 1979. pp. 496-497.

Abbreviated bio and filmography in this massive edition.

**B89.**    Keylijn, Arlene and Fleischer, Suri. Hollywood Album - <u>Lives And Deaths Of Hollywood Stars From The Pages Of The New York Times</u>, New York, Arno Press, 1977. p. 129.

Reprint of Grable's obituary and "My Legs Made Me" by Alden Whitman from the <u>New York Times</u>. Ironically, after all of the negative reviews Grable received from Bosley Crowther, the <u>New York Times</u> reviewer, the article shakily states: "Reviewers thought Miss Grable's films pleasant and bouyant. In World War II and the years that immediately followed, she could be counted on to tantalize and divert audiences, to take their minds of the grimness of armed conflict. She was, as a <u>New York Times</u> reviewer said, 'a lot of fun.'"

**B90.**    Kobal, John. <u>50 Super Stars</u>, New York, Bounty Books, 1974. pp.78-90.

Complimentary bio, filmography, unusual pin up photos and excellent color reproductions of two of her film posters in this poster-size book. Because the book was printed in England, it mentions her basically "American" appeal and states her name at birth as "Elizabeth Grasle."

**B91.**    Kobal, John. <u>Gotta Sing, Gotta Dance</u>, London, Hamlyn Publishing Group, 1970 (revised edition 1983).

Chatty bio, insightful comments by Hermes Pan and Dan Dailey, and Grable's contribution and place in the movie musical, including her work in Busby Berkeley films. Many excellent photos. Hermes Pan is quoted as saying in an interview: "The numbers I did for Betty were just things I dreamt up...The story just told you what you needed, and you went ahead and thought 'Wouldn't this be fun to do in dance form' or 'Nobody has ever done that, I wonder why?' and so I'd try it...There's only one number that stands out in my mind from that time, because I was very unhappy about it! It was a number I did with Betty Grable. It was the worst number that I've done, that Grable's ever done, that anybody has ever done! It was one of those horrible things which is just forced on you because of the song. It was during the war and it was called 'I'LL BE MARCHING TO A LOVE SONG' and it was just the most awful number." The number was deleted from <u>Footlight Serenade</u>, but was salvaged for <u>All Star Bond Rally</u> and exists on Video (V12).

**B92.**    Kobal, John. <u>People Will Talk</u>, New York, Alfred A. Knopf, 1985. pp. 210, 389, 442-443, 597, 629-631.

Comments about Grable from Madison Lacy, Melba Marshall, Lois Lindsay, Loretta Young, Jean Louis, Jack Cole and Hermes Pan in a very unique collection of interviews gathered by Kobal. In the interviews with film dancers Lacy, Marshall and Lindsay, they offer the following statements as they struggle with their memories - Lacy: "No, Betty Grable didn't begin as a Berkeley Girl." Lindsay: "She was singing with a band." Lacy: "She started in the Collegiates, shorts, they were made at Universal, suppposed to be a bunch of high-school kids or

college kids. Long time ago. And she was one of the extras on
the picture. And the leading lady, the girl playing the lead,
was a total flop...The director, whom I've forgotten, picked
Betty Grable to do the lead in this picture. And *she* was
terrible. But she was better than the other girl, the results
were better-looking." John Kobal: "But she did begin as a
Berkeley Girl in '29." Lacy: "Oh, but she had been around for
a long time by then." Loretta Young is quoted: "Let's say,
take the period of Betty Grable. She was the biggest star in
the business for ten years. Betty Grable was never an
actress, never pretended to be. Per se. Like Garbo or Bette
Davis or Joan Crawford or any of the big stars. She was
still, however, the biggest star in the business. Because
more people could identify with Betty Grable...than they
could do with Garbo."

**B93.**   Koster, Henry, <u>A Director's Guild Of America Oral
Historv</u>, Metuchen, New Jersey, Scarecrow Press, 1987.
pp. 3, 97-99.

Director Koster talks about his work with Grable (<u>My Blue
Heaven</u> and <u>Wabash Avenue</u>), his affection and admiration for
her and her sense of humor: "I want to say that Betty was the
funniest, the most natural movie actress I ever saw...
certainly not the greatest. She was not a great dancer, not a
great singer, not a great actress, but altogether such a
likeable personality. She couldn't say a phony word. Maybe
that made her as an actress not too great."

**B94.**   Kozicharow, Eugene. "You're Looking Swell, Betty,"
<u>Kansas City Times</u>, October 4, 1966.

When Grable arrived in Kansas City to star in <u>Hello Dolly</u>,
she gave an interview describing how happy she was with her
life. On the subject of Lillian, she had this to say: "She
never became a stage mother...Of course, I would rather have
gone to parties when I was young instead of taking music and
dancing lessons but everything has worked out marvelously."
She concludes the interview with: "I am not wrapped up in
myself...I'm proud of what I've done and I enjoy what I'm
doing now. I've never taken myself seriously one bit."

**B95.**   Kreuger, Miles. <u>The Movie Musical From Vitaphone To
42nd Street</u>, New York, Dover Publications, Inc. 1975.

Articles and revues reprinted from <u>Photoplay</u> of <u>Happy Days</u>,
<u>Fox Movietone Follies of 1930</u>, <u>Palmy Days</u>, <u>Whoopee</u> and <u>The
Kid From Spain</u>. A wonderful book containing priceless
material about early film musicals.

**B96.**   Lamour, Dorothy and McInnes, Dick. <u>My Side Of The
Road</u>, Englewood Cliffs, N.J., Prentice-Hall, Inc.
1980. pp. 23, 59, 61, 80-81, 172, 208-209, 216.

Kindly reminiscences about Lamour's work and friendship with
Grable. Among the memories: "...back in 1937 Betty and I were
just a blonde and brunette chosen by Wally Westmore who
needed a blonde and brunette so he could test some new makeup

for something called television. They put a very vivid blue
on me; Betty looked Irish in a bright Kelly Green. It was
fortunate that they perfected the television cameras only
later, because even in black and white we really looked like
two ladies from outer space."

**B97.** Lane, Lydia. "Betty Grable Discusses Care of
Complexion, Figure, Hair," <u>United Press</u>, 1955.

Under the topic of "Hollywood Beauty," Betty's glamour tricks
are revealed: "I've never scrubbed my face with soap and
water. My Mother used to say 'Wash your face and your beauty
goes down the drain.' I guess there is something to it,
because her skin is lovely even now and she has always used
hand lotion on her face." For her sun tan, Betty uses Cocoa
Butter, a suggestion given to her by her doctor to soften the
scar after she had her appendix removed. Mascara is the first
thing she applies each morning and she only diets when she is
working.

**B98.** Loney, Glenn. <u>Unsung Genius, The Passion of Dancer-
Choreographer Jack Cole</u>, New York, Franklin Watts,
1984. pp. 21, 124, 127-128, 159-163, 176-177, 211-213.

Detailed description of Jack Cole's relationship and work
with Grable in <u>Moon Over Miami</u>, <u>Meet Me After the Show</u>, <u>The
Farmer Takes a Wife</u> and <u>Three For the Show</u>.

**B99.** <u>Los Angeles Daily News</u>. "Betty Grable Helps Mother
Win Divorce," July 13, 1939.

Betty Grable Coogan testifies at her parent's divorce trial.
After being "assisted to the witness stand because of
lameness..." Lillian describes Conn as "arrogant, domineering
and critical and refused to work...He supported me for awhile
but Betty has been the sole support of myself and Mr.
Grable...Two weeks after Betty had an appendicitis operation,
he drove her from the house despite the fact she had been
supporting us for years...he said he wanted Betty's money -
his share."

**B100.** <u>Los Angeles Daily News</u>. "Rita, Betty Give Their Gangs
Big Fight Talk For Game at Coliseum," October 1942.

A newspaper article which relates that Betty Grable and Rita
Hayworth are the captains for football teams composed of
Hollywood celebrities for a charity football game to be held
on October 18, 1942 at the Los Angeles Coliseum. The proceeds
from the game will go to the U.S.O. and Mt. Sinai Hospital.
Rita Hayworth leads the "Leading Men" team, containing such
stars as Anthony Quinn, Broderick Crawford, Dennis Morgan,
Dick Powell and George Montgomery. Betty leads the
"Comedians": Buster Keaton, Jack Oakie, J. Carroll Naish,
Arthur Lake, Andy Devine, Allen Jenkins, Alan Mowbray and
Billy Gilbert. Prior to the 2 p.m game, there was "The Parade
of Stars," featuring more than 150 celebrities. Admission was
55 cents.

**B101.** <u>Los Angeles Daily News</u>. "Betty Grable Weds James," July 6, 1943.

All of the details of the hectic James-Grable wedding: A five minute ceremony; performed at the Little Church of the West in the Hotel Last Frontier at 4:15 a.m. on July 5; officiated by Rev. C. S. Sloan, Baptist minister and Nevada County Clerk Lloyd Pains; witnessed by Mrs. Edith Wasserman, Betty Furness and Emmanuel Sacks and the costumes: "Miss Grable, remarking that she was very happy but a little nervous, wore a 'something new' hat at a dangerous angle atop her curly hair-do, and twisted a 'something borrowed' handkerchief given to her by Alice Faye." Harry's train from New York had been an hour and a half late, adding to the anxiety and they would not be able to enjoy a "Honeymoon," as the Bride was working on a film and the Groom had a radio broadcast the following morning from Hollywood. One of James' best wedding gifts was his reclassification by his local Beaumont, Texas draft board as a "family man."

**B102.** <u>Los Angeles Daily News</u>. "Threat to Kidnap Grable Baby; FBI Jails Woman Here," January 9, 1948.

Newspaper article detailing the latest extortion plot against Grable. Mrs. Jane Bean, of Los Angeles, sent a threatening note to Betty, demanding $5000 in cash, or daughter Jessica would be kidnapped. The FBI quickly apprehended the woman. Three previous extortion plots against Grable were noted: In 1941, a Pennsylvania youth, calling himself "The Yellow Hornet," demanded $2000; in 1942, an 18 year old Omaha boy, calling himself "The Leopard," demanded $5000. In 1943, while on probation, "The Leopard" tried to get an additional $500.

**B103.** <u>Los Angeles Daily News</u>. "Betty Grable Suspended," May 2, 1951.

On May 1, 1951, Grable was suspended "without salary for a maximum of eight weeks" for refusing to start filming on <u>The Girl Next Door</u>. "She complained she hasn't been getting enough time off to be with her family," a studio spokesman was quoted.

**B104.** <u>Los Angeles Herald and Express</u>. "Betty Grable Makes 'Kid' Divorce Final," November 19, 1940.

Newspaper article about Grable receiving her final decree from Jackie Coogan. Reasons for the divorce were stated as: "Miss Grable testified that the famous 'Kid' of silent screen days had quarreled with her without cause, had stayed out late at night on many occasions and that finally one day when she came down to breakfast, she found 'some men moving our furniture out of the house'..." which Coogan had sold to pay bills he owed. The last paragraph of the article states that Grable denied she was engaged to Victor Mature.

**B105.** <u>Los Angeles Times</u>. "Betty Grable Ordered To Rest To Gain Strength For Operation," May 20, 1942.

Grable is ordered to stop work so that she could gain strength for an operation, which had "aggravated her condition" by strenuous dance routines. Neither the "condition" nor the operation is ever named.

**B106.** <u>Los Angeles Times</u>. "Betty Grable and Harry James Become Parents of Daughter," March 3, 1944.

"Legs-famous Betty Grable and trumpet-toting Harry James yesterday became the parents of a 7-pound 12-ounce baby girl - Victoria Elizabeth - born to the actress at Cedars of Lebanon hospital." Dr. George Harris, performed a Caesarian operation for Victoria, who was premature (not due until March 31st).

**B107.** <u>Los Angeles Times</u>. "Grable-James Horse Trainer, Ousted, Sues," April 26, 1947.

Newspaper article which tells that horse trainer Donald Jefferson, hired by the James' with a one year contract, signed Sepember 12, 1946, was fired by the couple on February 9, 1947, without just cause. Jefferson was seeking $14,500 in damages, plus a complete accounting of the winnings of the horses he had trained, as he had been promised ten per cent of their winnings.

**B108.** <u>Los Angeles Times</u>. "Harry James, Betty Grable End Turf Suits," May 25, 1947.

Less than a month after the previously listed article, this article appeared stating that the James' had settled with Horse Trainer Donald Jefferson for a "satisfactory amount". The article also mentions that the James' had dropped a $68,000 suit previously filed against C.H. Jones and Sons over the sale of seven horses, which the James' claimed were "unfit for competition."

**B109.** <u>Los Angeles Times</u>. "Betty Grable Ordered to Appear in Court," December 8, 1950.

In December, 1950, Grable had two court cases pending. One regarded a "breach of contract" issue when she changed talent agencies from MCA Artists, Ltd. to Nat Goldstone. The other was due to a squabble Betty and Harry were having with neighbors Perry and Virginia Snow over a fence. The Snows claim that the James'(with Conn Grable, the ranch manager) had constructed concrete and wire barriers which prevented the Snows from "access to joint irrigation installations."

**B110.** <u>Los Angeles Times</u>. "Suit Names Betty Grable, Harry James," April 11, 1955.

Another article about a law suit involving the ranch - which seemed to plague Betty and Harry. This time, the law firm of Pacht, Tannenbaum and Ross demanded back salaries of $24,195 from the James' for services performed over the last four years. The Sheriff attached the Calabasas Ranch for payment.

**B111.** <u>Los Angeles Times</u>. "Hotel in Las Vegas Sues Grable,

Harry James," March 15, 1956.

Yet another troublesome article describing that the El Rancho
Hotel in Las Vegas filed suit against the couple for $53,000.
The hotel claimed that this was the amount due for advanced
salaries and rent for accomodations for the couple and their
entourage during their engagements at the hotel. It disclosed
that the couple was earning $12,750 per week in a 20-weeks-
per -year contract, but had far exceeded the salary due with
advances and rental for four bedrooms and five separate
cottages (for family, mother, two managers, band members and
guests). Betty and Harry were handed a summons as they left
the stage after completing a four-week engagement at the
Hotel.

**B112.**   Los Angeles Times. "Wedding Bells Ring for Belles of
Filmland," August 17, 1964.

August 15, 1964 was a day filled with "Show Biz" weddings:
Amanda Blake, Connie Francis and Betty and Harry's first
daughter, Vicki (Victoria). At the age of twenty, she married
William Bevins in Las Vegas. The couple had met while they
were both students at the University of Arizona.

**B113.**   Los Angeles Times. "Miss Grable Ignores Bad Stage
Reviews," May 3, 1969.

An article quoting the ugly reviews Betty received in London
in Belle Starr. "A spokesman for the 52-year-old Hollywood
star of the 40's quoted her as saying: 'I gave up reading
reviews years ago and I'm not going to start reading them
now. The British audiences are wonderful, and that's more
important.'"

**B114.**   Louisville Courier-Journal, "Betty Grable, With
$208,000, Leads All Women Salary Earners in 1945,"
August 26, 1946.

An article which lists the highest salaries of 1945. Grable
led American females, followed by Olivia De Havilland
($206,994), Maureen O' Hara ($190,666.67) and Gene Tierney
($114,916.67). Grable also out-earned the top salaried film
actor Fred MacMurray ($203,526) but not Charles P. Skouras,
of the Fox West Coast Agency Corporation, who earned
$568,144. Harry James' salary is quoted at $111,667, making
Mr. and Mrs. James America's highest earning couple.

**B115.**   Lowrance, Dee. "Movieland's Misunderstood Miss,"
Oakland Tibune, July 25, 1943.

Grable reacts to the untruths printed by the press about her
romantic life and all of the feuds with female costars that
have been started by the press. About Alice Faye, she said:
"Alice has her own following and we are two different
personalities. I couldn't fill Alice's shoes even if I wanted
to...she has everything I'd like to have. Not only her acting
ability and the way she can put over a song, but she has a
home, a husband and a baby. I'd be the happiest girl in the

world if I could follow in her footsteps." About the supposed feud with Carole Landis during the filming of I Wake Up Screaming, she said: "Carole and I are the best of friends and we have a habit of sharing our servicemen visitors now. When I have a group I take them over to meet Carole - and Carole does the same with hers." Another supposed feuding co-star, Carmen Miranda, is phonetically quoted about Betty: "I am mad for leetle Betty...she is so cutey, sooch wonderful dancing, how she seengs. Eef she would onlee come to my countree, her sensation would be volcanoed. In Brazeel they would have great eruptions of joy and admeeration for Betty!"

B116.  Lynch, Richard Chigley. Movie Musicals on Record, Westport, Conn., Greenwood Press,1989.

Detailed discography of several of Grable's films.

B117.  Mann, May. "The Startling Truth About Betty Grable," Screen Stars, July, 1947. pp. 20-21, 52.

Fan magazine writer reveals that Betty is pregnant with her second child, while filming Mother Wore Tights. "Harry said to me one day, 'Betty, seems to me you're getting a little plump. Why don't you go and see the doctor?...He didn't have to look to tell me, and to my surprise, mind you, the James would have a new heir in another few months." When asked why she felt she had been awarded the "Sour Apple" by the Woman's Press Club for being one of the least cooperative stars of the year, she explained that when she spends time visiting Harry while he is on tour, she feels that the focus should be on him, not on her. She also adds: "Somehow I think it is bad taste to exploit one's family and children to further the box office...If pictures ever conflict with the happiness of my home and family, well, it would be goodbye pictures." About her nomination as "most uncooperative star," she quipped: "But at least I was in good company; they also nominated Crosby, Bergman and Sinatra. All good people to be with."

B118.  Manners, Dorothy. "Snappy Shots - The Four Jameses," Los Angeles Examiner, April 9, 1948.

Description of the home life of the Harry James': "She has a special clause in her contract that she may stop work promptly at 6 o'clock in order to be home for 6:30 dinner with 4-year-old Vicki, 10-month-old Jessica and pappy Harry James...Right after dinner, the baby is put to bed then Betty and Harry go into Vicki's room to listen to her sing her two nightly songs 'YES, JESUS LOVES ME' and 'GOD BLESS AMERICA,' followed by her prayers." Harry then goes out to his latest band date and Betty reads a novel. Summer vacations are spent at Del Mar and Winters are spent at their ranch in Calabasas. On Friday night, the girls are allowed to stay up late to listen to their Father on his radio broadcasts.

B119.  Manville, Roger. Love Goddesses of the Movies, New York, Crescent Books, 1985. pp. Title Pages, 96-99.

Brief bio and nice photos. This book mentions another theory

about Betty's name change to "Frances Dean":"...and a number
of two-reelers with her identity hidden under the name of
Frances Dean, in order to avoid trouble with RKO studios, who
had put her under a five-year contract in 1933 but were
unable to find enough work to keep her occupied."

**B120.**   Martin, Pete. "The World's Most Popular Blonde,"
        Saturday Evening Post, April 15, 1950.

Long, detailed article about Grable's popularity and appeal
to the common man. In interviews with hair-stylist Marie
Brasselle and dance-coach Angie Blue, details are given about
Grable's "down to earth" attitudes and behavior on the set.
Blue states that Grable has a tendency to gain weight between
pictures (she describes her as:"Saftig") and the crash diets
she must go before she starts each film role. In a
description of Dan Dailey's nervousness over co-starring with
Betty, she is quoted as saying to him: "Relax, Dan. I've got
mine. Go get yours." The article then details most of her
life, concluding with a snide quote from an unnamed Columnist
of the time when she was expecting first daughter, Victoria:
"Wouldn't it be terrible if that blonde musical star and her
musician husband have a child with her brain and his legs?"
Grable's retort was:"He has good legs!"

**B121.**   Mason, Jerry. "I Danced With Grable," This Week,
        September 26, 1943.

"Betty Grable sings softly in your ear when she's dancing
with you. She is also a very good dancer. It is also a very
great pleasure to hold her in your arms. I know because I
took Betty Grable dancing" is the opening paragraph as a
reporter spends a night on the town with Miss Grable, the
evening that Coney Island premiered. He tells about Grable's
request to drive by the theater before the Premiere "...to
see if anybody's waiting in line to buy tickets." He writes
at great length about her common appeal ("I'm the kind of
girl truck drivers like") and the many hours she spends at
the Hollywood Canteen, dancing with servicemen and signing
autographs. The article concludes with a recollection by
Grable about visiting a hospital and a wounded soldier who
did not believe she was Betty Grable: "So Betty stepped back,
held her sport dress an inch above the knees, put those
famous legs together and waited. The boy looked carefully.
Then: 'Yep. You're Betty Grable!'"

**B122.**   Maynard, John. "Call Her Betty James - What Is Betty
        Grable Really Like?," Motion Picture, August 1950. pp.
        40-41,59-60.

A fan-mag article which talks about Grable's desire for
anonymity when she is with her family. In describing the
"Real" Betty Grable, it discusses her love of the children
and their ranch. While talking about her career, it states:
"In the matter of certain unimportant aspects of Miss
Grable's professional life, studio and outside sources are
not in complete agreement. Fox spokesmen contend that on the
set or in choice of scripts she is docile as a lamb, whereas

others understand she can raise quite a commotion when
crossed. Again, both studio and Miss Grable were honestly
hurt and puzzled when a story in a national magazine inferred
that Miss Grable's mother, Lillian, was a domineering sort
where Betty is concerned. Daughter and employer alike,
doubtless in the best position to know, deny it."

**B123.**    McClelland, Doug. Forties Film Talk, Jefferson,
          N.C., McFarland and Co., 1992. pp 5, 58, 155, 372-75,
          379-80

Anecdotes from Grable co-stars Robert Arthur, Alice Faye, Dan
Dailey, Douglas Fairbanks, Jr. and Grable herself in this
enjoyable book. Grable tells her version of the "Pin Up"
photo session and praises Frank Powolny for his photographic
talents: "He'll tell you it was nothing...but the picture was
Mr. Powolny and his camera genius."

**B124.**    Michael, Paul. The American Movies Reference Book: The
          Sound Era, Englewood Cliffs, N.J., Prentice-Hall, Inc.
          1969.

Statistics, cast, credits and photos of nine of Grable's
films.

**B125.**    Minneapolis Star Journal, "Jitterbugging Sends Grable
          To Hospital," April 6, 1943.

A newspaper report about Grable going into the hospital on
April 7, 1943 for an operation. "Production recently was
suspended when the star began suffering pains in her right
side, recurrence of the trouble which bothered her in another
picture a year ago." She cites too much "Jitterbugging" at
the Hollywood Canteen, and expects to be back at work in
three or four weeks.

**B126.**    Moore, Christopher. "Hollywood's Most Famous Photo-
          graph," Hollywood Studio Magazine - Then And Now,
          September 1981.

One page description and accompanying photo of Grable's
famous pin up pose. It states that the pose was a result of
photographer Frank Powolny saying: "Look this way, Betty" and
that the shot was intended for the use of Fox studio artists
to create artwork for Sweet Rosie O'Grady, complete with
black garter on her left thigh, which had to be removed
through retouching, by request of the Hays office.

**B127.**    Mordden, Ethan. The Hollywood Musical, New York, St.
          Martin's Press, 1981. pp. 61, 63, 65, 93, 94, 113,
          143, 161, 165, 168, 182, 186, 195.

Breezy observations on some of Grable's roles and films:
"Zanuck thought the story musical too much bother, but the
public was happy - Grable made the top-ten list from 1942-
1951, number one in 1943. The year is crucial: Grable was
essentially the nation's wartime mascot and Grable knew it.
'I'm strictly an enlisted man's girl' she explained, 'just

like this has got to be an enlisted man's war.' Like Faye, Grable was a working-class Cinderella."

**B128.**   Mordden, Ethan. <u>The Hollywood Studios</u>, New York, Alfred A. Knopf, 1988. pp. 84, 165, 264, 272, 284-288, 313.

Excellent analysis of Fox's "Grable Musical Film" formula, written in Mordden's highly entertaining style: "...the Grable musicals are pleasurable. Consider <u>Coney Island</u> (1943). This is absolute Grable: a costume show (in as many incorrect costumes as possible), a Technicolor show...a backstage show (with all numbers in a performing context) ...It moves, it's funny, and it has everything: old standards...old novelties...and some new songs; two big dark men (Montgomery and Romero); two stage-trained comics (Charles Winninger and Phil Silvers); some Irish savor; a competent director (Walter Lang); and Grable. Nothing unusual here. These films ran not on surprise but on familiarity."

**B129.**   Mordden, Ethan. <u>Movie Star - A Look At The Women Who Made Hollywood</u>, New York, St. Martin's Press, 1983. pp. 101, 168, 194-195, 198, 212, 216, 218, 233, 287.

In the chapter "Maidens and Pinups," Grable is compared to the other leading female stars of the 1940's: Rita Hayworth, Judy Garland, Deanna Durbin, Shirley Temple, Elizabeth Taylor and Ava Gardner in this highly pleasurable study of women in film. "Grable was the quasi-virgin pinup, closer to Garland than to Hayworth, even if the postmaster general felt driven to ban her famous bathing suit from the mails. Grable was a family pinup, a wife and daughter, and thus very close to the wrapped-up tone of the times."

**B130.**   Morella, Joe, Epstein, Edward Z. & Griggs, John. <u>The Films Of World War II</u>, Secaucus, N.J., Citadel Press, 1973. pp. 54-56, 182-183, 187-189.

Cast, credits, photos, discussion and reviews (usually devastating) of <u>A Yank in the R.A.F.</u>, <u>Four Jills In a Jeep</u> and <u>Pin Up Girl</u>, Grable's three films with a World War II theme and setting.

**B131.**   Morella, Joe & Clark, Eleanor. <u>Those Great Movie Ads</u>,

New Rochelle, N.Y., Arlington House, 1972. pp. 93, 175, 234, 238, 253-254.

Reprints of the original ads for <u>Beautiful Blonde From Bashful Bend</u>, <u>Tin Pan Alley</u>, <u>Pin Up Girl</u>, <u>Down Argentine Way</u>, <u>The Dolly Sisters</u> and <u>Cavalcade</u>.

**B132.**   Moshier, W. Franklin. <u>The Alice Faye Movie Book</u>, Harrisburg, Pa., Stackpole Books, 1974. pp.15-17, 137-139, 156, 169-170.

Synopsis, credits, reviews and many photos from <u>Tin Pan Alley</u>; anecdotes about Grable's relationship with Alice Faye;

plus the author's assessment about the relationship of three of the "Fox Blondes": "Film historians through the years have been quick to point out that it was Grable who 'replaced' Faye and ultimately Monroe who 'replaced' Grable. A closer examination of the facts proves that both Faye and Grable projected quite a different personality from the screen. Down Argentine Way was changed to fit the Grable temperament of a more extroverted blonde and to concentrate on her natural talents for dancing. In all fairness one cannot claim that Monroe 'replaced' Grable. Their styles were markedly different. Grable was bright, breezy, bold and brash. Monroe was a smoldering sexpot, a unique personality not essentially a singer like Faye nor a dancer like Grable."

**B133.**   Nash, Jay Robert and Ross, Stanley Ralph. The Motion Picture Guide, Chicago, Cinebooks, Inc. 1985.

All of Grable's films described in this mammoth multi-volume set, giving cast and abbreviated credits, as well as synopsis, comments, behind-the-scenes details and often insightful critiques.

**B134.**   New York Daily News, June 14, 1982.

In a Hollywood gossip column, it is announced that TV producer Bob Banner will film the book Pin-Up with actresses Loni Anderson and Ann Jillian being considered to play Grable. The TV movie was to be aired on CBS in 1983. It never happened.

**B135.**   New York Times, "Miss Grable Voted Leading 1943 Star," December 25, 1943.

Betty is hailed as "Motion-Picture Herald's Box-Office Champ" for the first time in 1943. Rising from #8 in 1942, she displaces Abbott and Costello as filmdom's most popular star. Bob Hope is anounced as #2 and Abbott and Costello slide to the third position.

**B136.**   New York Times.

Reviews:
Let's Go Places, 3.1.30
Kiki, 3.6.31
Greeks Had a Word For Them,The, 2.4.32
Hold 'Em Jail, 8.24.32
Cavalcade, 1.6.33
Child of Manhattan, 2.13.33
Melody Cruise, 6.23.33
What Price Innocence?, 6.26.33
Sweetheart of Sigma Chi,The 11.9.33
Hips, Hips, Hooray, 2.24.34
Student Tour, 10.31.34
Gay Divorcee,The, 11.16.34
Collegiate, 1.23.36
Follow the Fleet, 2.22.36
Don't Turn 'Em Loose, 9.25.36
Pigskin Parade, 11.14.36

This Way Please, 10.8.37
Thrill of a Lifetime, 12.9.37
College Swing, 4.28.38
Give Me A Sailor, 8.11.38
Campus Confessions, 9.23.38
Man About Town, 6.29.39
Day the Bookies Wept, The, 9.14.39
DuBarry Was a Lady, 12.7.39
Down Argentine Way, 10.18.40
Tin Pan Alley, 11.22.40
Moon Over Miami, 7.5.41
Yank in the R.A.F..A, 9.27.41
I Wake Up Screaming, 1.17.42
Song of the Islands, 3.12.42
Footlight Serenade, 8.10.42
Springtime in the Rockies, 11.12.42
Coney Island, 6.17.43
Sweet Rosie O'Grady, 10.21.43
Four Jills in a Jeep, 4.6.44
Pin-Up Girl, 5.11.44
Billy Rose's Diamond Horseshoe, 5.3.45
Dolly Sisters, The, 11.15.45
Shocking Miss Pilgrim, The, 2.12.47
Mother Wore Tights, 8.21.47
That Lady in Ermine, 8.25.48
When My Baby Smiles at Me, 11.24.48
Beautiful Blonde From Bashful Bend, 5.28.49
Wabash Avenue, 4.29.50
My Blue Heaven, 8.16.50
Call Me Mister, 2.1.51
Meet Me After the Show, 8.16,51
Farmer Takes a Wife, The, 6.13.53
How To Marry a Millionaire, 11.11.53
Three For the Show, 2. 25.55
How to Be Very, Very Popular, 6.23.55
Hello Dolly!, 6.14.67
Belle Starr, 5.3.69
Obituary -   7.4.73

**B137.**   Oakie, Jack. Jack Oakie's Double Takes, San Francisco, Strawberry Hill Press, 1980. pp. 62, 66, 69, 96, 109-110.

Photos and reminiscences by Oakie about his film work with Grable.

**B138.**   Othman, Frederick C. "Betty Grable Has Sun-Tan Trouble After Layoff For Operation," St. Louis Star-Times, May 24, 1943.

During the filming of Sweet Rosie O' Grady, the filming is halted "...because its star, Betty (Peaches and Cream) Grable, got a pain in her side. So Betty had an operation, went to the desert to recuperate and returned to work as good as new. Only she wasn't peaches and cream any more. More of a handsome bronze." Daily baths in lemon juice are suggested, but solutions were found by the makeup department with pale make-up and more lighting from the photographic department so that she could "Match" the previous footage.

**B139.**    Othman, Frederick C.. "Legs Grable Puts Them In
Concrete," <u>United Press</u>, February 17, 1943.

Article describing the ceremony enshrining Grable's right leg
imprint at Grauman's Chinese Theater. "Getting the imprints
of Miss Grable's legs in the cement was an engineering
project that took an hour and a half, and the army, navy and
marine corps. The problem was to get the legs in the goo and
keep 'em there while the concrete set, without getting Miss
Grable's skirt too high for the Hays office." Betty was
assisted by Naval Gunner's Mate J.O. Buchanan; Marine
Sergeant B. L. Duckett and Army Sergeant Albert Woas (whose
last name is printed in various articles about the ceremony
as "Woab," "Woas" and "Moss.") During the intricate
choreography necessary to only lower Miss Grable's right leg
into the cement, they almost dropped her and succeeded in
sitting her in the wet cement, covering her dress with
cement. "She said she guessed she'd have to hurry home and
get off that dress before it set."

**B140.**    Parish, James Robert. <u>The Fox Girls</u>, New Rochelle,
N.Y., Arlington House, 1971. pp. 339-409.

Excellent bio chapter, filmography and photos, containing
many interesting anecdotes: "Betty would also innocently
recall that as a child she had a recurring dream that she was
hitting her mother over the head with the bedside lamp - Mrs.
Grable and Betty took its obvious implications jokingly...
Among the other problems the couple had were Coogan's failure
to come home nights, his selling at auction of most of their
wedding gifts, and his alleged hampering of her career. In
fact, claimed Betty at the court hearing, he once sold their
furniture to buy a car to leave town."

**B141.**    Parish, James Robert. <u>The Paramount Pretties</u>, New
Rochelle, New York, Arlington House, 1972. pp. 332,
337, 339, 352, 354, 375, 546.

Facts about Grable in relationship to her work at Paramount
and Dorothy Lamour.

**B142.**    Parish, James Robert & Pitts, Michael R., <u>Hollywood
Songsters</u>, New York, Garland Publishing, Inc. 1991.
pp. 299-306.

Another excellent bio chapter, expanded filmography and
discography in this tribute to Hollywood's singing stars.

**B143.**    Parsons, Harriet. "Failure Six Months Ago, Betty
Grable's On Way To Stardom," <u>Omaha World Herald</u>, June
30, 1940.

Written by the daughter of famous Hollywood Gossip Queen
Louella O. Parsons, this newspaper article describes Betty's
new contract with 20th Century Fox and her New York success
in <u>Dubarry Was a Lady</u>. Betty confesses that Darryl Zanuck is

the first studio executive she has ever spoken to after her contracts with RKO and Paramount. "At Para, however, her juvenile appearance caused her to be continually cast as a collegiate rah-rah girl. She played so many sophomores that she began to believe she was doomed to a perpetual life on campus. She's pretty tickled, therefore, to find that her new boss, Zamuck (sic), is going to let her graduate and plans to put her in Ginger Rogers-ish roles."

**B144.**   Parsons, Louella O. "Betty Grable, James To Wed," Los Angeles Examiner, June 30, 1943.

This newspaper article by the Hollywood Gossip Queen herself, describes the many details of the upcoming wedding: Mrs. Louise James, Harry's former wife, would obtain a divorce within the next few days, and both Betty and Harry were trying desperately to secure train reservations to Las Vegas. Betty was coming from Hollywood and Harry would be arriving from New York.

**B145.**   Parsons, Louella O. "Betty Grable and Children," Los Angeles Examiner, December 21, 1947.

As part of Parsons' regular "In Hollywood" series of newspaper articles, Betty's career and home life are described, with an emphasis on Christmas activities at the James' home. "Last year, Harry put on old tired whiskers that were almost gray and played Santa Claus...This year we will get a stranger to do the honors. Vicki will be three and a half and she would surely recognize her daddy." Betty describes her pleasure in working with famed directors Ernst Lubitsch on That Lady in Ermine and Walter Lang on Mother Wore Tights. When asked if she has any plans for retirement, Betty says: "Oh, no, of course not...Harry has to be away on tour with his orchestra and that's the time I try to get in my picture making. With two children, I can't go with him."

**B146.**   Parsons, Louella O. "In Hollywood," Los Angeles Examiner, October 9, 1949.

In this profile on Betty and Harry James' relationship written while Parsons was enjoying a one month long vacation at Del Mar with the couple, Grable admits to introducing Horse Racing to Harry: "Harry had never been to a horse race in his life until he met me. I guess I'm responsible for his interest in horses. We bought a couple of horses to ride, and had no place to keep them. So, we bought a little place in the country. The little place turned out to be 62 acres!" It goes on to discuss the expenses of raising horses: "Of course, it's expensive to start with...but our horses have pretty well paid for their keep. I can't truthfully say we have made any money yet, but that doesn't worry us." The article ends with Grable voicing her unhappiness with The Beautiful Blonde From Bashful Bend, which she calls "the Sturges atrocity."

**B147.**   Parsons, Louella O. "Betty Grable," Los Angeles Examiner, May 14, 1950.

Grable discusses her dedication to her fans and thoughts on acting in musical films with gossip-writer Parsons. While appearing on Parsons' radio program, they review her acting abilities: "'You really don't think I am a good actress' she said. 'No one ever said that of me.'" Louella replies:'Oh, yes, they did. I for one, and other critics thought you gave a beautiful acting performance in <u>Mother Wore Tights</u>." The on-going discussion about performers being nominated for Oscars in musical films is ended with Grable saying that she felt Ginger Rogers deserved an Oscar in <u>The Barkleys of Broadway</u>.

**B148.**   Parsons, Louella O. "Glamour Girls Can Be Friends," <u>Los Angeles Examiner</u>, June 28, 1953.

Gossip doyenne Louella's version of the Grable-Monroe "feud": "At Walter Winchell's party, given for me, the two glamour queens of the 20th lot, Betty and Marilyn, walked in arm in arm, and I had an opportunity to talk to Betty, whose husband, Harry James, was out of town. Marilyn Monroe's devoted Joe Di Maggio was also among the absent, hence they arrived together...Marilyn, who I see often, had told me of Betty's great kindness to her and how she went out of her way to help her. Marilyn isn't one who expresses herself on any subject that she doesn't mean."

**B149.**   Parsons, Louella O. "Grable Given 20th Release," <u>Los Angeles Examiner</u>, July 1, 1953.

Parsons' account of the end of the Fox/Grable partnership. The article erroneously states "She has been under contract to the studio since 1936, when she made her first musical <u>Pigskin Parade</u>." It mentions her third and last suspension (for refusing to be loaned to Columbia for something called <u>The Pleasure is All Mine</u>, which Parsons said would be filmed with Rita Hayworth). "But she recently told me that she had wanted her release from 20th because she felt she'd be better off choosing her own stories. One by one, these big-salaried stars are leaving the studios: June Allyson, Jeanne Crain and now Betty."

**B150.**   Pascall, Jeremy & Jeavons, Clyde. <u>A Pictorial History Of Sex In The Movies</u>, London, Hamlyn, 1975. pp.95, 98-100.

Contains the author's thesis of Grable's status as "Pin Up Supreme" in the sexual development of films; her allure and the changing image of women as objects of lust. "If anyone in films had gold beating beneath their bosom it was Betty Grable."

**B151.**   Pastos, Spero. <u>Pin-Up - the Tragedy Of Betty Grable</u>, New York, G.P. Putman's Sons, 1986.

Extensively researched book-length biography with many photos; personal comments from sister Marjorie, daughter Jessica and good friends Betty Ritz, Paula Stone and former beau, Charles Price; Reviews; personal anecdotes. Several people interviewed for this book told this author that they felt they had been greatly misquoted in Pastos' book. The title itself is indicative of the sensational tone the author has taken. Despite the hardships of financial and emotional difficulties and poor health in her later years, this author feels that the life of a lady who happily worked at her craft for four decades and was rewarded with fame, friends, love and a family does not fully warrant the "Tragedy" title.

B152.   Peak, Mayme Ober. "Betty Grable-George Raft in Romantic Triangle," Boston Globe, September 18, 1941.

Lengthy newspaper article detailing the complications in Betty and George's romance. Betty is quoted as saying that she has asked Grace Mulrooney, Raft's wife, to meet with her so that she can plead for his freedom. It also mentions "The best lawyers in the country have tried to bring about a settlement. Even Raft has 'balked' at the terms she has demanded." It also chronicles Raft's previous romances with Virginia Peine and Norma Shearer.

B153.   Peary, Danny. Close Ups - The Movie Stars Book, New York, Workman Publishing, 1978, pp.161-165.

Insightful Bio-profile: "Betty Grable: Soldier's Delight" by Jeanine Basinger, photos, filmography. "Grable's appeal to men seems obvious. Her appeal to women is more complex. Her personality was modern by forties standards. At a point in American history when women first began to flood the job markets, Betty Grable almost always played a woman who worked. She belonged out in the world, earning her own living."

E154.   Peary, Danny. Cult Movies - 3, New York, Fireside, 1988. pp. 92-93.

Yet more discussion about Grable's loss to Monroe of the role in Gentlemen Prefer Blondes in this hip, humorous book which is part of a series: "So Zanuck changed his mind about Grable and gave the part of 'Lorelei Lee' to Monroe. The deciding factor in his decision was that Grable would have cost about $150,000 to play Lorelei, while Monroe's contract would limit her to just $18,000." A questionable decision from a man who had so often claimed that Grable's earnings had saved his studio!

B155.   Photoplay. "Grab Bag On Grable," December 1944. pp.42-42, 113.

Fan magazine article listing miscellaneous trivia about Grable and her life: Favorite Food - gooey desserts; Favorite book - The Good Earth by Pearl Buck; Best Woman Friend - Paula Stone, daughter of Fred Stone, godmother to Victoria James; Worst Lie She Ever Told - stating that she wasn't pregnant during the filming of Pin Up Girl so that she could do the film; Favorite Flower - Orchids and any kind of flower in her hair and "What Betty knows but the public doesn't: That by this time any interest she had in giddy night life is over. She's shed her sequins for an apron!"

**B156.**  Pickard, Roy. <u>The Hollywood Story</u>, Secaucus, New
Jersey, Chartwell Books, Inc. 1986. pp. 80-87, 101,
133, 146, 190, 200.

Well written profile in relationship to her success for Fox;
excellent color photos.

**B157.**  Pike, Bob & Martin, Dave, <u>The Genius of Busby
Berkeley</u>, Reseda, Calif. Creative Film Society, 1973.
pp.104, 145, 157, 177.

This photo-bio of Berkeley includes rare photos of Grable in
<u>Whoopee</u>, <u>Palmy Days</u>, <u>The Kid From Spain</u> and <u>Call Me Mister</u>,
as well as a description of Berkeley "discovering" her and
giving her the vocal solo in <u>Whoopee</u>.

**B158.**  <u>Pittsburgh Sun Telegraph</u>, "Betty Grable Threat Holds
Phila. Waiter," February 5, 1941.
.
Another extortion plot involving a demand for $8,500 from a
24 year old singing waiter with a prison record. United
States Commissioner Norman J. Griffin said at the hearing:
"I'll fix your bail at the same price you placed on Miss
Grable's piece of mind." The prisoner tried to escape the
courtroom, striking one of the deputies.

**B159.**  Ragan, David. <u>Movie Stars of the 40's</u>, Englewood
Cliffs, N.J., Prentice-Hall Inc. 1985. pp. 65-66.

Concise bio and movie highlights.

**B160.**  Ringgold, Gene. <u>Screen Facts</u>, Vol. 1, Number 4, Fall
1963. pp. 1-44.

Full biography and filmography with many photos. Describes in
detail her early years in St. Louis, even discussing a
special platform being built in the foyer of the the family's
apartment at the Forest Park Hotel where she could practice
her dancing. "Sifted out of the pre-debs of Mary's Institute
selected to participate in the annual Fortnightly dances,"
because of Betty's show business aspirations, it claims
Lillian was furious, making her wish to get Betty out of St.
Louis and on to Hollywood even greater. After elucidating her
film career into the 1950's, it states that she had a year
away from the screen and spent it all at the racetrack:
"Anyone trying to discuss her film work on these occasions
would always discover she was more interested in what horse
they were betting in the next race. Her knowledge of workout
charts and her ability to scan a racing form in seconds and
retain all important informations is wonderful." When asked
about film plans, she stated: "I'm lazy. I never retired but
I just sort of laid off for a few years. But I get submited
scripts all the time. They wanted me to play the vamp in
<u>Please Don't Eat the Daisies</u> but I didn't like the part." The
article ends with her triumph playing <u>Guys and Dolls</u> in Las
Vegas.

**B161.**   Rogers, Miriam. "Betty's Other Life," <u>Photoplay</u>, February, 1953. pp. 55, 90.

A description of Grable's favorite role as "Mommie" with her two daughters. During her recent suspension, she enjoyed spending all day with her daughters, having picnics, taking them to the playground and the races. Betty explains that after Lillian's strict routine of multiple classes for young Betty, she had only given Vicki piano lessons. When Vicki showed no interest, the lessons were stopped. "I didn't see any point in forcing her...I was coaxed to take dancing lessons. My Mother would promise that I could ride horseback if I would take them. That bribe never failed!"

**B162.**   Rosen, Marjorie. <u>Popcorn Venus</u>, New York, Avon Books, 1973. pp.168, 192, 221-223, 227, 261, 284, 322.

Grable's role as "The Pin Up Girl" in women's development through American films is explored by the author. "Grable, blonde and pink and glowing healthy, celebrated the joy of being a girl untouched by war, work, gray serge, or brains. Because she so seriously embodied both familial and maternal warmth and 'all-American sex appeal,' she outdistanced all box-office competitors."

**B163.**   Ross, Sid. "An Oscar For Grable?," <u>Parade Magazine</u>, June 3, 1951.

The article begins with the author telling about a test he had been conducting: to ask every male you know to name five top women movie stars. When Betty Grable's name kept being mentioned (along with Bette Davis and Gloria Swanson) he decides to visit her on the set and asks what she thinks about never receiving an "Oscar" for her work: "Actually, I don't think I've ever had a role that would bring me within hollering distance of an award...There are lots of wonderful stars in Musicals...Stars like Gene Kelly and Vera-Ellen, for instance. Don't you think Gene Kelly's worth a musical Oscar?...the regular Oscars are strictly for acting ability - and you don't find dramatic acting in musicals, or in westerns, either. Yet the musicals and westerns make a lot of money." She mentions wanting the screen version of <u>Gentlemen Prefer Blondes</u>, but:"...she says (generously, it seemed to me) that the lead role would be a 'natural' for Judy Holliday." Quotes from Hollywood co-workers about an "Oscar" for Betty: Nunnally Johnson: "I don't know what Betty would want with an Oscar on her mantel when she has every Tom, Dick and Harry at her feet!;" Henry Koster: "A girl like Grable, who's been carrying the box office for seven straight years, ought to have some very special recognition. Her money-earning musicals have made possible many Oscar-earning films. Maybe there should be a small credit line engraved on each Oscar 'Betty Grable helped pay for this;'" George Jessel: "Every year she gets her own Oscar from the American public."

**B164.**   St. John, Adela Rogers. "Love, Laughter and Tears," <u>Los Angeles Examiner - "American Weekly"</u> - April 1, 1951.

Account of Betty's business acumen and her love of horses.

**B165.**   Schickel, Richard & Hurlburt, Allen, <u>The Stars</u>, New York, The Dial Press, 1962. pp. 216-217.

A particularly mean-spirited portrait of Grable and her place in film stardom: "Miss Grable's beauty - if that is the word for it - was of the common sort. Nor did she offer much in the way of character or maturity. She was, at best, a sort of great American floozie, and her appeal to lonely G.I.s was surely that of every hash-house waitress with whom they had ever flirted...The two of them, Grable and Lamour, represented democratic womanhood's lowest common denominator. It is not surprising that they reached the heights of popularity in a nation at war to protect democratic values, or that once the crisis passed and there was time for the finer things they disappeared from view with hardly a trace."

**B166.**   Schroeder, Carl. "Miss Grable Steps Out," <u>Modern Screen</u>, March 1954. pp. 53, 88-89.

In this fan magazine article about Betty's activities after leaving 20th Century Fox, she is quoted as saying: "I figured it was time to leave the studio. I had wonderful years there, but I don't think it's smart to stay with one studio for more than ten years. Enthusiam begins to wane and executives lose their excitement over your possibilities every time they see a newcomer." It chronicles the opening of Betty and Harry's act at the Chicago Theatre, staged by Billy Daniel. Daniel declares that Betty is his idol and says: "People always ask what it's like to dance with Betty. All I can say is that when she begins to sing 'Put your arms around me, Baby,' and struts into your vest pocket looking you right in the eye, it's like taking a great big living doll in your arms. You start dancing and you're gone, man, all gone."

**B167.**   Sennett, Ted. <u>Hollywood Musicals</u>, New York, Harry N. Abrams, Inc. 1981.

Detailed descriptions of Grable's musicals, excellent color photos, selected filmography in this lavish volume.

**B168.**   Sheppard, Gene. "Betty Grable - She Lived A Lot!," <u>Hollywood Studio Magazine - Then and Now</u>, August 1986. pp. 4-9.

Feature article about Grable's life and career with photos. Filled with many details, such as: "...a nationwide World War II bond drive sold a pair of silk stockings that Betty Grable had worn for an unprecedented $110,000, accompanied by a certificate of authenticity from Miss Grable, of course."

**B169.**   Sheridan, Jack. "James-Grable Show To Close in City Tonight," <u>Lubbock, Texas Avalanche-Journal</u>, March 1960.

In this newspaper article written when Betty and Harry came together to appear in a special show at the Lubbock Municipal

Auditorium, the writer states that their "Reunion" was short lived and after the engagement, they would both go their separate ways with their night club tours. In discussing the show, Betty says: "In the supper clubs...I am working right in front of the people. I can see their faces and there is an intimacy. I have never played big halls and the Lubbock Auditiorium is immense. The distances across the stage, over the big pit and the blinding lights seem to rob me of that contact with the audiences which I love."

**B170.** Shipman, David. <u>The Great Movie Stars - The Golden Years</u>, New York, Crown Publishers, 1970. pp. 250-253.

Excellent, concise bio with photos.

**B171.** Siegel, Scott & Siegel, Barbara. <u>The Encyclopedia of Hollywood</u>, New York, Avon Books, 1991. pp. 177-178.

Well written profile.

**B172.** Silverman, Stephen M. <u>The Fox That Got Away</u>, Seacaucus, N.J., Lyle Stuart, 1988. pp. 72, 74, 138, 153, 300.

Interesting quotes about Grable's strength and position at 20th Century Fox in this book about the last days of Darryl F. Zanuck at Fox. Zanuck's brusque, commercial attitudes are captured in this quote from 1970: "One of the gossip columnists got what I think was a clever line, although it caused me a lot of trouble...that Alice was fading and Zanuck was grooming Grable to take over her roles. Fading! Christ, all hell broke loose. Alice was a little bit hurt by it. But she was a very nice girl. In time, she and Betty became quite friendly, and I used them together in a picture, the name of which - God, I can't remember."

**B173.** Skolsky, Sidney. "Tintypes," <u>Hollywood Citizen News</u>, May 20, 1942.

Article which covers her early years, romance with George Raft and personal likes, dislikes and beauty hints: "She is peaches and cream to look at - but she loves onions. She likes onions in any form, raw or fried. She will also nibble at a bit of garlic in the raw, if she hasn't a special engagement that evening...She insists on getting eight hours sleep...She likes plain American cooking but highly seasoned ...The soap she uses is of the inexpensive variety which can be purchased in any store for 5 cents a bar...She hates showers and likes to take a tub bath at least twice a day...She abhors slinky clothes and anything that makes her look obviously sirenish...She wears a nightgown to bed... She's the kind of girl who can walk barefooted, wear a sweater and please the public."

**B174.** Skolsky, Sidney. <u>Hollywood Citizen News</u>, October 2, 1952.

Another Skolsky "profile," written ten years after the

previously listed one, begins with Grable's reasoning behind going on suspension rather than making <u>Blaze of Glory</u>: "I don't go for that dramatic stuff...I'm no actress." Other gossipy details noted: "She eats at the same table in the studio commissary every day when working, and with practically the same group of people. She says 'I'm comfortable with them. Can say what I please. I don't have to put on company manners'...She owns her own stable. Last season, one of her entries, 'Big Noise' collected stakes totalling more than $100,000. She usually arranges her film schedule so she can spend the racing season at the important nearby tracks...She is a great believer in new talent and has gone out of her way to help Dan Dailey and Mitzi Gaynor when they were just starting. It is often asked how she and Marilyn Monroe get along. When she met her, she said: 'Relax, Marilyn. I've got mine, Go get yours.'"

**B175.** Snyder, Leslie. "There is No Betty Grable!," <u>Motion Picture</u>, October 1951. pp. 47, 75-76.

One of the rare fan magazine articles which talks about Grable's negative personality traits: laziness; unwillingness to give interviews on her days off; a quick temper: "...Betty's character, the character so rarely described in magazine articles. The ingredients of moodiness and reticence, combined with a really genuine stubborn streak, have caused Betty much unhappiness, and indeed the loss of many a friendship." In discussing her laziness, Betty is quoted: "I've never had any great desire to be a star. I was happy when I was dancing in the chorus, and I was happy when I was singing with a band. Actually, it was my mother who had the ambition and kept pushing me toward success." The article ends with the softening statement: "You can't help admiring a girl, at that, who tells you 'Stop writing all that tripe about me, will you? Tell the truth about Betty Grable. I'm just an ordinary girl who came up with a lot of luck,' And a very swell personality."

**B176.** Springer, John. <u>All Talking! All Singing! All Dancing!</u>, New York, Citadel Press, 1966. pp. 141, 142, 146-148, 155, 167.

Brief section with many photos in this lushly illustrated look at film musicals.

**B177.** Springer, John & Hamilton, Jack D. <u>They Had Faces Then</u>, Seacaucus, N.J., Citadel Press, 1974. pp. 120, 123.

Contains this assessment of Grable's future fame: "In the Thirties, who would have thought that Betty Grable would be the Musical Comedy Queen and the Pin Up Girl of World War II. It might as well have been Toby Wing or Mary Carlisle - Toby was as perky and blonde, and Mary had bigger parts." A brief listing and two "Cheesecake" photos in this photo-packed encyclopedia of women in films in the 30's. It is interesting to compare the rather severe "Look" of the Thirties to the successful make-up and hairstyles that Grable and many of the other female stars evolved into.

**B178.**  Stars and Stripes, <u>Betty Grable Weeps as Scots Cheer</u>,
April 3, 1969.

Press release describing the five minute standing ovation
Grable received on Opening night at the Alhambra Theater in
Glasgow after the World Premiere of <u>The Piecefull Palace</u>
(later titled <u>Belle Starr</u>.) In a curtain call speech, she
said: "I have been in show business for many years, but this
is the highlight of my whole long career. I just want to
thank you very much for this wonderful reception."

**B179.**  Stern,  Lee  Edward.  <u>The Movie Musical (Pyramid
Illustrated History of the Movies)</u>, New York,
Pyramid Communications Inc., 1974. pp. 53, 108-
113.

Profile with photos.

**B180.**  Stine,  Whitney  and  Hurrell,  George,  <u>50 Years of
Photographing Hollywood</u>, New York, Greenwich House,
1983. pp. 126, 169.

Description of a photo shoot that Hurrell had for <u>Esquire</u>
Magazine with Grable in 1942 that was so cold, her teeth were
chattering. As she cheerfully thanked him and hurriedly left
the cold studio, he looked at the proofs through a magnifying
lens and found "Betty Grable's magnificent gams were covered
with goosebumps!" One small, unflattering photo from the
session is printed. It is unfortunate that they only worked
together once, for Hurrell was one of the masters of
photography, as the rest of the photos in the book reveal.

**B181.**  Strick, Philip. <u>Great Movie Actresses</u>, New York, Beech
Tree Books, 1985. pp. 11, 107.

One page in this oversized photo tribute containing a
miniscule bio and two interesting photos, plus a rare photo
of Grable in ice-skates in a "Pin Up" section. Grable was an
excellent skater and at one time Fox reportedly considered
making a skating themed film for her but she was intimidated
by Sonja Henie's expertise and demured.

**B182.**  Taylor, John Russell & Jackson, Arthur. <u>The Hollywood
Musical</u>, New York, McGraw-Hill, 1971.

Profile, statistics, filmography and descriptions of fourteen
of her films with photos.

**B183.**  Terrace, Vincent. <u>Encyclopedia Of Television - Series,
Pilots And Specials 1937 - 1984</u>. Vol. #1 and #3, New
York, Zoetrope, 1986.

Listing of TV "Special" credits with cast list and air dates.

**B184.**  Thomas, Bob. "Back To Footlights For Betty Grable,"
<u>Herald Examiner</u>, December 21, 1962.

As Betty prepared to open in Las Vegas in <u>Guys and Dolls</u>, this article detailed her feelings after a two-year layoff. "I haven't done a thing but play golf for two years...I figured as long as the course was right there, I'd better use it...but when I reported for costume fittings, I found the dimensions were exactly the same as when I was making pictures at Fox." It also states that the engagement is very convenient for her since the James' lived in Vegas: "It's a cinch for me...I just report to the show at 8 and go home at 11." In a statement about playing the role of "Adelaide" on the stage, after the disappointment of not getting the role in the film: "Here's how she tells the story:'I had a date one day to talk to Sam Goldwyn about doing the picture. It happened that on the same day my dog, who was 14 years old and like one of the family, hurt his paw and I had to rush him to the hospital. So I sent word that I could not keep the date. When Mr. Goldwyn heard that I broke a date with him because of a sick dog, he sent word that he never wanted to see me.' Vivian Blaine got the role."

**B185.**   Thomas, Tony & Terry, Jim. <u>The Busby Berkeley Book</u>, New York, New York Graphic Society, 1973. pp. 38, 40, 163.

Photos, synopses and details on <u>Whoopee</u>, <u>Palmy Days</u>, <u>The Kid From Spain</u> and <u>Call Me Mister</u> in this book chronicling director Berkeley's career.

**B186.**   Thomas, Tony. <u>The Films Of The Forties</u>, Secaucus, N.J., Citadel Press, 1975. pp. 38-39.

Brief biographical information, photos, cast and credits and comments about <u>Moon Over Miami</u>: "Grable's singing was modest, but her dancing, particularly her tapdancing with the Condos Brothers, was very pleasing, as was all of the film."

**B187.**   Thomas, Tony. <u>Harry Warren and the Hollywood Musical</u>, Secaucus, N.J. Citadel Press, 1975. pp. 168-170, 192 199, 203-207, 209.

Detailed descriptions, photos and music from the films composer Harry Warren wrote for Grable, with personal comments about their working relationship in this very special book about one of Hollywood's greatest composers. Warren had this to say about her: "I don't remember her ever objecting to a song or causing any problems...I signed with MGM in early 1944 but came back to Fox soon afterward to do this picture (<u>Billy Rose's Diamond Horseshoe</u>) because Billy Rose asked that I do the music. I imagine Betty might also have had something to do with it - she was a very shrewd girl, a real pro."

**B188.**   Thomas, Tony. <u>That's Dancing!</u>, New York, Harry N. Abrams, Inc., 1984. pp. 15, 17, 32-35, 51, 219, 220.

Brief profile, photos and descriptions of dance numbers in some of Grable's films.

**B189.**   Thomas, Tony & Solomon, Aubrey. <u>The Films Of Twentieth Century Fox</u>, Secaucus, N.J., Citadel Press, 1979.

Photos, synopses and abbreviated credits for all of Grable's Twentieth Century Fox films.

**B190.**   "Ham and Legs," <u>Time</u>, April 13, 1959.

In an article/review of her successful appearance at New York's Latin Quarter, the writer states that the nightclub had "Booked her for nostalgia." The writer continues: "But for a packed house at her opening in New York, it was the night the old nostalgia burned down." Mentioning that she had not been on the screen since <u>How To Be Very, Very Popular</u>, Betty describes the film as "a turkey."

**B191.**   <u>Toledo Times Parade</u>, "Her Heart Beats In Jive Time," 1944.

Using Jackie Coogan, Artie Shaw and Harry James as examples, the article states that all of the men in Grable's life have been musicians. Her multiple Wartime awards are mentioned: "An enterprising press agent has figured out that one of every 15 men in the armed services of the United states belongs to a camp, regiment, company or other unit which has elected Miss Grable its mascot, dream girl, honorary commander or to some similar position." It goes on to discuss her famous legs, to which she says: "People seem to have forgotten that I have a face, a form, and perhaps some ability as an actress. I'd like them to forget my legs." Advice is then given to men who want to "make a hit with her, don't mention her legs. Sit down at the piano instead and dash off a bit of boogie-woogie, a trifle of Chopin, a little something from Stravinsky."

**B192.**   <u>Twentieth Century Fox Press Release</u>, Untitled, July 11, 1940.

"Betty Grable got her way. She will not have to take off the ankle bracelet she has worn for three years for her starring role in the Technicolor production <u>Down Argentine Way</u>." This ankle bracelet, a gift from George Raft ("She admits it was a gift from an admirer, but refuses to name him") also is very evident in her famous "Pin Up" pose, taken several years later. The press release states that Betty is very superstitious and "...was fearful of the consequences if she followed studio orders." The situation was solved when the ankle bracelet was written into the script as a gift from her screen aunt, Charlotte Greenwood.

**B193.**   <u>Twentieth Century Fox Press Release</u>. "On the Set of <u>Springtime in the Rockies</u>," July 8, 1942.

Betty is appointed "Captain" by the Screen Actor's Guild for the current film industry charity drive for contributions to the Navy, Chinese, Dutch and Russian Relief funds. She will be responsible for soliciting money from her co-workers and has devised some new charity-raising tactics: "Just wait till

this love scene,' Betty discloses.' I'm going to kiss that
Payne lad (costar John Payne - author) as he's never been
kissed before. When I finish with him he'll be so dizzy that
he'll sign on the dotted line for his shirt and everything
else."

**B194.**  Twentieth Century Fox Press Release. Untitled, 1942.

"Betty Grable has just broken an all-time Hollywood record in
fan-photo correspondence, by sending a grand total of 54,000
four-by-five inch pictures of herself to the soldiers of Camp
Robinson, Arkansas." Six months earlier, she had been elected
the Camp's "Official Sweetheart" and never received the
notification. After reading that the soldiers felt she might
be "High-hat" in a local news clipping, she began receiving a
letter from each and every soldier. She responded with a
photo for each soldier, with a personal note on the back. She
said: "I suppose if the boys wanted to now they'd be able to
pave the company streets with my pictures...I don't want any
soldier boy to get the notion I'm high-hat."

**B195.**  Twentieth Century Fox Press Release. Untitled, 1943.

In this studio press release, Grable reveals her most
embarassing moment. She describes an audition at the
Hillstreet Theatre in Los Angeles for a musical revue
starring Paul Ash and his Orchestra when she was fifteen
years old. The auditions were held in front of the audience
as soon as the show was over and while dancing, the buttons
on her halter top popped off and she had to complete the
dance routine holding her top on. "I was purple as a petunia
from embarrassment, but the audience's laughing at me just
made me stick it out to the end. I guess that made 'em feel
sorry for me, because when I finished they were applauding as
though I were Pavlova." P.S.: She got the job!

**B196.**  Twentieth Century Fox Press Release. Untitled, April
4, 1943.

A listing of Grable's accidents and injuries during recent
filming: A black-and-blue hand caused from shutting a window
on it during Sweet Rosie O'Grady; impacted wisdom tooth on
Moon Over Miami; another swollen tooth on A Yank in R.A.F.;
bump on the head during Springtime in the Rockies; sprained
ankle on Coney Island and appendix attack on Song of the
Islands with eventual removal of her appendix after
completing Footlight Serenade.

**B197.**  Twentieth Century Fox Press Release. Untitled, 1947.

While filming That Lady in Ermine, Betty reveals that she
once used the stage name "Frances Dean": "I was all of 14 and
just a line chorine under contract to Sam Goldwyn when
someone got the idea my name ought to be changed
...Fortunately, since I didn't last long at Goldwyn, no one
ever confused me with Frances Dean, and I've since gotten by
all right with my real name!" She credits author Vicki Baum
(Grand Hotel) with coming up with the name.

**B198.**   Ursini, James. <u>Preston Sturges, An American Dreamer</u>,
New York, Curtis Books, 1973.

Detailed notes, synopsis and dialogue from <u>The Beautiful
Blonde From Bashful Bend</u> in this assessment of the work of
Sturges and his place in American film history.

**B199.**   Vallance, Tom. <u>The American Musical (Screen Series)</u>,
London, A. Zwemmer Ltd., 1970. pp. 69-71.

Concise bio and filmography in a nice little book with info
about performers, composers, choreographers and directors of
American musical films.

**B200.**   <u>Variety</u>. "20th Suspends Grable For Refusing Her First
Dramatic Role In 11 Years," September 11, 1952.

When Grable refuses to do <u>Blaze Of Glory</u>, Fox, once again,
places her on suspension without pay. Her previous suspension
(May 1, 1951, for refusing to do <u>The Girl Next Door</u>) lasted
11 months. The article mentions that the studio will hold off
starting filming until October 5th ("...and if Miss Grable
hasn't reported for part by then, will angle for another
femme.") Jean Peters eventually took the role.

**B201.**   <u>Variety</u>.

Film Reviews:
<u>Happy Days</u>, 2.19.30
<u>Let's Go Places</u>, 3.5.30
<u>Movietone Follies of 1930</u>, 6.25.30
<u>Whoopee</u>, 10.8.30
<u>Kiki</u>, 3.11.31
<u>Palmy Days</u>, 9.29.31
<u>Greeks Had a Word For Them, The</u>, 2.9.32
<u>Probation</u>, 4.12.32
<u>Hold 'Em Jail</u>, 8.23.32
<u>Kid From Spain, The</u>, 11.22.32
<u>Cavalcade</u>, 1.10.33
<u>Child of Manhattan</u>, 2.14.33
<u>Over the Counter</u> (S), 5.9.33
<u>Melody Cruise</u>, 6.27.33
<u>What Price Innocence?</u>, 6.27.33
<u>Sweetheart of Sigma Chi, The</u> 11.14.33
<u>Business is A Pleasure</u> (S), 2.6.34
<u>Student Tour</u>, 10.16.34
<u>Gay Divorcee, The</u>, 11.20.34
<u>By Your Leave</u>, 1.1.35
<u>Nitwits, The</u>, 6.26.35
<u>Old Man Rhythm</u>, 9.25.35
<u>Collegiate</u>, 1.29.36
<u>Follow the Fleet</u>, 2.29.36
<u>Don't Turn 'Em Loose</u>, 9.30.36
<u>Pigskin Parade</u>, 11.18.36
<u>This Way Please</u>, 9.15.37
<u>Thrill of a Lifetime</u>, 11.10.37
<u>College Swing</u>, 4.27.38
<u>Give Me A Sailor</u>, 8.3.38

Campus Confessions, 9.14.38
Man About Town, 6.14.39
Million Dollar Legs, 7.12.39
Day the Bookies Wept, The, 9.29.39
Down Argentine Way, 10.9.40
Tin Pan Alley, 11.27.40
Moon Over Miami, 6.18.41
A Yank in the R.A.F., 9.10.41
Hot Spot, 10.22.41
Song of the Islands, 2.11.42
Footlight Serenade, 7.8.42
Springtime in the Rockies, 9.23.42
Coney Island, 5.19.43
Sweet Rosie O'Grady, 9.22.43
Four Jills in a Jeep, 3.15.44
Pin Up Girl, 4.19.44
Billy Rose's Diamond Horseshoe, 4.11.45
Dolly Sisters, The, 9.26.45
Do You Love Me?, 4.17.46
Shocking Miss Pilgrim,The, 1.1.47
Mother Wore Tights, 8.20.47
That Lady in Ermine, 7.14.48
When My Baby Smiles At Me, 11.10.48
Beautiful Blonde From Bashful Bend, 5.25.49
Wabash Avenue, 4.5.50
My Blue Heaven, 8.23.50
Call Me Mister, 1.24.51
Meet Me After The Show, 8.3.51
Farmer Takes a Wife,The, 4.22.53
How To Marry A Millionaire, 11.11.53
Three For The Show, 2.16.55
How To Be Very, Very Popular, 7.20.55
Obituary - 7.4.73

**B202.**  Vermilye, Jerry. More Films Of The Thirties, Secaucus, N.J., Citadel Press, 1989. pp. 198-199.

Synopsis, credits and rare photos of Grable in Pigskin Parade.

**B203.**  Vespa, Mary. People, March 9, 1987.

Review of Spero Pastos biography Pin-Up: The Tragedy of Betty Grable (B151): "...another saga of disillusionment out of the Mommie Dearest school of celebrity biography...Pastos does a journeyman's job telling Grable's tragic story, mixing in a bit too much nickle-and-dime psychoanalysis. What makes his book such a good read is both the wealth of information he has gathered about this Hollywood phenomenon and the empathy and compassion he has for her and her family."

**B204.**  Walker, Leo. Big Band Almanac, Hollywood, Vinewood Books, 1978. pp. 129, 131, 160.

Notations of her work with Ted Fiorito and Hal Grayson's bands and a rare photo with Fiorito. It contains one erroneous statement about Ted Fiorito: "Somewhat later he hired Betty Grable, who had been singing with a local San

Francisco band."

**B205.**   Wanamaker, Marc. <u>The Hollywood Reporter Star Profiles</u>, London, Octopus Books, 1984. pp. 74-75.

Brief bio-profile with color photos.

**B206.**   Warner, Alan. <u>Who Sang What On The Screen</u>, North Ryde, Australia, Angus & Robertson Publishers, 1984.

Detailed notation of many songs Grable sang in her films in this interesting, specialized book.

**B207.**   Warren, Doug. <u>Betty Grable - The Reluctant Movie Queen</u>, New York, St. Martin's Press, 1981.

Another book-length biography with filmography, many photos and a more objective point of view on Grable's life and work. Includes interviews and observations from sister Marjorie Arnold; agent Kevin Pines; photographer Frank Powolny; fan Michael Levitt and many co-workers. Many of Grable's "human frailties" (alcohol, gambling, etc.) are emphasized in a bid for commercial appeal.

**B208.**   Wilkerson, Tichi & Borie, Marcia. <u>Hollywood Reporter</u>, <u>The Golden Years</u>, New York, Howard-Mc Cann Inc., 1984.

Nice bio-profile, gossip "mentions" throughout the years and article "From the Cradle to the Grable" (B54) by Betty in this compilation from one of Hollywood's two important trade papers. In describing her love affair with George Raft, the profile states: "She had three-dimensional pictures of George plastered all over the walls of her home. The photos were virtually the only things which weren't put there by the interior decorator...In 1941, Betty and George made a serious attempt to secure his freedom. There was a meeting set up with Grace (Raft's wife - auth.) in the hopes that Betty could implore her to give George the divorce. Grace retained her stiff terms. Betty, who was earning good money, didn't care that George would lose everything. But Raft could not, and would not, give in to the untenable terms."

**B209.**   Wilson, Earl. "Gabriel In Jive," <u>Liberty Magazine</u>, July 3, 1943.

Informative article about the popularity of Harry James at the height of his success as one of America's Big Band Leaders. Filled with statistics of how many records the Band had sold (15 to 20 million) and what the weekly costs were for operating the Band ($6000 in salaries), it mentions that at the time the article was written, James was in the midst of divorcing his wife: "The gossips say James wants to marry Betty Grable but then who doesn't?"

**B210.**   Wilson, Ivy Crane. <u>Hollywood in the 1940's - The Star's Own Stories</u>, New York, Frederick Ungar Publishing Co., 1980. pp. 144-147.

"Thanks to My Dancing," an article by Grable and color photo in this book of reprinted photos and articles from Hollywood fan magazines.

B211.    Woll, Allen L. The Hollywood Musical Goes To War, Chicago, Nelson-Hall, 1983. pp. 101, 112, 141, 147.

An interesting discussion of several of Grable's films (Tin Pan Alley, Moon Over Miami, Springtime in the Rockies, Four Jills in a Jeep and The Dolly Sisters); the Fox musical formula; the effect of the "Good Neighbor Policy" and the musicals of the World War II period and how the War influenced those films.

B212.    Woodcock, Joan. Paper Dolls Of Famous Faces - Vol. II, Cumberland, Md., Hobby House Press, 1980.

Contains Betty Grable "Movie Star Dressographs" from the St. Louis Post Dispatch, 1935.

B213.    Wynn, Ned. We Will Always Live In Beverly Hills, New York, William Morrow and Company, Inc., 1990. pp.13-15, 51, 188.

In Keenan Wynnn's son's biography of growing up among the stars, Grable is described as a charming sexual fantasy of his youth and one of the few true friends of the family who was still supportive after step-father Van Johnson and mother Evie Wynn's divorce.

B214.    Yablonsky, Lewis. George Raft, New York, McGraw-Hill, 1974. pp. 156-162, 171, 180.

Well-researched description of Grable's relationship with Raft, as well as a brief profile of her life. Mary Livingstone, Jack Benny's wife, is identified as the one who brought Grable and Raft back together after their initial friendship. Raft is quoted as saying: "My dates with Betty - well, they were different. Virginia Peine went to the games and fights to please me. Norma Shearer went for the novelty. But Betty Grable went because she, personally, liked sports as much as I did, and she proved this by helping me organize my contribution to the war effort - 'George Raft's Cavalcade of Sports.'"

B215.    Yates, Paula. Blondes, London, Michael Joseph, 1983.pp.86-87.

Snide profile with photos in this comical British evaluation of the Blonde's contribution to history.

B216.    Zeitlin, Ida. "The Love Story of Betty Grable and Harry James," Modern Screen, October, 1943, pp.30-32, 107-109.

Fan magazine article describing how Betty had been in love with George Raft for three years when she met Harry in Chicago. Their romance blossomed at the Hollywood Canteen and

he continued to woo her while on tour with his band with
letters and phone calls, even romancing her on his radio
shows by saying "Hello Betty" sometime during the broadcast.
As soon as Harry's divorce became final, they quickly planned
the ceremony, telling only Lillian about their plans. Sister
Marjorie heard the announcement on the radio and from co-
workers at Douglas Aircraft.

**B217.**   Zilner, Dian. <u>Hollywood Collectibles</u>, West Charter,
Penn., Schiffer Publishing, 1991. pp. 99-106.

Entire chapter devoted to Grable's life and career, many
color photos of sheet music, fan magazine covers, paper dolls
and other collectibles.

**B218.**   Zolotow, Maurice. <u>Marilyn Monroe</u>, New York, Harper &
Row, 1960 (Revised Edition, 1990). pp. 187-192.

In this, one of the best books about Marilyn Monroe, Zolotow
writes about Marilyn's campaign to get the starring role in
<u>Gentlemen Prefer Blondes</u>: "The studio had bought for $500,000
the Broadway musical version of <u>Gentlemen Prefer Blondes</u>. It
had been announced as a vehicle for Betty Grable. Marilyn was
conducting a quiet campaign to get the role of Lorelei Lee
assigned to her. From the volume of fan mail, the front
office knew that Miss Grable's popularity had declined as
much as Marilyn's had increased. But could Marilyn sing and
dance? She proved, at (Camp) Pendleton, that she could sing
and had enough acting ability to delude an audience into
thinking that she was an accomplished dancer." There are also
charming anecdotes about the two women's work and
relationship during the filming of <u>How To Marry A
Millionaire</u>.

# Index

The index refers to page numbers as well as codes in the various sections. Entries with roman numerals xi-xvi may be found in the "Preface." Page numbers 1 - 28 will be found in the "Biography" section. "F" will be found in "Filmography," "T" in "Television," "S" in "Stage," "N" - "Nightclubs," "R" - "Radio," "V" - "Videography," "D" - "Discography," "M" - "Miscellaneous" and "B" in "Bibliography." For the sake of brevity, only creative personnel who worked frequently with Miss Grable or who contributed significantly to her career are noted for their film, stage and television credits.

B11
Universal Pictures, F10
**Unsinkable Molly Brown,
The**, S17
Unsung Genius, The Passion
of Dancer-Choreographer,
Jack Cole, B98
**Up in Arms**, F4
U.S.O., 12, B8, B100


Vallee, Rudy,  F75, S23
Van, Bobby, N11, N14-16
Van, Vera, S6
Vance, Vivian, T16
Van Doren, Mamie, 23
Variety, 15, B201
Vaudeville, 2, 6-7, S9-12,
   S14-15
Veloz and Yolanda, B20
Veloz, Frank, B20
Venuta, Benay, 18-19, F78,
   D5, B16
Vera-Ellen, F55, B163
Verdon, Gwen, 19, F79-80,
   D29, B60
**Vicki**, F57
Victor, Lucia, S19
Virgil, Jack, F31
Von Stroheim, Eric Jr.,
   F37


**Wabash Avenue**, 18, F76,
   R57, S15, D1-2, D26,
   D44, M10, B93
Waggoner, Lyle, T33
Wallis, Hal, T3
Walsh, Raoul, F46
**Walt Disney World's
Diamond Horseshoe
Revue**, F65
Walters, Charles, F63,
   S13, B16, B39
Walters, Flo, N5-8
**Walter Winchell Show,
The**, 22, T1
Walsh, Bridget, B1
Warner Brothers Studios,
   6, 11, F28, F62, F76,
   S7
Warner, Harry, 15
Warren, Harry, 10, F52-53
   F58, F62, F65, F71,
   D23, B75, B187
Washburn, Bryant Jr., F37
Wasserman, Edith, B101
Wayne, David, F77, F81, D32

Webb, Jack, F23
Webb, Roy, F34-38
**Weekend in Havana**, 12,
   F60
Weld, Tuesday, 23
Welles, Orson, T7
Wences, Senor, F71
West, Mae, T18, M8, B12
Westmore, Wally, B96
We Will Always Live in
   Beverly Hills, B213
Whalen, Harold, S9
**What Price Innocence?**,
   6, F23, B78
**What's My Line?**  T29,
   T32
Wheeler and Woolsey, 4-6,
   F16, F34, S2, S9
Wheeler, Bert, 4-6, F16,
   F34-35, S1-2, S9
**When My Baby Smiles At
Me**, 17, F74, F77, R51,
   R53, R56
Whidden, Jay, 5, S8
White, Jules, F26
White, Marjorie, F1, F3
White, Sam, F25
Whitman, Alden, B89
Whitney, Eleanor, F45, F48,
   R18
Whitty, Dame May, R36, R47
**Whoopee**, 3, F4, V33, D1,
   B11, B65, B95, B157,
   B185
Who Sang What on the Screen,
   B206
Widmark, Richard, 19
Wilder, Marc, F79
Wilder, Thornton, S19
Williams, Andy, T26
Williams, Chilli, 11
Williams, Frances, S13
Williams, Kenny, F65, F71,
   F74, B8
Wilson, Dorothy, F15
Wilson, Mary, S12
Winchell, Walter, B148
Wing, Toby, F19, S10, B177
Winninger, Charles, F61, D9,
   B128
Winters, Shelley, 19
Woas, Albert, B139
Wood, Dee Dee, 24, T27-28
Woolsey, Robert, F16, F34,
   S9
Wray, John, T14
Wright, Cobina Jr., F59, D15
Wyatt, Jane, F77

## About the Author

LARRY BILLMAN is a writer, director, and producer of live entertainment in international theme parks. His previously published works include numerous scripts.

**Titles in**
**Bio-Bibliographies in the Performing Arts**

Milos Forman: A Bio-Bibliography
*Thomas J. Slater*

Kate Smith: A Bio-Bibliography
*Michael R. Pitts*

Patty Duke: A Bio-Bibliography
*Stephen L. Eberly*

Carole Lombard: A Bio-Bibliography
*Robert D. Matzen*

Eva Le Gallienne: A Bio-Bibliography
*Robert A. Schanke*

Julie Andrews: A Bio-Bibliography
*Les Spindle*

Richard Widmark: A Bio-Bibliography
*Kim Holston*

Orson Welles: A Bio-Bibliography
*Bret Wood*

Ann Sothern: A Bio-Bibliography
*Margie Schultz*

Alice Faye: A Bio-Bibliography
*Barry Rivadue*

Jennifer Jones: A Bio-Bibliography
*Jeffrey L. Carrier*

Cary Grant: A Bio-Bibliography
*Beverley Bare Buehrer*

Maureen O'Sullivan: A Bio-Bibliography
*Connie J. Billips*

Ava Gardner: A Bio-Bibliography
*Karin J. Fowler*

Jean Arthur: A Bio-Bibliography
*Arthur Pierce and Douglas Swarthout*

Donna Reed: A Bio-Bibliography
*Brenda Scott Royce*

Gordon MacRae: A Bio-Bibliography
*Bruce R. Leiby*

Mary Martin: A Bio-Bibliography
*Barry Rivadue*

Irene Dunne: A Bio-Bibliography
*Margie Schultz*

Anne Baxter: A Bio-Bibliography
*Karin J. Fowler*

Tallulah Bankhead: A Bio-Bibliography
*Jeffrey L. Carrier*

Jessica Tandy: A Bio-Bibliography
*Milly S. Barranger*

Janet Gaynor: A Bio-Bibliography
*Connie Billips*

James Stewart: A Bio-Bibliography
*Gerard Molyneaux*

Joseph Papp: A Bio-Bibliography
*Barbara Lee Horn*

Henry Fonda: A Bio-Bibliography
*Kevin Sweeney*

Edwin Booth: A Bio-Bibliography
*L. Terry Oggel*

Ethel Merman: A Bio-Bibliography
*George B. Bryan*

Lauren Bacall: A Bio-Bibliography
*Brenda Scott Royce*

Joseph Chaikin: A Bio-Bibliography
*Alex Gildzen and Dimitris Karageorgiou*

Richard Burton: A Bio-Bibliography
*Tyrone Steverson*

Maureen Stapleton: A Bio-Bibliography
*Jeannie M. Woods*

David Merrick: A Bio-Bibliography
*Barbara Lee Horn*

Vivien Leigh: A Bio-Bibliography
*Cynthia Marylee Molt*

Robert Mitchum: A Bio-Bibliography
*Jerry Roberts*

Agnes Moorehead: A Bio-Bibliography
*Lynn Kear*

Colleen Dewhurst: A Bio-Bibliography
*Barbara Lee Horn*

Helen Hayes: A Bio-Bibliography
*Donn B. Murphy and Stephen Moore*

Boris Karloff: A Bio-Bibliography
*Beverley Bare Buehrer*